Modern Welsh

A Comprehensive Grammar

Modern Welsh: A Comprehensive Grammar is the ideal reference source for all speakers and learners of Welsh. Focusing on contemporary spoken Welsh, it presents the complexities of the language in a concise and readable form. Common grammatical patterns and parts of speech are discussed in detail and without jargon and extensive cross references make the book comprehensive and easy to use.

Now in its third edition, the *Grammar* has been thoroughly revised and updated throughout. Changes include an increased number of illustrative examples, additional appendices for easy reference, inclusion of IPA phonetic symbols and expanded sections on further reading.

Features include:

- full use of authentic examples
- particular attention to areas of confusion and difficulty
- extensive index and cross referencing
- initial consonant mutations marked throughout
- separate sections on communicative functions
- notes on variation between dialects and on formal written language.

Modern Welsh: A Comprehensive Grammar is the most thorough, detailed and user-friendly Welsh grammar available in English today. It is suitable for use in schools, colleges, universities and adult classes at all levels and will, as its predecessors, prove an invaluable aid for Welsh language learning and teaching.

Gareth King is an experienced teacher of Welsh and the author of *Modern Welsh: A Comprehensive Grammar* (1993, 2003, 2015), *Basic Welsh: A Grammar and Workbook* (1995, 2014), *The Routledge Intermediate Welsh Reader* (2013), *Colloquial Welsh: The Complete Course for Beginners* (2009) and *Intermediate Welsh: A Grammar and Workbook* (1996). All are published by Routledge.

Routledge Comprehensive Grammars
Comprehensive Grammars are available for the following languages:

Bengali
Cantonese
Catalan
Chinese
Danish
Dutch
Greek
Indonesian
Japanese
Modern Welsh
Modern Written Arabic
Polish
Slovene
Swedish
Turkish
Ukrainian

Titles of related interest

Colloquial Welsh: A Complete Course for Beginners
By Gareth King

Basic Welsh: A Grammar and Workbook
By Gareth King

Intermediate Welsh: A Grammar and Workbook
By Gareth King

Routledge Intermediate Welsh Reader
By Gareth King

Business Welsh: A User's Manual
By Robert Dery

Modern Welsh

A Comprehensive Grammar

Third edition

 **Gareth King**

 Routledge
Taylor & Francis Group

LONDON AND NEW YORK

First published 2016
by Routledge
2 Park Square, Milton Park, Abingdon, Oxon OX14 4RN

and by Routledge
711 Third Avenue, New York, NY 10017

Routledge is an imprint of the Taylor & Francis Group, an informa business

© 1996, 2003, 2016 Gareth King

British Library Cataloguing-in-Publication Data
A catalogue record for this book is available from the British Library

Library of Congress Cataloging-in-Publication Data
A catalog record for this book has been requested

ISBN: 978-1-138-82629-8 (hbk)
ISBN: 978-1-138-82630-4 (pbk)
ISBN: 978-1-315-73941-0 (ebk)

Typeset in Sabon and Gill Sans
by Saxon Graphics Ltd, Derby

Contents

English words causing particular translation problems 466

Affirmative and negative responses 473

Preface to the third edition

The indulgence with which readers and critics have favoured the first and second editions of this grammar of the modern Welsh language, and the heartening response it has drawn from those it has always been primarily intended for, have encouraged me to risk a third.

Once again I have taken the opportunity for expansion and improvement. I have significantly added to the illustrative examples throughout, and have adopted a more generalised approach to dialect indication. Four appendices have been added, dealing with the verb system, mutation system, and Welsh linguistic and grammatical terminology. Naturally I have updated and slightly expanded the Further Reading section to include works that have appeared since the previous editions, and I have also this time added links for some reliable and useful internet resources.

My debt to those already acknowledged in the previous editions of course remains. For this third edition I would like to add my thanks and appreciation to Isabelle Cheng, Lilian Edwards, Andrea Hartill, Kat Kiraly and Samantha Vale Noya.

G.K.
Cambridge
December 2014

Preface to the second edition

With this new edition of *Modern Welsh* I have taken the opportunity to make some changes and improvements. Chief among these are: the extension of typographic marking of initial consonant mutations to cover the entire text of the new edition – I hope that this provision will enhance the user-friendliness of the grammar by making more transparent the distribution and syntactic patterns of this difficult aspect of the language; and the addition of an entire new section dealing with the practical aspects of function and situation, by which I have aimed to set the language even more firmly in a context that reflects its status as a living and flourishing medium of modern everyday communication. The order and numbering of the grammar sections remains unchanged from the original edition, except that the concluding sections 514–530 of the original have now been incorporated in the new 'Function' part of the book, and have been accordingly redesignated. References for original and new material have been conflated into a revised and somewhat expanded Index. I have also taken the opportunity to correct a small number of typographical errors that slipped through in previous reprints. The text of the grammar section of the book remains otherwise essentially the same.

The bibliography has been slightly amended to record the happy fact that Fynes-Clinton's work referred to in the acknowledgements of the original edition has indeed now achieved its reprinting.

I am glad that this grammar has found so many friends among those for whom it was written, and I hope that in its new and expanded incarnation it will win many more.

G.K.
East Sussex
February 2002

Acknowledgements

First and foremost I should like to thank the many native speakers of Welsh from all over Wales from whose speech a large proportion of the illustrative material in this grammar has been drawn. Their anonymity here belies the importance of their contribution. I am especially indebted to those Welsh-speaking friends and acquaintances who, in the later stages of writing, were interested and patient enough both to answer all manner of questions and to gently correct me when I went wrong.

Thanks must also go to my students, mainly in Llanafan, Llanilar and Aberystwyth, for not being afraid to ask awkward questions, and thereby bringing to my attention many gaps and areas for improvement in the explanations.

Special thanks are due to James Fife, not only for innumerable discussions over the years on questions of Welsh grammar and semantics, but also for his meticulous and conscientious reports on the grammar in its earlier stages which saved me from not a few slips and oversights, those remaining being entirely my own responsibility. He also discharged his responsibilities in periodically reminding me, when my resolve showed signs of faltering, of our shared conviction that, for the serious student of any language, grammar is a key to understanding and not an obstacle.

The writer of any descriptive work of this kind owes an immeasurable debt to his predecessors in the field. I have listed the main works that have been of help to me (see References) but I would like to single out for particular mention the study by O.H. Fynes-Clinton, published eighty years ago and a model of objective fieldwork untarnished by any disesteem of the language of ordinary people. Its reprinting is long overdue.

I wish to thank Simon Bell of Routledge for having faith in this project from the very start, and for his enthusiasm, encouragement and practical help along the way. I thank also Helen Coward and Louisa Semlyen.

Acknowled-gements

The planning and writing of this grammar, which of necessity was done largely in my spare time, would not have been possible without the practical and moral support of my wife, Jonquil, who was a constant source of encouragement and constructive criticism; and of our sons, Adam and Liam, who helped me keep things in perspective, and put up with having a recluse for a father more often than I had any right to expect of them. I owe much to my own mother and father, not least the education that empowered me to undertake such a project in the first place; my father's strength of character and independence of mind and spirit have been an unfailing inspiration to me in writing this book, and I therefore dedicate it to his memory.

G.K.
Llanafan
Mis Chwefror, 1993

The linguistic relationship of Welsh

Of all the languages currently spoken in the British Isles, Welsh has been here the longest. Others preceded it, in pre-Celtic times, but none of these have survived – we may take it that the Celtic invaders were thorough in their assimilation of the indigenous population of these islands, and that the speech of these pre-Celtic peoples, whatever its nature and affinities, was quickly overwhelmed. Isolated traces of these languages may be preserved in certain place-names or, more likely, river-names.

Welsh, then, is a member of the Celtic branch of the Indo-European language family, and is therefore related, albeit distantly, to most of the languages of Europe today, including French, German, Russian and, of course, English. All these languages can be traced back to a single parent language, or at least a closely interconnected 'community' of very similar dialects, which are referred to as Indo-European, since they subsequently spread East and West over almost the entire continents of Europe and India. It is thought that the process of splitting off and going their separate ways did not affect all dialects uniformly or simultaneously, and that some language groups may have delayed their departure from the original homeland. This may have been the case with what were later to become Celtic and Romance. These two groups of speakers may have coexisted for a while longer after their cousins had departed, and this theory has been put forward as an explanation for a number of important shared characteristics between the Celtic and Romance languages to this day. Celtic also shows unexplained similarities with certain languages of North Africa.

Within the Celtic family, Welsh has as its closest relatives: Breton (Welsh name **Llydaweg**), spoken in Brittany – estimates of number of speakers vary, but probably somewhat under half a million active users, of which perhaps a little under a half of those are native speakers; and Cornish (**Cernyweg**), which died out in the late eighteenth century, but which has lately enjoyed a modest but determined revival and a gradually increasing public profile in Cornwall. More distantly related are Irish (**Gwyddeleg**), Scottish Gaelic (**Gaeleg yr Alban**) and Manx (**Manaweg**), whose last native speaker died only in 1974, but which, like Cornish, has recently undergone a modest but notable revival in use and status on the Isle of Man. Welsh, Breton and Cornish constitute the Brythonic group, while Irish, Scottish Gaelic and Manx form the Goidelic group. There are strong similarities within each group, and considerable differences between the two groups. All six languages share certain basic characteristics which mark them out as Celtic languages – notably the mutation system (see §§**3–12**), and inflected prepositions (see §**446**).

While most of the Celtic languages today face at best an uncertain future, Welsh and Scottish Gaelic at least are in a better position in that they can still claim to be the everyday language of particular and well-defined communities. Breton, with its number of native speakers putting it easily into second place after Welsh, has also experienced a marked improvement in status, both cultural and political, in recent decades, and its future looks brighter than it used to not so long ago. Irish, despite long-standing official status as national and first language of the Republic of Ireland (and more recently official status as a minority language in Northern Ireland), finds itself in perhaps the most precarious position of the main four modern Celtic languages; yet it too has seen a modest revival in fortunes in recent decades.

As things stand at the start of the twenty-first century, by far the most secure and solidly established of all the Celtic languages, both culturally and sociopolitically, is Welsh.

Types of Welsh – colloquial, modern standard and literary

A distinction must be made between the Colloquial (or Spoken) Welsh in this grammar and Literary Welsh. The difference between these two is much greater than between the virtually identical colloquial and literary forms of English – so great, in fact, that there are good grounds for regarding them as separate languages – certainly the verb systems at least are radically different.

One telling difference is as simple as it is fundamental: Colloquial Welsh is a first language for native speakers of Welsh. They do not have to make an active effort to learn it, any more than English speakers have to do for colloquial English. It is acquired automatically from childhood, and native speakers have an intuitive feel for what sounds 'right' or 'wrong'.

Literary Welsh, on the other hand, is no-one's native language. All those who know how to read it, whether Welsh speakers or not, have been taught. In this sense it is an artificial language – consciously planned and designed to standardize the written language at the time of the translation of the Bible into Welsh (sixteenth century), and by and large with a deliberate disregard for the native speech of ordinary people. It is mainly in the verb system that the literary construct most diverges from all natural and unaffected spoken varieties. Its subsequent undoubted success as the medium of a prolific literature has been at the expense of Colloquial Welsh, neglected and relentlessly disparaged by a powerful (Welsh-speaking) minority who had much to gain from putting the main means of expression of the cultural identity out of the reach of the majority. In this way a sense of inferiority was engendered among ordinary Welsh speakers with regard to their language – one which persisted for a very long time, with native speakers routinely dismissing their own spoken language as something 'inferior' (i.e. to the artificial Literary Welsh) and 'not proper Welsh'. Only in very recent decades has this situation begun to be redressed, and it is at last becoming the norm to hear and, particularly important, see and read in the media in

Types of
Welsh –
colloquial,
modern
standard and
literary

all but the most formal of contexts a type of Welsh that conforms much more closely to the form and spirit of the living spoken language in all its diversity – a diversity which, nevertheless, maintains as it always has done a plainly apparent degree of internal consistency and homogeneity in its differentiation from the more extreme manifestations of the literary construct. This official form of written Welsh, used generally and with a high degree of consistency in all public spheres these days, may be termed Modern Standard Welsh – a standardised written form of the language that more closely corresponds to spoken norms and therefore more faithfully reflects the realities of the living language. Dialect variation (see below), being far more a matter of pronunciation than of form or spelling, is easily and effectively accommodated.

Literary Welsh, then, while it merits study in its own right, is of marginal importance in a book based on native Welsh speech patterns. Those who wish to study the literary construct will find manuals and grammars aplenty to meet their needs, and it would certainly do the user of this book a disservice to attempt to somehow reconcile what are essentially two differently based forms of the language, and to try to pass them off as one. A small number of Literary Welsh forms have everyday currency in the more formal Welsh of the media, however, and so are included in the grammar (see for example §§367–374).

I have sought to accommodate the main aspects of dialect variation by following the consensus in dividing Colloquial Welsh into two major dialects – North (N) and South (S). In one sense, of course, this is a simplistic analysis, since there are many distinct dialects in the North, and in the South. On the other hand, considerations of vocabulary and pronunciation *do* allow us to make a broad distinction between Northern and Southern varieties of the spoken language, and it is this distinction which most obviously strikes the learner of the language. Native Welsh speakers share this perception, incidentally. That said, the substantive differences between North and South Welsh are sometimes made too much of – divergence is mainly in pronunciation, much less in vocabulary and hardly at all in syntax.

The guidelines I have set myself in according equal status to N and S variants are as follows:

vocabulary – differences have been noted in the text of the grammar and the two variants given side by side and labelled N and S. In fact, this involves only a relatively small number of common words – a list is given in section **XLIV**;

Types of
Welsh –
colloquial,
modern
standard and
literary

pronunciation – differences are likewise easily dealt with, since for the most part they are predictable and in any case are of marginal relevance in a book of this kind;

syntactic – differences are also relatively few in number, though again they occur in some of the most basic patterns. I have simply drawn attention to these where they arise in the text of the grammar, and given both variants;

citations in Welsh present a more awkward problem, since there is usually no obvious reason for choosing N or S in any particular instance, and often there would be no difference anyway – as mentioned above, N and S are not that different overall. This being the case, I have simply aimed at evenhandedness in the book as a whole, and have restricted labelling to the minority of cases where vocabulary and/or sentence structure distinctively marks the example sentence out as N or S – but it will be seen that most cases, in their written form at least, are not region-specific.

In general, the citations are intended as illustrations of usage, not of dialect variance unless specifically stated.

An asterisk (*) preceding an example indicates an incorrect form or construction.

SPELLING CONVENTIONS

In the body of the grammar, I have remained faithful, by and large, to standardized spellings. Guidelines for these were published as *Ffurfiau Ysgrifenedig Cymraeg Llafar* ['Written Forms of Spoken Welsh'] by the Welsh Joint Education Committee in 1991, and remain broadly accepted and in force. But in citations, particularly from speech, I have followed the practice of an increasing number of publishers and at least one weekly magazine (*Golwg*) in using, for certain types of word, spellings which reflect regional pronunciation rather than compromise. These instances fall into two types:

1   Commonly used words whose traditional or standardized spelling does not reflect pronunciation anywhere. A good example is **eisiau** *want*, which is pronounced in different parts of the country **isio, isie** or **isse.**

2   A whole class of words where a vowel is heard between two final consonants in speech, but not shown in writing: **pobl** (spoken: **pobol**), **ochr** (spoken: **ochor**), **cwbl** (spoken: **cwbwl**).

This does complicate the picture slightly, of course, but it should not represent an insuperable problem for the serious user for whom this

Types of Welsh – colloquial, modern standard and literary

grammar is primarily intended. Indeed, a certain amount of deliberate inconsistency in this regard is warranted, I feel, in a descriptive grammar of this kind, reflecting as it does a diversity of the language that is one of its most fascinating aspects.

Glossary of technical terms

adjective a word that describes a noun; answers the question 'What kind of . . . ?' – *red, heavy, international*; also *my, this*, etc.

adverb a word that gives additional information about how, when or where an action takes place – *quickly, tomorrow, outside*

AFF affirmative – any **verb-form** used in making statements as opposed to questions or negatives. Compare **INT** and **NEG**

article in Welsh, the words corresponding to English *the* (definite article). English also has an indefinite article *a/an*, for which there is no equivalent in Welsh

auxiliary a verb used in conjunction with a **verb-noun** (*VN*) – the VN gives the meaning, while the auxiliary gives information such as tense, person, etc.

clause a part of a complex sentence, containing at least a subject and a verb, and usually joined to the rest by a **conjunction**

conditional a **tense** in Welsh and English that indicates an action which is hypothetical at the time of speaking – *we would go*

conjunction a word joining two **clauses** in a sentence – *and, but, whether, because, whereas*

dynamic a term describing a positive action as opposed to an unchanging state. *Go, write, learn, run* are all dynamic verbs. Compare **stative**

focused sentence in Welsh, a sentence where a particular element, usually non-verbal, is placed first in the sentence to give it focus or emphasis. See §§17–21

inflected	any **verb**-form with endings attached to the verb. Compare **periphrastic**
INT	interrogative – any **verb**-form used in making questions as opposed to statements or negatives. Compare **AFF** and **NEG**
mutation	a change in the initial letter of a word, for example *bara* to *fara*. See §§3–12 for full explanations
NEG	negative – any **verb-form** used to make negative statements as opposed to (positive) statements and questions. Compare **AFF** and **INT**
non-past	a set of verb-endings in Welsh that place the action of the verb in the present or (more often) future. Compare **past** and **unreality**
non-specific noun	a **noun** used in a general sense, and not referring to any individual or particular thing. Compare **specific noun**
noun	any word that names an object, place or person – *cat*, *Camden*, *Kate Bush*
object	in a sentence, the thing or person that receives or suffers the action of the verb. In *The man ate the sandwich*, *the sandwich* is the object of the verb *eat*. Compare **subject**
passive	a sentence construction in which the **subject** is the receiver, and not the doer, of the action – *an old sword was dug up*
past	a set of **verb**-endings that place the action of the verb in the past. Compare **non-past** and **unreality**
periphrastic	any tense of a **verb** that is expressed not by endings on the verb itself, but by the use of an **auxiliary**. Compare **inflected**
person	a way of identifying the relationship of something to the speaker: the first person is the speaker (*I*, *we*); the second person is the one spoken to (*you*); and the third person is the one spoken about (*he*, *she*, *they*)
possessive adjective	words like 'my', 'their', 'your', etc. – they are adjectives because, like all adjectives, they describe nouns (just as a 'red coat' is a particular kind of coat, so 'my coat' is also a particular coat); in Welsh, however, the possessive adjectives behave rather differently from ordinary adjectives
preposition	a word which indicates a relationship, usually spatial, between two things – *in*, *on*, *at*, *between*

preterite	a **tense** which indicates a completed action in the past. Examples in English are: she *swam*, he *jumped*
pronoun	a word like *he, you, they*, etc. that stands for a **noun** previously mentioned
quantifier	a word or phrase that indicates how much or how many of something is being referred to – *many, a few, enough, too much*
radical	the basic, dictionary form of a Welsh word without any **mutation** to the initial letter
specific noun	any **noun** that refers to a specific thing or person as opposed to a general one. In practice this means nouns preceded by the definite **article** or a **possessive adjective**; also personal names and **pronouns**
stative	a term describing not an action, but an unchanging condition or state. *Know, belong, hope, exist* are all stative verbs. Compare **dynamic**
subject	in a sentence, the thing or object that performs the action of the verb, as opposed to what receives or suffers the action. In *The man ate the sandwich, The man* is the subject of the verb *eat*. Compare **object**
syntax	sentence structure; the order of words in a sentence
tense	an indication within the form of the **verb** as to when an action happened in relation to the speaker
underlying form	a form of a word (usually a **verb** in Welsh) from which differing spoken regional variants have developed, and which itself is now confined mainly to the written language
unreality	a set of verb-endings in Welsh which imply that the action of the verb will not, may not or cannot happen. Compare **non-past** and **past**
verb	usually the action or doing word in the sentence – *eat, run, speak*. Also words denoting a physical or mental condition or state – *be, exist, belong, know*
verb complement	the part of the sentence dependent on the **subject** and **verb** – it can be the **object**, or an **adjective** or **adverb**, or a phrase of some kind: I saw *the end of the film*; This soup is *too hot*; The rest of the crew are *waiting outside*
verb-noun (VN)	in Welsh, the basic dictionary form of the **verb**. It expresses the meaning alone, without reference to **tense** or **person**

Abbreviations

abbr.	abbreviation
adj.	adjective
AFF	affirmative
AM	Aspirate Mutation
condt	conditional
c/u	collective/unit
descr.	descriptive
E	English
exist.	existential
f	feminine
fut.	future
ident.	identification
impf	imperfect
infl.	inflected
INT	interrogative
lit.	literally
m	masculine
MM	Mixed Mutation
n	noun
N	North, Northern
NEG	negative
NM	Nasal Mutation
obj.	object
perf.	perfect
peri.	periphrastic
pers.	person
pl.	plural
pluperf.	pluperfect
poss.	possessive
prep.	preposition

pres.	present
pret.	preterite
S	South, Southern
sing.	singular
SM	Soft Mutation
subj.	subject
SVO	subject-verb-object
v	verb
VN	verb-noun
VSO	verb-subject-object
W	Welsh
<	derived from

GRAMMAR SECTION

Sounds and spelling

This is a brief summary of the relationship between sounds and spelling in modern Welsh, giving attention only to the main differences from English.

1   Alphabet

All of the following are *separate letters* for dictionary and other alphabetical purposes:

a b c ch d dd e f ff g ng h i j l ll m n o p ph r rh s t th u w y

The IPA phonetic symbol correspondence is broadly as follows (but see more detailed comments under Vowels and Consonants below):

a b k x d ð ɛ v f g ŋ h ɪ dʒ l ɬ m n ɔ p f r ʰr s t θ i/ɨ u ə *or* i/ɨ

Notes:

(a)   there is no **k, q, v** or **z**

(b)   digraph combinations of letters (**ch dd ff ng ll ph rh th**) are separate letters with their own independent place in the alphabet, and are so treated in dictionaries: so, for example, **cysgu** appears before **chwaer**, **teclyn** before **technoleg**; **lori** appears before **llawr**, **palu** before **pallu**. Note particularly the position of **ng-** between **g** and **h** – so, for example, **angen** comes before **anabl**.

(c)   **a e i o u w y** are all vowels, the rest are consonants. In some circumstances, **i** and **w** can be consonants. Vowels can be long or short, and long vowels are sometimes marked with an accent – see Spelling and Accents below.

Vowels

u is pronounced as **i** in the S, while in the N it resembles more the French **u**, German **ü**, but with unrounded lips – IPA [ɨ].

w is like English 'took'; when long it resembles English *cool*, but pronounced further back in the throat.

y has two sounds:

(a)   in the final (or only) syllable of a word, it sounds like **u** above;

(b)   otherwise it sounds like the neutral 'uh' vowel written *-a* in *sofa* – IPA [ə]

So **ynys** [ənɪs] ('uh-niss') has both sounds – 'i' in the final syllable, 'uh' in the preceding one.

Several common one-syllable words contravene these rules and have the [ə] 'uh' sound, e.g. **y(r)** *the*, **yn** *in* (also a particle), **dy** *your* and **(f)y(n)** *my*.

Diphthongs, or combinations of vowels, are mostly a simple running together of the two parts: for example, **ew** is **e** + **w** [ɛu]; **aw** is **a** + **w** (English '*cow*' – [au]). But note the following:

  au only sounds as expected (i.e. like '-igh' in English *sigh* – [aɪ]) when it is not a plural ending (see §2)

  oe is English 'oy' – [ɔɪ]

  wy (unless preceded by **g-** or a vowel) is usually 'oo-ee' with the first element long and the second short – ([uːɪ])

Consonants

Consonants cannot be doubled except for **nn** and **rr** (and even here there is no change in pronunciation). **Dd**, **ff** and **ll** are separate letters in their own right, not doubled versions of **d**, **f** and **l**.

  ch is like Scottish *loch*, German **ach** or Spanish **jefe** - [x]

  dd is like English *this* – a voiced sound - [ð]

  f is English *v*

  ff is English *f*

  g is always as in *goal* (never as in *gem*)

  h is always sounded

  ll is an aspirated *l* – the articulation is the same as for **l**, but with an outward breath instead of voicing - [ɬ]

  ph is as in English *physical* – much less common in Welsh, which uses **ff** in all radical words

r is a rolled or 'flapped' *r*, not the Southern English or American type

rh is an aspirated rolled *r* – in practice the aspiration comes first, and the sound is *hr* – [ʰr]

s is always *s* (never a *z* sound), except in the combination **si** + vowel, where it stands for the sound spelt in English *sh* [ʃ] – **siop** *shop*

th is the unvoiced equivalent of **dd**, like English *think* - [θ]

i + vowel is like English *y*: **iard** *yard*

w + vowel is usually like English *w*: **Gwent**

Stress accent is nearly always on the penultimate syllable: **dàrllen, darllènodd, darllenàdwy**. But verbs ending (h)au and some words where two vowels have merged into a diphthong are stressed on the final syllable – **mwynhàu** *enjoy*, **Cymràeg** *Welsh language*; so are some adverbs that were originally two words (e.g. **ynghỳd** *together*, **ymlàen** *forward*).

2　Spelling and accents

Welsh spelling is a more consistent guide to pronunciation than is the English system. However, there are three general instances where spelling and pronunciation do not agree:

(a) **-au** as a plural marker (it is the commonest) sounds like **-a** in the N and like **-e** in the S. So what is written **pethau** *things* (sing. **peth**) is pronounced **petha** in the N and **pethe** in the S

Note that this is also true for the 3rd pers. sing. unreality verb-ending **-ai** (see §291). This historical (and indeed standard) spelling (as with pl. **-au**) has been retained in the body of the grammar for succinctness, but the user should always bear in mind that it stands for two pronunciations

(b) in most N areas, an unstressed **-e-** in a final syllable sounds like **-a-**, and is sometimes so written. Standard **rhedeg** *run* but N **rhedag**; standard **(ba) sen nhw** *they would be*, N **san nhw**

(c) final **-f** is usually silent except in very careful speech, and so is often omitted in informal writing, giving for example **tre** for **tref** *town*, **gaea** for **gaeaf** *winter*.

Other isolated cases will be pointed out as they occur in the grammar.

Vowels can be made long by adding a circumflex accent ^ : **tan** [tan] *until*, **tân** [ta:n] *fire*. But not all long vowels are so marked: many one-syllable words have a long vowel but no accent – **nos** [noːs] *night*, **ceg** [keːg] *mouth*, **dyn** [diːn] *man*.

As well as indicating a long vowel (see above), the circumflex accent is also occasionally encountered in the plural ending -**âu**, where it indicates that the singular noun ends in -**a**, which is merged with the plural ending -**au**; in other words, -**âu** = -**a** + **au**. So, for example, **camera**, pl. **camerâu** *cameras*. Note that, unlike the usual -**au** plural ending (see above), this variant -**âu** is always pronounced as written, i.e. like 'igh' [ai] in English *sigh*.

A similar function is performed by the diaeresis, i.e. two dots, usually over an **i** in the plural endings -**ïau** and -**ïon**, to indicate the the -**i**- is the final letter of the singular noun and not part of the ending, so for example **copi**, pl. **copïau** *copies*, **egni**, pl. **egnïon** *energies*. In these cases, the pronunciation is the same as the normal endings -**iau** and -**ion**. See also §60 (b), (c).

3–12

Mutations in Welsh

3 Different mutations in Welsh

In common with its sister Celtic languages, Welsh is characterized by a particular phenomenon that affects the form of words. This phenomenon is traditionally designated the mutation system, and will be so referred to here.

The mutations are phonological (and corresponding spelling) changes that affect (predominantly) the initial consonant of a word. For example, in the standard formal language, the word **plant** *children* can appear also as the following: **blant, phlant** or **mhlant**. Similarly, a word like **bara** *bread* sometimes appears as **fara** or **mara**. The reasons and conditions for these changes will be dealt with in the course of the grammar, but it is worth emphasizing here that the mutation system so briefly described here, or parts of it, pervade the entire structure of the language, and cannot be divorced from any aspect of it. These initial changes to words are as integral a part of Welsh as, say, the endings to words are in German or Russian.

In fact, the mutation system in Welsh, to all appearances at least, is one of the most complex found in any of the living Celtic languages – although, as will be indicated later, appearances can be deceptive. There are three different mutations in Welsh – the Soft Mutation (henceforth SM), the Aspirate Mutation (AM) and the Nasal Mutation (NM), and each of these operates a different set of sound changes on certain consonants, where circumstances require. There is also a Mixed Mutation (MM) which combines elements of the SM and AM. Note that not all consonants (and none at all of the vowels – though in very restricted circumstances they can add an h-) in Welsh are affected by mutation, and even fewer are affected by all three (**p**, as in **plant** above, is one). Also, again taking the example of **plant** above, different mutations have different effects on the same consonant – **p** can turn into **b**, **ph** or **mh** under SM, AM and NM respectively.

4 List of mutations

The mutations can be shown in their entirety (certain spoken usages excepted) in tabular form:

Original consonant	SM	AM	NM
c	g	ch	ngh
p	b	ph	mh
t	d	th	nh
g	(disappears)	–	ng
b	f	–	m
d	dd	–	n
ll	l	–	–
m	f	(mh)	–
rh	r	–	–
n	–	(nh)	–

In this table the dash (–) signifies that the original consonant does not change, i.e. it is not affected by that particular mutation.

The changes **mh** and **nh** in brackets under AM represent common spoken practice of long standing which, however, is not presently accepted as part of the standard written language.

5 General principles governing mutations

(a) Letters of the alphabet not appearing in the *Original consonant* column of the table above are not liable to mutation, and words beginning with them are invariable, whatever the circumstances. So the following Welsh words, for example, never undergo initial mutation: **arth, egni, fferm, halen, ildio, lôn, osgoi, siop, sothach, ŵy, ysgol**. It is important to note, however, that **ch** is a separate letter from **c** in Welsh (see Alphabet section), and while **c** can be mutated, **ch** cannot. So to the list of immutable words above we can add, for example, **chwaer**. Similarly **ll** and **l** are separate, as are **rh** and **r**.

(b) The changes that each mutation causes to each consonant are consistent, i.e. SM of **d**, for example, is always **dd**. The original nonmutated form of a word is called the radical.

(c) A consonant that has been mutated already cannot undergo a second mutation (in the standard language at least). For example, (SM) **t** gives **d**; and (SM) **d** gives **dd**; but while **tegell** *kettle* can become (SM) °**degell**, this cannot receive a second SM and become *ddegell.

(d) Where a mutation is 'triggered' by a particular word (as in the majority of cases in Welsh – lists of these are given in §9), its effect can be blocked, and thereby cancelled out, if another word gets in the way. For instance, **neu** *or* causes SM of the following word – so the phrase *a window or a door* would be **ffenest neu °ddrws** in Welsh (there is no word for *a*); but *the window or the door* would be **y ffenest neu'r drws** (no SM of **drws** because the intervening **'r** *the* blocks it).

(e) Where a mutation is triggered by sentence construction (a less frequent occurrence), this mutation cannot be neutralized by any other factors. For example, constructions with **rhaid** to convey the idea of *must* (§349) always require SM of the main verb:

Rhaid i mi °fynd yn °gynnar I must go early

It might be thought that this SM is simply triggered by the pronoun **mi** (pronouns are traditionally included on the 'trigger' list for SM), but if a name is substituted the mutation still applies:

Rhaid i Emrys °fynd yn °gynnar Emrys must go early

even though Emrys is of course not one of the relatively small number of words on the trigger list. Here then, it is clearly the sentence construction that is operating the mutation. In fact the SM is required after the actual or notional subject of the sentence (see §14 for a full discussion of this), and 'blocking' does not come into the matter.

6 Mutation differences between Literary and Colloquial Welsh

Literary Welsh and Colloquial Welsh (see pp. xv–xvi) differ in how they apply mutation rules, with the literary standard showing a more complex and rigidly applied system. Broadly speaking, the SM is far more generalized in the spoken language, at the expense of both AM and NM. This grammar reflects the more fluid situation in the language of most native speakers.

7 Indication of mutations in this grammar

All instances of mutation will be typographically indicated, both in the text of the grammar and in the illustrative examples, except instances of fixed soft mutation like **ddoe** *yesterday* (the radical **doe** is not found).

The Soft Mutation is by far the most prevalent of the three mutations in spoken Welsh. Its presence will be indicated by °:

(a) *after* a word which causes SM of the following letter. So, for example, **heb°** tells the reader simply that **heb** causes SM on the following word where possible;

(b) *before* a word to show that the word is here seen in its mutated form – °**fara** is to warn the reader that this form is not the radical (**bara**) but the SM-version of the word.

The Aspirate Mutation and Nasal Mutation are similarly indicated [h] and [n] throughout.

So, for example, the radical word **cegin** will have its mutated variants shown as follows:

(Soft Mutation)	°**gegin**
(Aspirate Mutation)	[h]**chegin**
(Nasal Mutation)	[n]**nghegin**

8 Reasons for mutation

All instances of the mutations in Welsh can be classified as either:

(a) contact mutations – where a mutation of a word is 'triggered' by the word preceding. This involves a relatively small number of high-frequency words. They are listed below.

(b) grammatical mutations – where the mutation (almost invariably SM) is not 'triggered' by a particular word, but fulfils some grammatical function.

9 Words causing contact mutation

Soft Mutation *(SM)*

Prepositions:

am° ar° at° dan° dros° gan° heb° hyd° i° o° tan° trwy°/drwy° wrth°

Other types of word:

a°	[relative] (see §481)	**mi°**	[particle] (see §213)
dacw°	*(over) there is/are . . .*	**mor°**	*so* [not **ll-, rh-**]
dau°	*two* (m)	**(y)na°**	*there*
dwy°	*two* (f)	**neu°**	*or*
dy°	*your*	**pa°...**	*which . . . . . . ?*
dyma°	*here is/are . . .*	**pan°**	*when*
dyna°	*there is/are . . .*	**pur°**	*very*
ei°	*his*	**rhy°**	*too*
fe°	[particle] (see §213)	**un°**	*one* (f) (not **ll-, rh-**)
go°	*fairly*	**y°**	*the* (f) (not **ll-, rh-**)
(y)ma°	*here*	**yn°**	[complement marker – nouns and adjectives only; not **ll-, rh-**]

Adjectives preceding nouns, e.g. hen °ddyn *old man*, Prif °Weinidog *Prime Minister*

Nos with days of the week, e.g. **Nos °Fawrth** *Tuesday night*

Several common prefixes used in word-formation cause internal SM:

af- *un-*:

afresymol *unreasonable* [**rhesymol** *reasonable*]

aflwyddiannus *unsuccessful* [**llwyddiannus** *successful*]

di- *un-*, *-less*, *without*:

didrafferth *without problems* [**trafferth** *trouble, problems*]

di-Gymraeg *non-Welsh-speaking* [lit. *Welshless*]

dibaid *ceaseless* [**paid, peidio** *cease*]

cyd- *co-, con-*:

cydbwysedd *balance* [**pwysedd** *weight, pressure*]

cyd-ddigwyddiad *coincidence* [**digwydd** *happen*]

cydweithwyr *colleagues* [**gweithio** *work*]

gwrth- *anti-, counter-, against*

gwrthblaid *opposition party* [**plaid** *(political) party*]

gwrthgynhyrchol *counterproductive* [**cynhyrchu** *produce*]

hunan- *self-*

hunanbarch *self-esteem* [**parch** *respect*]

hunanladdiad *suicide* [**lladd** *kill*]

rhag- *pre-, fore-*

rhagweld *foresee* [**gweld** *see*]

rhagfarn *prejudice* [**barn** *judgment*]

ym- [reflexive – often meaning *self* or *each other*]

ymolchi *wash (oneself)* [**golchi** *wash*]

ymladd *fight* [**lladd** *kill*]

as does a noun attached to the front of another noun to make a compound, e.g. llys + mam = llysfam *stepmother*.

Aspirate Mutation (AM)

a[h]	*and*	**gyda**[h]	*with*
â[h]	*with*	**tri**[h]	*three (m)*
chwe[h]	*six*	**tua**[h]	*towards, about*
ei[h]	*her* [poss.]		

AM is not consistently applied after any of these words in many areas, though it is fairly common after **ei**[h] *her*. It should also be noted that in many areas the incidence of AM is much more consistent with words beginning c- than with words beginning p- or (particularly) t-. So, for example, it is common enough, and natural, to hear **bws a** [h]**char** *a bus and a car*, but **bws a** [h]**thacsi** *a bus and a taxi* is unusual and, indeed, sounds affected to many speakers. Similarly, **tri** [h]**cheffyl** *three horses* sounds perfectly natural and normal to native speakers, while **tri** [h]**thwll** *three holes* generally does not, or at least sounds distinctly affected.

Nasal Mutation (NM)

fyⁿ, **'(y)n**ⁿ *my*   **yn**ⁿ *in*

NM is not consistently applied after these two words in many parts of Wales – see relevant sections for details.

In addition, some time words (notably **blynedd** *year* and **diwrnod** *day*) undergo NM after certain numerals (see §176).

One word-formation prefix – **an-** (*un-, in-*) – causes internal NM:

an-	+ **tebyg**	*likely*	**annhebyg**	*unlikely*
	+ **darllenadwy**	*legible*	**annarllenadwy**	*illegible*
	+ **cyson**	*consistent*	**anghyson**	*inconsistent*
	+ **cofio**	*remember*	**anghofio**	*forget*
	+ **posib**	*possible*	**amhosib**	*impossible*

Words like these with internal NM are regarded as radical words in their own right, and this is the only case in modern Welsh where the NM is consistently applied.

The **-n** of **an-** drops when mutating **b-** to **m-**, **c-** to **ngh-** or **p-** to **mh-**: an + pendant (*definite*) becomes **amhendant** *indefinite*. Note also that radicals beginning **tr-** cause one of the resulting **n**'s to drop – **tebyg** becomes **annhebyg** but **trefn** *order* becomes **anhrefn** *chaos* (not **annhrefn*). This does not affect pronunciation, since doubled consonants (i.e. -nn- and -rr-) are not pronounced double in Welsh.

10 Mixed mutation (MM)

This involves using AM where possible (i.e. on **c**, **p** and **t**), and SM otherwise. This mutation is more a feature of the literary language than of the spoken, though it is heard in the speech of some speakers. It is primarily used with NEG inflected verbs – for example, ʰ*pharith* hi °ddim *it won't last* uses AM on **p-** (para *last*), but °*ddylset* ti °ddim *you shouldn't* uses SM, because **d-** cannot undergo AM.

11 Grammatical mutation

There are five main instances where SM is present for grammatical reasons:

(a) After the subject of the sentence – **Naethon nhw° fynd** *They went.* See §14 for full discussion

(b) With adverbs of time, and occasionally of manner – **°ddwy °flynedd yn ôl** *two years ago* (see §403)

(c) Where a noun is used in addressing or calling someone – **Dewch fan hyn, °blant!** *Come here, children!*

(d) Generally with all inflected verbs – **°Golles i'r tocyn** *I lost the ticket*; **°Allwch chi °weld e o fan hyn** *You can see him from here.* This spoken usage is not reflected in the written language, where more complex mutation rules apply (see §6).

(e) After an 'intrusive' word that is not part of the basic VSO pattern (see §13). Compare:

> **Fe °alla i °weld darn o °bapur**
>
> I can see a piece of paper
>
> **Fe °alla i °weld hefyd ° ddarn o °bapur**
>
> I can also see a piece of paper [**hefyd** *also* inserted]

12 Words that cannot undergo mutation

These are:

(a) words that are already mutated, like **beth?** *what?* (from **peth** *thing*) or **dros** *across, over* (originally **tros**)

(b) miscellaneous words: **dy°** *your*, **pan°** *when*, **mae** *is/are*, **mai** and **taw** *that* (in focused sentences), **mor°** *so*, **tua** *towards, about*, **byth** *ever/never*, **lle** *where* – usage varies with the last two; and certain adverbs like **tu allan** *outside* that originally had **y** preceding

(c) non-Welsh place-names: **i Birmingham**, **i Bonn**. But places outside Wales which nevertheless have special Welsh names are subject to mutation: **i °Fanceinion** *to Manchester* (**Manceinion**), **i °Fryste** *to Bristol* (**Bryste**). In speech, examples like **i °Firmingham** are not uncommon, however, with some speakers at least.

(d) personal names – **i Dafydd** usually, rather than **i °Ddafydd**

(e) foreign words, especially those beginning with **g-**: **garej**, **gêm**. Also some very short Welsh words in **g-**: **ar gro'r afon** *on the (pebble-) bank of the river* (not: **ar °ro . . .*). But note **glo** *coal* – **lori °lo** *coal-lorry*

Note also that occasionally a d- does not mutate as expected if the preceding word ends in -s: **nos da** *good night*, **wythnos diwetha** *last week* – SM of the adjectives **da** and **diwetha** would be expected here (i.e. **nos °dda*, **wythnos °ddiwetha*) as they follow singular feminine nouns **nos** and **wythnos**, but this is overridden probably for reasons of euphony.

Words that cannot undergo mutation

15

Word order and sentence structure

Note: for this important and fundamental aspect of the mechanics of Welsh, it is important to have a clear understanding of the concepts of *subject*, *object* and *complement*. If in doubt, you should check the **Glossary** for definitions before proceeding.

13 General principles

Welsh shares with all the other Celtic languages (see p. xiii) one striking aspect of sentence structure that sets it apart from other European languages: the verb occupies the first main position in neutral sentences, with the subject following. This is the reverse of the normal situation in languages like English:

Fred	*arrived*
[subj.]	[verb]
°Gyrhaeddodd	**Fred**
Arrived	Fred
[verb]	[subj.]

In other European languages, including English, the verb is the second main idea (not necessarily second word) in the sentence, separating the subject (first position) from the complement – either the object or a phrase dependent on the verb (and following the verb). Compare:

The man	opened	the door
[subj.]	[verb]	[obj.]
Agorodd	**y dyn**	**y drws**
Opened	the man	the door
[verb]	[subj.]	[obj.]

This sentence structure is traditionally known as VSO (verb-subject-object – though verb-subject-complement would be more accurate), while the English type is SVO. The VSO rule in Welsh, however, is more general than the SVO rule in English. Consider the following English sentences:

(AFF) Fred *is* here

(INT) *Is* Fred here?

(NEG) Fred *is* not here

In the AFF (affirmative – i.e. statement) and NEG (negative) sentences, the subject (*Fred*) comes first, with the verb (*is*) in second place, and a complement (*here*) following. *Not* is added for the NEG, but otherwise the two sentences are structurally identical. In the INT (interrogative – i.e. question) sentence, the verb and the subject change places.

Now compare the Welsh versions (**ddim** corresponds to *not* in NEG):

   (AFF) *Mae* **Fred fan hyn**

   (INT) *Ydy* **Fred fan hyn?**

   (NEG) *Dydy* **Fred °ddim fan hyn**

Note that the verb (in italics) comes first regardless of whether the sentence is AFF, INT or NEG. The changing form of the verb in this example (**mae–ydy–dydy**) is a secondary feature unique to the verb *to be* (see §218(b)); the important point here is its fixed position at the start – and this would be true of any verb, for example °**gaeth** *got*:

   (AFF) °**Gaeth Fred °wobr**   *Fred got a prize*

   (INT) °**Gaeth Fred °wobr?**   *Did Fred get a prize?*

   (NEG) °**Gaeth Fred °ddim gwobr**   *Fred didn't get a prize*

From this it is clear that the main reason for shifting the verb from its usual position in English (in INT sentences) has no bearing whatever on Welsh. In this sense, the VSO rule can be seen as a much more general rule.

14 Mutation implications of VSO word-order

An obvious consequence of VSO word-order is that the subject of the sentence has nothing to separate it from the complement, because the verb has already preceded it. But in Welsh the boundary between the subject and the complement is marked by the presence of SM (°). A truer picture of neutral word-order in Welsh, therefore, would be VS°O, with whatever follows the subject receiving SM if possible, i.e. unless it:

(a)   begins with an immutable letter (see §5(a));

or

(b)   is permanently resistant to mutation (see §12).

This is probably the most important, and simplest, mutation rule in modern Welsh, and may be summarized as:

[SUBJECT] °

It accounts for most incidences of SM that are not simply contact mutations (i.e. triggered by certain words, e.g. **neu**°, **pan**°, **am**° etc.), and if we extend the idea of subject to include cases (such as the command forms of verbs – §380) where:

(a)   the subject is not stated but is understood

and

(b)   the doer of the action is clear in the speaker's mind, even if it is not technically the grammatical subject of the sentence – this may be viewed as a 'notional' or semantic subject

then virtually all incidences of grammatical mutation are covered. Examples:

(a)   **Collodd Aled °ddwy °bunt**
Aled lost £2
[Aled is the stated subject of the sentence]

(b)   **Naeth Aled °golli dwy °bunt**
Aled lost £2
[Aled is the stated subject again, but in this different construction it is the VN (**colli**) that follows the subject, so this receives the SM, and not **dwy**]

(c)   **Rhaid iddo fe °fynd**
He must go
[**fe** *he/him* is technically not the grammatical subject of the Welsh sentence, but it is clearly he who has to do the going, therefore notional or semantic subject]

(d)   **Rhaid i Aled °fynd**
Aled has to go
[same as previous example, except with a proper name instead of a pronoun]

(e)   **Rho °ddwy °bunt i mi!**
Give me £2! [lit. Give £2 to me]

[subject not expressed after a command form, but the idea of *you* is understood in the mind of the speaker, and if stated would follow the verb: **Rho di °ddwy °bunt i mi!**]

It is worth noting that many textbooks wrongly place the pronouns among the list of words causing 'contact' SM. This might account for example (c) above (with **fe** ostensibly causing contact mutation), but not for example (d), where **mynd** still becomes °**fynd**, even though the pronoun has been replaced. The [**subject**]° rule neatly deals with the apparent anomaly.

15   Complement-marker yn in VSO bod-sentences

Where the verb at the front of the sentence is some part of **bod** *be* (as is frequently the case in Welsh), an additional indicator **yn**° (see §473) is (usually – see below) placed between subject and complement. Compare:

(a) Naethon   nhw   °**wastraffu'u harian**

    [verb]   [subj.]°   [complement]

    They wasted their money

(b) Maen   nhw°   'n   **gwastraffu'u harian**

    [verb]   [subj.] °   [yn]   [complement]

    They are wasting their money

In example (a), the verb at the front is not part of **bod** (it is the preterite of **gwneud**), so SM alone is used to mark the boundary between subject and complement. The first word of the complement (*waste their money*) is the VN **gwastraffu** *waste*, so this takes the SM and becomes °**wastraffu**. In example (b), the verb at the front is a part of **bod** (3rd pers. pl. pres. – **maen**), so an **yn** (here **'n** because of preceding vowel) is inserted just before the complement. This has the effect of blocking the SM, and the VN **gwastraffu** remains as it is.

There is a further complication with the complement-marker **yn**: depending on what type of word begins the complement (in the above example it was a VN – **gwastraffu**), it appears either as **yn** or as **yn**°. The rule is simple:

In sentences beginning with some part of **bod** *be*:

yn before a complement beginning with a VN;

yn° before a complement beginning with a noun or adjective;

all other cases – no **yn** at all.

19

In practice this means that:

(a) the particle written **yn** mutates nouns and adjectives, but leaves VNs unchanged;

(b) complements beginning with some other part of speech (almost invariably an adverb) MUST NOT have a preceding **yn**.

These principles can be seen in the following, where complement 1 begins with a VN (**tynnu**), complement 2 with an adjective (**tost**), and complement 3 with an adverb (**tu allan**):

[verb]	[subj.]		[complement]
1 **Mae'r**	**ffotograffydd**	*yn*	**tynnu llun**
The photographer's			*taking a picture*
2 **Mae'r**	**ffotograffydd**	*yn*	**°dost**
The photographer's			*ill*
3 **Mae'r**	**ffotograffydd**		**tu allan**
The photographer's			*outside*

16 Exceptions to VSO word-order in Welsh

There are two special types of sentence in Welsh where the VSO rule is broken and the verb displaced from its first position. All other sentence types are 'neutral', and in this grammar 'neutral sentence' means any sentence with normal VSO word-order.

The two exceptions are:

(a) identification sentences

(b) focused sentences

Identification sentences represent a particular use of the verb **bod** *be*, and they are explained in §220. Remember also that sentences involving the superlative of adjectives (*the . . . -est, the most . . .*) are a type of identification sentence in Welsh (see §108).

Focused sentences constitute a far more fundamental element in the grammatical structure of Welsh, and are dealt with in detail below.

17–21 FOCUSED SENTENCES

17 Definitions and general remarks

A focused sentence is any sentence where one particular element (whether a single word or a number of words making up a single idea) is given prominence or highlighted. This may be for emphasis, or to contradict something already said, or in giving a specific (i.e. singled out) piece of information in answer to a question. Focused elements can occur in English and Welsh, but the two languages deal with them in very different ways. The best way of approaching this important aspect of Welsh grammar is to look first at how it is dealt with in English.

Consider the following dialogues in English:

(a) What happened next?   Iwan broke the window.

(b) Who broke the window?   Iwan broke the window.

We are concerned here with the responses, which in the English examples above look the same in writing, but do not sound the same in speech – the word *Iwan* is given a more forceful intonation in (b), and this is how English very often indicates a focused element. We could represent this in writing by, say, italicizing the element, but structurally there is no modification to the neutral response (a) to turn it into the focused response (b). In (a) no element is particularly highlighted for attention – the whole sentence is new information. But in (b) *Iwan* is highlighted as the only new piece of information, as a window being broken has already been mentioned in the question. Intonation, then, is an important factor in English sentence structure, and especially where focused elements are involved. This is as a result of the very fixed and rigid nature of word-order in English: all AFF sentences need some kind of subject at the start, then the verb, and all other elements following on behind. It is worth noting that the only way to focus an element in English without resorting to intonation change is to completely alter the structure of the sentence:

It was Iwan *who* broke the window

18 Principles of focused sentences in Welsh

As regards sentence structure, Welsh (like many other European languages) has more flexibility and 'room for manoeuvre' than English. For example, although there is a general rule that the verb comes as first main element in a Welsh sentence (see §13), it is not an absolute rule (as is, for example, the 'subject' rule in English), and there is nothing to stop some other element coming in first position if need be. However, the 'verb first' rule in Welsh is fundamental enough to make any deviation from it quite noticeable, and this factor makes verb-position an ideal way of indicating a focused element – quite simply, Welsh places focused elements in what is usually the verb slot, where normally they would least be expected. This is what draws attention to them. We can see this principle in action in the Welsh versions of the two English examples (a) and (b) in §17 above:

(a) **Be' °ddigwyddodd wedyn?**   **°Dorrodd Iwan y ffenest**
     What happened next?   Iwan broke the window

(b) **Pwy °dorrodd y ffenest?**   **Iwan °dorrodd y ffenest**
     Who broke the window?   *Iwan* broke the window

This technique pushes the verb into second place, an unusual position in itself from the point of view of Welsh, but correct and natural where focus is intended on the element preceding it. Note that this is one of the very few circumstances where **mae** *is/are*, a start-of-sentence word if ever there was one, can be dislodged (for another, see §140). Compare:

	1	2	3
(a)	**Mae**	**'ch llyfrau**	**ar y bwrdd**

     Your books are on the table   [neutral statement]

	1	2	3
(b)	**Ar y bwrdd mae**	**'ch llyfrau**	

     Your books are *on the table*   [focused element italic]

Example (b) answers the notional question *Where are my books?* In the Welsh version, position 1 is occupied by an element (in this case a phrase) that is not a verb, and so this element must be the object of focus. In the neutral sentence (a), on the other hand, position 1 is occupied by the verb (**Mae**), and this fact alone indicates right at the outset that no special focus or emphasis is intended in the rest of the sentence.

The same principle operates in Welsh for INT sentences. Compare:

I	2	3
(a) Ydy	**'ch gwraig**	**yn siarad Almaeneg?**

Does your wife speak German?

I	2	3
(b) Eich gwraig	**sy**	**'n siarad Almaeneg?**

Is it your wife who speaks German?

Example (a) is neutral, because it simply asks whether something is true or not; example (b) focuses on **eich gwraig**– the questioner knows, perhaps, that someone here speaks German, and wants to narrow it down to exactly who. Once again, English alters the sentence structure to put focus on *your wife*, with dummy subject *it* in front, and relative *who* immediately after. Intonation would again be a possible, but here less likely, option.

Focused INT sentences can optionally be preceded by a particle **Ai**, so for above:

Ai eich (or **Ai'ch**) **gwraig sy'n siarad Almaeneg?**

Further examples:

Ai nhw sy'n °gyfrifol?

(Is it) they (who) are responsible?

Ai'r Cynulliad ei hun °ddylai talu am hyn?

(Is it) the Welsh Assembly itself (that) should pay for this?

This particle ai is also used to introduce INT focused indirect sentences (see §493).

Difficulties with present tense of bod *be in* **focused sentences**

In focused sentences where the verb is 3rd pers. sing. of **bod**, either **mae** or **sy(dd)** is possible, depending on the sense. Compare:

Heledd sy'n siarad Almaeneg

(It is) Heledd (who) speaks German

[i.e. not Angharad – focus on Heledd]

Almaeneg *mae* Heledd yn siarad

It is German that Heledd speaks

[i.e. not Russian – focus on German]

Both the above examples are focused sentences, but in the first one the focused element (Heledd) is the *subject* of the sentence (she is doing the speaking), while in the second the focused element (German) is the *object* (it is the thing spoken).

Given that some form of 3rd pers. sing. present of **bod** is required, there are three choices: **ydy/yw**, **mae** and **sy** (all 3rd pers. sing. present). The criterion for choosing between **sy** and **mae** (i.e. is the preceding word the subject or the object?) is the same as in questions beginning with **Pwy . . .?** *Who . . .?* or **Beth . . .?** *What . . .?* (see §140). **Ydy/yw** is not relevant here, since its use in second position indicates an identification sentence (see §223).

All other parts of **bod**, and all other verbs, are straightforward because only the 3rd pers. sing. present of **bod** has these distinct forms. For example, with the imperfect of **bod** we would have in spoken Welsh:

Heledd *oedd* yn siarad Almaeneg

(It was) Heledd (who) spoke German

Almaeneg *oedd* Heledd yn siarad

It was German that Heledd spoke

Here the only difference other than the focused elements is the position of complement-marker **yn**, which always immediately precedes the first word of the complement (**siarad**).

20   Removal of yn in focused sentences

If the element to be focused immediately follows the **yn** in the neutral sentence, then the **yn** is removed in the focused version:

Neutral   **Maen nhw'*n* codi tatws**

            They're digging potatoes

Focused   **Codi tatws maen nhw**

            They're *digging potatoes* [i.e. not doing something else]

            [not: *Yn codi tatws maen nhw]

Neutral   **Dw i'n mynd i'r °dafarn**

            I'm going to the pub

Focused   **Mynd i'r °dafarn dw i**

            I'm *going to the pub*

            [i.e. I don't know what *you're* doing, but . . .]

            [not: *Yn mynd i'r °dafarn dw i]

This rule (see §473) applies to complement-marker **yn** only – the preposition **yn** *in* cannot be removed:

Neutral   **Mae ei rhieni'n byw yn Llangefni bellach**

            Her parents live in Llangefni now

Focused   **Yn Llangefni mae ei rhieni'n byw bellach**

            Her parents live *in Llangefni* now

21   'that . . .' followed by focused sentence

Where a focused sentence is the second half of a two-part *that . . .* sentence (for example: *I think + that + Iwan broke the window*), special words for *that* are required because of the abnormal word-order. This is explained fully in §§492–494.

Articles

22   The indefinite article

There is no indefinite article in Welsh, so English *a* and *an* are not translated – the indefiniteness of a noun is indicated by the absence of any preceding article. This means there is no difference in Welsh between *apple* and *an apple*. This distinction matters only in English, and whether or not to include *a/an* in translating is a question that English speakers will have no trouble deciding.

afal apple, an apple   **gorsaf** station, a station

English possesses 'substitute' indefinite articles for use with plural nouns and uncountable nouns such as *bread* (we do not normally speak of *breads* except in a very restricted sense). These words are *some* and (with questions and negatives) *any*. They similarly have no equivalent in the Welsh system. Where they occur in this use in English, they must be left untranslated in Welsh.

23   'Substitute' indefinite articles

Look, I bought *some apples* when I was in town this morning

but: **Edrychwch, nes i °brynu *afalau* pan o'n i yn y °dre bore 'ma**

Have you got *any white bread* today?

but: **Oes *bara gwyn* 'da chi heddiw?**

Fred hasn't paid *any tax* on his car for years

but: **Dyw Fred °ddim wedi talu *treth* ar ei °gar ers blynyddau**

In other words, *I bought some apples* is rendered in Welsh as *I bought apples* which, after all, means the same thing. It is merely a rule of English that prefers an article substitute in these cases. Welsh, having no concept of an indefinite article, is consistent in ignoring it. Note also that sometimes, as in the last example above, the article substitute is optional in English (*Fred hasn't paid tax on his car*), and even in the other examples, omission of *some* or *any*, while perhaps sounding slightly odd, makes no difference to the sense in English. This is the test for whether or not these words are article substitutes and therefore to be left untranslated.

24 Cases where 'some' and 'any' must be translated in Welsh

Where *some* and *any* are not simply used as article substitutes, but as words with their own meaning, then they will of course appear in Welsh too. Compare the following:

(a) I bought *some apples* in town this morning

(b) *Some apples* are green, and *some apples* are red

We have seen that omitting *some* in sentence (a) makes no difference to the meaning. But in (b) such an omission is not possible – the *some* carries distinctive meaning that is necessary to the sense. Further examples:

(a) Have you bought *any books* lately?

(b) Take *any books* that you want

(a) Do they want *any help*?

(b) *Any help* is better than no help at all

Rhai, rhyw° and **unrhyw°** are all possible translations for *some* and *any*. Their use is explained under §§115, 148.

25 The definite article

The underlying form of the definite article *the* is **yr** in Welsh, but this appears in three different forms depending on the words around it:

yr	when the following word begins with a vowel or **h-**
y	when the following word begins with a consonant
'r	when the preceding word ends with a vowel

Clearly, there is a potential conflict of interests in this arrangement as it stands, because the article could have a consonant following, for example, but also a vowel preceding. In these cases, the third option 'r always takes precedence. Therefore in isolation we find:

alarch	swan	**yr alarch**	the swan	[begins with a vowel]
hebog	hawk	**yr hebog**	the hawk	[begins with **h-**]
barcud	kite	**y barcud**	the kite	[begins with a consonant]

but:

i'r alarch	to the swan
i'r hebog	to the hawk
i'r barcud	to the kite

because in all these cases the preceding word ends in a vowel, nullifying all other considerations as to the form of the article.

26   The definite article with singular and plural nouns

Whether the following noun is singular or plural makes no difference to the form of the definite article in Welsh, and the principles outlined in §25 above are operated independently of this factor.

yr alarch the swan	**yr elyrch** the swans
i'r alarch to the swan	**i'r elyrch** to the swans, etc.

27   The definite article and gender of the noun

The gender of the following noun (see §44) similarly makes no difference to the form of the definite article, and the principles outlined in §25 above are operated independently of whether the noun is masculine or feminine.

28   Mutations and the definite article

The effect of the definite article on the following noun differs with gender:

Masculine nouns, whether sing. or pl., do not change after the definite article.

Feminine singular nouns undergo SM when preceded by the definite article, while feminine plural nouns remain, like all masculines, unaffected. Compare:

bardd (*m*)	bard, poet	**y bardd**	the bard
baner (*f*)	flag	**y °faner**	the flag
beirdd	bards, poets	**y beirdd**	the bards
baneri	flags	**y baneri**	the flags
ci (*m*)	dog	**y ci**	the dog
cath (*f*)	cat	**y °gath**	the cat
cŵn	dogs	**y cŵn**	the dogs
cathod	cats	**y cathod**	the cats
drych (*m*)	mirror	**y drych**	the mirror
draig (*f*)	dragon	**y °ddraig**	the dragon
drychau	mirrors	**y drychau**	the mirrors
dreigiau	dragons	**y dreigiau**	the dragons
geiriadur (*m*)	dictionary	**y geiriadur**	the dictionary
gorsaf (*f*)	station	**yr °orsaf**	the station
geiriaduron	dictionaries	**y geiriaduron**	the dictionaries
gorsafoedd	stations	**y gorsafoedd**	the stations
mab (*m*)	son	**y mab**	the son
merch (*f*)	daughter	**y °ferch**	the daughter
meibion	sons	**y meibion**	the sons
merched	daughters	**y merched**	the daughters
pennaeth (*m*)	chief	**y pennaeth**	the chief
pabell (*f*)	tent	**y °babell**	the tent
penaethiaid	chiefs	**y penaethiaid**	the chiefs
pebyll	tents	**y pebyll**	the tents
traeth (*m*)	beach, strand	**y traeth**	the beach
tylluan (*f*)	owl	**y °dylluan**	the owl
traethau	beaches	**y traethau**	the beaches
tylluanod	owls	**y tylluanod**	the owls

Notes:

(a) Since **g-** disappears under SM, the definite article in isolation will be **yr** (except with some feminines beginning **gw-** where the **w** is a consonant: **gwlad** (one syllable) *country*, **y °wlad** *the country*). This loss of initial **g-**, incidentally, makes identification of an unknown feminine noun difficult for the learner, since there is no way of telling whether, for example, **yr ardd** is a masculine or feminine noun **ardd** (with basic form beginning with a vowel), or a feminine noun **gardd** (with **g-** dropped by SM because of the preceding definite article). Where there are no other clues, look the word up first as it stands, and if it is not listed, then assume a missing **g-**.

(b) Feminine singulars beginning with **ll-** and **rh-** do not undergo SM after the definite article:

lloeren	satellite	**y lloeren**	the satellite
rhodfa	avenue	**y rhodfa**	the avenue

This case of 'selective' application of SM is unusual, however. Generally, when SM is required, all nine consonants are liable, whatever the circumstances.

29 The numeral 2 and the definite article

Both forms (i.e. masculine and feminine) of the numeral *two* (dau° m, dwy° f) undergo SM after the definite article, becoming y °ddau°, y °ddwy° – see §162.

30 Divergence of use of definite articles in Welsh and English

The circumstances where the definite article is used are broadly parallel in English and Welsh – more so, in fact, than is the case between other languages. Even so, there are instances where one language omits the article while the other requires it.

31 Definite article in Welsh, none in English

There are three main instances of this:

(a)   Names of places (particularly countries) are often used with the definite article in Welsh. English has a few examples – The Netherlands, The Gambia, The United States – but Welsh has many more. The commonest names of countries that diverge from English in this regard are:

Yr Alban	Scotland	**Yr Eidal**	Italy
Yr Aifft	Egypt	**Y Ffindir**	Finland
Yr Almaen	Germany	**Y Swisdir**	Switzerland
Yr Ariannin	Argentina		

Iwerddon *Ireland* is sometimes heard with a definite article, though more often not. An alternative for *Scotland*, the loanword **Sgotland**, is sometimes heard in speech, but is very unusual otherwise – the Welsh name **Yr Alban** is exclusively used in the media these days, and is becoming more and more prevalent generally.

Place-names in Wales and the Marches often include a definite article where the English equivalent does not. Common examples:

Y Barri	Barry	**Y Trallwng**	Welshpool
Y Drenewydd	Newtown	**Yr Wyddfa**	Snowdon
Y Fenni	Abergavenny	**Y Gelli**	Hay
Yr Wyddgrug	Mold	**Y Garn**	Roch (Pembs)

(b)   With certain adverbial expressions of movement to and location at a place. English has a preference for dropping the article in phrases such as *in town*, *at work*, *to school*, etc., where the place is gone to on a regular or routine basis. This omission is obligatory, and applies only with certain words – we have to say, for example, *I am going to bed*, but we cannot say *I am going to bank*. But Welsh does not make this distinction, and uses the article regardless: **Dw i'n mynd i'r gwely**; **Dw i'n mynd i'r banc.**

motion:	to bed	**i'r gwely**
location:	in bed	**yn y gwely**
motion:	to school	**i'r ysgol**
location:	at school	**yn yr ysgol**
motion:	to work	**i'r gwaith**
location:	at work	**yn y gwaith**
motion/location:	upstairs	**i fyny'r grisiau** (N), **lan y grisiau** (S)
motion/location:	downstairs	**lawr y grisiau**

Note for the last two examples, however, that the common loanword alternative **staer** follows the English practice without the article: **i fyny staer; lan staer; lawr staer**.

Note also that both motion towards and location at home is usually expressed without a preposition in Welsh (see §421):

motion:	(to) home	**adre**
location:	(at) home	**gartre**

Means of transport (*by bus, car, train*) are likewise rephrased as *with/on <u>the</u> bus*, etc.

°**Ddes i fan hyn ar y bws**	I came here by bus
°**Ddaethoch chi gyda'r trên?**	Did you come by train?

(c)   The various expressions for *this, that, these, those*, both spoken **y . . .'ma**, **y . . .'na** and literary **y . . . hwn**, etc. (see §117) require the definite article. Pronouns **y rhain** *these* (ones), **y rheiny** *those* (ones) (see §136) often drop the article in speech. See paragraphs indicated for details of all these.

32   Definite article in English, none in Welsh

Instances of this fall into two categories:

(a)   When two nouns are in a genitive relationship, as in, for example, *the car of your neighbour* (= *your neighbour's car*), the first definite article is dropped in Welsh: **car eich cymydog**. This important construction is dealt with fully under §40.

(b)   Names of rivers in Welsh, unlike English, do not normally have the definite article: **Hafren** *the Severn*; **Tafwys** *the Thames*; **Gwy** *the Wye*; **Dyfrdwy** *the Dee*. The word **afon** *river* may be prefixed to the river-name in a genitive relationship (see (a) above), but the name itself remains without an article – **Afon Ystwyth** *the River Ystwyth*; **Afon Dyfrdwy** *the River Dee*.

The same principle applies to other named geographical features, e.g. mountains – **Mynydd Talfan** *Mount Talfan* – but here English follows the same usage as Welsh anyway.

33 Definite article in Welsh corresponding to indefinite in English

In expressions of price/quantity and time/distance, **yr** is used where English requires either *a* or *per*:

hanner can ceiniog y dwsin — fifty pence a dozen

ugain milltir yr awr — twenty miles per hour

Note **yr un** *each*:

°Werthes i nhw i gyd am °dair punt yr un
I sold them all for three pounds each

not to be confused with **°bob un,** which generally implies every single one:

°Werthes i nhw °bob un
I sold every single one of them

Money and prices are discussed generally under §181.

Nouns

34   Definitions and general remarks

Nouns are words that name things, ideas, places or people. They are the largest category of words in the language, and fall into two broad groups:

(a) proper nouns. These are names, either of places or people, and are written with a capital letter. Examples in English would be *Fred*, *Argentina*, *Mrs Williams*, *Thames*, *Hastings*, *William the Conqueror* and *Battle Abbey*; and examples in Welsh would be **Dafydd**, **Norwy**, **Mrs Williams**, **Hafren**, **Cilmeri**, **Llywelyn Tywysog Cymru** and **Abaty Ystrad Fflur**.

(b) common nouns – all the rest. These are not written with a capital letter, and come in two main groups, known as count nouns and mass, or uncountable, nouns.

> count nouns denote countable, tangible or otherwise perceptible objects and living things, e.g., **cath** *cat*, **tŷ** *house*, **llenni** *curtains*, **gwlad** *country*, **gaeaf** *winter*, **awel** *breeze*.

> mass nouns denote (normally) uncountable things, or abstract ideas and concepts, e.g., **siwgwr** *sugar*, **mêl** *honey*, **bara** *bread*, **te** *tea*, **aur** *gold*, **llawenydd** *happiness*, **anufudd-dod** *disobedience*, **oerfel** *cold(ness)*, **chwilfrydedd** *curiosity*.

> Generally, count and mass nouns act the same way, except that mass nouns are not usually found in the plural (they are sometimes – for example we can talk about different 'breads', meaning different types of bread, or three 'teas', meaning three cups of tea), and the abstracts among them are often used without the definite article.

The above definitions are as true for Welsh as for English. In addition, Welsh has a large category of verbal nouns (VNs). These are dealt with separately in §§198–209.

35   'Specific' words

This is an important concept in Welsh, and the distinction between specific and non-specific words is crucial to the understanding of certain aspects of Welsh grammar, notably the use of the preposition **yn** *in* (see §473) and the negator **mo** (see §295).

A word counts as 'specific' in Welsh if it is:

(a)   preceded by the definite article **y(r)** (see §25)

(b)   a proper name (see §34(a))

(c)   a pronoun (see §119)

(d)   preceded by a possessive adjective (*my, his,* etc.) (see §109).

For example, **tŷ** (*a*) *house* is non-specific (it could refer to any house), while **y tŷ** *the house* is specific (the speaker has a particular house in mind). **Ei °dŷ** *his house* is specific for the same reason – in saying this we must have a particular house in mind. Pronouns are used to refer to a person or thing already mentioned, so are by definition specific. And proper names are labels that we use to refer to specific people or places – **Harlech** refers to a particular place.

36   Mutations with Welsh proper nouns

It is a general rule of the modern language that personal names are not subject to mutation. Compare these sentences, with a proper and a common noun following **i°** *to*:

> **°Roddes i'r manylion i °bennaeth yr adran ddoe [pennaeth]**
>
> I gave the details to the head of the department yesterday

> **°Roddes i'r manylion i Pedr ddoe [Pedr]**
>
> I gave the details to Pedr yesterday

37   Mutations with Welsh geographical names

Welsh geographical names, on the other hand, *are* susceptible to mutation – this means not only places in Wales, but locations outside Wales for which a Welsh name is in common use, including many towns throughout England which still retain their original Celtic names in Welsh. Examples with **i°** *to*:

Caerdydd	i °Gaerdydd	to Cardiff
Llandeilo	i °Landeilo	to Llandeilo
Dyfed	i °Ddyfed	to Dyfed
Bangor	i °Fangor	to Bangor
Machynlleth	i °Fachynlleth	to Machynlleth
Manceinion	i °Fanceinion	to Manchester
Caergrawnt	i °Gaergrawnt	to Cambridge
Caerliwelydd	i °Gaerliwelydd	to Carlisle
Porthaethwy	i °Borthaethwy	to Porthaethwy
Rhydaman	i °Rydaman	to Rhydaman
Llundain	i °Lundain	to London
Dyfnaint	i °Ddyfnaint	to Devon

This occurs similarly for AM (usually after a *and*), e.g. **Caerfyrddin a** [h]**Che-redigion** *Carmarthen and Ceredigion*; and for NM after **yn**[n] *in*, e.g. **yn** [n]**Nhalybont** *in Talybont*, though with certain complications – see §472.

38   Mutations with non-Welsh geographical names

It should be noted that sometimes this principle extends in speech to non-Welsh place-names, e.g. **i** °**Firmingham**. This is regarded as sub-standard in the written or formal language (both of which prefer **i Birmingham** or **i** °**ddinas Birmingham** *to the city of Birmingham*), but it is widely heard everywhere.

39   Mutations with points of the compass

The points of the compass (see §423) are also susceptible to mutation when used in geographical names, e.g. **i** °**Ogledd Cymru** *to North Wales*, **yng** [n]**Ngorllewin Morgannwg** *in West Glamorgan*.

40   Genitive noun phrases

Two (or more) nouns can be used together in a genitive relationship. This is done in two ways in English:

(a)   the doctor's car

(b)   the end *of* the road

In Welsh, only option (**b**) is available, so all English expressions involving *'s* or *s'* must first be mentally rephrased using *of*, even where this is unnatural in English. So *Fred's book* will be *the book of Fred*. Expressions using option (**b**) in English need not be rephrased, of course.

Welsh, like the other Celtic languages, has a special way of expressing the genitive (or possession) relationship between two nouns. This construction must be mastered early on by learners, not only because it is of frequent occurrence in everyday speech, but also because it has mutation implications.

Taking *the doctor's car* as our example, we must first convert it into a phrase using *of*:

The car of the doctor

We then remove the word *of*:

The car   **the doctor**

And finally we remove any *the* except the one before the last element of the phrase (if there is one):

car   **the doctor**

These elements are now ready for translation into Welsh

car   **y meddyg**

Starting from an . . . *of* . . . phrase, then, two operations, both involving removal of elements, are required:

operation 1:   the removal of all instances of *of*

operation 2:   the removal of all occurrences of *the* except if it occurs
                         before the last noun in the phrase

In effect, the two nouns are linked simply by the intervening **y**, and it is particularly important to remember that *there is no definite article at the beginning of genitive noun phrases*. Examples like *y gyrrwr y bws *the driver of the bus* or **y canol y dre** *the centre of the town* are serious and basic errors, as are attempts to use **o** *of*, as in *y gyrrwr o'r bws, *y canol o'r °dre – **o** *does* mean *of* in certain contexts (see §185), but *not* in genitive relationships between nouns, where *of* must not be translated.

The two operations given above work for all noun-noun genitive relationships, regardless of how many nouns are involved:

(three nouns) the bank manager's daughter

= the daughter of the manager of the bank

operation 1:

the daughter the manager the bank

operation 2:

daughter	manager	the	bank
merch	**rheolwr**	**y**	**banc**

(four nouns) the bank manager's daughter's cat

= the cat of the daughter of the manager of the bank

operation 1:

the cat	the daughter	the manager	the bank

operation 2:

cat	daughter	manager	the bank
cath	**merch**	**rheolwr**	**y banc**

The second noun in an *of* construction can be indefinite:

	the middle of	a	city
operation 1:	the middle	a	city
operation 2:	middle	a	city
	canol		**dinas**

Here only two words are left in the Welsh version, because the first *the* and the *of* are removed by operations 1 and 2, and the indefinite article *a* does not have a counterpart in Welsh: **canol dinas**.

Examples with proper nouns:

	Dafydd's house		
	the	house of	Dafydd
operation 1:	the	house	Dafydd
operation 2:		house	Dafydd
		tŷ	**Dafydd**
	The capital of France		
operation 1:	the	capital	France
operation 2:		capital	France
		prifddinas	**Ffrainc**

41   Mutation implications of genitive noun phrases

These have to do with the fact that an initial definite article is dropped in this construction. Compare:

Nes i °adael y papurau *ar y bwrdd*

I left the papers on the table

but: **Nes i °adael y papurau *ar °fwrdd* y bos**

I left the papers on the boss's table [i.e on the table of the boss]

These two phrases (apart from necessary restructuring of the second to include *of*) are essentially the same in English, but look different in Welsh because the absence in Welsh of the first *the* in *the table of the boss* places **bwrdd** immediately after **ar°**, which causes SM. In *on the table* in the first sentence, there is no reason to remove the first *the* (because we are not saying whose table it is), and so the **y** blocks the SM. Further examples:

the centre of the town

canol y °dre

in the centre of the town

yng ⁿghanol y °dre (NM after **yn** – §472)

the door of the bedroom

drws y stafell °wely

by the door of the bedroom

wrth °ddrws y stafell °wely

the majestic plains of Nebraska

gwastadoedd mawreddog Nebraska

across the majestic plains of Nebraska

dros °wastadoedd mawreddog Nebraska

42–53 GENDER

42   Principles of grammatical and natural gender systems

Welsh, like French, German, Russian and many other European languages, operates a system of grammatical gender. As it happens, one of the few European languages that does not use this system is English, and this makes grammatical gender a strange concept for English-speaking students. The English system is one of natural or semantic gender (gender dictated by the meaning of the noun).

The two systems classify the world around us in fundamentally different ways, though both start from the premise that everything that needs a name (i.e. a noun) can be identified as either:

(a)   animate (a living thing or organism); or

(b)   inanimate (anything that does not come under **(a)**).

From this premise, the natural gender process of classification (the English system) is simple enough:

Animates are either masculine or feminine, as they are in real life (with a catch-all 'common' category for concepts such as *child* which can be either sex). In other words, gender = sex. Animates are thought of and referred to as *he* and *she* (with *it* possible for common nouns).

Inanimates are genderless (not neuter – see below under grammatical gender). They have no sex, so they have no gender, and are thought of and referred to as *it*.

This is the essence of the gender system in English. Note that most nouns (the inanimates) do not even fall within the gender system at all.

From the same animate/inanimate premise, grammatical gender operates on either a two-way system (masculine and feminine – as in Welsh or French) or three-way system (masculine, feminine and neuter – as in German or Russian). Either way, the fundamental principle is that every noun is assigned a gender, and on this principle the classification process is as follows:

Animates are usually (not always) assigned grammatical gender according to sex – therefore they will be masculine or feminine just as in the natural gender system.

Inanimates must be assigned a gender. This cannot be done by the criterion of sex (they have none), so it is done more or less arbitrarily (at least from the learner's point of view), with both or all three genders represented. Note that neuter does not mean 'genderless' (cf. the natural gender system above), but is simply a conventional term for the third gender in a three-way system.

43   Drawbacks of a grammatical gender system

In a natural gender system, meaning is everything; in a grammatical gender system, meaning is not the sole arbiter of gender (because of the inanimates), and this means that sometimes the assigning of gender is bound to be either apparently arbitrary, or based on other considerations, of which the most likely is the form of the word itself. For example, all French nouns ending in **-oir** are masculine; so are all German nouns ending in **-ig;** and so are all Welsh nouns ending in **-iant**. But such absolute reliability is rare.

This unpredictability is the essential disadvantage of a grammatical gender system for the learner – it complicates the learning process, in that the student of the language has to learn not only the word itself, but also its gender. This is a matter of logic for animate nouns (though not infallibly), but, as pointed out above, the gender of inanimates defies logic because such a classification is not based on the real world, but only on the language's internal system. The remaining discussion of gender in Welsh will therefore concentrate on practical aspects of identification and implementation.

44 **Gender of the noun in Welsh**

Nouns in Welsh are either animate or inanimate, and masculine (m) or feminine (f). Where predictable, this can be done either by form or meaning. Meaning comprises two sub-groups:

(a) nouns that denote male or female things or people;

(b) nouns of the same gender within a generic group (e.g. months – all masculine).

Animate nouns usually have their gender determined by meaning – male things are generally m, and female things f.

Inanimate nouns (including abstracts) sometimes have their gender determined by form – the shape of the word, or some part of it (usually the ending), is associated with one or other gender.

In addition, some types of animate nouns can have their gender changed by altering the form of the word.

45 **Features of feminine nouns**

Feminine nouns behave differently from masculine nouns in three main respects:

(a) When singular, they undergo initial SM after the definite article (see §28)

(b) When singular, they cause SM of a following adjective (see §102)

(c) Special forms of some numbers and adjectives are used with them (see §§100, 162).

46–49 DETERMINATION OF GENDER BY MEANING

Note: this involves animates only, and does not include nouns with gender-specific endings – these are treated as 'gender by form' below (see §§50–51).

46   Names of male persons and animals

Names of male persons and specifically male animals are masculine. Examples:

bachgen	boy	**tad**	father
dyn	man	**brawd**	brother
gŵr	man, husband	**nai**	nephew
brenin	king	**tarw**	bull
tywysog	prince	**ceiliog**	cock
meistr	master	**maharen**	ram

Nouns which can refer to either sex

47   Names of female persons and animals

Names of female persons and specifically female animals are feminine. Examples:

merch	girl, daughter	**modryb**	aunt
geneth	girl (N)	**buwch**	cow
gwraig	woman, wife	**iâr**	hen
mam	mother	**mamog**	ewe
chwaer	sister	**caseg**	mare
nith	niece	**gast**	bitch
nain	grandmother (N)		

These undergo mutation with preceding definite article: y °ferch, y °wraig, y °fuwch, y °gaseg etc.

48   Nouns which can refer to either sex

Many nouns of this type, especially animals, are applied to either sex without altering their grammatical gender. For example, **cath** *cat* is f even when the animal referred to is a male. Similarly with **ci** (m) *dog*. This is when speaking in general terms of the species, where the sex of the animal is not important. The same situation exists in English, where we can say *Our neighbours have a black cat* without regard to sex. We only need say *tom-cat* when we wish to draw attention to the sex of the animal in question.

The Welsh equivalents of *he-* . . . and *she-* . . . are . . . **gwryw** and . . . **benyw**: **cath** °**wryw** *tom-cat* (mutation of **gwryw** occurs because **cath** is still grammatically a f noun); **draenog benyw** *female hedgehog*. Some nouns, of course, like **ci**, have special terms for one or other sex (**gast** *bitch*), while occasionally two different words are used with no general term available for the species, as with **ceiliog** and **iâr**.

Examples of gender-fixed nouns denoting human beings of either sex:

plentyn (m)	child
baban (m)	baby
gwestai (m)	guest

and nouns ending **-ydd** (m) denoting doers of actions or professions:

cyfieithydd	translator
cadeirydd	chairman/woman
llefarydd	spokesman/woman

Note, however, that some nouns in **-ydd** form feminine equivalents by adding **-es**. Those that do this must simply be noted as they are come across. Examples:

ysgrifennydd (m)	(male) secretary
ysgrifenyddes (f)	(female) secretary
teipydd (m)	(male) typist
teipyddes (f)	(female) typist

Sometimes there is inconsistency in applying this principle, however – for example, **teipydd** is often used for both sexes.

49 Verbal nouns

Verbal nouns (VNs) (see §198), when used as nouns, are always masculine:

canu da	good singing
marchnata deallus	intelligent/clever marketing
cwyno dibaid	ceaseless complaining
ysgrifennu gwael	bad writing

An exception is **gafael** (f) *grip, grasp*.

50–51 DETERMINATION OF GENDER BY FORM

This involves both animates and inanimates, though the animates are usually also identifiable by meaning as well.

50   Nouns masculine by form

The following types are masculine by form:

(a)   Nouns ending in **-wr**, **-ydd** and **-yn**. Examples:

cyfreithiwr	lawyer
actiwr	actor
cyfieithydd	translator
gwleidydd	politician
gwresogydd	heater
teimlydd	antenna (of insect)
hogyn	boy (N)
rhwymyn	bandage
mochyn	pig

Care should be taken with nouns in **-yn**, which, as in the last example, is sometimes the indicator of a masculine collective unit (c/u) noun (see §**92**).

(b)   Nouns (usually but not always abstract) derived from adjectives and verbs, ending in:

-deb	**-had**
-der	**-iad**
-did	**-iant**
-dod	**-ni**
-dra	**-rwydd**
-edd	**-wch**

Examples:

purdeb purity	< **pur** pure
balchder pride	< **balch** proud
glendid hygiene	< **glân** clean
plentyndod childhood	< **plentyn** child
twpdra stupidity	< **twp** stupid
edmygedd admiration	< **edmygu** admire
mwynhad enjoyment	< **mwynhau** enjoy
ysgariad (marital) separation	< **ysgaru** separate (vb)
hyfforddiant training	< **hyfforddi** train
culni narrowness	< **cul** narrow
dwyieithrwydd bilingualism	< **dwy iaith** two languages
tristwch sadness	< **trist** sad

51   Nouns feminine by form

The following types are feminine by form.

(a)   Nouns ending in **-en** and **-es**. Examples:

rhaglen	programme
teisen	cake
meistres	mistress
tywysoges	princess

There are exceptions in **-en**, e.g. **talcen** (m) *forehead*, **maharen** (m) *ram*. Note also that many feminines in **-en** are c/u nouns (see §90).

(b)   Many derived nouns (mostly abstract) ending in **-aeth** and some in **-as**. Examples:

cenhedlaeth	generation
swyddogaeth	function, duty
priodas	wedding
perthynas	relation(ship)

Several commonly used nouns in **-aeth** are masculine, however, notably **gwasanaeth** *service,* **gwahaniaeth** *difference* and **hiraeth** *longing.*

(c)   Nouns ending in **-fa** denoting places where actions or events happen. These are derived mostly from verbs, sometimes from nouns. Examples:

arhosfa	waiting room	< **aros** *wait*
meithrinfa	nursery	< **meithrin** *nurture*
meddygfa	surgery	< **meddyg** *doctor*
swyddfa	office	< **swydd** *job*

(d)   Two-syllable words with **-e-** in the second syllable (excluding suffixes listed under masculine above) are very often feminine, especially if the vowel of the first syllable is **-a-**. Like all rough rules, this one is fallible, but surprisingly reliable all the same. Examples:

tabled	tablet
sianel	channel
colled	loss
siwmper	jumper
ornest	combat, duel

Endless rules can be formulated for predicting the gender of nouns, but hardly any of these are absolute, and a point is reached where it is less of a burden for the learner simply to try and remember the gender of a noun as it is encountered. In practical terms, apart from a few fairly safe indicators (**-wr** or **-fa** above, for example) gender is largely unpredictable in Welsh unless sex is relevant (even here there are traps, like **cennad** *messenger*, always f).

A few other circumstances are of help to the learner, however, based on certain natural groupings of words and concepts:

(a)   names of the days, months, seasons and points of the compass are masculine

(b)   names of countries, rivers and languages are generally feminine

(c)   units of time from *second* to *year* alternate in gender:

eiliad (f)	second
munud (m)	minute
awr (f)	hour

dydd (m)	day
wythnos (f)	week
mis (m)	month
blwyddyn (f)	year

but **munud** is feminine in some dialects, and sometimes vacillates within a dialect.

52   Words with differing genders in different regions

This phenomenon happens in all grammatical gender languages. In some cases, one gender is accepted as standard, with the other as a variant, though in Welsh at least the choice between the two is often arbitrary.

Munud above (§51) is one example – officially masculine, but frequently feminine in many parts of Wales. Otherwise both variants co-exist, often as N–S alternatives. Common words of 'undecided' gender (with standard or more frequent gender noted where possible) are:

braich (m)	arm
clust	ear
rhyfel	war
troed (m)	foot
cinio (m)	lunch, dinner
cyflog (m)	pay, salary

Note that **gwaith** is masculine when it means *work*, and feminine when it means *time*, *occasion* (**dwywaith** *twice*, **weithiau** *sometimes* – see §§183, 402).

53   Use of dictionaries

Many Welsh–English dictionaries, especially those designed primarily for Welsh speakers, use Welsh terminology in indicating gender of a noun (**enw**):

eg (enw gwrywaidd)	masculine
eb (enw benywaidd)	feminine
ell (enw lluosog)	plural (used generally for c/u nouns)

Where a dictionary is not to hand, and there are no clues to gender, the only option is to guess – masculine is the safer bet, because (a) they are statistically more numerous, and (b) new words and loanwords tend to be adopted as masculines.

54–92 NOUN NUMBER

54 Comparison of noun number systems in English and Welsh

The number system for nouns in English is a simple singular/plural opposition, of which the singular is the base form. Any noun in English can be classified into one of three sub-classes within this two-way system:

(a) nouns that can be used in either the singular or plural (the vast majority of non-abstract things – *cat, star, radiator*)

(b) nouns that can normally only be used in the singular (mainly abstract ideas and 'uncountable' things – *honesty, milk*)

(c) nouns that can only be used in the plural (often denoting things that are or have two parts – *trousers, scissors*)

Welsh has mutually exclusive twin systems:

system 1: singular/plural

system 2: collective/unit

System 1 works on much the same lines as in English, with the same three sub-classes. The difference from English is that these do not account for all nouns in Welsh, because a certain number lie outside the singular/plural system and belong instead to the collective/unit (c/u) system, which has its own rules of operation. It should, however, be pointed out that most grammar books treat Welsh c/u nouns as anomalous singular/plurals, a misleading approach which distorts the logic of the Welsh system.

55 Distinction between singular/plural and collective/unit

As already indicated, the sing./pl. system in Welsh mirrors that in English and other European languages – the basic form of the noun is the sing., with the pl. (where a pl. is possible – abstract nouns, for example, rarely form

49

plurals) formed from it by one method or another. It does not matter if a particular noun cannot form a plural – the base noun is still the sing., and that is enough to classify it as part of the sing./pl. system. The collective/unit system, on the other hand, comprises mostly living things that are primarily associated with being in a group. This includes many trees and plants, animals (especially those kept or living in groups, and swarming or colony insects), and other miscellaneous items often associated with these categories. The base form of all these nouns has collective meaning, with the unit form (indicating one individual member of the group) built from it in ways similar to the formation of pl. from sing. in the other system.

Examples of both systems:

sing./pl.:	**cath**	cat	**cathod**	cats
c/u:	**moch**	(group of) pigs	**mochyn**	pig
sing./pl.:	**llyfr**	book	**llyfrau**	books
c/u:	**coed**	wood (group of trees)	**coeden**	tree

From the English speaker's single sing./pl. point of view, 'collective' seems little different from 'plural', with 'unit' obviously corresponding to 'singular', and it is tempting to make the c/u nouns fit the familiar sing./pl. arrangement:

Singular	*Plural*
cath	**cathod**
llyfr	**llyfrau**
mochyn	**moch**
coeden	**coed**

and this would be all well and good but for two considerations:

(a) Such an arrangement leaves the c/u nouns (**moch** and **coed**) apparently forming their 'singular' from their 'plural' – by addition of **-yn** and **-en** respectively. This goes against the sing./pl. principle of forming the pl. from the sing.

(b) While, for example, **coed** can be translated as *trees* (because English has only the plural to fall back on in any case), it has a strong sense of a homogeneous group about it that *trees* on its own does not convey. The alternative translation *wood* (sing. in English) conveys the idea of a single item or group, but cannot include any idea of the units that make up that group (the trees). Both English translations are perfectly adequate as far as they go, but the relationship between the group and its individual components is neatly expressed only in the c/u system. Perhaps an even clearer example is **dail/deilen** – **deilen** is *leaf*, while **dail** is often translated as the plural *leaves*, which it does indeed mean:

Mae'r dail yn troi

The leaves are turning

but it also carries the connotation of *foliage*, i.e. a single group meaning that, unusually, has a corresponding English term.

The singular/plural and collective/unit systems are dealt with in detail separately below (see §§56–89; §§90–92).

56–89 SINGULAR/PLURAL NOUNS

56 Formation of noun plurals in Welsh

The different methods of turning a sing. noun into a pl. in Welsh are so various and, for the most part, unpredictable, that the simplest approach for the non-native speaker is to learn the pl. form with each noun as it is met. In this regard, Welsh is more complicated than languages like English or Spanish with their almost universal -s ending for pl.

There are two main principles involved in forming plurals in Welsh – addition of endings, and internal vowel change. These principles are used separately and in combination.

(a) Adding endings to the noun – about a dozen are in common use. Examples:

Singular	Plural	
siop	**siopau**	shop/shops
mur	**muriau**	wall/walls
geiriadur	**geiriaduron**	dictionary/dictionaries
colled	**colledion**	loss/losses
capel	**capeli**	chapel/chapels
merch	**merched**	daughter/daughters
mynydd	**mynyddoedd**	mountain/mountains

(b) Changing one or more vowels of the original noun in some way (like English *man*, *men*, but much commoner in Welsh). Examples in this category include:

Singular	Plural	
castell	cestyll	castle/castles
car	ceir	car/cars
corff	cyrff	body/bodies
brân	brain	crow/crows

(c) Many nouns use a combination of (a) and (b), changing an internal vowel and adding an ending. Examples:

Singular	Plural	
mab	meibion	son/sons
gardd	gerddi	garden/gardens
cyfaill	cyfeillion	friend/friends
iaith	ieithoedd	language/languages

(d) A relatively small group of nouns ending in **-yn** and **-en** in the singular replace these with plural endings of various types. Examples:

Singular	Plural	
blodyn	blodau	flower/flowers
oedolyn	oedolion	adult/adults
sleisen	sleisys	slice/slices

(e) Nouns ending in **-wr**, and some in **-ydd**, denoting persons and professions replace these with **-wyr**. Examples:

Singular	Plural	
trydanwr	trydanwyr	electrician/electricians
siaradwr	siaradwyr	speaker/speakers
cyfieithydd	cyfieithwyr	translator/translators
but: llefarydd	llefaryddion	spokesman/woman spokesmen/women

(f) A few nouns form their pl. from an extended or derived form of the sing. Examples:

Singular	Plural	
dosbarth	**dosbarthiadau**	class/classes
llif	**llifogydd**	flood/floods

These are best learnt as they are encountered.

There are a number of nouns which do not come under any of the above, and are best regarded as irregular (see §85).

57 Plurals of compound nouns

Compound nouns – i.e. words made up of noun + noun, verb + noun or adjective + noun – form their pl. in the same way as the second element: e.g. **mam** – **mamau** *mothers*, **llysfam** – **llysfamau** *stepmothers*; **taith** – **teithiau** *journeys*, **gwibdaith** – **gwibdeithiau** *excursions*; **ffordd** – **ffyrdd** *roads*, **priffordd** – **priffyrdd** *highways, motorways*.

58 Plural endings

There are a dozen different pl. endings in use in spoken Welsh, some of them rather restricted and others very common. They may be grouped as follows:

-au	-on	-i	-edd	-ed	-aint
-iau	-ion		-oedd	-iaid	
			-ydd	-od	

Of these, -au/-iau is the most common (see §2(a) for pronunciation), and is normally also the choice for plurals of borrowed and new words. -on/-ion and -i are all quite common as well. All variants with -i- are liable to involve change of internal vowel as well, especially -a- to -e- or -ei-, but other vowels may change as well (see under internal vowel change §77 for full analysis).

59 Endings and stress pattern

Addition of an ending may alter the stress pattern of the original word, since Welsh has very consistent penultimate stress. This in turn may cause slight alteration in the base-form of the noun, particularly where -nn- and -rr- are present, reducing them to -n- and -r-, or changing them to -nh- and -rh-: peiriannydd *engineer*, pl. peirianwyr; torrwr *cutter*, pl. torwyr.

Furthermore, final -n and -r may be doubled. This happens when an originally monosyllabic word with a short vowel adds a syllable – ton, pl. tonnau *waves*; but tôn, pl. tonau *tones*.

60 Plural endings and the final letter of the singular

Sometimes the addition of a pl. ending can affect the final letter of the sing. noun. There are three main circumstances for this, the first representing a change in pronunciation, and the other two, spelling conventions only:

(a) Before **-au**, final **-nt** changes to **-nn-**: **peiriant – peiriannau** *machines*.

(b) Words ending in **-i** in the sing. (mostly, but not exclusively, loan-words) make their plurals in **-ïau** and **-ïon**, with the two dots signifying that the **-i-** is part of the original word, and not of the pl. ending: **stori – storïau** *stories*, **egni – egnïon** *energies*.

(c) Loanwords ending in **-a** in the sing. make their pl. in **-âu**, with the accent performing the same function for **-a** as the two dots for **-i** in (b) above: **camera – camerâu** *cameras*, **drama – dramâu** *dramas*. Note that the ending **-âu** is always pronounced as spelt, and does not come under the **-a/-e** pronunciation rule (see §2(a)).

An exhaustive listing for the common pl. formations is impractical. The following examples will serve to show presence or absence of internal vowel change, and other modifications to the base-word.

61 au/-iau **plural ending**

This is the most common pl. ending in Welsh. Internal vowel change is possible with either variant. Examples:

Singular	Plural		
llyfr	**llyfrau**	book/books	Nouns with predictable **-au** plural ending
siop	**siopau**	shop/shops	
cloch	**clychau**	bell/bells	
bwrdd	**byrddau**	table/tables	
gwefus	**gwefusau**	lip/lips	
trên	**trenau**	train/trains	
taith	**teithiau**	journey/journeys	
drws	**drysiau**	door/doors	
bws	**bysiau**	bus/buses	

62   Nouns with predictable -au plural ending

The -au pl. ending can be predicted for the following types of noun:

(a) Nouns ending in **-iad** (made from verbs) and **-aeth** (made from nouns or verbs) in the sing. take **-au** in the pl. Examples:

Singular	Plural	
cyfieithiad	**cyfieithiadau**	translation/translations
argymhelliad	**argymhelliadau**	recommendation/ recommendations
gwasanaeth	**gwasanaethau**	service/services
trafodaeth	**trafodaethau**	discussion/discussions

(b) Nouns ending in **-iant** (usually from verbs). In these cases the final **-t** is changed to **-n-** before the ending. Examples:

Singular	Plural	
llwyddiant	**llwyddiannau**	success/successes
gwelliant	**gwelliannau**	improvement/ improvements
peiriant	**peiriannau**	machine/machines

(c)   Feminine nouns in **-es** denoting persons, derived from male equivalent. Examples:

[tywysog]	tywysoges	tywysogesau	princess/ princesses
[athro]	athrawes	athrawesau	teacher/ teachers (f)
[Sais]	Saesnes	Saesnesau	Englishwoman/ Englishwomen

(d)   Abstract nouns in **-deb** (from adjectives), where a pl. is possible. Examples:

Singular	Plural	
cyfrifoldeb	cyfrifoldebau	responsibility/ responsibilities
ffurfioldeb	ffurfioldebau	formality/formalities

63   -on/-ion **plural ending**

The **-ion** ending is much more frequent than **-on**, and often changes a preceding -a- or -ai- to -ei-. Examples of both variants:

Singular	Plural	
modur	moduron	car/cars
rhagolwg	rhagolygon	forecast, prospect/forecasts, prospects
awel	awelon	breeze/breezes
cennad	cenhadon	envoy, messenger/envoys, messengers
cenau	cenawon	cub/cubs
ystyr	ystyron	meaning/meanings
mab	meibion	son/sons
ysgol	ysgolion	school/schools
colled	colledion	loss/losses
claf	cleifion	patient/patients
dyn	dynion	man/men

Note also Sais – Saeson *Englishman/Englishmen*.

Nouns with predictable -ion **plural ending**

The -ion pl. ending can usually be predicted for the following types of noun:

(a) Nouns ending in **-og** denoting persons. Examples:

Singular	Plural	
swyddog	**swyddogion**	officer, official/officers, officials
tywysog	**tywysogion**	prince/princes
marchog	**marchogion**	horseman/horsemen

(b) Nouns ending in **-or** denoting persons. Examples:

Singular	Plural	
canghellor	**cangellorion**	chancellor/chancellors
telynor	**telynorion**	harpist/harpists

In addition, many nouns ending in -ydd denoting persons and implements add -ion for the plural. But note that, for persons, -wyr is often preferred. Occasionally both options are heard. Examples:

Singular	Plural	
cadeirydd	**cadeiryddion**	chairman/woman/chairmen/women
teipydd	**teipyddion**	typist/typists
gwleidydd	**gwleidyddion**	politician/politicians
cysodydd	**cysodyddion** or **cysodwyr**	compositor/compositors
gohebydd	**gohebyddion** or **gohebwyr**	correspondent/correspondents (newspaper)

but:

cyfieithydd	**cyfieithwyr**	translator/translators

65 -i plural ending

This is a limited class, but includes many commonly encountered nouns. Nearly all have -e- as final vowel in the sing., or change an -a- into an -e-. Some have final diphthong -wy-, which remains unchanged.

The following are the most frequent nouns with -i plural:

Singular	Plural	Singular	Plural
allwedd	allweddi (keys)	llwyth	llwythi (loads)
arglwydd	arglwyddi (lords)	maen	meini (stones)
baner	baneri (flags)	meistr	meistri (masters)
basged	basgedi (baskets)	modfedd	modfeddi (inches)
bisged	bisgedi (biscuits)	paced	pacedi (packets)
blanced	blancedi (blankets)	pamffled	pamffledi (pamphlets)
bwced	bwcedi (buckets)	parsel	parseli (parcels)
cadwyn	cadwyni (chains)	pêl	peli (balls)
camles	camlesi (canals)	pensaer	penseiri (architects)
capel	capeli (chapels)	pentre(f)	pentrefi (villages)
cartre(f)	cartrefi (homes)	perth	perthi (hedges)
cerdd	cerddi (songs, poems)	plwy(f)	plwyfi (parishes)
cawr	cewri (giants)	poced	pocedi (pockets)
clogwyn	clogwyni (cliffs)	potel	poteli (bottles)
clwyd	clwydi (gates)	roced	rocedi (rockets)
coelcerth	coelcerthi (bonfires)	rhes	rhesi (rows)
cofrestr	cofrestri (registers)	rhestr	rhestri (lists)
cornel	corneli (corners)	rhiant	rhieni (parents)
cyfres	cyfresi (series)	rhwyd	rhwydi (nets)
eglwys	eglwysi (churches)	saer	seiri (carpenters)
ffenest(r)	ffenestri (windows)	sbaner	sbaneri (spanners)
galwyn	galwyni (gallons)	sgert	sgerti (skirts)

Singular	Plural	Singular	Plural	
gardd	gerddi (gardens)	siaced	siacedi (rackets)	-i plural ending
lodes	lodesi (girls, lasses)	sianel	sianeli (TV channels)	
llechen/ llech	llechi (slates)	soser	soseri (saucers)	
llen	llenni (curtains)	sylfaen	sylfeini (bases)	
llestr	llestri (dishes)	ticed	ticedi (tickets)	
llwyn	llwyni (groves)	tunnell	tunelli (tons)	

Of these, the following have alternative plurals in -au:

allwedd	cyfres
cadwyn	rhes
clogwyn	rhestr
clwyd	rhwyd

Notes:

(a) In the spoken language, **ffenest(r)**, **plwy(f)** and **tre(f)** (+ compounds) usually drop the final consonant in the singular, but restore it before the plural ending. Hence in speech **ffenest – ffenestri**, etc.

(b) **Llwyth** means *tribe* as well as *load*, but differentiates between them in the pl.: **llwythau** *tribes*, **llwythi** *loads*. Other double-meaning nouns distinguished in the pl. are given in §86.

(c) The great majority of nouns with **-i** pl. are feminine.

Also in this class are feminines ending in -en (but not c/u nouns), often denoting sheets or printed papers. They double the -n- before adding the -i ending. Examples of nouns belonging to this category include:

Singular	Plural	Singular	Plural
amlen	amlenni (envelopes)	lloeren	lloerenni (satellites)
bwydlen	bwydlenni (menus)	rhaglen	rhaglenni (programmes)
dogfen	dogfenni (documents)	taflen	taflenni (leaflets)
ffurflen	ffurflenni (forms)		

-edd/-oedd/-ydd **group of plural endings**

Of these, **-edd** is the least numerous, with less than twenty simple nouns (i.e. not including compound nouns). These are listed below. There are rather more nouns forming their plural with **-ydd**, but again the class is sufficiently limited to allow a fairly comprehensive listing. The **-oedd** class is larger overall, but includes many nouns not often encountered in speech, or whose pl. is formed differently in the spoken language. The listing for **-oedd,** then, will confine itself to commonly used nouns only.

-edd **plurals**

The following nouns have **-edd** plurals. Many also have internal vowel change or other modifications. Variant plurals are noted at the end of the list.

Singular	Plural	Singular	Plural
adain	**adanedd** (wings)	**gwraig**	**gwragedd** (women)
bys	**bysedd** (fingers)	**mign**	**mignedd** (marshes)
celain	**celanedd** (carcasses)	**modryb**	**modrybedd** (aunts)
dant	**dannedd** (teeth)	**neidr**	**nadredd** (snakes)
edau	**edafedd** (threads)	**rhiain**	**rhianedd** (maidens)
elain	**elanedd** (fawns)	**teyrn**	**teyrnedd** (monarchs, lords)
ewin	**ewinedd** (nails, claws)	**ysgithr**	**ysgithredd** (tusks, fangs)
ewythr	**ewythredd** (uncles)		

Variants:

Singular	Plural	Singular	Plural
adain	**adenydd**	**neidr**	**nadroedd**
ewythr	**ewythrod**	**teyrn**	**teyrnoedd**

-ydd **plurals**

The following nouns form their plurals in **-ydd.** Internal vowel change is less common in this class. Variant plurals are noted at the end of the list.

Singular	Plural	Singular	Plural
adain	adenydd (wings)	heol	heolydd (roads)
aelwyd	aelwydydd (hearths, homes)	helm	helmydd (hayricks)
afon	afonydd (rivers)	lôn	lonydd (lanes)
bwyd	bwydydd (foods)	lle	llefydd (places)
bord	bordydd (tables, (S))	llif	llifogydd (floods)
bro	bröydd (regions)	llofft	llofftydd (lofts)
bron	bronnydd (breasts of hills)	maes	meysydd (fields, squares)
cawod	cawodydd (showers)	moel	moelydd ((bare) hills)
camlas	camlesydd (canals)	mynachlog	mynachlogydd (monasteries)
clod	clodydd (praises)	mynwent	mynwentydd (cemeteries)
clos	closydd (yards)	myswynog	myswynogydd (barren cows)
cors	corsydd (bogs)	nant	nentydd (streams, brooks)
crofft	crofftydd (crofts)	palmant	palmentydd (pavements)
cyfarfod	cyfarfodydd (meetings)	plwy(f)	plwyfydd (parishes)
chwaer	chwiorydd (sisters)	pont	pontydd (bridges)
diod	diodydd (drinks)	rhew	rhewogydd (frosts)
dôl	dolydd (meadows; dales)	rhos	rhosydd (moors)
egwyd	egwydydd (fetlocks)	siglen	siglennydd (swings)
fferm	ffermydd (farms)	storm	stormydd (storms)
fforest	fforestydd (forests)	taflod	taflodydd (lofts)
gallt	gelltydd (cliffs; woods)	tomen	tomennydd (dunghills)
gofer	goferydd (streams)	tre(f)	trefydd (towns)
gwern	gwernydd (alder-groves)	twynen	twynennydd (sandhills)
gwaun	gweunydd (meadows)		

61

Variants:

bord, bordau

bron – when meaning anatomical breast, pl. is **bronnau**

camlas, camlesi

dôl, dolau

gallt also appears as **allt**, pl. **elltydd**

gwern, gwerni

heol also appears as **hewl**, pl. **hewlydd**

lle, lleoedd (a predominantly S pl.)

plwy(f), plwyfi

rhew, rhewiau (and sometimes also **rhewydd**)

siglen, siglenni

tre(f), trefi; and note that the compound **pentre(f)** *village* only has pl.
  pentrefi

69   -oedd **plurals**

The following are the commonest nouns taking a pl. **-oedd**. Internal vowel
change is rare with this ending, though some nouns show other changes in
the base-form when the ending is added.

Singular	Plural	Singular	Plural
aber	**aberoedd** (estuaries)	**llys**	**llysoedd** (courts)
amser	**amseroedd** (times)	**mantell**	**mantelloedd** (mantles)
ardal	**ardaloedd** (region(s), areas)	**marchnad**	**marchnadoedd** (markets)
blwyddyn	**blynyddoedd** (years)	**metel**	**meteloedd** (metals)
brenin	**brenhinoedd** (kings)	**mil**	**miloedd** (thousands)
byd	**bydoedd** (worlds)	**môr**	**moroedd** (seas)
byddin	**byddinoedd** (armies)	**mynydd**	**mynyddoedd** (mountains)

Singular	Plural	Singular	Plural
cant	cannoedd (hundreds)	neidr	nadroedd (snakes)
cell	celloedd (cells)	nef	nefoedd (heavens)
cenedl	cenhedloedd (nations)	nerth	nerthoedd (strengths, powers)
coedwig	coedwigoedd (woodlands)	nifer	niferoedd (numbers)
cyfle	cyfleoedd (chances)	nith	nithoedd (nieces)
cylch	cylchoedd (circles)	niwl	niwloedd (mists)
darlith	darlithoedd (lectures)	oes	oesoedd (ages)
dinas	dinasoedd (cities)	pobl	pobloedd (peoples)
dŵr	dyfroedd (waters)	porthladd	porthladdoedd (ports)
ffatri	ffatrïoedd (factories)	punt	punnoedd (pounds; currency)
ffi	ffïoedd (fees)	rheng	rhengoedd (ranks)
gallu	galluoedd (abilities)	rhyfel	rhyfeloedd (wars)
glyn	glynnoedd (glens)	safle	safleoedd (sites)
gorsaf	gorsafoedd (stations)	silff	silffoedd (shelves)
gwin	gwinoedd (wines)	sir	siroedd (counties)
gwisg	gwisgoedd (costumes)	stryd	strydoedd (streets)
gwledd	gwleddoedd (feasts)	teulu	teuluoedd (families)
gwynt	gwyntoedd (winds)	tir	tiroedd (lands)
gwrych	gwrychoedd (hedges)	ymgyrch	ymgyrchoedd (campaigns)
iaith	ieithoedd (languages)	ynys	ynysoedd (islands)
lle	lleoedd (places)	ysbryd	ysbrydoedd (ghosts)
llu	lluoedd (hosts, multitudes)	ystafell	ystafelloedd (rooms)
llyn	llynnoedd (lakes)		

-oedd plurals

Variants:

amser, **amserau** (this variant is the more usual nowadays)

blwyddyn, **blynyddau** (but see §176 for further variants used in time expressions)

cylch, **cylchau**

lle, **llefydd**

mantell, **mentyll**

metel, **metelau**

neidr, **nadredd**

punt, **punnau**

rheng, **rhengau**

ysbryd, **ysbrydion**

70   Plurals of nouns ending in -fa

In addition, many nouns ending in the suffix **-fa** (often, though not necessarily, indicating place where an action happens) add **-oedd** for the pl.

Examples:

Singular	Plural	
agorfa	**agorfaoedd**	opening (aperture)/openings (apertures)
meithrinfa	**meithrinfaoedd**	nursery/nurseries
gyrfa	**gyrfaoedd**	career/careers
cynulleidfa	**cynulleidfaoedd**	audience/audiences

Others, however, change **-fa** to **-feydd,** and there seems no hard-and-fast rule for deciding between the two. Examples:

Singular	Plural	
swyddfa	**swyddfeydd**	office/offices
arddangosfa	**arddangosfeydd**	exhibition/exhibitions
tollfa	**tollfeydd**	toll-house/toll-houses

71   Plural ending -od

This ending is mainly associated with names of animals (though not all animals have plurals in -od). Some birds and fishes are represented here as well. In some cases, a singular ending is removed before the -od is added, and some nouns undergo a change in the base-form. Examples:

Singular	Plural	Singular	Plural
cath	cathod (cats)	draenog	draenogod (hedgehogs)
cwningen	cwningod (rabbits)	crwban	crwbanod (tortoises)
llwynog	llwynogod (foxes)	eliffant	eliffantod (elephants)
asyn	asynnod (asses, donkeys)	chwilen	chwilod (beetles)
buwch	buchod (cows)	hwch	hychod (sows)
llew	llewod (lions)	gwiwer	gwiwerod (squirrels)
ysgyfarnog	ysgyfarnogod (hares)	twrci	twrcïod (turkeys)
tylluan	tylluanod (owls)	ystlum	ystlumod (bats)
broga	brogaod (frogs)	colomen	colomennod (doves)
brithyll	brithyllod (trout)	teigr	teigrod (tigers)

It is also used with some nouns denoting persons, and a few nationalities:

Singular	Plural	Singular	Plural
baban	babanod (babies)	gwrach	gwrachod (witches)
geneth	genethod (girls – N)	benyw/ menyw	benywod/menywod (women)
Gwyddel	Gwyddelod (Irishmen)	Ffrancwr	Ffrancod (Frenchmen) (also Ffrancwyr)

Note that in modern usage **baban, babanod** is used of *babies* generally, but *babies* personally known to the speaker are generally referred to as **babi, babis**.

A few non-animate nouns take this ending as well:

Singular	Plural
nionyn	**nionod** (onions)
nyth	**nythod** (nests)
bwthyn	**bythynnod** (cottages)

72 Collective nouns ending in -od

While they do not strictly belong here, it is worth noting three collective nouns (see §90) that end in -**od**:

Singular	Plural
pioden	**piod** (magpies)
llygoden	**llygod** (mice)
pysgodyn	**pysgod** (fish)

Note that they make their unit form by adding -**en**/-**yn** in the usual way, rather than removing the -**od**, so we do not have *pi (at least in the standard language), *llyg or *pysg for *magpie*, *mouse* and *fish*. There is a sing. noun **llyg** (pl. **llygod**), used in the related sense of *vole* or *shrew*.

73 Plurals in -iaid

This, like -**od** in §§71 and 72, is an ending primarily associated with animate beings; but while -**od** is for the most part used with animals, -**iaid** has predominantly human connotations. It is invariably pronounced -**ied** in natural speech, and is used with names of peoples, nationalities, tribes, etc., and with surnames. In all these instances, it is added to a proper name that normally has no plural, or sometimes to an adjective. It is sometimes accompanied by a vowel-change. Examples:

Rhufeiniaid, Romans   (< **Rhufain**, Rome)

Rwsiaid, Russians   (< **Rwsia**, Russia)

(y) ffyddloniaid, (the) faithful   (< **ffyddlon**, faithful)

(y) Morganiaid, (the) Morgans

It is also used with many loanwords descriptive of persons or professions:

Singular	Plural	Singular	Plural
doctor	doctoriaid (doctors)	person	personiaid (parsons)
cwsmer	cwsmeriaid (customers)	biwrocrat	biwrocratiaid (bureaucrats)
prentis	prentisiaid (apprentices)	capten	capteiniaid (captains)
partner	partneriaid (partners)	ffŵl	ffyliaid (fools)
fandal	fandaliaid (vandals)	ficer	ficeriaid (vicars)
pagan	paganiaid (pagans)		

Nouns ending -adur from verbs and denoting the doer of the action usually take this plural ending:

Singular	Plural	
ffoadur	ffoaduriaid	(refugees < ffoi, flee)
pechadur	pechaduriaid	(sinners < pechu, sin)
cachadur	cachaduriaid	(cowards < cachu, shit)

Note that nouns ending in -adur denoting things cannot take this animate plural ending, and instead take -on, e.g. gwyddoniadur, gwyddoniaduron (encyclopedias); gliniadur, gliniaduron (laptop computers); trefniadur, trefniaduron (personal organisers).

Some animals, including anifail *animal*, also come under the -iaid class. Examples:

Singular	Plural	Singular	Plural
anifail	anifeiliaid (animals)	ffwlbart	ffwlbartiaid (polecats)
cimwch	cimychiaid (lobsters)	blaidd	bleiddiaid (wolves) (also bleiddiau)
fwltur	fwlturiaid (vultures)	barcud	barcutiaid (kites)
gwennol	gwenoliaid (swallows)		

Note also gefell, gefeilliaid *twins*, which unusually takes SM in the plural after the definite article – yr °efeilliaid. This may be due to its original status as a dual rather than a plural. See §88 for other duals.

74 Plurals in -ed

This is a very small subclass of the -iaid plurals (themselves pronounced -ied), and comprises only two nouns in the spoken language:

merch – **merched** (girls, daughters)   **pry(f)** – **pryfed** (insects)

75 Plurals in -aint

These are very few in the spoken language:

go(f)	**gofaint** (blacksmiths)	**nai**	**neiaint** (nephews)
euro(f)	**eurofaint** (goldsmiths)	(no sing.)	**ysgyfaint*** (lungs)

Sometimes a sing. form **ysgyfant** is found corresponding to **ysgyfaint**, but this is probably formed by analogy with pairs of the type **sant, saint; llyffant, llyffaint,** which are instances of internal vowel-change and do not belong to this category.

76 English plural ending -ys

Some loan-words from English retain their English pl., but in Welsh spelling:

bws	**bysys** (buses)	(but more usually **bysiau** nowadays)
mats(i)en	**matsys** (matches)	(**-ts-** pronounced as Eng **ch**)
nyrs	**nyrsys** (nurses)	

Note that **trowsus** (trousers) is a sing. noun with an unusual spelling in Welsh.

77 Plural by internal vowel-change only

This class is larger in Welsh than in English (which has only a few survivals: *man – men*; *goose – geese*; *mouse – mice*; etc.). It is, however, still very much a limited class. (The much more general principle of using vowel change in combination with a pl. ending has already been seen in the various sections above). Nouns in this class fall into two main categories:

(a) Nouns where one vowel only is changed;

(b) Nouns where two vowels in consecutive syllables are changed.

These two categories will be dealt with separately, with indications of the most common vowel alternation patterns. In all cases, a general principle is followed of converting a *back vowel* (i.e. one pronounced towards the back of the mouth – **a**, **o** or **w** in Welsh) to a *front vowel* (pronounced towards the front of the mouth – **e**, **i** or **y**). This principle in internal plural formation goes back to the very origins of Welsh and related languages in Europe, and was once a more widespread feature of the language than it is today. In the written language, internal plurals are often encountered where the spoken language has long since replaced them by endings, or at the very least internal change + endings (this last is a very wide category in the modern language).

78 Plural formation by single change of vowel

There are three main alternation patterns where only one syllable in the sing. is changed:

(a)   **a** to **ei**

(b)   **a** to **ai**

(c)   **o** to **y**

Examples of each type follow. These listings, and those for two-vowel internal plurals, can be taken as fairly complete for the spoken language, though as noted above it is impossible to be exhaustive where some nouns have an internal plural in written and formal spoken Welsh, but not in everyday speech.

79 Plural formation by changing a to ei

Commonly occurring nouns of the type changing a to ei include:

Singular	Plural	Singular	Plural
bardd	**beirdd** (bards, poets)	**gwalch**	**gweilch** (hawks)
car	**ceir** (cars)	**iâr**	**ieir** (hens)
carw	**ceirw** (deer, stags)	**tarw**	**teirw** (bulls)
gafr	**geifr** (goats)		

Note: **Gwalch** is used colloquially to mean *rascal* or *rogue* – **yr hen °walch!** *you rascal! Hawk* is usually **hebog** (pl. **hebogau**) nowadays.

80   Plural formation by changing a to ai

Nouns changing a to ai include:

Singular	Plural	Singular	Plural
brân	brain (crows)	llyffant	llyffaint (toads)
hwyad	hwyaid (ducks)	sant	saint (saints)
llygad	llygaid (eyes)		

Notes:

(a)   In the N the pl. of **llygad** is usually **llgada** (i.e. **llygadau** – regular pl. ending)

(b)   **Hwyad** has an alternative sing. **hwyaden**, and in this form is therefore a c/u noun (**hwyaden** – **hwyaid**).

Note where -ai- is in a monosyllable (e.g. **brain**) it is pronounced as written, but in the last syllable of a polysyllabic word (e.g. **llygaid**) it is normally pronounced -e-.

81   Plural formation by changing o to y

Nouns changing o to y include:

Singular	Plural
corff	cyrff (bodies) (all meanings)
corn	cyrn (horns)
ffon	ffyn (sticks)
fforc	ffyrc (forks) (cutlery)
fforch	ffyrch (forks) (agricultural implement)
ffordd	ffyrdd (roads, ways)

Also to be mentioned here is **Cymro** – **Cymry** *Welshmen* – the plural not to be confused with the name of the country **Cymru**, which in many parts of Wales sounds identical.

82   Plural formation by other single vowel changes

Miscellaneous internal single vowel change plurals that do not correspond to any of the three types above are:

Singular	Plural
croen	crwyn (skins)
cyllell	cyllyll (knives)
oen	ŵyn (lambs)
troed	traed (feet)

83   Plural formation by change of two consecutive vowels

This almost always involves a change from -a-e- in the last two syllables of the sing. to -e-y- (spelt -e-i- in the occasional word). A very few exceptions are noted separately. Most of this type are feminine.

Singular	Plural	Singular	Plural
alarch	elyrch (swans)	llannerch	llennyrch (glades)
asgell	esgyll (wings)	llawes	llewys (sleeves)
bachgen	bechgyn (boys)	maneg	menig (gloves)
carreg	cerrig (stones)	pabell	pebyll (tents)
castell	cestyll (castles)	padell	pedyll (bowls, pans)
gwaell	gweill (knitting needles)		

Variants are: alarchod, llanerchau, padelli/padellau.

Maharen – meheryn *rams* is a three-vowel change broadly conforming to this pattern.

84   Plurals formed by miscellaneous two-vowel changes

Miscellaneous two-vowel internal plurals are:

asgwrn, esgyrn	(bones)	
dafad, defaid	(sheep)	(pl. usually pronounced **defed**)

85 **Irregular and miscellaneous plurals**

The following do not fit into any established type:

Singular	Plural	Singular	Plural
brawd	**brodyr** (brothers)	**llo**	**lloi/lloeau** (calves)
ci	**cŵn** (dogs)	**pennog**	**penwaig** (herrings)
gwayw	**gwewyr** (pangs, pains)	**tŷ**	**tai** (houses)
gŵr	**gwŷr** (men)	**ych**	**ychen** (oxen)
llaw	**dwylo** (hands) (see §88)		

Some nouns drop a syllable in the pl. Examples:

Singular	Plural
cymydog	**cymdogion** (neighbours)
cystadleuaeth	**cystadlaethau** (competitions)
gorchymyn	**gorchmynion** (orders)
perchennog	**perchnogion** (owners)

Note also the unusual formation of **hosan** in the plural, **sanau** (socks), with the loss of the first syllable.

Some nouns form their pl. from a derivative of the sing. (often -(i)ad):

Singular	Plural
dechrau	**dechreuadau** (beginnings)
diwedd	**diweddiadau** (ends)
dosbarth	**dosbarthiadau** (classes)
golau	**goleuadau** (lights)

Noson *evening* takes for its pl. **nosweithiau** (from the related word **noswaith** of the same meaning).

Note:

gwestai (pl.)	**gwesty** (sing.) (hotel)
gwestai (sing.)	**gwesteion** (pl.) (guests)

86 Double plurals with different meanings

Some Welsh nouns have more than one meaning. Welsh occasionally distinguishes the two meanings by forming different plurals. A good example is **llwyth**, which means *tribe* (pl. **llwythau**) or *load* (pl. **llwythi**). Other examples:

bron	**bronnau** (breasts, i.e. anatomical);	**bronnydd** (breasts, i.e. of hills)
cyngor	**cynghorau** (councils);	**cynghorion** (counsels)
llif	**llifogydd** (floods);	**llifiau** (saws)
person	**personau** (persons);	**personiaid** (parsons)
pryd	**prydau** (meals);	**prydiau** (times)
ysbryd	**ysbrydion** (ghosts);	**ysbrydoedd** (spirits, i.e. other senses)

87 Nouns with no singular

Some nouns have no sing. form, or are not used in the sing.:

creision	(potato) crisps
gwartheg	cattle
nefoedd	heaven
pigion	selections (i.e. extracts)
trigolion	inhabitants

Aroglau *smell* looks like a plural but is not, even though the written language has now developed a sing. *arogl* from it. The spoken language keeps the original as a sing., though in a variety of forms, e.g. **ogle, rogla, hogla**. Note that *to smell* in this context is **clywed**:

'Na'r ogle rhyfedd °glywson ni ddoe

There's that funny smell we smelt yesterday

88 Duals

A very few nouns have a special dual form denoting 'two' rather than 'many'. All are made up of the element **deu-** or **dwy-** *two* + noun:

73

dydd,	deuddydd	day, (period of) two days
mis,	deufis	month, (period of) two months
llaw,	dwylo	hand/hands (generally when thought of as a pair but there is a regular pl. **llawiau**)

89   Special plural for 'three days'

Dydd *day* also has a special form for *three* which is still widely used – tridiau (stress on first **i**, -au as -a/-e):

Mi °fydd y °gynhadledd yn para am °dridiau

The conference will go on for (a period of) three days

90–92 COLLECTIVE/UNIT NOUNS

See §55 for an explanation of the principles behind c/u nouns, and the difference between them and sing./pl. nouns. Because of their relatively small number, it is best simply to identify those in common use so that the learner can recognize them when encountered. Feminines, as by far the larger group, are given first, with a separate listing for trees, and then masculines. Except where noted otherwise, feminine unit nouns are formed by adding -en to the collective form, masculines by adding -yn.

90   Feminine collective/unit nouns

In the following list, which is fairly complete but omits trees (dealt with separately below) and rarely used or obsolete items, the collective term is given as the base form (which it is), with unit forms in brackets where some change other than the simple addition of -en is needed.

afan	raspberries	**gwythi (gwythïen)**	veins
blodfresych	cauliflower	**hwyaid (hwyaden)**	ducks
bresych	cabbage	**letys**	lettuce
briallu (briallen)	primrose	**llau (lleuen)**	lice
brics	bricks	**lluched**	lightning

cacwn (**cacynen**)	wasps	**llus**	bilberries	
ceirch	oats	**llygod**	mice	
cennin (**cenhinen**)	leeks	**llyngyr**	worms (in body)	
cesair (**ceseiren**)	hail	**madarch**	mushrooms	
clêr (**cleren**)	flies	**mafon**	raspberries	
cnau (**cneuen**)	nuts	**maip** (**meipen**)	turnips	
coed	trees	**mefus**	strawberries	
crach	scabs	**mellt**	lightning	
cylion	flies, gnats	**mes**	acorns	
chwain (**chwannen**)	fleas	**moron**	carrots	
dail (**deilen**)	leaves, foliage	**mwyar**	blackberries	
drain (**draenen**)	thorns	**mwyarafan**	loganberries	
ffa (**ffäen**)	beans	**nedd**	nits	
gweill (**gwellen**)	knitting needles	**piod**	magpies	
gwenith	wheat	**plu**	feathers	
gwenyn	bees	**sêr** (**seren**)	stars	
gwiail (**gwialen**)	twigs	**tywyrch** (**tywarchen**)	turfs	
gwrysg	stalks	**tywys**	corn	
gwŷdd (**gwydden**)	trees	**ysgall**	thistles	

Notes:

(a)   The true relationship between collective and unit nouns is particularly clear in the English translations for some of the above pairs. As mentioned earlier, *foliage*, for example, is a very close approximation to the actual sense of **dail**, conveying as it does the idea of 'leaves' as one homogeneous body. The translations for some of the unit forms (i.e. in -**en** here) are revealing: **tywysen** means *an ear of corn*; **llucheden** *a flash of lightning*; **mefusen** *a strawberry*, as opposed to **mefus** (*bed of*) *strawberries* (or *plate of strawberries*).

75

(b)   **Gweill** and **hwyaid** are alternatively members of the sing./pl. system: **gwäell – gweill** and **hwyad – hwyaid**.

(c)   Though anomalous in that it appears with an ending (**-i**) in the base-form, **mieri – miaren** *bramble* probably belongs here as well.

91   Collective nouns for trees

The following are the commonest collective terms for native trees. All of them add -**en** to the collective to give the name for a single tree of the species – changes are noted where required. So, for example, **bedwen** is *birch tree*.

bedw	birch	**gwern**	alder
ceirios	cherry	**helyg**	willow
celyn (celynnen)	holly	**llwyf**	elm
cerddin	rowan	**marchredyn**	fern
cyll (collen)	hazel	**meryw**	juniper
derw	oak	**onn/ynn (onnen)**	ash
eirin	peach	**poplys**	poplar
gellyg	pear	**ysgaw**	elder
gwaglwyf	lime	**yw**	yew

Notes:

(a)   **afallen – afallennau** *apple* (*tree*) is *not* a c/u noun – there is no form ****afall** for a group of apple trees.

(b)   Other trees, including non-native species, are formed with the suffix -**wydd** (unit: -**wydden**) *tree*. Examples: **castanwydd** *chestnut*, **cedrwydd** *cedar*, **cypreswydd** *cypress*, **ffawydd** *beech*, **ffynidwydd** *fir, pine*, **llarwydd** *larch*, **sycamorwydd** *sycamore*.

abwyd	worms (in earth)	gwellt	grass, straw
adar (aderyn)	birds	gwybed	gnats
blagur	shoots, buds	lindys	caterpillars
briwsion	crumbs	moch	pigs, swine
blew	fur	morgrug	ants
crabys	crabapples	plant (plentyn)	children
cnewyll	kernels	pysgod	fish
dillad (dilledyn)	clothes	rhos	roses
graean (greyenyn)	gravel, shingle	sgadan (sgadenyn)	herrings

Note: **dilledyn** is used for an item of clothing or garment, again showing the distinction between the 'generality' of the collective noun and the 'individualization' of the unit noun.

Adjectives

93 Definitions

Adjectives are those words which *describe* people or things. Broadly speaking, they answer the question 'what kind of . . .?' (what kind of man is he? – a *tall* man; what kind of house is it? – a *semi-detached* house; what kind of book is it? – a *Welsh* book). Mostly they are adjectives in their own right, but any word, even if it usually has a different function, can be said to be an adjective if it used for this job of describing, or narrowing down, something. Nouns and verbs are the most likely candidates for this, both in English and Welsh (what kind of room? – a *living* room: *verb* – ystafell °fyw; a *bed*room: *noun* – ystafell °wely).

The idea of narrowing down is also seen in certain special adjectives which identify something as belonging to an individual (English *my*, *your*, etc. – see §109).

94 Position of adjectives

The normal position for the adjective in Welsh is after the noun, like French and unlike English:

car *newydd*	a *new* car
yr ysgol °*fawr*	the *big* school

In adjective sequences of the type 'big red bus' or 'dear little creatures', Welsh is more consistent than English, preferring always to place the size term closest to the noun: **bws mawr coch, creaduriaid bach annwyl.**

95 Adjective modifiers

The most common adjective modifiers are:

iawn	very	**mor°**	so
eitha	quite, fairly	**rhy°**	too
go°	pretty	**tra°**	pretty
pur°	very	**reit°**	very, really
braidd	rather	**digon**	enough

The modifying word **iawn** *very* comes after the adjective:

ysgol °fawr iawn a very big school

plant hapus iawn very happy children

rhaglen °wael iawn a very poor programme

but other words used to modify adjectives generally come before:

Mae'r °gadair 'ma'n *rhy isel* i mi

This chair is *too low* for me

Oedd petrol yn *eitha rhad* °bryd hynny

Petrol was *fairly cheap* in those days

°Ddes i'n *reit agos* fan'na

I came *really close* there

***Pur anaml* y bydda i'n mynd yno dyddiau 'ma**

Very rarely do I go there now

Sut dach chi heddiw? Yn °o *lew*, diolch

How are you today? OK, thanks

In **braidd yn°** *rather* . . ., the **yn°** is an integral part of the expression and the two cannot be separated. Compare the following:

Mae'r parsel yn eitha trwm	The parcel is quite heavy
Mae'r parsel braidd yn °drwm	The parcel is rather heavy

and the **yn°** is needed with **braidd** even in constructions where it would not be needed otherwise:

Parsel eitha trwm	Quite a heavy parcel
Parsel braidd yn °drwm	A rather heavy parcel

With **mae** . . . sentences there is an alternative possibility with **braidd**, however, and that is to place it after the adjective:

Mae'r parsel yn °drwm braidd

The parcel is rather heavy/on the heavy side

Mor° *so* . . . has its own peculiarities, see §105.

96 Adjectives that precede the noun

Although the vast majority of Welsh adjectives come after the noun they are describing, there are a few which always come before, and some that are found in both positions, just as in French.

(a) The most common adjectives which always come before are

hen	old	**prif**	main, chief
ambell	occasional	**holl**	all
pob	every, each (see §97)		

Examples:

hen °ddyn *old man*, **ambell °gawod** *(the) occasional shower*, **pob gair** *every word*, **prif °bwrpas** *main purpose*, **yr holl °blant** *all the children*

(b) The interrogative adjective **pa°** *which . . .?* always precedes the noun:

Pa °lyfr °bryni di?

Which book will you buy?

Ym ⁿmha °wlad mae hi'n byw bellach?

What country does she live in now?

Pa ieithoedd dach chi'n siarad yn rhugl?

What languages do you speak fluently?

Pa °fath o °gar sy gynnoch chi dyddiau 'ma?

What kind of car have you got these days?

Note incidentally that English often substitutes *what . . .?* for *which . . .?* – but **pa°** (and not **beth**, see §139) is always required in these instances in Welsh. In many S areas, **pwy°** is substituted for **pa°**: **Pwy °lyfr . . .?**

(c) In addition, the following are attached directly to a noun in the particular meanings given:

cyn-	ex-, former	**uwch**	senior, superior
dirprwy	deputy	**is-**	sub-, vice

Examples:

cyn-°**lywydd** *former president*, **dirprwy** °**bennaeth** *deputy head*, **uwch** °**olygydd** *senior editor*, **is-**°**lywydd** *vice-president*

(d) **Cryn** *considerable*, used in certain quantity expressions, always precedes the noun: **cryn** °**dipyn (o)** *quite a bit (of)*, **cryn nifer (o)** *quite a number (of)*.

Note that adjectives which come before the noun always cause SM, except for **pob**. Examples: hen °gastell *an old castle*; Prif °Weinidog *Prime Minister*; ambell °air *an occasional word*; yr holl °waith *all the work*; 'y ⁿghyn-°wraig *my ex-wife*; uwch-°gapten *major (rank)*; y dirprwy-°lyfrgellydd *the deputy librarian*; Is-°Lywydd yr Unol Daleithiau *the Vice-President of the United States*; is-°olygydd *sub-editor*; cyn-Is-°Lywydd yr U.D. *the ex-Vice-President of the U.S.*

But: **pob dyn** *every man*, **pob gardd** *every garden*.

A more general alternative for *all* is **i gyd** which, however, follows the noun it refers to:

yr holl °**blant** or **y plant i gyd**	all the children

In many cases, including with pronouns, only **i gyd** can be used:

chi i gyd	all of you
y gweddill i gyd	all the rest

Where preceding and following adjectives are used at the same time, they will go in their proper places:

hen °**dŷ gwag**	an old empty house
pob iaith °**Geltaidd**	every Celtic language

Pob

Pob always comes before the noun, but does not cause SM. It corresponds to *every* or *each* and should not be confused with the pronoun **pawb** *everyone* (see §158).

Ofer oedd pob ymdrech i °wrthdroi'r penderfyniad

Every attempt to overturn the decision was in vain

Mae pob ffordd trwy'r pentre bellach ar °gau

Every road through the village is now closed

Pob llwyddiant!

Good luck! [lit. Every success!]

The combination **yn** *in* + **pob** is usually written and pronounced **ymhob**:

Bydd hyn yn °flaenoriaeth ymhob ardal

This will be a priority in every region/all regions

Pob also appears in a number of idioms:

°**bob dydd**	every day
°**bob wythnos**	every week
pob dim	every (single) thing
°**bob yn ail**	alternately
yn ôl pob tebyg	in all likelihood
pobman/ymhobman	everywhere
°**bob amser**	always

For **popeth** *everything*, see §159.

(Yr) hen° . . .

(Yr) hen° is often used colloquially in terms of address, either as an insult or to express endearment, but in either case bearing no relationship to age. In this usage it corresponds to English *you* . . .:

Yr hen °fochyn!	You pig!
Yr hen °blentyn bach!	You poor little child!

Also as an intensifier:

Hen lol!   (What) nonsense!

Hen °bethau gwirion!   Stupid things!

99   Adjectives that can precede or follow the noun

These are relatively few in number, and you cannot just do as you please – their meanings differ depending on whether they come before or after. The only one in common use is **unig**:

unig °blentyn   an only child

plentyn unig   a lonely child

100   Feminine forms of adjectives

Generally, the gender of a noun makes no difference to the form of the adjective (but see §102 for mutation differences), but in the older language, many one-syllable (and some two-syllable) adjectives had different forms for masculine and feminine. Nowadays only a few adjectives preserve this distinction in normal speech:

gwyn (*m*)	**gwen** (*f*) white	**tlws** (*m*)	**tlos** (*f*) pretty
byr (*m*)	**ber** (*f*) short	**cryf** (*m*)	**cref** (*f*) strong
bychan (*m*)	**bechan** (*f*) small	**gwyrdd** (*m*)	**gwerdd** (*f*) green
crwn (*m*)	**cron** (*f*) round	**llym** (*m*)	**llem** (*f*) severe
trwm (*m*)	**trom** (*f*) heavy	**melyn** (*m*)	**melen** (*f*) yellow

Examples (note mutation of adjective after feminine singular noun):

cyfnod byr	a short period	**stori °fer**	a short story
tŷ bychan	a small house	**gardd °fechan**	a small garden
parsel trwm	a heavy parcel	**ergyd °drom**	a heavy blow
adeilad crwn	a round building	**ffenest °gron**	a round window
dyn llym	a severe man	**profedigaeth °lem**	a severe trial
ceffyl cryf	a strong horse	**caseg °gref**	a strong mare

Note: even these few adjectives that do have a feminine form often revert to the masculine when separated from the noun by other words, particularly yn°. Compare:

	Stori °fer	a short story
but:	**Roedd y stori'n °fyr iawn**	the story was very short
	Pêl °wen	a white ball
but:	**Roedd y °bêl yn °wyn**	the ball was white

101   Plural forms of adjectives

Some adjectives have special plural forms. Again, this phenomenon was more widespread in the older language, and today it is very much the exception. Many of these adjectives form their plural by adding -ion or -on, or by changing a vowel, or by both:

doeth (wise):	**doethion**	**gwyrdd** (green):	**gwyrddion**
bychan (small):	**bychain**	**ifanc** (young):	**ifainc**
dall (blind):	**deillion**		

These plural adjectives are nowadays more commonly found on their own than with a noun, to denote . . . *people*:

(**parchus**): **y parchusion** – the respectable people

(**tlawd**): **y tlodion** – the poor

(**cyfoethog**): **y cyfoethogion** – the rich

(**dall**): **cŵn y deillion** – guide-dogs (for the blind)

(**enwog**): **yr enwogion** – the famous; celebrities

(**gwybodus**): **y gwybodusion** – the experts; people in the know

(**ffyddlon**): **y ffyddloniaid** – the faithful

(**ifanc**): **yr ifainc** – the young

(**meddw**): **meddwon** – drunks

(**marw**): **y meirw, y meirwon** – the dead

Otherwise, plural-form adjectives are, to all intents and purposes, confined to set phrases, e.g. **mwyar duon** *blackberries*; **gwyntoedd cryfion** *strong winds*. But in normal speech (and writing), *black horses*, for example, would be **ceffylau du** (not . . . **duon**); *strong objections* would be **gwrth-wynebiadau cryf** (not . . . **cryfion**).

One adjective that is always changed for plural, however, is **arall** *(an)other*, plural **eraill** (pronounced **er*i*ll**):

merch arall	another girl
y °ferch arall	the other girl
merched eraill	other girls
y merched eraill	the other girls

But note that it is not usual to say *yr eraill for *the others* even though we have seen that this is perfectly all right with other adjectives (e.g. **yr ifainc** *the young*). Instead **rhai** (see §115) is inserted: **y rhai eraill** *the others* ('other ones'), or the pronoun **y lleill** is used (see §142). Similarly, the other one is either **yr un arall** or **y llall**.

Mae'r °gath 'ma'n ifanc, ond mae'r llall yn hen

Mae'r °gath 'ma'n ifanc, ond mae'r un arall yn hen

This cat is young, but the other one is old

°Ddaeth y llythyrau 'ma heddiw, ond °ddaeth y lleill ddoe

°Ddaeth y llythyrau 'ma heddiw, ond °ddaeth y rhai eraill ddoe

These letters came today, but the others came yesterday

102   Mutation of adjectives

Adjectives following a feminine singular noun require SM. Neither masculine nouns (singular or plural) nor feminine plural nouns cause mutation:

bwrdd	table (*m*):	**bwrdd mawr**	a big table
byrddau	tables:	**byrddau mawr**	big tables
torth	loaf (*f*):	**torth °fawr**	a big loaf
torthau	loaves:	**torthau mawr**	big loaves

This rule holds good regardless of whether or not the noun is used with **y(r)**, (though of course this in its turn will mutate a feminine singular noun, see §28):

y bwrdd mawr	the big table
y byrddau mawr	the big tables
y °dorth °fawr	the big loaf
y torthau mawr	the big loaves

Nouns and verbs used adjectivally – i.e. to describe another noun (see §93) – are subject to the same rule. If the noun they are attached to is feminine singular, then they undergo SM:

> [ystafell (f) – *room*] + [byw – *to live; living*] = ystafell °fyw – *living room*
>
> [cyllell (f) – *knife*] + [bara – *bread*] = cyllell °fara – *bread-knife*
>
> [siop (f) – *shop*] + [blodau – *flowers*] = siop °flodau – *flower-shop*
>
> [rhaglen (f) – *programme*] + [teledu – *television*] = rhaglen °deledu – *television programme*

but note the plurals: ystafelloedd byw, cyllyll bara, siopau blodau, rhaglenni teledu

103   Comparison of adjectives

As in English, there are two ways of expressing this in Welsh, and choice depends largely on whether the adjective is a short word or not. Short words (one or two syllables) add endings that correspond to English -*er*, -*est*: -ach, -a. Examples:

coch red	cochach redder	cocha reddest
ysgafn light (weight)	ysgafnach lighter	ysgafna lightest
tal tall	talach taller	tala tallest
hardd beautiful	harddach more beautiful	hardda most beautiful

Note in the last example that the English equivalent does not use endings, but rather *more*, *most*, because it is a longer word – we can say *prettier* but not *beautifuller*. The same thing applies in Welsh – if the adjective is longer than two syllables, mwy (*more*) and mwya (*most*) must be used:

cyfforddus (comfortable)	mwy cyfforddus	mwya cyfforddus
siaradus (talkative)	mwy siaradus	mwya siaradus
darllenadwy (legible)	mwy darllenadwy	mwya darllenadwy

Again as in English, two-syllable adjectives fall on the line and can often take either endings or mwy/mwya, though there may be a local preference:

hapus happy	hapusach/mwy hapus	hapusa/mwya hapus
doniol funny	doniolach/mwy doniol	doniola/mwya doniol

If in doubt as to which method to use, the safer option is mwy/mwya. Derived adjectives (see §118) almost invariably use it.

Than is na[h] (nag before vowels):

Mae aur yn °fwy gwerthfawr nag arian

Gold is more valuable than silver

Roedd y ffermwyr yn °dlotach na'r dinasyddion

The farmers were poorer than the city-dwellers

Bydd rhaid inni °fod yn °gyflymach na hynny

We'll have to be quicker than that

Ysgafnach nag aer

Lighter than air

104   Internal mutations with -ach, -a

When these endings are added to words whose last letter is -b, -d or -g, these letters undergo a kind of reverse SM, changing to -p, -t and -c respectively:

gwlyb	wet	**gwlypach**	wetter	**gwlypa**	wettest
rhad	cheap	**rhatach**	cheaper	**rhata**	cheapest
teg	fair	**tecach**	fairer	**teca**	fairest

Notes:

(a)   By a rule of Welsh spelling, final **-n** and **-r** are often doubled when an ending is added. So **byr** (*short*) becomes **byrrach**, and **gwyn** (*white*) becomes **gwynnach**. Cf nouns, §59.

(b)   Some adjectives change an **-w-** or an **-aw-** to **-y-** and **-o-** respectively as they add these endings, e.g. **trwm – trymach; tlawd – tlotach.**

(c)   *even . . . -er, even more . . .* is expressed by adding **fyth** to the comparative adjective: **tlotach fyth** – *even poorer*; **mwy cyfoethog fyth** – *even richer.*

(d)   *much . . . -er, much more . . .* can be done by putting **llawer** (*much*) before the adjective, or **o °lawer** (*by much*) after it: **llawer gwlypach** or **gwlypach o °lawer** *much wetter*; **llawer mwy doniol** or **mwy doniol o °lawer** *much funnier*

(e)   *a bit . . . -er, a bit more . . .* requires **ychydig** or **tipyn** before the adjective: **ychydig rhatach** *a bit/little cheaper*; a very common colloquial alternative is **bach yn°: bach yn oerach** *a bit colder*, **bach yn °fwy defnyddiol** *a bit more useful.*

(f) *rather . . ., somewhat . . .* is usually **rhywfaint** (a certain amount): **rhywfaint mwy costus** *rather more expensive.*

105 Equative adjectives ('as . . . as . . .')

As . . . as . . . is usually expressed in Welsh by **mor° . . . â**[h]**/ag . . . :**

mor °wyn ag eira	as white as snow
mor °ddu â'r °frân	as black as a (the) crow
mor °dal â [h]**choeden**	as tall as a tree
mor °gystadleuol ag erioed	as competitive as ever
mor °dlawd â llygoden eglwys	as poor as a church mouse

There also exists a more stylized way of expressing *as . . . as . . .*, where **mor°** is replaced by **cyn°** and **-ed** is usually added to the adjective itself:

Mor °ddu â'r °frân	As black as a crow
or **Cyn °ddued â'r °frân**	

For the most part, the method with **cyn . . . -ed** is nowadays found only in set expressions, such as:

cyn °belled â[h] **. . .**	as far as . . .
cyn °gynted ag y bo modd	as soon as possible

Cyn °belled ag y gwela i, does dim gobaith am °welliant

As far as I can see, there's no hope of any improvement

Danfonwch y siec ata i cyn °gynted ag y bo modd

Send me the cheque as soon as possible

and with certain very common irregular adjectives (see §106). In normal speech, **mor°** is by far the more likely option.

Mor °belled, a combination of the two methods, is commonly used for *so far*:

Mae pethau'n mynd yn °dda	**Ydyn, mor °belled**
Things are going well	Yes they are, so far

In some areas, a third option is available for expressing *as . . . as . . .* using the colloquial **fatha**[h] (i.e. **fath â**[h] 'type as') *like* between adjective and noun:

Oedd o'n °wan fatha [h]**chath**

He was as weak as a cat [lit. 'He was weak like a cat']

Notes:

(a)   *just as . . . as . . .*, or *every bit as . . . as . . .* is normally expressed in Welsh
with °**lawn** *full*:

> **Dw i °lawn mor °grac â ti**
>
> I'm just as cross as you
>
> **Mae hyn °lawn mor °bwysig â'r hyn wedsoch chi**
>
> This is every bit as important as what you said
>
> **Yn anffodus, mae'r sianeli eraill °lawn cynddrwg**
>
> Unfortunately the other channels are just as bad

(b)   **mor** also means *so . . .*, and so can be used without **â/ag**:

> **Mae'r peth 'ma mor °drwm, °alla i °ddim °gario fe**
>
> This thing is so heavy, I can't carry it

It is important to remember that, in sentences of this type, **mor°** *replaces*
the expected **yn°**. Compare:

> **Mae'r peth 'ma 'n °drwm**
>
> This thing is heavy
>
> **Mae'r peth 'ma mor °drwm**
>
> This thing is so heavy

Finally, note that **cyn** does not have this double use.

(c)   *How . . .?* with adjectives is **Pa mor° . . .?**

> **Pa mor °fawr yw'ch tŷ newydd, 'te?**
>
> How big is your new house, then?
>
> **Pa mor anodd ydi'r °Wyddeleg o'i ʰchymharu a'r °Gymraeg?**
>
> How difficult is Irish compared with Welsh?
>
> **Pa mor °ddrud ydy Stockholm?**
>
> How expensive is Stockholm?

Note that **Sut?** *How?* is not appropriate here. The English *how?* covers
two distinct meanings: *in what way?* (= **sut?**) , and (with adjectives) 'to
what extent?' (= **pa mor°?**)

(d) There is a convenient colloquial phrasing for *not much . . . -er*, involving **fawr°** (fixed mutation **f-**) before the comparative:

> **Oeddan ni fawr nes i'r bwthyn ar ôl awr o °gerdded**
>
> After an hour of walking we were not much nearer (**nes**) to the cottage

> **Wedi'r holl siarad 'na, dan ni fawr °gallach**
>
> After all that talk, we're not much (the) wiser

(e) **mor°** generally does not mutate words beginning **ll-** and **rh-** (so: **mor llawn** *so full*, **mor rhad** *so cheap*).

106 Comparison of adjectives: irregular formations

A few common adjectives have irregular *-er, -est* forms that must simply be learnt:

	comparative	*superlative*	*equative*
da good	**gwell** better	**gorau** best	**cystal** as good
drwg bad	**gwaeth** worse	**gwaetha** worst	**cynddrwg** as bad
mawr big	**mwy** bigger	**mwya** biggest	**cymaint** as big
bach small	**llai** smaller	**lleia** smallest	**cynlleied** as small
uchel high	**uwch** higher	**ucha** highest	
isel low	**is** lower	**isa** lowest	
hen old	**hŷn** elder	**hyna** eldest	
ifanc young	**iau** younger	**fenga** youngest	
hawdd easy	**haws** easier	**hawsa** easiest	
agos near	**nes** nearer	**nesa** nearest	

In the spoken language particularly, **hen, ifanc, hawdd** and **agos** are often heard with regular formations instead – so, for example, hena *oldest*, ifanca *youngest*, hawdda *easiest*, agosa *nearest*.

Notes:

(a) **hŷn** is often replaced by **henach**, especially when the sense is *older* rather than *elder*:

> **Dw i'n henach na chi**   I am older than you
>
> **Brawd hŷn**   an elder brother

Similarly, **hyna** is sometimes replaced by **hena**.

(b)   **ifanc** presents the learner of the spoken language with a bewildering variety of slightly differing forms: **iau** is often replaced by **ifancach** (i.e. regular formation), but this is often heard as **fancach**, **fangach** or **fengach**. Similarly, **fenga** is sometimes heard as **ienga** or **ieuenga**. Some of these differences are regional, and will cause no problems once the preferred variant for an area has been ascertained.

(c)   These days, at least in many parts of Wales, **haws** and **hawsa** seem to be less current than the regularized formations **hawddach** and **hawdda**. To some extent the same is true of **nes** and **nesa** (**agosach** and **agosa**) – this may have something to do with the fact that **nesa** also means *next*, and this meaning has come to predominate:

> **Pwy sy nesa?** Who's next?

> **Ble mae'r blwch post agosa?** Where's the nearest post-box?

(d)   It is important to note that **mwy** and **mwya** double for *more/bigger* and *most/biggest* respectively:

> **Roedd ein tŷ ni'n °fwy na'u tŷ nhw**

> Our house was *bigger* than theirs

> **Roedd ein tŷ ni'n °fwy moethus na'u tŷ nhw**

> Our house was *more* luxurious than theirs

By the same token, **cymaint** can mean *so much/many* as well as *so big*, and **cynlleied** can mean *so little/few* as well as *so small*:

> **Mae cymaint o sbwriel fan hyn, on'd oes?**

> There's so much rubbish here, isn't there?

> **Dw i erioed wedi gweld cynlleied o °bobl mewn cyfarfod**

> I've never seen so few people in a meeting

107   'Less . . . than'/'the least'

Llai *smaller* and **lleia** *smallest* (see §106) also do the work of *less* and *least* – in much the same way, incidentally, as **mwy** and **mwya** do for *bigger/more* and *biggest/most* respectively (see §106(d)). Compare:

> **Mae'r llyfr 'ma'n *llai***

> This book is *smaller*

Mae llyfrau cloriau meddal yn *llai* costus na ʰchloriau caled

Paperbacks are *less* expensive than hardbacks

Hwn ydy'r un *lleia*

This is the *smallest* (one)

Hwn ydy'r un *lleia* costus

This is the *least* expensive (one)

108 Sentence structures with comparatives and superlatives

While expressions involving *-er* are simple statements of fact:

Tokyo is larger than London

those with *-est* are *identification* sentences:

Tokyo is the largest city in the world

Note that in the first of these two examples, Tokyo is not being singled out for particular attention – one could just as easily say *London is smaller than Tokyo*, and the meaning would be the same. In the second sentence, however, we are identifying Tokyo as having some particular quality in its own right (no other city could be the largest, because largest implies 'different from all the others'). In Welsh, where the form of the verb *to be* differs as to whether the sentence is an identification sentence or not (see §§220, 223), this distinction comes out in both the form of the verb *to be*, and in the word order:

Mae Tokyo'n °fwy na Llundain

but: **Tokyo ydy'r °ddinas °fwya yn y byd**

because identification sentences require **ydy** (or **yw**), and in this use **ydy** cannot stand first in the sentence.

Obviously the distinction explained above holds good whether you are using **mwy/mwya** or **-ach/-a** comparisons:

Mae Tseineg yn °galetach na'r °Gymraeg

Chinese is harder than Welsh

Tseineg _ydy_'r iaith °galeta yn y byd

Chinese is the hardest language in the world

In tenses other than the present there is no separate identification form of
the verb **bod**, but the difference in sentence structure remains:

Bydd y °daith yfory'n hirach na heddiw

The journey tomorrow will be longer than today

Y daith wythnos nesa °fydd yr un hira

The journey next week will be the longest

Roedd y Nissan yn °ddrutach na'r Honda

The Nissan was more expensive than the Honda

Y Toyota oedd yr un druta ohonyn nhw i gyd

The Toyota was the most expensive of them all

For reported speech with sentence patterns which shift the verb from its
normal position at the front, see §492 (**mai/na/taw**).

109–114 POSSESSIVE ADJECTIVES

109 Forms and mutation patterns

The possessive adjectives (*my, your, his, her, our, their*) come before the
noun, with an optional element after it (here shown in brackets). Care must
be taken with pronunciation of these words, which does not correspond
very well to spelling.

fy, '(y)nⁿ . . . (i)	my	**ein . . . (ni)**	our
dy° . . . (di)	your	**eich . . . (chi)**	your
ei° . . . (e/fe)	his	**eu . . . (nhw)**	their
eiʰ . . . (hi)	her		

Examples with **plant** *children*:

'y ⁿmhlant i	my children	**ein plant ni**	our children
dy °blant di	your children	**eich plant chi**	your children
ei °blant e	his children	**eu plant nhw**	their children
ei ʰphlant hi	her children		

The above is the standard system for the spoken language, but there are
variations from region to region, and particularly with regard to the use of
Aspirate and Nasal Mutations (see §§4, 9), which are often avoided in
natural speech by many speakers. Thus it is common enough to hear **ei
plant hi** for *her children*, or even **plant fi** for *my children* (this latter is

93

widely regarded as sub-standard, but is certainly gaining ground in some S areas). The Soft Mutation, however, is an integral part of the spoken language, and we would certainly expect to hear **ei °blant e** rather than anything else for *his children*.

You may hear **ei** (*her* only!), **ein** and **eu** causing an **h-** to be added to the front of a following word if it begins with a vowel, e.g.: (**anrheg**) **ei hanrheg hi** *her present*; (**ysgol**) **ein hysgol ni** *our school*; (**oriau gwaith**) **eu horiau gwaith nhw** *their working hours*. There is little consistency about this, however, in the spoken language, and many speakers seem not to do it. It is required, however, in the standard written form of the language.

Conversely, and because of uncertainty among many speakers, an incorrect **h-** after **eich** is sometimes encountered, even in writing: *eich hysgol. Try not to imitate this.

The practice of 'echoing' the pronoun of the possessor after the thing possessed is widespread, and may have arisen from the fact that **ei** (*his* or *her*) and **eu** (*their*) sound the same ('ee'/[i] – see §**112**). This meant that, with words not susceptible to mutation of any kind, *his*, *her* or *their* could not be differentiated on their own: **ei/eu radio**, to the ear, could mean a radio belonging to him, her or them. By putting the relevant pronoun on the end, the ambiguity is eliminated: **ei radio fe, ei radio hi, eu radio nhw.** This device has now become generalized, though it is by no means obligatory.

The following paragraphs give a more detailed treatment of these adjectives individually.

110   Fy, '(y)n ('my')

The pronunciation represented by **fy**: [və], in so far as it is ever heard in natural, unaffected speech at all, seems usually to be confined to use with words beginning with (non-mutated) **m-**: **fy mam**. It is the standard spelling, however.

'yn reflects the actual pronunciation far more closely, even though it is hardly ever seen so written. This is how *my* is heard before words that cannot undergo NM, or where NM is avoided in normal speech. So **fy ewythr i** generally sounds like **'yn ewythr i** *my uncle*; **fy siop i** as **'yn siop i** *my shop*; **fy llaw i** as **'yn llaw i** *my hand*.

If NM is used (and this, of course, can only be with words beginning **b- c- d- g- p-** or **t-**, see §4), the word for *my* tends to disappear altogether, leaving the NM to do the job: instead of **fy mhlant** (i), or **'y mhlant** (i), you are likely to hear simply **mhlant** (i). Note that the usual expression for referring to one's father is **nhad**.

111   Dy ('your')

The only two things to note here are that

(a)   the 'echoing' pronoun used is not **ti** but the mutated variant **di**

(b)   before vowels the **dy** is usually shortened in speech to **d'**.

> **Lle wyt ti wedi rhoi d' arian di?**
> Where have you put your money?

112   Ei ('his'; 'her'); eu ('their')

These words, despite their spelling, have always been pronounced [i]. Pronunciations that follow the spelling (giving these words the same sound as in **tei** or **cynlleied**, i.e. [əi]), although increasingly heard on the media and at formal occasions, are essentially hypercorrections. They sound and are very affected, and should not be imitated. It is much safer always to sound **ei** and **eu** as if they were written **i**, as they originally were.

A change occurs in these words when they are preceded by the preposition **i** (*to* or *for*) – they are replaced by **'w**, and so pronounced. Examples:

> °**Roddes i °ddeg punt i'w °frawd e** (i + *ei °frawd e*)
> I gave his brother £10 (gave £10 *to his* brother)

> **Mae Sioned yn °debyg iawn i'w chwaer hi** (i + *ei chwaer hi*)
> Sioned is very like her sister (similar *to her* sister)

> °**Gawson ni °wahoddiad i'w priodas nhw** (i + *eu priodas nhw*)
> We got an invitation to their wedding

113   Ein ('our'); eich ('your')

Ein is yet another word that sounds as if it were written **yn**. Partly for this reason, it is nearly always accompanied in speech by the 'echoing' pronoun **ni**.

Similarly, **eich** sounds as though it were written **ych** (i.e. 'uh-ch') [əx].

95

These two words lose the **ei-** when following a word ending in a vowel:

Ewch â'ch sbwriel adre (*â + eich*)

Take your rubbish home (*go with your* rubbish)

Dyn ni eisiau helpu'n plant ni (*helpu + ein*)

We want to help our children

There are no mutations with **ein** or **eich** (or the other plural possessive adjective **eu** either).

114 Possessive adjectives as pronoun objects of VNs

Where the object of a VN is a pronoun, this is usually expressed in Welsh by the corresponding possessive adjective – in other words, *see(ing) him* will literally be *his seeing* **ei °weld** (VN **gweld** *see*). This usage will be encountered:

(a) in periphrastic tenses (see §§210, 262) involving an auxiliary + VN

(b) where the VN stands on its own, either:
because it shares its subject with a preceding inflected verb (see §325), or:
because the action of the verb is itself the subject of the sentence.

In all cases, the mutation patterns after the possessive adjectives are unchanged, e.g. (**fy**) ⁿ**nanfon** *send(ing) me*, **ei danfon** *send(ing) her*, **ei °ddanfon** *send (ing) him*, etc.

The 'echoing' pronoun of the possessive adjective usually appears after the VN in speech, though not invariably. It is frequently omitted in writing. Many speakers go a stage further, and drop the possessive adjective while keeping the echoing pronoun, giving a construction more reminiscent of English. Examples of types (**a**) and (**b**) above:

(a)	**Wyt ti'n ⁿngweld i?**	Can you see *me?*
	Dw i am *eu cynnwys* nhw	I want to *include them*
	Oedd hi'n *ei °dwyllo* fe	She was *deceiving him*
	°Alla i'ch *helpu* chi?	Can I *help you?*

(b) **Llenwch y ffurflen a'*i dychwelyd* erbyn diwedd y mis**
Fill in the form and *return it* by the end of the month

Mi °fyddai *eu hargyhoeddi* (nhw) yn anodd ar ôl be' °ddigwyddodd ddoe
Convincing them would be difficult after what happened yesterday

Rhyw° and **rhai** both translate English *some*, but with this distinction of meaning: **rhyw°** is always followed by a singular noun, and so corresponds to English *some . . . (or other)*; whereas **rhai** (no mutation) is always followed by a plural noun, and is simply the plural of **un** (*one*). Compare:

Mae rhyw °ddyn wedi syrthio oddiar y llong

Some man [or other] has fallen off the ship

Mae rhai dynion wedi syrthio oddiar y llong

Some men [more than one] have fallen off the ship

Note that, if English *some* does not correspond to either of these possibilities, then it should probably be left untranslated:

Rhaid i mi °fynd allan i °brynu bara

I've got to go out to buy *some* bread

Dw i angen dillad newydd

I need *some* new clothes

Here the *some* is normally required by a rule of English grammar – if it were left out, it would make no difference to the sense, and indeed it *can* be left out. In the first two examples above, however, *some* cannot be left out of the English, and so will be present in the Welsh as well, either as **rhyw°** or **rhai**.

The use of **rhai** also extends to being a plural 'tag' to hang other adjectives on. §101 dealt with the use of plural adjectives as nouns, e.g. **y cyfoethogion** *the rich*. This is a generalized term encompassing all rich people as a whole, but if we want to narrow it down to particular rich people, we can say: **y rhai cyfoethog** (note singular adjective!) *the rich ones*.

Maen nhw i gyd yn hardd, ond °well gen i'r rhai coch

They're all beautiful, but I prefer the red ones

This highlights the use of **rhai** as a plural form of **un**, corresponding to English *ones*. The singular version of the example above would be:

Maen nhw i gyd yn hardd, ond °well gen i'r un coch

They're all beautiful, but I prefer the red one

Sometimes **rhai** *some* contrasts with **eraill** *others* (plural of **arall**, see §101):

Mae rhai'n cerdded, tra bod eraill yn dod ar y bws

Some are walking, while others are coming by bus

Bydd rhai yn mynd, ac eraill yn aros

Some will go, and others will stay

Or the **rhai** can simply be repeated, as in English *some . . ., some . . .* with **eraill** added optionally:

Roedd rhai yn siarad Ffrangeg, rhai (eraill) yn siarad Almaeneg

Some were speaking French, and some were speaking German

Note also **unrhyw°** . . . *any* . . .

Unrhyw °lyfr

Any book

116   Amryw, ambell; y cyfryw, y fath . . .; Yr un

Amryw° means *several*, and is followed in the modern language by a plural: **amryw °ddynion** *several men*, **amryw °lyfrau** *several books*.

Ambell° means *occasional*, and is mostly heard nowadays in the expressions **ambell un** *an occasional (one)* and **ambell °waith** *occasionally, sometimes*. This last is similar in meaning to the adverbial expression **o °bryd i'w gilydd** (see §402).

Y cyfryw *such a . . .* was once more common than now. Mostly it is heard in the set expression . . . **fel y cyfryw** . . . *as such*:

Does gen i °ddim cysylltiad â'r byd addysg fel y cyfryw

I have no connection with the world of education as such

For *such a . . .* the usual modern expression is **y fath°** . . . (SM). So *such a thing*, which might be encountered in writing as **y cyfryw °beth**, is more likely to be **y fath °beth** in modern speech:

Dw i erioed wedi clywed y fath °beth

I've never heard such a thing

A very common colloquial alternative to **y fath°** is the loanword **ffasiwn°** (*fashion*):

°Ddylwn i °ddim dweud ffasiwn °beth, na °ddylwn?

I shouldn't say such things, should I?

While **un** means *one*, **yr un** specifically means *the same*. Its usage corresponds closely to its English equivalent:

> **O'n i yn *yr un stafell* â ti heb °wybod**
>
> I was in *the same room* as you and didn't know it [lit. 'without knowing']

> **Mae'r stafell 'ma'n edrych *yr un* ag oedd hi ugain ⁿmlynedd yn ôl**
>
> This room looks *the same* as it did twenty years ago

For **yr un** meaning *not one*, see §143.

For **yr un** meaning *each*, see §33.

117   Demonstrative adjectives

In spoken Welsh *this . . .* is phrased as *the . . . here*, and *that . . .* as *the . . . there*. The definite article (see §25) is placed in front of the noun, and the word **'ma** *here* or **'na** *there* after it:

> **y llyfr 'ma** this book [lit.: the book here]

> **y llyfr 'na** that book [lit.: the book there]

With this phrasing, there is no need to distinguish between *this* (sing.) and *these* (pl.) in Welsh, or between *that* (sing.) and *those* (pl.). If *this book* is *the book here*, then *these books* will be *the books here* – the only change needed is to turn the word for the object itself from sing. to pl.:

y llyfr 'ma	this book
y llyfrau 'ma	these books
y llyfr 'na	that book
y llyfrau 'na	those books

In formal and written Welsh a different system generally operates, using true demonstrative adjectives. They work like any other adjective and come after the noun they refer to. Like the spoken versions already explained, they need the definite article before the noun; unlike the spoken versions, they have differing forms for m and f in the sing. only:

	Singular		*Plural*	
	this	that	these	those
m	**hwn**	**hwnnw**	**hyn**	**hynny**
f	**hon**	**honno**	**hyn**	**hynny**

This gives:

Masculine		Feminine	
y llyfr hwn	this book	**y °daflen hon**	this leaflet
y llyfr hwnnw	that book	**y °daflen honno**	that leaflet
y llyfrau hyn	these books	**y taflenni hyn**	these leaflets
y llyfrau hynny	those books	**y taflenni hynny**	those leaflets

All these written demonstrative adjectives also function as pronouns (*this one*, *that one* etc.), and in this use they are part of the spoken language as well (see §**136**).

118   Adjectives derived from nouns and verbs

Apart from -**adwy** and -**edig** (see below), it is difficult to determine specific meanings for most of the adjective endings in common use in Welsh, and it is probably simpler just to learn each word as it is encountered.

By far the most productive ending is -**ol** (sometimes -**iol**), which forms huge numbers of adjectives in Welsh, mostly from nouns:

anobeithiol	hopeless	(**an** un- + **gobaith** hope)
beirniadol	critical	(**beirniad** critic)
cydwybodol	conscientious	(**cydwybod** conscience)
gogleddol	northerly	(**gogledd** north)
ieithyddol	linguistic	(**ieithydd** linguist)
moesol	moral	(**moes** morality)
perthnasol	relevant	(**perthynas** relationship)
rhagrithiol	hypocritical	(**rhagrith** hypocrisy)
swyddogol	official	(**swyddog** (an) official)
troseddol	criminal	(**trosedd** crime)
wythnosol	weekly	(**wythnos** week)

but also from verbs:

anfarwol	immortal	(**an-** un- + **marw** die)
cefnogol	supportive	(**cefnogi** support)
ymgynghorol	consultant (adj)	(**ymgynghori** consult)

Examples of the other main formations are given below:

-aidd can be added to adjectives to moderate their sense, as English -ish (coldish):

oeraidd	coldish
trymaidd	heavy, close (weather) (**trwm** heavy)

or to a noun, turning it into an adjective (like English childish):

plentynaidd	childish
benywaidd	feminine (**benyw** female)
hafaidd	summery
rhamantaidd	romantic (**rhamant** romance)

In borrowed or international words it often corresponds to English -ic, -ical:

biwrocrataidd	bureaucratic
economaidd	economic
piwritanaidd	puritanical
stoicaidd	stoic(al)

-adwy is added to verb-stems, and corresponds to English -able, -ible:

anghredadwy	unbelievable	< **an-** un- + **credu** believe
annealladwy	incomprehensible	< **an-** un- + **deall** understand
annarllenadwy	illegible	< **an-** un- + **darllen** read
clywadwy	audible	< **clywed** hear
cofiadwy	memorable	< **cofio** remember
gweladwy	visible	< **gweld** see
trosglwyddadwy	transferable	< **trosglwyddo** transfer

-edig can be added to hundreds of verbs to mean -ed, but is more restricted in use than its English counterpart in that it is used strictly as an adjective:

amgaeëdig	enclosed	< **amgau**
blinedig	tired	< **blino**
cyfyngedig	limited	< **cyfyngu**
etholedig	elect(ed)	< **ethol**
unedig	united	< **uno**

In many cases in Welsh, other constructions, involving for example **wedi** and **i'w**, also translate the English participle -*ed*, depending on the circumstances. Compare:

Y llywydd etholedig

The president-elect [i.e. the elected president – adjectival use]

Mae'r llywydd wedi'i ethol

The president has been elected

Mae'r llywydd i'w ethol

The president is to be elected

These alternative constructions are dealt with in §§364–366.

-**gar** forms adjectives mostly from verbs, denoting possession of the quality:

dioddefgar	patient, forbearing	< **diodde(f)** suffer
enillgar	lucrative	< **ennill** gain
meddylgar	thoughtful, pensive	< **meddwl** think
anfaddeugar	unforgiving	< **maddau** forgive
gweithgar	active	< **gweithio** work
gafaelgar	enthralling, gripping	< **gafael** grip, grasp
ymroddgar	eager to apply oneself	< **ymroi** apply oneself

but also from nouns:

blaengar	prominent	< **blaen** front
cyfeillgar	friendly	< **cyfaill** friend
croesawgar	welcoming	< **croeso** welcome
dialeddgar	vengeful	< **dialedd** vengeance
gwlatgar	patriotic	< **gwlad** country

-**ig** (as opposed to -**edig** – see above) forms adjectives from nouns, often with slight changes in the word:

brwdfrydig	enthusiastic	< **brwdfrydedd** enthusiasm
gwledig	rural	< **gwlad** country
lloerig	lunatic	< **lloer** – *old word for* moon

It appears in many loan-words from English adjectives ending -*ic*:

academig	**athletig**
awtomatig	**deinamig**

Some -**ig** adjectives do not derive from any obvious base-noun:

gwrthnysig	rebellious
styfnig	stubborn

-**lon** forms a limited number of adjectives from nouns:

anghyfreithlon	illegal	< **an-** un- + **cyfraith** law
ffrwythlon	fruitful, fertile	< **ffrwyth** fruit
heddychlon	peaceful	< **heddwch** peace
maethlon	nourishing	< **maeth** nutrition, nourishment
prydlon	punctual	< **pryd** time

-**llyd/-lyd** forms adjectives mostly from nouns, sometimes from verbs:

cysglyd	sleepy	< **cysgu** sleep *v*, **cwsg** sleep *n*
drewllyd	stinking	< **drewi** stink
dychrynllyd	frightful	< **dychryn** fright, frighten
rhagfarnllyd	prejudiced	< **rhagfarn** prejudice
seimlyd, seimllyd	greasy	< **saim** grease
swnllyd	noisy	< **swˆn** noise

-**og** forms adjectives mostly from nouns. It often has the sense of 'possessing (a quality)':

barfog	bearded	< **barf** beard
cyfoethog	rich	< **cyfoeth** wealth
galluog	able, capable	< **gallu** ability
gwyntog	windy	< **gwynt** wind
niwlog	foggy	< **niwl** fog, mist
talentog	talented	< **talent** talent

-us forms adjectives from nouns:

anffodus	unfortunate	< **anffawd** misfortune, accident
arswydus	horrible, horrific	< **arswyd** horror
blasus	tasty	< **blas** taste
costus	expensive	< **cost** cost
dawnus	gifted	< **dawn** gift, talent
dolurus	painful, grievous	< **dolur** pain
gelyniaethus	hostile	< **gelyniaeth** hostility
gwarthus	disgraceful	< **gwarth** disgrace
llwyddiannus	successful	< **llwyddiant** success
peryglus	dangerous	< **peryg(l)** danger
pleserus	pleasant, pleasurable	< **pleser** pleasure
poenus	painful	< **poen** pain
stormus	stormy	< **storm** storm
trefnus	orderly, tidy	< **trefn** order

A few adjectives in -us are from verbs:

drwgdybus	suspicious	< **drwgdybio** suspect
gwybodus	informed	< **gwybod** know
siaradus	talkative, loquacious	< **siarad** talk

Pronouns

119 Definitions

Pronouns are words that stand in place of nouns. Examples in English are *I*, *she*, *them*, *who?*, *this one*. While the noun names the person or thing, the pronoun simply refers back to it, once identity has been established: 'Mary sat down at the table, and then *she* ate her dinner'.

Pronouns come in several categories, and they will be discussed separately as follows:

personal pronouns: *I, you, he, she* etc. – §§120–131

reflexive pronouns: *myself* etc. – §§132–135

demonstrative pronouns: *this (one), these (ones)* etc. – §§136–138

interrogative pronouns: *who?, what?* etc. – §§139–141

miscellaneous – §§142–159

120–131 PERSONAL PRONOUNS

120 Personal pronouns

The personal pronoun system in Welsh differs from English in five main respects:

(a) English distinguishes subject and object forms for all pronouns except *you*: *I – me, he – him, we – us* etc. Welsh simply does not make this distinction, and uses, for example, **hi** to mean either *she* or *her* depending on the context:

Mae hi wedi chwarae'r rôl 'ma o'r blaen

She has played this part before

°Weles i *hi* yn y rôl 'ma llynedd

I saw *her* in this part last year

When, however, the pronoun is the object of a VN, an alternative construction is also available (see §114).

(b) Welsh, like French, carries its two-way gender system (see §44) over into the pronouns, and there is consequently no pronoun corresponding to English *it*. Problems with translating *it* are dealt with below (§128). In the 3rd pers. pl. (*they*), however, Welsh departs from this principle and resembles English in having only one form (**nhw**) for both genders (compare French *ils* and *elles*).

(c) Welsh distinguishes between a sing. *you* (**ti**) and a pl. *you* (**chi**) – these are likewise used in a manner very much reminiscent of French, with the pl. form also doubling as a formal or polite sing. See §127 for details of usage.

(d) The 1st pers. sing., 2nd pers. sing. and 3rd pers. sing. (m) have variant forms used in different circumstances. These are explained under the relevant sections, but note the important point, often misunderstood, that the difference between, say, **e** and **fe** is not that of subject and object – both can mean either *he* or *him*, and it is other considerations that determine the choice between them.

(e) All the personal pronouns have extended forms used in a contrastive or emphatic sense (see §131).

121 Personal pronouns – forms

	Singular		*Plural*	
1st	**i, fi, mi**	I, me	**ni**	we, us
2nd	**ti, di**	you	**chi**	you
3rd	**e/o, fe/fo**	he, him	**nhw**	they, them
	hi	she, her		

The form i is used:

(a)   after verbs – **dw i** *I am*, **wedes i** *I said*, **bydda i** *I will be*, **dylwn i** *I ought to*, °**wela i** *I'll see*, **galla i** *I can*. The apparent exception to this – where the Future I forms of the four irregulars **mynd**, **dod**, **cael** and **gwneud** (see §**305**) are sometimes heard as **a fi**, **do fi**, **ga fi** and **na fi** – probably represents the restoration of the old **-f** ending (i.e. these are really **af i** etc.).

(b)   with compound prepositions (see §§**475–476**) – **o ⁿmlaen i** *in front of me*, **ar ⁿghyfer i** *for me*, **er 'y mwyn i** *for my sake*.

The form fi is used:

(a)   after conjunctions and other miscellaneous words, e.g. **pawb ond fi** *everyone but me*, **ti a fi** *you and me*, **pam fi?** *why me?*, **yn iau na fi** *younger than me*, **fe neu fi?** *him or me?*

(b)   after non-inflecting prepositions e.g. **(gy)da**, **efo**, **â**, **heblaw**: **dewch 'da fi** *come with me*, **pawb heblaw fi** *everyone except me*.

(c)   as the object of an inflected verb:

°**Welodd e fi yn y °dre**	He saw me in town
Credwch chi fi	Believe you me
Stopiodd yr heddlu fi	The police stopped me

i and fi are interchangeable:

(a)   in inflected prepositions (see §**446**), but with **i** considered the standard usage:

arna i or **arna fi**	on me
wrtha i or **wrtha fi**	by/to me

(b)   as the object of a VN, though if the VN ends in a vowel there is a preference for **fi**:

Wyt ti'n ⁿghlywed i/fi?	Can you hear me?
Dach chi wedi ⁿghamddeall i/fi	You have misunderstood me
°**Allwch chi ('n) helpu fi?**	Can you help me?
Naeth yr heddlu stopio fi	The police stopped me

(c)   as the 'echoing' pronoun after **(f)y('n)** *my* (see §110), again with a preference in some regions for **fi** after a vowel:

yn 'yn stafell i/fi	in my room
gyda ⁿnheulu fi	with my family

mi is confined to two uses in spoken Welsh:

(a)   after the preposition **i** *to/for*: **Rho hwnna i mi** *Give that to me.* Even here many regions use **i fi** instead.

(b)   after the N preterite auxiliary verb **ddaru** (see §301): **Ddaru mi °weld o neithiwr** *I saw him last night* (originally **ddaru i mi °weld . . .** – cf. use of **mi** in (a) above).

For the affirmative particle mi, see §213.

123   ti/di **(2nd pers. sing. pronoun)**

In the overwhelming majority of cases, **ti** is the singular form for *you*, with **di** confined to the following circumstances:

(a)   as the subject in Future I: **os gweli di fe** *if you see him,* **pan °gyrhaeddi di** *when you arrive,* **°Fyddi di °ddim yn hir, na °fyddi?** *You won't be long, will you?*

(b)   in the reinforced singular command-form (see §379): **Aros di fan hyn am eiliad** *You wait here a moment,* **Dechreua di** *You start.* But note the exception with **Paid ti â . . .!** *Don't you . . .!*: **Paid ti ag edrych arna i fel 'na!** *Don't you look at me like that!*

(c)   as the 'echoing' pronoun after **dy°** *your*: **dy °gar di** *your car,* **d'allwedd di** *your key.*

In many parts of the N, an alternative form **chdi** is very common in speech: **°Wela i chdi** *I'll see you;* **°Ddo i hefo chdi rŵan** *I'll come with you now;* **Mae gen i ffydd ynochdi** *I've got faith in you.* It is *not* used as the subject in the preterite – so not *°Welest chdi hwnna? but °Welest ti hwnna? *Did you see that?*

124   e/fe, o/fo **(3rd pers. sing. pronoun)**

E/fe are used in the S, while **o/fo** are found in the N. The criteria for choosing between the short form **e/o** and the long form **fe/fo** are almost exactly the same as for 1st pers. sing. i or fi already given (see §122). But in two minor instances there is divergence:

(a)   after one verb-ending only, the 3rd pers. sing. non-reality **-ai**, the long form is used – **dylai fo °fynd** *he ought to go*;

(b)   after the N auxiliary **ddaru**, the short form **o** is usually found.

Note: *with him* = (**gy**)**da fe** or (**gy**)**dag e**.

For the affirmative particle fe, see §213.

125   Pronouns with no variant forms

The remaining pronouns – **hi** *she/her*, **ni** *we/us*, **chi** *you* and **nhw** *they/them* – have no variant forms. Note, however, that the normal unaffected pronunciation of **nhw** is **nw**.

126   Variant forms in literary Welsh

In literary Welsh, several of the personal pronouns have different forms: **ef** (= **e/fe**); **chwi** (= **chi**); and **hwy** (= **nhw**). None of these are in any way natural to the spoken language, and sound affected to varying degrees – **hwy** in particular verges on the ridiculous. All are common enough in more formal writing, however.

Furthermore, LW possesses a subset of infixed object pronouns which appear before the verb and are attached to the AFF particle **Fe** (*not* **Mi**)

Fe'*ch* telir yn °fisol

You will be paid monthly [lit. 'There will be a paying (of) you . . .']

Fe'*i* hyfforddwyd yn y °brifddinas

He was trained in the capital

Fe'*m* dysgwyd gan °ddyn sydd yn adnabyddus i chi

I was taught by a man who is well known to you

Fe'*th* °garaf di (song title)

I love you

None of this is part of the spoken language, and these infixed variants should not be used in speech. They are encountered in formal styles of writing, most often with autonomous/impersonal forms of the verb (see §367–374).

127   Ti **or** chi?

The use of the 2nd pers. sing. and 2nd pers. pl. pronouns in Welsh closely follows the practice of other European languages, e.g. French, Russian etc. **Ti** is the more restricted.

Ti, being singular, can only be used of one person. It is not only singular, but also familiar, and these two considerations combine to give a very narrow field of use. It is appropriate with:

(a)   a close member of the family

(b)   a close friend

(c)   a child, whether related or not

(d)   an animal

(e)   certain goddesses and gods

To use **ti** to an individual not from one of these categories can be construed, and can equally be intended, as offensive or, at the very least, deprecating. **Chi** is used in all other cases, i.e. not only for all instances where more than one individual is being addressed, but also with single individuals not coming under any of the **ti** categories above.

Obviously, the use of **ti** is very much a matter of personal choice – some people have more occasion to use **ti** than others, and use it more readily. Furthermore, the question of what constitutes, for example, a 'close' friend is a very subjective one. For the learner, it is safer to stick with **chi** in cases of doubt.

128   **Translation of 'it'**

Where *it* refers to a concrete object the identity of which is known, then the choice of **e** or **hi** depends on the grammatical gender of the word in Welsh:

°Fedrech chi symud y °gadair 'ma? Mae *hi*'n rhy °drwm i mi

Could you move this chair? It's too heavy for me

°Dries i °godi'r peiriant, ond oedd e'n rhy °drwm

I tried to lift the machine, but it was too heavy

Where *it* has an abstract or intangible sense, as in *it was raining*, or *it will be too late by then*, hi is used and *not* e:

Oedd hi'n bwrw (glaw)

Bydd hi'n rhy hwyr erbyn 'ny

Note that, in speech, **Mae hi'n** usually loses the pronoun in any case:

Mae'n bwrw

It's raining.

Mae'n rhewi bore 'ma

It's freezing this morning

129 Use of personal pronouns after prepositions

Most simple prepositions alter their form when used with the personal pronouns – for example am + fe gives **amdano fe**; i + nhw gives **iddyn nhw**. These are the inflected prepositions referred to above, and they are dealt with in full elsewhere (§446).

130 Personal pronouns as first elements in focused sentences

When used as the first element in a focused sentence (see §§17–18), the personal pronouns sometimes have a preceding y: **y fi, y ti, y fo/fe, y ni, y chi** and **y nhw**.

Y fo ydy tad Meirion, 'ta? (N)

He's Meirion's father, then?

Y nhw sy'n °gyfrifol am °drefnu'r lluniaeth

They are responsible for organizing the food and drink

131 Contrastive/emphatic personal pronouns

These are extended forms of the personal pronouns, used in certain circumstances as explained below. All end in -au, which is pronounced -a in the N and -e in the S (see §2(a)):

	Singular	Plural
1st	**innau, finnau, minnau**	**ninnau**
2nd	**tithau, dithau**	**chithau**
3rd (m)	**yntau, fintau**	**nhwthau**
3rd (f)	**hithau**	

These are used either when some idea of contrast (or sometimes balance) with a preceding pronoun or noun is present, or when emphasis is required. In both cases, as shown in the examples following, Welsh conveys by these special forms of the pronoun what English, as usual, conveys by stress and/or intonation.

[Contrast]

°Elli dithau °fynd yno os ti eisiau, ond dw innau'n aros fan hyn

You can go there if you want, but *I'm* staying here

Mae hynny'n iawn i chithau, efallai, ond beth amdanon ninnau?

That's fine for *you*, perhaps, but what about *us*?

[Balance]

°Welsoch chi mono innau, a °weles i monoch chithau

You didn't see me, and I didn't see you

Nadolig Llawen i chi! Ac i chithau!

Merry Christmas to you! And to you!

[Emphasis]

°Well i tithau °ofyn y tro 'ma

You'd better ask this time

. . . ond does 'na °ddim galw amdani bellach, chadal nhwthau

. . . but there's no call for it any more, so *they* say

These extended forms of the pronouns are not encountered all that often, but they should certainly be known for recognition purposes. Two common phrases use **finnau**: **A finnau** *Me too*, and **Na finnau (chwaith)** *Me neither*:

O'n i'n bwriadu mynd allan heno.	**A finnau.**
I was intending to go out tonight.	Me too.
°Alla i 'm diodde operâu sebon.	**Na finnau.**
I can't stand soap operas.	Me neither.

They are also used with **a(c)** *and* in a construction corresponding to . . . *being . . .*, *. . . having (done) . . .*, or *sincelas*.

°Flwyddyn yn °ddiweddarach, a nhwthau heb °fod ar °faes Eisteddfod yr Urdd, roedd maint eu dylanwad ar °Gymru'n amlwg

A year later, (with them) not having been on the Urdd Eisteddfod field, the scale of their influence on Wales was obvious

Ac yntau newydd °lofnodi cytundeb gydag EMI, mae ei °ddyfodol yn edrych yn °ddisgleiriach nag y bu erioed

(And he) having just signed a contract with EMI, his future looks brighter than ever

A ninnau wedi bod allan o °Gymru am °bum ⁿmlynedd, profiad go arbennig oedd gweld y Franks ar y teledu am y tro cynta

(And we) having been out of Wales for five years, seeing the Franks on TV for the first time was a special experience

Where appropriate to the sense as outlined above, the extended pronouns can be used also in place of the 'echoing' pronouns of the possessive:

Tybed a oes bai yn ein dull ninnau o °fyw hefyd?

I wonder if there are things wrong with *our* way of life as well?

(Cf. non-emphatic **ein dull ni**)

132–135 REFLEXIVE PRONOUNS

132   Reflexive pronouns

These are formed with **hun** (N) or **hunan** (S) *self* in conjunction with the possessive adjectives *my*, *your*, etc. (see §109). There is no 'echoing' pronoun following the word for *self*, and so there is no difference either in speech or writing between *himself* and *herself*. Forms for N areas:

	Singular	Plural
1st	**(f)y(n) hun**	**ein hun**
2nd	**dy hun**	**eich hun**
3rd	**ei hun**	**eu hun**

In the S, **hunan** changes to **hunain** in the plural, and so gives a rather more complex pattern:

	Singular	Plural
1st	**(f)y(n) hunan**	**ein hunain**
2nd	**dy hunan**	**eich hunain** (or **eich hunan** for sg.)
3rd	**ei hunan**	**eu hunain**

With **hunan**, as opposed to the invariable **hun**, the double function of the 2nd pers. pl. (pl., or formal sing.) can be differentiated: **eich hunain** *yourselves*, **eich hunan** *yourself* (polite or formal).

Note that standard English uses possessive adjectives for some reflexive pronouns (*myself*), but personal pronouns for others (*him*self, not **his*self). Welsh consistently uses the possessives.

Examples of the reflexive pronouns:

A i yno 'n hun

I'll go there myself

Bydd rhaid i ti °wneud 'ny dy hun, mae ofn arna i

You'll have to do that yourself, I'm afraid

Gwnewch eich hunain yn °gartrefol wrth i mi °drefnu'r te

Make yourselves at home while I organize the tea

Maen nhw'n hoff o °dwyllo'u hunain bod nhw dal yn sosialwyr

They like to kid themselves that they're still socialists

Maen nhw'n °dueddol o °gadw eu hunain at eu hunain

They tend to keep themselves to themselves

Pam nad ewch chi'ch hun ato fo?

Why don't you go to him yourself?

Byddwn ni'n cyflawni'r gwaith ein hunain os bydd eisiau

We'll get the work done ourselves if need be

When used with inflecting prepositions (see §446), usage varies.

Ei hoff °beth oedd gwrando ar ei hun ar y radio

Ei hoff °beth oedd gwrando arno 'i hun ar y radio

Ei hoff °beth oedd gwrando arno fe ei hun ar y radio

His favourite thing was listening to himself on the radio

133 Idiom expressing 'on my own,' etc.

A common idiom involving hun/hunan is ar 'y mhen 'yn hun(an) *on my own*, which goes as follows:

ar 'y mhen 'yn hun(an)	on my own
ar dy °ben dy hun(an)	on your own
ar ei °ben ei hun(an)	on his own
ar ei ʰphen ei hun(an)	on her own
ar ein pennau'n hun(ain)	on our own
ar eich pen eich hun(an)	on your own (sing.)
ar eich pennau'ch hun(ain)	on your own (pl.)
ar eu pennau eu hun(ain)	on their own

Examples:

Am y tro cynta aeth y °ddau onyn nhw allan ar eu pennau eu hun

For the first time the two of them went out on their own

Y cwbwl mae hi eisiau ar hyn o °bryd yw bod ar ei ʰphen ei hunan

All she wants at the moment is to be on her own

Gad inni °fod ar ein pennau ein hunain am °funud, nei di?

Let us be on our own for a minute, will you?

134 Hun/hunan **meaning 'own'**

Hun/hunan is used with nouns to mean . . . *own* . . .

Dyn ni °ddim eisiau cymryd y °gyfraith i'n dwylo ein hunain

We don't want to take the law into our own hands

Eich car eich hun 'dy hwn, 'te?

Is this your own car, then?

Siarad am 'y ᵐmhrofiadau 'n hun ydw i nawr, cofia

I'm talking about my own experiences now, mind

Man a man iddyn nhw °ddefnyddio'u harian eu hunain, 'te

They might as well use their own money, then

135 Hunan **in combination with nouns or adjectives**

Hunan (but not **hun**) combines with nouns and adjectives, causing SM in the usual way where possible – hunan-hyder *self-confidence*, hunanfeddiannol *self-possessed*, hunangyflogedig *self-employed*.

Yn rhyfedd iawn, roedd hi'n swil ac weithiau'n °brin o hunan-hyder

Strangely enough, she was shy and sometimes lacking in self-confidence

'Sdim eisiau iddo edrych mor hunangyfiawn, nag oes?

He needn't look so self-righteous, need he?

Mae'n system newydd ni bellach ar °gael ar y °ddwy °derfynell hunanwasanaeth

Our new system is now available on the two self-service terminals

136–138 DEMONSTRATIVE PRONOUNS

136 **Demonstrative pronouns**

This, *that*, *these* and *those* are pronouns when they stand alone without a following noun, e.g. *How much are these?*, *I like the look of this*. When used with a noun (*How much are these apples?*, *I like the look of this picture*) they are demonstrative adjectives, which are different in form and use in Welsh – see §**117**.

For concrete and other non-abstract ideas, the demonstrative pronouns vary for number and (in the sing.) gender:

	Masculine	*Feminine*
this	**hwn**	**hon**
that	**hwnnw**	**honno**
these	**y rhain**	
those	**y rheiny**	

Notes:

(a) **hwnnw** has a spoken variant **hwnna**, and **honno** a spoken variant **honna**; **y rheiny** similarly has a spoken variant **y rheina**

(b) **y rheiny** and **y rheina** often lose the initial definite article in rapid speech: **rheiny**, **rheina**

(c) these demonstrative pronouns can refer to either persons or things.

Examples:

Beth dych chi'n galw hwn yn °Gymraeg?
What do you call this in Welsh?

Beth dych chi'n galw rheina yn °Gymraeg?
What do you call those in Welsh?

Ai'r athrawes newydd ydy honno?
Is that the new [female] teacher?

Mae'r rhain i chi
These are for you

°Gymera i °ddau °bwys o'r rheiny, os gwelwch yn °dda
I'll have two pounds of those, please

Honna sy °well gen i, rhaid cyfadde
I prefer that one, I must admit

137 Demonstrative pronouns referring to non-tangible ideas

Welsh has a separate pair of singular demonstrative pronouns for use when referring to general, non-tangible ideas or pieces of information, or abstract concepts:

this	**hyn**
that	**hynny**

Note: **hynny** has a spoken variant **hynna**, usually pronounced 'hinna' [hɪna] rather than the 'huhna' [həna] that we might expect from the spelling – because really this word is **hyn** [hɪn] + **'na**

Examples:

Mae hyn oll yn °wastraff llwyr o amser

All this is a complete waste of time

Fe °allen ni i gyd °ragweld hyn

We could all see this coming

Beth mae hynny i °fod i °feddwl, 'te?

What is that supposed to mean, then?

Weithiau fel hyn, weithiau fel arall

Sometimes like this, sometimes another way

Hyn sy'n °gywir, a hynna sy'n anghywir

This is right, and that is wrong

Hwyrach °fod hynny'n °wir, ond serch hynny tydy hi °ddim yn °deg

Perhaps that is true, but all the same it isn't fair

138   **Idiomatic expressions with** hyn **or** hynny

Many idiomatic expressions involve the pronouns **hyn** or **hynny**, as for instance **serch hynny** *despite that, all the same* in the last example above.

ar hyn o °bryd	at the moment
erbyn hyn	by now; these days
erbyn hynny	by then
hyd yn hyn	up till now
hyn-a-hyn	so-and-so (as example)
°bob hyn a hyn	every so often; once in a while
o hyn ymlaen	from now on
hynny yw	that is; i.e. (abbr. **h.y.**)
hyn oll	all this
hynny i gyd	all that

The very common location adverb **fan hyn** *here* may also be mentioned here, though technically the **hyn** in this expression is an adjective (variant of **hon** – see §117).

Examples:

Dyma'r prif °ddatblygiadau ar hyn o °bryd

These are the main developments at the moment/for now

Mae hynny i gyd yn iawn

That is all well and good

Addysg °fydd ein prif °flaenoriaeth o hyn ymlaen

Education will be our main priority from now on

Sut mae'ch teulu erbyn hyn?

How are your family these days?

Does dim byd wedi'i °gyflawni hyd yn hyn

Nothing has been achieved so far

Mae hyn oll yn mynd yn °groes i ysbryd y cytundeb

All this goes against the spirit of the agreement

**. . . cael effaith hir-°dymor – hynny yw, sydd wedi parhau am
°flwyddyn o °leiaf**

. . . having a long-term effect – that is, (one) which has lasted at least a year

Hyn and hynny appear in many other time expressions where **hyn** corresponds to *now*, and **hynny** to *then* – see §402 for full list of common time expressions.

139–141 INTERROGATIVE PRONOUNS

139   **Interrogative pronouns**

These are **pwy?** *who?*, **beth?** *what?*, **pa un?** *which (one)?* and **pa °rai?** *which (ones)?* Note that in speech **beth** is very frequently pronounced **be'**, and similarly **pa un** is pronounced, and sometimes written, either **p'un** or **p'r'un**.

The meanings of **pwy?** and **beth?** are straightforward, but note that **pwy** means *who?* with a question mark. There is another *who* in English which is not an interrogative but a relative pronoun (see §144), and the distinction must be made in Welsh – only where a question is intended can **pwy** be used. Compare:

Pwy sy'n sgrifennu'r cofnodion heno?

Who is taking down the minutes tonight?

Dyna'r dyn *sy'n* sgrifennu'r cofnodion heno

That's the man *who is* taking down the minutes tonight

The second example is not a question, and **pwy** would be wrong, even though both English sentences contain the word *who*. Relative sentences of this type are dealt with in detail elsewhere (see §§479–85).

140 Mae, ydy/yw **or** sy **after** pwy **and** beth?

All three words corresponding to *is/are* are found after **pwy . . .?** and **beth . . .?** – the choice depends on the type of sentence. To understand the difference, one must simply be aware of the difference between subject and object in a sentence, and of what an identification sentence is. Definitions of subject and object may be found in the glossary of technical terms, while identification sentences are explained under §220.

Ydy/yw is used in identification sentences, of the type *Who is that? What is that colour?* They are easy to spot because they contain no other verb (nor adverb) in the clause, only a pronoun or noun referring back to the question-word:

Pwy ydy/yw hwnna?	Who is that?
Beth ydy/yw'r lliw 'na?	What is that colour?

But if the remainder of the English sentence (after *is/are*) includes a verb form with *-ing*, or some expression of location, then this is not an identification sentence, and **ydy/yw** is ruled out in Welsh.

With the identification sentence option ruled out, the choice between **mae** and **sy** is determined by a simple question: is the **pwy** or **beth** the subject of the verb or the object?

If **pwy** or **beth** is the subject of the sentence, then **sy(dd)** will follow for the present tense.

If **pwy** or **beth** is the object of the sentence, then **mae** will follow with the subject immediately after that.

Pwy sy'n helpu gyda'r llestri heno?

Who [subj.] is helping with the dishes tonight?

Pwy mae Sioned yn helpu gyda'r llestri heno?

Who(m) [obj.] is Sioned helping with the dishes tonight? [subj. – Sioned]

Beth sy'n cuddio o dan y gwely?

What [subj.] is hiding under the bed?

Beth mae Elwyn yn °guddio o dan y gwely?

What [obj.] is Elwyn hiding under the bed? [subj. – Elwyn]

In the object sentences (i.e. with **mae**) above, the following VN often has SM.

The **mae/sy** principle outlined above also applies, of course, where the tense of the English verb is simple present (e.g. *help/s*) rather than the continuous present (*is/are helping*), since both types of present are done the same way in Welsh, viz. **mae/sy** + **yn** + VN. And indeed the same principle also applies to the perfect tense, which in Welsh is similarly formed with **mae/sy**, but with **wedi** instead of **yn**. See §211.

Examples:

Pwy *sy'n siarad* Ffrangeg fan hyn?

Who [subj.] *speaks* French here?

Pwy *mae* Elin *yn nabod* fan hyn?

Who(m) [obj.] *does* Elin *know* here? [subj. – Elin]

Beth *sy'n digwydd* nesa?

What [subj.] *happens* next?

Beth *mae* hyn *yn °feddwl?*

What [obj.] *does* this *mean?* [subj. – this]

Pwy *sy wedi gwahodd* Gwen?

Who [subj.] *has invited* Gwen?

Pwy *mae* Gwen *wedi °wahodd?*

Who(m) [obj.] *has* Gwen *invited?* [subj. – Gwen]

Beth *sy wedi digwydd?*

What [subj.] *has happened?*

Beth *mae'r* heddlu *wedi °ddweud?*

What [obj.] *have* the police *said?* [subj. – the police]

Although this subject/object/identification distinction is usually found with pwy? and beth?, the principle is the same with the other interrogatives. Examples with faint?:

> **Faint sy'n dŵad hefo ni heno?** (N)
>
> How many [subj] are coming with us tonight?

> **Faint mae Gwilym yn gwahodd i'r °briodas?**
>
> How many [obj] is Gwilym [subj] inviting to the wedding?

> **Faint yw hwnna?**
>
> How much is that? [ident]

141 Which

Pa un (often p'un) and pa °rai are used where English *which* is not followed by a noun – otherwise pa° is used (see §96). Compare:

> **Dw i °ddim yn gwybod *pa °lyfr* y dylwn i (ei) °brynu**
>
> I don't know *which book* I should buy

> **Rhaid i mi °brynu un ohonyn nhw, ond dw i °ddim yn gwybod *p'un***
>
> I've got to buy one of them, but I don't know *which* (one)

> ***Pa ffilmiau* °welsoch chi yn yr °Ŵyl eleni?**
>
> *What films* did you see at the Festival this year?

> **Oedd dwy ohonyn nhw'n °dda iawn, ond °alla i °ddim cofio *pa °rai***
>
> Two of them were very good, but I can't remember *which*

> ***Pa ieithoedd* mae Tony yn siarad?**
>
> *What languages* does Tony speak?

> **Mae'n siarad nifer o ieithoedd, ond dw i °ddim yn siŵr pa °rai**
>
> He speaks a number of languages, but I'm not sure which ones

Note in the above example that colloquial English often uses *what* for *which* when used with a noun. If the meaning is *which*, then pa° must be used in Welsh.

142 Y llall, y lleill ('the other/s')

These are the pronoun counterparts of the adjectives **arall** (sing.), **eraill** (pl.) *other* (see §101). **Y llall** is a neater way of saying **yr un arall** *the other* (*one*), while the plural **y lleill** similarly corresponds to **y rhai eraill** *the others/other ones*. Examples:

Ewch chi i gyd rŵan, ac mi arhosa innau fan hyn am y lleill

You lot go on, and I'll wait here for the others

Dw i'n leicio'r un yma, ond dw i °ddim yn siŵr am y llall

I like this one, but I'm not sure about the other

143 Yr un (un), yr un °rai ('the same (one/s)'; 'none', 'not any')

Used with an AFF verb, these present no problems:

Maen nhw'n edrych yr un i mi

They look the same to me

Yr un °rai °welson ni llynedd yw'r rhain

These are the same ones we saw last year

But when used with a NEG verb, **yr un** means (*not*) *the one*, i.e. *not* (*any*) *one*, *not a single one*, *none*. This negative sense often escapes the attention of non-native users of the language, especially since the apparently ubiquitous negative marker °**ddim** is rarely present. Examples:

ʰChlywais i'r un sŵn neithiwr

I didn't hear a single sound last night

Dw i heb °feddwl am yr un ohonyn nhw trwy'r ha'

I haven't thought about any of them all summer

Tydi'r un ohonyn nhw'n siarad Cymraeg, 'sti (N)

Not one of them speaks Welsh, you know

Erbyn wythnos y perfformiadau doedd yr un tocyn ar ôl

By the week of the performances there was not a single ticket left

Sometimes the °ddim is present, however – mainly with **wedi**-tenses:

Dyn nhw °ddim wedi deud wrth yr un ohonon ni 'to

They haven't told any of us yet

Tydi Aled °ddim wedi gwerthu'r un llyfr hyd yma

Aled hasn't sold a single book so far

144 **Relative pronouns**

In English, these look like interrogatives (*who?*, *which?*, *what?*), but are used instead to refer back to something already mentioned. Examples:

That's the woman *who* does the weather on TV

Have you seen the parcel *which* came this morning?

I don't like *what* he said just then

In these examples, *who* refers to *woman*, *which* refers to *parcel*, and *what* stands for *the thing which* . . .

But in Welsh there is no real equivalent to the English relative pronouns, and instead the language uses either a special relative form of the verb **bod** where appropriate (**sy(dd)** – see §229), or preverbal particles to convey the relative sense. These are dealt with in all their aspects under complex sentences (see §§479–485).

In one case only, that of the third English example above, spoken Welsh has something approaching a relative pronoun: **yr hyn** meaning *that which* . . . or *the thing which* . . .. It usually corresponds to *what* in natural English, and **beth** is often an acceptable alternative in Welsh. Examples:

Beth dach chi i gyd yn °feddwl am yr hyn °welson ni ar y llwyfan heno?

What do you all think about what we saw on the stage tonight?

Bydd rhaid ymchwilio i'r hyn °ddigwyddodd neithiwr

What happened last night will have to be investigated

Yr hyn sy isio ar °fyrder ydy ymateb uniongyrchol a ʰchadarn

What is urgently needed is a direct and firm response

Yr hyn ydy *Uned °Gelf* ydy cylchgrawn misol newydd

What *Uned Gelf* is, is a new monthly magazine

Note in the last two examples that **yr hyn**, like *what*, can be used at the front of a sentence to anticipate something that is about to be mentioned.

145   Y sawl ('those . . . who')

Sawl? *how many?* is a quantity expression (see §187); but **y sawl** is used colloquially with a following relative construction to mean (*all*) *those* (*people*):

°Alla i °ofyn i'r sawl sy eisiau ymuno am aros yn y neuadd?

Can I ask those who wish to join to wait in the hall?

Bydd rhaid i'r sawl sy heb °docynnau °geisio 'u prynu nhw wrth y drws nos yfory

Those (who are) without tickets will have to try and buy them at the door tomorrow night

146   **Reciprocal pronouns ('each other')**

The basic form is **ei gilydd**, literally meaning (*each*) *his fellow*. This is used in all instances (regardless of gender) except where the context implies *us* or *you*, in which case **ein gilydd** and **eich gilydd** respectively are used instead. Examples:

Siaradwch â'ch gilydd am °ddeng munud

Talk to each other [amongst yourselves] for ten minutes

Dan ni'n mynd i helpu'n gilydd hyd y gallwn ni

We're going to help each other as far as we can

Naethon nhw °gerdded yn syth heibio i'w gilydd

They walked straight past each other

In the last example, **ei** becomes **'w** after **i** as is normal (see §112). Similarly, **ein gilydd** and **eich gilydd** appear as **'n gilydd** and **'ch gilydd** after vowels.

147   **'Together'**

Efo'i gilydd (N) and **gyda'i gilydd** (S) are used in Welsh for *together* (literally *with his fellow*), and again 1st and 2nd pers. pl. variants are available where appropriate. English does not make this distinction, and it is important to make the right choice when translating *together* in Welsh.

efo'i gilydd, gyda'i gilydd	(they) together
efo'n gilydd, gyda'n gilydd	(we) together
efo'ch gilydd, gyda'ch gilydd	(you) together

Dan ni isio eistedd efo'n gilydd os ydy hynny'n iawn

We want to sit together if that's all right

°Ellwch chi °ddim eistedd efo'ch gilydd, achos na sedd rhywun arall 'dy honna

You can't sit together, because that's someone else's seat

Maen nhw wedi bod yn chwarae'n hapus gyda'i gilydd trwy'r bore

They've been playing happily together all morning

Gweithiwch gyda'ch gilydd mewn parau am °ddeng munud

Work together in pairs for ten minutes

Maen nhw'n arfer cerdded lawr i'r siop efo'i gilydd bob bore

They usually walk down to the shop together every morning

Together after verbs is usually **at ei gilydd**:

Naethon ni °gasglu'n holl °bethau at ei gilydd

We gathered together/collected up all our things

As an idiom, **at ei gilydd** means *on the whole* or *all in all*:

At ei gilydd, does dim rhaid gwneud môr a mynydd o'r amrywiadau

On the whole, there's no need to make a big deal of the variations

At ei gilydd, ŷn ni'n croesawu'r °fenter 'ma

All in all, we welcome this enterprise

Neu'i gilydd corresponds to . . . *or other*:

°Ddaeth hi â rhywbeth neu'i gilydd i'w °ddangos iddyn nhw

She brought something or other to show them

°Fydd e'n ôl °rywbryd neu'i gilydd yfory, mae'n °debyg

He'll probably be back sometime or other tomorrow

Fel ei gilydd means . . . *alike*, where two dissimilar things are shown to have something in common:

°Fydd y llyfryn 'ma'n apelio at °Gymry a Saeson fel ei gilydd

This booklet will appeal to Welsh and English alike

Mae'r adnoddau yma wedi'u hanelu at bobol iau a hŷn fel ei gilydd

These resources are aimed at younger and older people alike

148 Pronouns with rhyw- ('some-') and unrhyw- ('any-')

These are rhywun *someone*, rhywbeth *something*, unrhywun *anyone* and unrhywbeth *anything*. Examples:

Mae rhywun wrth y drws, on'd oes?

There's someone at the door, isn't there?

Cadwch eich llygaid ar agor, rhag ofn i °rywbeth annisgwyl °ddigwydd

Keep your eyes open in case something unexpected happens

°Fedr unrhywun â geiriadur digon da °ddarllen Tseineg

Anyone with a good enough dictionary can read Chinese

Oes rhywun wedi dweud rhywbeth wrthat ti, 'te?

Has someone said something to you, then?

**'Sai unrhywbeth yn °well na gorfod aros fan'ma am °weddill y
bore, on' basai?**

Anything would be better than having to stay here for the rest of the
morning, wouldn't it?

Rhywun has a plural rhywrai *some people*:

Mae rhywrai yn meddwl bod hi ar °ben ar atomfeydd bellach

Some people think that atomic power stations are finished now

Although not pronouns, other words involving rhyw- and unrhyw-, some more common than others, may conveniently be mentioned here:

rhywbryd	(at) some time	**unrhywbryd**	(at) any time
rhywle	(in) some place, somewhere	**unrhywle**	(in) any place
rhywsut	somehow	**unrhywsut**	anyhow, in any fashion

Rhywle *somewhere* is often heard with a preceding yn *in*: yn rhywle *somewhere*.

The set with **rhyw-** are commonly heard with SM, e.g. °**rywbryd**. See §403.

Note also **rhywfaint** (or **rhyw** °**gymaint**), which is used to mean *a certain amount*:

Mae rhywfaint o °Gymraeg 'dag e, ond dyw e °ddim yn rhugl o °bell ffordd

He has a certain amount of Welsh, but he's nowhere near fluent

Mae hi wedi cynhesu °rywfaint ers bore 'ma, on'd yw hi?

It's warmed up a bit since this morning, hasn't it?

Yn naturiol, mae rhywfaint o °gyfaddawdu wedi bod

Naturally there has been a certain amount of compromise

149 Bynnag ('-ever')

Interrogative pronouns **pwy?** *who?* and **beth?** *what?* (see §139) combine with **bynnag** to give **pwy bynnag, beth bynnag** *whoever, whatever*.

Pwy bynnag °fyddan nhw, dw i'm isio siarad â nhw

Whoever they are/may be, I don't want to speak to them

Beth bynnag °fo'r canlyniadau, rhaid gweithredu'n °benderfynol

Whatever the consequences, (we) must act decisively

This element can also be used with non-pronoun interrogatives (see §441): **lle?** (**lle bynnag** *wherever*); **pryd?** (**pryd bynnag** *whenever*); **sut?** (**sut bynnag** *in whatever way*); **faint?** (**faint bynnag** *however much/many*). *Whichever . . . before nouns* uses the interrogative adjective **pa°** (see §96): **pa °lyfr bynnag** *whichever book*. **Pa°** is often omitted in **ffordd bynnag** *whichever way*:

Bydd dogfen ymgynghori °gychwynnol yn cael ei ʰchyflwyno pryd bynnag y bo modd

An initial consultation document will be presented whenever possible

Ffordd bynnag dach chi'n mynd, mi °fyddwch chi'n hwyr

Whichever way you go, you'll be late

150 Neb ('no-one'; '(not) . . . anyone')

The predominantly negative sense of **neb** is straightforward enough (but see §151 below), and the main area of uncertainty for non-native speakers lies in whether or not to use °ddim. This question can be resolved by looking at the relative positions of °ddim and **neb** in the sentence: where the °ddim would appear next to **neb**, it disappears. Otherwise it remains.

Therefore, as the subject or direct object of an inflected verb, **neb** does not require a °ddim, because with inflected verbs the subject immediately precedes °ddim, and the object immediately follows:

°Ddaeth neb i'r parti [subj]

No-one came to the party

°Weles i neb o °bwys o °gwbwl ar °Faes yr Eisteddfod 'leni [obj]

I saw nobody at all of importance on the Eisteddfod field this year

But in periphrastic constructions (see §§210, 262), while the subject still immediately precedes the °ddim, the object is separated from it by the main (non-auxiliary) verb. So with **neb** as the object of a periphrastic verb, the °ddim remains. Compare:

°Fyddai neb yn honni °fod y sefyllfa 'ma'n °foddhaol [subj]

No-one would claim that this situation was satisfactory

Dw i °ddim yn clywed neb yn sibrwd [obj]

I don't hear anyone whispering

Where **neb** is preceded by a preposition, °ddim is optional:

Weda i wrth neb or **Weda i °ddim wrth neb**

I won't tell anyone

°Gwrddes i â neb or **°Gwrddes i °ddim â neb**

I didn't meet anyone

There is no-one is **Does neb**:

Does neb ar ôl ond ninnau

There's no-one left but us

Does neb yn gwybod sut yn y byd °ddaethon nhw fan hyn

Nobody knows how on earth they got here [lit. There is no-one who knows . . .]

With other tenses:

Doedd neb yn °fodlon ein helpu ni

No-one was willing to help us

°Fydd neb yn gwybod hynny

No-one will know that

151 Neb ('anyone')

Originally **neb** meant either *no-one* or *anyone* according to context (rather like **erioed/byth** meaning either *never* or *ever* – see §409), but nowadays *no-one* clearly predominates. The most likely circumstance where **neb** means *anyone* these days is in comparative expressions after **â/ag** *as*:

Mae o °gystal â neb am °wneud pethau fel 'ny

He's as good as anyone at doing things like that

Oedd ⁿmrawd mor °gyflym â neb yn yr ysgol adeg 'ny

My brother was as fast as anyone at school at that time

and in constructions involving **cyn** *before*, **rhag ofn** *in case* etc.

Rhowch y dogfennau yn ôl yn y °ddesg cyn i neb °weld

Put the documents back in the desk before anyone sees

°Well inni °fod yn °dawel rhag ofn i neb °ddod

We'd better be quiet in case anyone comes

Note also the idiomatic expression **yn anad neb** *more than anyone*:

Sioned, yn anad neb, °fyddai'n addas i'r swydd

Sioned more than anyone would be suited for the job

See also §156.

152 Fawr neb

Hardly anyone **fawr neb** (fixed mutation of **mawr**) or **fawr o neb**:

Pwy °welsoch chi yno?   **Fawr neb**

Who did you see there?   Hardly anyone

Does fawr neb yn credu hynny

Hardly anyone believes that

. . . am nad oes fawr neb yn gwybod amdano

. . . since hardly anyone knows about it

Dim (**'nothing'**; **'(not) . . . anything'**)

As with **neb** above, **dim** has come to acquire a predominantly negative meaning. And as with **neb**, it 'absorbs' any negative °**ddim** that would occupy a position next to it, leaving the mutated or NEG-form verb on its own. When it is the subject or object of an inflected verb, it normally appears in the extended form **dim byd**. Examples:

°**Ddigwyddodd dim byd** [subj.]	Nothing happened
°**Glywais i** °**ddim byd** [obj.]	I didn't hear anything

The extension to **dim byd** is necessary in the second example because, in the spoken language, °**Glywais i** °**ddim** would be taken to mean *I didn't hear*, with °**ddim** simply as the negative marker of the verb.

In periphrastic constructions, **dim** or **dim byd** can be used with or without the negative marker °**ddim**, but this latter is not needed, and is often dropped:

Wi'n gwybod dim

I know nothing [Compare: **Wi** °**ddim yn gwybod** *I don't know*]

°**Fydd dim (byd) yn cael ei anghofio**

Nothing will be forgotten

Note that . . . °**ddim wedi** . . . expressions can be avoided with **heb**° (see §458):

Dan ni (°**ddim) wedi clywed dim (byd)**

or: **Dan ni heb** °**glywed dim (byd)**

We haven't heard anything

Elsewhere, though **dim** is usually sufficient, the extended variant **dim byd** *nothing* is very common, and has none of the ambiguity of **dim**.

'S gen i °**ddim (byd) yn ei erbyn**

I've got nothing against him

Faint yw'r tâl aelodaeth?	**Y peth nesa i** °**ddim (byd)**
How much is the membership fee?	Next to nothing

154 Fawr °ddim, fawr o °ddim

Not much is **fawr (o) °ddim** (fixed mutation of **mawr**):

Does 'na fawr o °ddim wedi digwydd yma ers y Canol Oesoedd
Not much has happened here since the Middle Ages

Be' nest ti yn y °brifysgol? Fawr o °ddim
What did you do at university? Not much

155 **Other idioms with** dim

Other idioms with **dim** include:

dim ond only (**'mond** in speech)
pob dim every single thing
i'r dim exactly, precisely; just so
dim un not a single one

Examples:

'Mond fi sy 'ma
It's only me here

O'n nhw wedi dwyn pob dim o'r tŷ
They had stolen every single thing in the house

Nawn ni °gwrdd yn y Llew Du yfory, 'te? - I'r dim!
We'll meet in the Black Lion tomorrow, then? - Perfect!

156 Dim (**'anything'**)

Sometimes **dim** corresponds to *anything*, especially in comparative expressions, e.g. **yn °well na dim** *better than anything*. Also in the idiom **yn anad dim** *more than anything* or *above all*:

Yn anad dim dw i'n gweld y swydd 'ma fel her
More than anything, I see this job as a challenge

Yn anad dim, mae rhaid i'n llywodraeth ni °fod yn atebol
Above all, our government must be accountable

Dim has two important non-pronoun uses:

(a) As a prohibitive marker for VNs, often seen on official notices and signs:

Dim Ysmygu	No Smoking
Dim Dymchwel Ysbwriel	No Dumping of Rubbish

Also in other common phrases:

Dim gobaith!

Not a hope!/Not a chance!

Diolch yn fawr! - Dim o °gwbwl!

Thanks a lot! - Not at all!/Don't mention it!

(b) As a negative marker in the spoken language for focused or emphasized elements at the front of a sentence (see §18):

Dim Ieuan °dorrodd y ffenest, ond fi

It wasn't Ieuan who broke the window, but me

158 Pawb ('everyone')

This pronoun must not be confused with the adjective **pob** *every* (see §97).

Mae pawb yn siarad Cymraeg ym ⁿMlaenau Ffestiniog

Everyone speaks Welsh in Blaenau Ffestiniog

Croeso i °bawb

Everyone welcome

Dw i wedi deud wrth °bawb yn °barod

I've already told everybody

Ydy pawb yn y cefn 'na yn gallu ⁿghlywed i'n iawn?

Can everyone at the back there hear me alright?

A more emphatic version is **pob un** (o°) *every* (*single*) *one*:

Mi °geith pob un ohonoch chi ei °bres yn ôl

Every one of you will get his money back

Note, however, that **pob un**, unlike **pawb**, can be used of objects as well as persons:

Edrychwch ar yr afalau 'ma – pob un wedi pydru!

Look at these apples – every one (of them) rotten!

159   Popeth ('everything')

This was originally **pob peth,** and is occasionally so found in written Welsh. It corresponds to **dim** (**byd**) *nothing* (see §153) as **pawb** corresponds to **neb** *no-one*.

Bydd popeth wedi newid yn °gyfangwbwl erbyn inni °ddod yn ôl

Everything will have changed completely by the time we get back

Byddwn ni'n siarad am °bopeth dan yr haul

We talk about everything under the sun

Mi na i °bopeth sy o fewn 'y ⁿnghyrraedd i

I'll do everything I possibly can [. . . which is within my reach]

Mae bron popeth fan hyn yn rhy °ddrud

Almost everything here is too expensive

Numerals and quantifiers

160 Cardinal numbers

Numbers 1–10 are fairly straightforward, though 2–4 have differing forms for masculine and feminine nouns, and some numerals cause mutations.

From 11 to 19, two counting systems co-exist in Welsh – the original one based on 20 (the vigesimal system), and a newer decimal system. The decimal system is simpler, and is promoted in schools. The vigesimal system is more awkward in some respects for non-native speakers, but is very much alive in ordinary speech, and is obligatory in certain circumstances. If anything, some of the shorter vigesimal numbers (particularly 12, 15, 18 and 20) seem to be regaining ground.

161 Syntax with numerals

With low numbers, a singular noun follows. This happens occasionally in English – *five head of cattle, I've lost two stone* – but it is the norm in Welsh. With higher numbers (except sometimes with money, weights and measures) a plural noun follows but with an intervening **o°**: **dwy °gath** *two cats* but **deg o °gathod** *ten [of] cats*, **pedwar drws** *four doors* but **cant o °ddrysiau** *a hundred [of] doors*. This principle generally does not apply with the vigesimal system. See examples in §§**165, 166**.

The dividing line between the two constructions, however, is hard to draw – **deg** is sometimes suggested, but few would argue with either **saith tŷ** or **saith o °dai** *seven houses*; **pum cath** or **pump o °gathod** *five cats*; or even with **tri dyn** or **tri o °ddynion** *three men*. And certainly *two children* is more usually **dau o °blant** than **dau °blentyn**. This is a question where 'feel' for the language is more reliable than any rules.

162 **Numbers 1–10**

Numbers 1–10 are as follows, m/f where appropriate:

1	un/un°	6	chweʰ(ch)
2	dau°/dwy°	7	saith
3	triʰ/tair	8	wyth
4	pedwar/pedair	9	naw
5	pum(p)	10	deg

Notes:

(a) **Un** is the same for m and f, but mutates a f noun (except those beginning with **ll-** or **rh-** see §9): **un ceffyl** (m) *one horse*, but **un °gath** (f) *one cat*.

(b) **Dau°** and **dwy°** both cause mutation of the following noun: **dau °geffyl** *two horses*, **dwy °gath** *two cats*. And both words themselves undergo mutation after **y** to mean *the two, both*: **y °ddau° geffyl** *both horses*, **y °ddwy °gath** *both cats*, **y °ddau ohonon ni** *the two of us*.

Used without a following noun, **dau°** can mean either two males or m objects, or a male and female (or m and f objects). **Dwy°**, being exclusively and specially feminine, can only mean two females or two f objects. So **y °ddau ohonyn nhw** *both of them* would be used with, for example, two boys or a boy and a girl, while **y °ddwy ohonyn nhw** would be required if there were two girls. This reflects a general ambiguity of the m forms of numerals, with the same principle applying to **tri** and **pedwar**.

(c) **Tri** causes AM, but erratically in the spoken language. It is definitely the rule in certain set combinations: **tri ʰchant** *300*. But the feminine **tair** is always followed by the radical: **tair ceiniog** *three pence*.

(d) **Pump** is used where there is no immediately following noun; otherwise **pum**:

> **Faint o °blant sy 'da chi erbyn hyn?** **Pump**
> How many children have you got now? Five
>
> **Wi wedi bod yn iste fan hyn am °bum awr** (S)
> I've been sitting here for five hours
>
> **Pum dyn / Pump o °ddynion.**
> Five men

(e) The difference between **chwe**[h] and **chwech** is the same as that between **pum** and **pump** (see previous note), except that some S regions use **chwech** even with a following noun.

Chwe can cause AM, but erratically in the spoken language, where both **chwe** [h]**cheffyl** and **chwe ceffyl** are likely to be heard for *six horses*. It is normal, however, in certain set phrases: **chwe** [h]**cheiniog**, *six pence*, **chwe** [h]**phunt** *six pounds*, **chwe** [h]**chant** 600.

(f) **Deg** has an alternative form **deng** which generally appears before time-words beginning with **m-**, either radical or NM-mutated: **deng munud** *ten minutes*, **deng mis** *ten months*, **deng** [n]**mlynedd** (NM of **blynedd**) *ten years*; and by the same token in the numerals **deng mil** *ten thousand* and **deng miliwn** *ten million*. Note also **deng** [n]**niwrnod** (NM of **diwrnod**) *ten days*, **deng milltir** *ten miles* and **deng modfedd** *ten inches*. In most other cases, **deg o°** is the preferred construction – **deg o °fapiau** *ten maps*.

163 Numbers from 11 upwards – decimal system

11	**undeg un**	101	**cant ag un**
12	**undeg dau** etc.	102	**cant a dau**
20	**dauddeg**	110	**cant a deg**
21	**dauddeg un** etc.	111	**cant undeg un**
30	**trideg**	140	**cant pedwardeg**
40	**pedwardeg**	200	**dau °gant**
50	**pumdeg/hanner cant**	300	**tri** [h]**chant**
60	**chwedeg**	1000	**mil**
70	**saithdeg**	2000	**dwy °fil**
80	**wythdeg**	10,000	**deng mil**
90	**nawdeg**	100,000	**can mil**
100	**can(t)**	1,000,000	**miliwn**
		2,000,000	**dwy °filiwn**

Notes:

(a) The tens can be written as two words – **dau °ddeg** instead of **dauddeg**, and so on.

(b)   **hanner cant** is a very common alternative for **pumdeg,** but *51* etc. is generally **pumdeg un** etc; **hanner cant ac un** (etc.) is, however, not unheard of.

(c)   **cant** *one/a hundred* and **mil** *one/a thousand* do not have **un** prefixed to them.

(d)   The first ten numbers after any hundred use **a/ac,** but thereafter do not: **cant ac wyth** *108*, **cant dauddeg tri** *123*; **wyth cant a chwech** *806*, **wyth cant nawdeg naw** *899*.

(e)   **can** and **cant** are differentiated in the same way as **pum/pump** and **chwe**[h]**/ chwech** (see §162): **cant o awyrennau** *a hundred aircraft*, but **can punt** *£100*.

(f)   Feminine variants must be used where appropriate: **trideg tri o °deirw** *thirty-three bulls*, but **trideg tair o °fuchod** *thirty-three cows*.

164   Numbers from 11 upwards – vigesimal system

11	**un ar °ddeg**	18	**deunaw**	32	**deuddeg ar hugain** etc.
12	**deuddeg**	19	**pedwar ar °bymtheg**		
13	**tri ar °ddeg**	20	**ugain**	40	**deugain**
14	**pedwar ar °ddeg**	21	**un ar hugain**	50	**deg a deugain**
15	**pymtheg**	22	**dau ar hugain** etc.	60	**trigain**
16	**un ar °bymtheg**	30	**deg ar hugain**	80	**pedwar ugain**
17	**dau ar °bymtheg**	31	**un ar °ddeg ar hugain**	100	**can(t)**

Notes:

(a)   There are special non-composite forms for *12, 15* and *18* (i.e. not, for example, **wyth ar °ddeg** for *18* but **deunaw**). These, and **ugain** *20*, are still very common in speech everywhere. **Deugain** *40* is not that unusual either, but **deg a deugain** for *50* is rarely heard. **Trigain** and **pedwar ugain** are not very common these days – indeed this is true generally for the vigesimal system above 50.

(b) **Deuddeg** and **pymtheg** have variants **deuddeng** and **pymtheng**, used in the same circumstances as **deng** for **deg** (see §162): **pymtheng milltir** *15 miles* (though **pymtheg milltir** etc. is heard as well).

(c) Numbers 21–39 are all added onto 20. So *33* is **tri ar °ddeg ar hugain** (*thirteen on twenty*) and *39* is **pedwar ar °bymtheg ar hugain** (*nineteen on twenty*). These may look cumbersome to the decimally-orientated, but they are to be heard every day on the lips of older native speakers.

(d) The teens can be, and often are, written as one word: **unarddeg**, **triarddeg** etc.

(e) **Ugain** adds an **h-** after **ar** in composite numbers. Note that **(h)ugain** (and compounds) is pronounced in many areas as **(h)ugian**. [igian]

(f) Occasionally a form **chweugain** *120* is heard, in the sense of *fifty pence* – this is a relic of pre-decimal currency, where 240 pence made a pound. Despite the abolition of the system long ago now, this expression is still current. Also **punt a chweugain** *£1.50*, etc.; **pisin chweugain** *50p piece*.

165 Uses of the vigesimal system

The vigesimal system is the norm in telling the time (see §173), and common with age and numbers of years (see §176), and with money. With many speakers, **deugain ⁿmlynedd** is far more likely for *40 years* than **pedwardeg o °flynyddoedd**. **Ugain** is to be recommended for learners for *20*, not only because it is widely used (an excellent reason on its own), but also because it is distinctive – the decimal alternative **dauddeg** sounds very like vigesimal **deuddeg** *12*, which is itself in common use.

166 Syntax of composite vigesimal numerals

Where a numeral contains **ar**, the noun directly precedes it. So, while *£18* is **deunaw punt**, *£19* is **pedair punt ar °bymtheg**. Similarly **tair buwch ar °ddeg** *thirteen cows*; **pum ⁿmlynedd ar hugain** *25 years*. Note that feminine numbers must be used where appropriate.

167   Un **in idiomatic expressions**

Un is used in various idiomatic expressions:

pob un	every (single) one
°**bob yn un**	one by one
fesul un	one by one
yr un (in NEG sentences)	not (a single) one (See §143)

Examples:

Dw i wedi treial pob un o'r rhain unwaith yn °barod

I've tried every one of these once already

Mi °ddaeth y disgyblion °bob yn un ar y llwyfan

The pupils came onto the stage one by one

°**Ddoth y plant i mewn fesul un**

The children came in one by one

°**Brynes i'r un llun**

I didn't buy a single picture

168   'Both'

y °ddau°/y °ddwy° are used in Welsh for *both*:

Mae'r °ddau isio dod ar yr un pryd

They both want to come at the same time

Ydi'r °ddwy ohonoch chi am °roi'ch enwau i lawr?

Do you both want to put your names down? [Do the both of you . . .]

°**Gymerwch chi'r °ddau?**

Will you have both?

Rhowch y °ddau °fag gyda'i gilydd yng ⁿnghefn y car

Put both bags together in the back of the car

169 **'You/we two, etc.'**

You two is chi'ch dau/dwy, and *we two* is ni'n dau/dwy. As usual, dwy is specifically for female persons while dau is ambiguous as to all-male or mixed company. Sometimes ill dau/dwy is encountered, meaning *they two*, and ill tri/tair *they three*:

Chi'ch dau, dewch fan hyn am eiliad!

You two, come over here a moment!

'Mond ni'n dau sy ar ôl

There's only us two left

Fe °gaethon nhw eu gwlychu ill dwy

The two of them [f] got soaked

170 **Ordinal numbers**

In practice, ordinals above *10th* are rarely needed (apart from dates – see §**177**). Note in the list below that *3rd* and *4th* have m and f forms (but not *2nd* – compare the cardinals).

1st	**cynta**
2nd	**ail°**
3rd	**trydydd/trydedd**
4th	**pedwerydd/pedwaredd**
5th	**pumed**
6th	**chweched**
7th	**seithfed**
8th	**wythfed**
9th	**nawfed**
10th	**degfed**

Notes:

(a) **Cynta** behaves like an ordinary adjective – it comes after the noun, and it undergoes SM when used after a feminine noun: **y mis cynta, yr wythnos °gynta**.

(b) All other ordinals come before the noun. **Ail°** mutates both m and f nouns: **yr ail °lyfr** (m) *the second book*, **yr ail °ddesg** (f) *the second desk*. From there on, ordinals with m nouns mutate neither themselves nor the following noun – **y Trydydd Byd** *the Third World*, **y pumed dosbarth** *the fifth class* while ordinals with f nouns mutate both themselves and the noun: **y °drydedd °goeden** *the third tree*, **y °bumed °orsaf** *the fifth station*.

(c) The usual, and simplest, method above *10th* is to use the cardinal after the noun, with or without **rhif** *number*: **y blwch (rhif) undeg tri** *the thirteenth box, box 13*. For *12th, 15th, 18th* and *20th*, a useful and neat alternative is provided by the non-composite vigesimals: **deuddegfed, pymthegfed, deunawfed** and **ugeinfed** (see §164): **y deuddegfed mis** *the twelfth month*, **yr ugeinfed °ganrif** *the twentieth century*.

(d) *100th* is **canfed**, and *1000th* is **milfed**.

171 Idioms using ordinal numbers

Note the idioms **gorau po °gynta** *the sooner the better*, and **yn °gyntaf oll** *first of all*. °Gynta is also used as a conjunction meaning *as soon as . . .*: °**Gynta daethon nhw . . .** *As soon as they came. . . .*

Ail is found in °**bob yn ail** *alternately, alternate*:

Na i °fwydo nhw °bob yn ail
I'll feed them alternately

°**Ddown ni °bob yn ail °benwythnos tan °ddiwedd yr Ha**
We'll come alternate weekends till the end of summer

172 'Last' – diwetha or ola?

These two words mean different things – **diwetha** means *most recent*, while **ola** means *last in a series*. So we say (**yr**) **wythnos diwetha** *last week*, but **wythnos ola'r gwyliau** *the last week of the holidays*. Further examples:

Dyna yn union be' wedodd hi tro diwetha
That's exactly what she said last time

Dyna'r tro ola i mi °geisio helpu fe
That's the last time I try and help him

Oedd ei llyfr diwetha'n °well o °lawer na'r un yma

Her last book was much better than this one

Mi °gafodd ei °lyfr ola ei °gyhoeddi °ddeufis yn unig cyn iddo °farw

His last book was published only two months before he died

173 Telling the time

The vigesimal system is routinely used for this. Note also that there is no equivalent in Welsh of the 24-hour clock, even for official use. *What time is it?* is **Faint o'r gloch ydy/yw hi?. . . .** Some speakers use the English phrasing **Beth ydy/yw'r amser?. . . .**

The hour in five-minute intervals is as follows:

3.00	**tri o'r °gloch**
3.05	**pum munud wedi tri**
3.10	**deng munud wedi tri**
3.15	**chwarter wedi tri**
3.20	**ugain munud wedi tri**
3.25	**pum munud ar hugain wedi tri**
3.30	**hanner awr wedi tri**
3.35	**pum munud ar hugain i °bedwar**
3.40	**ugain munud i °bedwar**
3.45	**chwarter i °bedwar**
3.50	**deny munud i °bedwar**
3.55	**pum munud i °bedwar**
4.00	**pedwar o'r °gloch**

Notes:

(a)   It is important to think of time in Welsh as a clock-face rather than numbers as above. We cannot say ***tri pumdeg pump** for *3.55*, as we can in English.

(b)   Although **awr** *hour* is feminine, the m numbers are used in telling the time, i.e. not ***tair o'r °gloch**.

(c)   Apart from the half- and quarter-hours, the word **munud** *minute* should strictly speaking be used, and not left out as is possible in English.

(d) While **chwarter wedi tri** exactly corresponds to English, *half past . . .* is always **hanner** *awr* **wedi . . .**

(e) There is SM after **i°**, but not after **wedi**.

(f) Accuracy to the minute simply involves using the appropriate number, vigesimal where appropriate, e.g. **saith munud ar hugain i naw** *8.33.*

(g) *11 o'clock* and *12 o'clock* use the vigesimal numbers: **unarddeg o'r °gloch, deuddeg o'r °gloch.**

Putting these principles into practice simply requires certain set phrases to begin the sentence. These are:

Mae (hi)'n° . . .	It's . . .
Mae hi newydd °droi . . .	It's just gone/turned . . .
Mae hi bron yn° . . .	It's almost . . .
Mae (hi)'n tynnu at° . . .	It's getting on for . . .

Examples:

Mae hi bron yn °ddeg o'r °gloch

It's almost ten o'clock

Mae'n °ddeng munud wedi wyth

It's ten past eight

Mae hi newydd °droi ugain munud wedi chwech

It's just gone twenty past six

Mae hi'n tynnu at °ddau (o'r °gloch)

It's getting on for two (o'clock)

174   a.m. and p.m.

Midnight and *midday* are **hanner nos** and **hanner dydd. Canol dydd** usually has a vaguer implication – *the middle of the day, around midday.* The abbreviations a.m. and p.m. are not used either in spoken or written Welsh – **(yn) y bore** *in the morning,* **(yn) y prynhawn/pnawn** *in the afternoon* and **(yn) y nos** *in the evening/night* are used as appropriate:

2.00 a.m.	**dau o'r °gloch (yn) y nos/bore**
8.00 a.m.	**wyth o'r °gloch (yn) y bore**
3.00 p.m.	**tri o'r °gloch (yn) y prynhawn**
9.00 p.m.	**naw o'r °gloch (yn) y nos**

The first two are sometimes abbreviated in writing: **yb, yp** – so, for example, 10.00 yb *10.00 a.m.*, 3.00 yp *3.00 p.m.*

175 Prepositions with time expressions

At what time? is **Am faint o'r gloch?**. *At* a time therefore is **am°**, while *at about* is **tua**. Also useful are **erbyn** *by*, **cyn** *before* and **ar ôl** *after*.

°Fydda i'n mynd i'r gwely °bob nos am °ddeg o'r °gloch

Every night I go to bed at ten o'clock

Dan ni'n bwriadu cyrraedd tua unarddeg o'r °gloch

We're aiming to arrive (at) about eleven o'clock

Gwnewch yn siŵr bod chi fan hyn erbyn hanner awr wedi saith

Make sure you're here by half past seven

Rhaid inni °fod yno cyn hanner nos

We've got to be there before midnight

Der i °ngweld i °rywbryd ar ôl pedwar

Come and see me some time after four

176 Years of age and number of years

The basic Welsh word for *year* is **blwyddyn** (f), pl. **blynyddoedd** or **blynyddau**, but the variant forms **blynedd** and **blwydd** are required in certain circumstances.

Nadolig Llawen a Blwyddyn Newydd °Dda i chi i gyd!

A Merry Christmas and a Happy New Year to you all!

°Dreulies i °flwyddyn a hanner yn crwydro Llydaw

I spent a year and a half roaming Brittany

Mae o wedi marw ers blynyddoedd

He died years ago

Un °flwyddyn yn unig ŷn ni wedi bod yma

We've only been here one year

Blynedd is the normal form for *year* after numbers (bearing in mind that the sing. is usual after numbers in Welsh – see §161), with **blwydd** used in the specialized sense of *years old*. Both these words are, like **blwyddyn**, feminine, so the appropriate numbers for *2, 3* and *4* are always used – **dwy°**, **tair** and **pedair** (see §162).

The low numerals cause mutations of **blynedd** (and of **blwydd** in exactly the same way) that, for *5* to *10,* do not hold true for non-time words:

dwy °flynedd	two years
tair blynedd	three years
pedair blynedd	four years
pum ⁿmlynedd	five years
chwe ⁿmlynedd	six years
saith ⁿmlynedd	seven years
wyth ⁿmlynedd	eight years
naw ⁿmlynedd	nine years
deng ⁿmlynedd	ten years

Notes:

(a) NM is present after 5–10 (with some variation – 6 and 8 are sometimes followed by the radical: **chwe blynedd, wyth blynedd**)

(b) **deg**, under the influence of the following nasal, becomes **deng**. This also happens, incidentally, with the non-mutated **munud** and **mis**

(c) **diwrnod** (m), the word used for *day* when counting, has NM in the same way after these numbers, e.g. **saith ⁿniwrnod**

Beyond 10, the traditional (vigesimal) numerals **deuddeg** *12,* **pymtheg** *15* **deunaw** *18,* **ugain** *20,* **hanner can** *50* and **can** *100* all cause NM of **blynedd/blwydd** and **diwrnod: deuddeng ⁿniwrnod, pymtheng ⁿmlynedd, ugain ⁿmlynedd, can ⁿmlwydd oed**, etc.

Blwydd usually appears with **oed**, but **oed** can optionally be used on its own, with the feminine of the number where appropriate:

Mae'r °ferch yn °dair (blwydd) oed

The girl is 3 years old

On its own, **blwydd** means *1 year old*:

Faint ydi ei oed rŵan?   **Blwydd a hanner**

How old is he now?   18 months

Hanner blwydd ydy o yfory

He's six months old tomorrow

At . . . years of age uses **yn°** when the subject of the main sentence is the same person:

Fe °adawodd °Gymru yn saith oed

He/she left Wales at the age of 7

Mi °gollodd ei ʰthad yn °flwydd a hanner oed

She lost her father at eighteen months old

177   Dates

Some of the months have Celtic names in Welsh, while others correspond to the more familiar international system:

Ionawr	January	**Gorffennaf**	July
Chwefror	February	**Awst**	August
Mawrth	March	**Medi**	September
Ebrill	April	**Hydref**	October
Mai	May	**Tachwedd**	November
Mehefin	June	**Rhagfyr**	December

In January is either **yn Ionawr**, or **ym mis Ionawr**. This second option avoids a NM with *July* and *November*: **ym mis Gorffennaf/yng ⁿGorffennaf, ym mis Tachwedd/yn ⁿNhachwedd**.

The preferred method of saying *the fifth November/November the fifth* is
with o° *of* – either **y pumed o °Dachwedd** or **y pumed o °fis Tachwedd**. The
vigesimal ordinals are needed for *eleventh* to *thirty-first*:

11th	**yr unfed ar °ddeg**	22nd	**yr ail ar hugain**
12th	**y deuddegfed**	23rd	**y trydydd ar hugain**
13th	**y trydydd ar °ddeg**	24th	**y pedwerydd ar hugain**
14th	**y pedwerydd ar °ddeg**	25th	**y pumed ar hugain**
15th	**y pymthegfed**	26th	**y chweched ar hugain**
16th	**yr unfed ar °bymtheg**	27th	**y seithfed ar hugain**
17th	**yr ail ar °bymtheg**	28th	**yr wythfed ar hugain**
18th	**y deunawfed**	29th	**y nawfed ar hugain**
19th	**y pedwerydd ar °bymtheg**	30th	**y degfed ar hugain**
20th	**yr ugeinfed**	31st	**yr unfed ar °ddeg ar hugain**
21st	**yr unfed ar hugain**		

Written abbreviations of these use **-eg**, **-fed** or **-ain** accordingly: **yr 11eg** *the
11th*, **y 15fed** *the 15th*, **yr 17eg** *the 17th*, **y 30ain** *the 30th*, **yr 31ain** *the
31st*. The simplified formula **30 Gorffennaf 1992** is usual in letters.

178 Years

Years are given in a different way from English. Instead of breaking a four-
digit year into two two-digit numbers (1789 – seventeen eighty-nine), Welsh
starts with **mil** (*thousand*) and then three single digits: **mil saith wyth naw**.
This means that *in . . .* any year between 1000 and 1999 will be **ym: ym
1907** (**mil naw dim saith**). Alternatively, some speakers simply use **un**
instead of **mil**, making a sequence of four one-digit numbers: **un naw dim
saith**. For the twenty-first century, *2000* is **dwy °fil**, *2001* **dwy °fil ag un**,
2009 **dwy °fil a naw**, etc. Years before 1000 are generally expressed as a
whole number, with **y flwyddyn** optionally preceding: **yn (y °flwyddyn)
chwe ʰchant trideg dau** *in 632*. B.C. is **C.C.** (**Cyn Crist**), and A.D. is **O.C.**
(**Oed Crist**).

Most of these bear more resemblance to French than English. The **Dydd** component is commonly pronounced **Dy'** in normal speech: **Dy' Llun, Dy' Mawrth**. The capital letter is obligatory with **Llun** etc., but not with **Dydd**.

Dydd Llun	Monday
Dydd Mawrth	Tuesday
Dydd Mercher	Wednesday
Dydd Iau	Thursday
Dydd Gwener	Friday
Dydd Sadwrn	Saturday
Dydd Sul	Sunday

To say 'on' a particular day simply use SM (see §403): °**Ddydd Llun** *on Monday*. **Ar°** (*on*) is not used in this instance, mainly because **ar °ddydd Llun** these days tends to mean *on Mondays* (i.e. *every Monday* – *on a Monday*, as some people say in English):

Mae 'na °gyfarfod pwyllgor °ddydd Mercher, on'd oes?

There's a committee meeting on Wednesday, isn't there?

Mae 'na °gyfarfod pwyllgor ar °ddydd Mercher

On Wednesdays there's a committee meeting

Replacing **Dydd** by **Nos°** gives . . . *day evening/night*:

°**Wela i chdi Nos °Fawrth, 'ta** (N)

I'll see you on Tuesday night, then

°**Fydd Nos Sadwrn am naw yn °gyfleus i ti, 'te?**

Saturday night at nine will be alright with you, then?

. . . *day morning* and . . . *day afternoon* usually include the **dydd**, as in English: **bore dydd Iau** *Thursday morning*, **pnawn dydd Gwener** *Friday afternoon*, but it is not obligatory in speech: **bore Iau, pnawn Gwener**.

180 Seasonal and religious festivals

Dydd Calan	New Year's Day
Gŵyl Santes Dwynwen	Welsh equivalent of St Valentine's Day (25th January)
Gŵyl °Ddewi	St David's Day (1st March)
Dydd Gwener y °Groglith	Good Friday
Pasg (m)	Easter
Sul y Pasg	Easter Sunday
Llun y Pasg	Easter Monday
Calan Mai	May Day
Y Sulgwyn	Whitsun
Y Dydd Hwyaf	Longest Day
Nos °Galan Gaeaf	Hallowe'en
Dydd Llywelyn yr Ail	Llywelyn II Day (11th December)
Y Dydd Byrraf	Shortest Day
Noswyl Nadolig	Christmas Eve
Nadolig (m)	Christmas
Dydd Nadolig	Christmas Day
Gŵyl San Steffan	Boxing Day
Nos °Galan	New Year's Eve

Seasons are: **Gwanwyn** *spring*, **Haf** *summer*, **Hydref** *autumn* and **Gaeaf** *winter*. The final -f of the last three words is often unpronounced, see §2(c).

181 Money

To begin with, note that **pwys** (m) means *pound (weight)*, while **punt** (f) means *pound (sterling)*. The plural of **punt** is either **punnoedd** or **punnau** depending on the area.

For *£1–£10* the sing. is used – note the feminine forms: **un °bunt** *£1*, **dwy °bunt** *£2*, **tair punt** *£3*, **pedair punt** *£4*. AM occurs with **chwe ʰphunt** *£6*. When listening to others, be aware that **°dair punt** (*£3*) can sound to the unwary like the incorrect but plausible **dau °bunt* (?*£2*):

°Wertha i hwnna i chi am °dair punt
I'll sell that to you for three pounds

Amounts over £10 can be expressed using the decimal system with o° + pl.
– undeg un o °bunnoedd *£11*, dauddeg tair o bunnoedd *£23* – but between
11 and 30 the vigesimal system + sing. is very common as well: un °bunt ar
ddeg, tair punt ar hugain. Above 30, the only vigesimal numbers you are
likely to need to recognize are deugain punt *£40*, hanner can punt *£50* and
possibly trigain punt *£60*. *£100* is either can punt or cant o °bunnoedd.
Then: mil o °bunnoedd *£1000*, deng mil o °bunnoedd *£10,000*, can mil o
°bunnoedd *£100,000*, miliwn o °bunnoedd *£1 million*, deng miliwn o
°bunnoedd *£10 million*.

Multiplicative
numbers

Ceiniog *penny* is feminine also. The pl. ceiniogau is not often used in giving
prices: pedair punt wythdeg tair ceiniog = *£4.83*; but pedair punt ag wythdeg
tair o °geiniogau would be possible too.

The following formulas are used in writing cheques:

Chwe^h phunt ar hugain 50c	Twenty-six pounds 50p
Hanner can punt yn unig	Fifty pounds only
Arian parod	Cash

The Welsh term for *PIN number* uses the English abbreviation: rhif PIN:

Cofiwch °guddio'ch rhif PIN wrth °ddefnyddio'r peiriant arian parod

Remember to conceal your PIN number when using the cashpoint

182   Fractions

The most common are hanner (pl. haneri or hanerau) *a half*, traean *a third*
and chwarter *a quarter*, all masculine. Other fractions are the same as the
corresponding ordinals (decimal system), e.g. un pumed *one fifth*, tri degfed
three tenths.

183   Multiplicative numbers

These are formed with gwaith (f) *time* (for other words meaning *time* see
§406): unwaith *once*, dwywaith *twice*, tairgwaith *three times*, pedairgwaith
four times, etc. Note also llawer gwaith *many times*, ambell °waith *occasionally*, sawl gwaith? (also written sawlgwaith) *how many times?* and
weithiau *sometimes*. SM is common in words ending in -waith because of
their adverbial meaning.

'Sdim angen i ti °ddeud °ddwywaith, 'sti

You don't need to say it twice, you know

°Dairgwaith yr wythnos y byddwn ni'n gwneud y gwaith siopa yn y °dre

We do the shopping in town three times a week

Dw i °ddim yn siwr weithiau ydi o o °ddifri

Sometimes I'm not sure whether he's serious

Bydd angen pumgwaith °gymaint â hynny cyn bod ni'n gallu dechrau hyd yn oed

We'll need five times as much as that before we can even start

Some phrases and idioms involve multiplicatives:

ar unwaith	at once
am unwaith	for once
unwaith neu °ddwy	once or twice
does dim dwywaith amdani	there's no two ways about it

Dewch yn ôl fan hyn ar unwaith!

Come back here at once!

Am unwaith, °allech chi °beidio â torri ar ⁿnhraws i?

For once, could you not interrupt me?

Once more is unwaith yn rhagor:

Nei di °ddarllen y °gerdd unwaith yn rhagor inni?

Will you read the poem once more for us?

Once… as a conjunction (see also §503), i.e. in the sense of 'after', is usually unwaith bod…:

Unwaith bod rhestr °derfynol 'da ni byddwn ni'n ymateb yn llawn

Once we have a final list we will give a full response

Twice as . . . as . . . etc. simply uses the equative form of the adjective (see §105) after -(g)waith:

Mae'r lle 'ma °dairgwaith cymaint ag o'n i'n °ddisgwyl

This place is three times as big as I expected

Ma' fe °ddwywaith cystal â neb arall yn y stafell

He's twice as good as anyone else in the room

184 Sequential numbers

These use the ordinals (see §170) and a different word for *time*: **tro** .

y tro cynta	the first time
yr ail °dro	the second time
y trydydd tro	the third time

For the . . . time uses am:

Am y tro cynta erioed, mae Norwy wedi ennill cystadleuaeth °ganeuon

For the first time ever, Norway has won a song contest

Am yr ail °dro mewn pedair awr ar hugain, mae daeargryn wedi digwydd yn ⁿNe Califfornia

For the second time in twenty-four hours, an earthquake has occurred in Southern California

Note the use of **dyma/dyna** and i to express *the . . . time that . . .*:

Dyma'r tro cynta i mi ymweld â ⁿmherthnasau yn yr Unol °Daleithiau

This is the first time that I've visited my relatives in the US

Dyna'r ail °dro iddo °dorri addewid

That is the second time he's broken a promise

Dyna oedd y tro ola iddo °roi ei °droed yng ⁿNghymru

That was the last time he set foot in Wales

185 Expressions of quantity

Nearly all quantity expressions are followed by **o°** + noun in Welsh, while this is only partially true of *of* in English (*a lot of potatoes* but *enough potatoes*). The sing./pl. distinction of *much* and *many* in English is not made in Welsh.

faint?	how much/many?		
sawl?	how much/many?		
sawl un?	how many?		
chwanag (N)	more	**rhagor**	more
digon	enough	**tamaid**	a bit
gormod	too much/many	**tipyn**	a bit
llawer	much/many; a lot	**ychydig**	a little; a few
peth	some, a bit		

186   Faint?

Faint? is the general-purpose term for both *how much?* (before sing. nouns) and *how many?* (before pl. nouns). It needs o° in either case.

Faint o °bobl sydd yn dal i aros fan hyn i °weld y meddyg?

How many people are still waiting here to see the doctor?

Faint o °fara sy angen dros y Sul?

How much bread do we need over the weekend?

It can also stand on its own with a specified noun, especially when asking the price of something:

Faint yw'r moron 'na?

How much are those carrots?

Faint mae Sulwyn eisiau archebu?

How much/many does Sulwyn want to order?

Rules for the use of **ydy/yw, mae** or **sy** after question words of this type are given in §140.

Sometimes **faint** is used to mean *however much*:

Cymerwch faint °fynnoch chi

Take however much you want

187   Sawl?

Sawl? means *how many?*, but is used with a singular noun and no o°. Where a noun is not specified, **sawl un?** is more usual:

Sawl gwaith °welsoch chi fe llynedd?

How many times did you see him last year?

Sawl llythyren sy yn yr wyddor °Gymraeg?

How many letters are there in the Welsh alphabet?

Sawl un sy 'da chi erbyn hyn?

How many have you got now?

Sawl also means *several*:

Mae sawl anifail 'da nhw

They've got several animals

For **y sawl**, see §145.

188   Chwanag

Chwanag (< ychwaneg) is used mostly in the N as an alternative to **rhagor** *more* (see §194):

°Gymeri di chwanag o °de?

Will you have some more tea?

189   Digon

Digon *enough* is used much as in English, but requires o° if a noun follows:

'S gynnoch chi °ddigon o °fwyd yn y tŷ? (N)

Have you got enough food in the house?

Mae hynny'n °ddigon am heddiw

That's enough for today

Digon is also used before adjectives/adverbs to mean . . . *enough*, or *quite/ fairly* . . .

Wyt ti'n mynd i'r gêm nos yfory?   **Digon tebyg**

Are you going to the game tomorrow night?   Quite likely

Dan ni'n °ddigon hapus lle ydan ni (N)

We're happy enough where we are

Note the idiom **hen °ddigon** for *quite enough, more than enough*:

Mae hen °ddigon o °waith 'da fi yn °barod, diolch (S)

I've got quite enough work already, thanks

190   Gormod

Gormod means *too much* or *too many* depending on whether a sing. or pl. noun follows. It requires **o°** in either case, but can stand on its own if need be:

Mae gormod o °fraster yn °beryg i'r iechyd

Too much fat is bad for your health

Dw i wedi cadw'n °dawel hyd yma, ond mae hyn yn °ormod

I've kept quiet so far, but this is too much

Mae gormod o °gwyno wedi bod yn °ddiweddar

There has been too much complaining lately

It can be used on its own adverbially:

Mae'n °fachgen digon dymunol, ond mae'n siarad gormod weithiau

He's a nice enough boy, but sometimes he talks too much

Dan ni °ddim wedi ffraeo gormod

We haven't argued too much

Far too much/many is gormod o °lawer, or llawer gormod.

Mae'n yfed gormod o °lawer

He drinks far too much

Mae trideg chwech ohonyn nhw i gyd yn y stafell 'ma, sy'n llawer gormod

There are thirty-six of them altogether in this room, which is far too many

Llawer means *a lot/much* or *many*, and requires o° with a following noun:

Mae llawer o °bobol yn dal heb °gofrestru

Many people still haven't registered

Bydd llawer o sŵn yn y °dre heno

There'll be a lot of noise in town tonight

Bu llawer o ymweliadau â'r °wefan newydd 'ma

There have been a lot of hits on this new website

Llawer iawn is *very much/many*:

Mae 'na °lawer iawn o °eiriau fan hyn sy'n anghyfarwydd

There are very many unfamiliar words here

In negative expressions, . . . °ddim . . . rhyw °lawer means . . . *not all that much* . . .:

Nes i °ddim dysgu rhyw °lawer yn y dosbarthiadau nos

I didn't learn all that much at evening classes

Much more . . . much . . . er is either done with llawer before the comparative adjective or adverb, or o °lawer after:

Dyn ni wedi gwerthu llawer mwy ers dechrau'r Ha

Dyn ni wedi gwerthu mwy o °lawer ers dechrau'r Ha

We've sold much more since the beginning of summer

Mae'n llawer hawddach ffordd hyn

Mae'n hawddach o °lawer ffordd hyn

It's much easier this way

Mae ei °Gymraeg e'n llawer gwell na'i Saesneg

Mae ei °Gymraeg e'n °well o °lawer na'i Saesneg

His Welsh is much better than his English

Mae hyn yn llawer pwysicach

Mae hyn yn °bwysicach o °lawer

This is much more important

Similarly, *Much too . . ., far too . . .* is either llawer rhy° . . . or rhy° . . . o °lawer:

Chi'n llawer rhy °bigog

Chi'n rhy °bigog o °lawer

You're far too touchy

192 Mwy

Mwy *more* is another alternative to **rhagor** (see §194):

Mae mwy o newyddion yma ar S4C am hanner awr wedi wyth

There's more news here on S4C at half past eight

Mae angen mwy o hygyrchedd

More accessibility is needed

193 Peth

Peth (*thing*) is used colloquially with sing. nouns to mean *some . . .*, *a bit* (*of*) *. . .*, *a certain amount of . . .* It is unusual in not having **o°** between it and a following noun.

Mae peth caws ar ôl yn yr oergell, dw i'n meddwl

There's a bit of cheese left in the fridge, I think

Aros eiliad, mae peth arian 'da fi fan hyn yn y °boced arall

Wait a minute, I've got a bit of money here in the other pocket

°Debyg iawn °fod peth biwrocratiaeth yn anochel yn hyn o °beth

A certain amount of bureaucracy is probably unavoidable in this

(note also in this example another idiom with **peth: yn hyn o °beth** *in this thing/matter*)

Ydy'r llaeth i gyd wedi mynd?   **Mae peth ar y bwrdd**

Has all the milk gone?   There's some on the table

194 Rhagor

Rhagor means *more* in the sense of *in addition*. It corresponds to French *encore* and German *noch*, and colloquial N Welsh **chwanag** (see §188). While the general word **mwy** more often replaces it in this sense (see §192), the reverse is not true. We can say either **rhagor o °de** or **mwy o °de** *more tea*, but *more exciting* is **mwy cyffrous** only, and not *rhagor cyffrous.

°Gymeri di °ragor o °gacen?

Will you have some more cake?

Mae rhagor o ymosodiadau'n rhwym o °ddigwydd cyn hir

More attacks are bound to happen before long

°Allwch chi °ddim gofyn rhagor o °gwestiynau

You can't ask any more questions

Note the related VN **rhagori (ar°)** *be better than*:

Does dim caws ym ⁿMhrydain yn rhagori ar °gaws Caerffili

No cheese in Britain is better than Caerphilly cheese

195 Tipyn **and** tamaid

Tipyn and **tamaid** are virtually synonymous for *a* (*little*) *bit*, and use **o°** with a following singular noun:

°Gaethon ni °dipyn o °drafferth ar y ffordd i fan'ma

We had a bit of trouble on the way here

°Gymeri di °gacen?	**Tamaid bach yn unig, diolch**
Will you have some cake?	Just a little bit, thanks

Where these two words diverge is that **tamaid** tends to have a literal or concrete meaning of *a piece*, while **tipyn** can also be used in a wider sense, for example with comparative adjectives – **tipyn** is *a little lower* – adverbially: **mae'n oeri °dipyn** *it's getting a little bit colder*, **fesul tipyn** *bit by bit*. It also appears in the set phrases **tipyn go lew** and **cryn °dipyn** *quite a bit* again used with sing. nouns:

Maen nhw wedi casglu tipyn go lew o °goed tân

They've collected a fair bit of firewood

Bydd hyn yn golygu y bydd pethau, fel arfer, yn cael eu newid fesul tipyn

This will mean that, as usual, things will be changed bit by bit

196   Ychydig

Ychydig (chydig) is similar to **tipyn/tamaid** (see §195), but can be used with pl. as well as sing. nouns, and therefore means either *a (little) bit* or *a few*. It requires **o°** before the noun in either case.

Basa ychydig o hunanhyder yn gwneud byd o °wahaniaeth iddi

A bit of self-confidence would make a world of difference to her

Naethon ni aros am ychydig ar ôl i'r cyngerdd °ddod i °ben

We stayed (around) for a bit after the concert had finished

Mae ychydig o °bethau ar ôl fyny'r grisiau

There are a few things left upstairs

Few (i.e. *not many*) is usually distinguished from *a few* by adding **iawn** after ychydig, or **go** before it; or, as in English, **'mond** or **yn unig** *only* can be used:

Ychydig iawn o ffoaduriaid sy'n cael croesi'r ffin ar hyn o °bryd

Few refugees are being allowed to cross the border at the moment

Faint sy ar ôl 'da chi?   **Go 'chydig**

How many have you got left?   Not (that) many

197   Cymaint **and** cynlleied

The equative adjectives **cymaint** and **cynlleied** (see §106) can also be used as quantity expressions – *so much/many, so little/few*:

Mae cymaint o °lanast fan hyn, dwn i °ddim lle i °ddechrau

There's so much mess here, I don't know where to start

Mae 'na °gymaint o °gwestiynau yn dal heb eu hateb

There are so many questions still unanswered

Mae cynlleied o amser ar ôl

There is so little time remaining

Mae cynlleied o ffenestri yn y lle 'ma!

There are so few windows in this place!

Verbs

198 Verbal noun (VN)

The verbal noun (VN) is the basic dictionary form of the verb. Grammatically it is in every respect a noun (masculine – there is, however, one feminine: **gafael**), and can function as one – for this reason it is possible to use the VN with the definite article, as well as with descriptive or possessive adjectives:

canu da	good singing
y canu gorau	the best singing
ymladd dibaid	ceaseless fighting
ysgrifennu gofalus	careful writing
safon ei ysgrifennu	the standard of his writing

Mae'*ch gyrru* wedi gwella'n °ddiweddar, on'd ydy?

Your *driving*'s improved lately, hasn't it?

Waeth i ti anghofio'r *holl siarad 'ma* am °*gyfaddawdu*

You might as well forget *all this talk* about *compromise*

Generally when the VN functions as a noun it corresponds to the *-ing* form of the verb in English, although, as the last example above demonstrates, sometimes the plain English verb without *-ing* can be more appropriate. This is usually a matter of deciding the better style in English for translation purposes – the VN is the same either way in Welsh.

When used as a noun, the VN can naturally occupy the same place in a sentence as an ordinary noun:

Dyw'r *rhaglen* °ddim wedi dechrau 'to   [noun]

The programme hasn't started yet

Dyw'r *dadlwytho* °ddim wedi dechrau 'to   [VN]

The unloading hasn't started yet

And, just as a noun can be used as an adjective, so can a VN:

Dogfen °*ddwyieithog* yw hon   [adjective]

This is a bilingual document

Dogfen *ymgynghori* yw hon   [VN]

This is a consultation document

199   Use of prepositions with the verbal noun

Like nouns, the VN can be used with prepositions, but with certain ones only, and in some cases with meanings particular to this VN use. These prepositions are:

am° ar° dan° gan° heb° trwy°/drwy° wrth°

and an example of each as used with the VN is given below. Fuller treatment will be found under the sections dealing with these prepositions individually.

Pwy sy *am* °ddŵad hefo ni i'r ffair heno?

Who *wants* to come to the fair with us tonight?

Brysiwch, mae'r trên *ar* °fynd!

Hurry up, the train's *about* to leave!

Eson nhw o amgylch y pentre *dan* °ganu

They went round the village sing*ing*

Aeth o °gwmpas y stafell *gan* °ofyn yr un cwestiwn i °bawb

She went round the room ask*ing* everyone the same question

Paid gadael *heb* ffarwelio â'r lleill

Don't leave *without* saying goodbye to the others

°Ddaethon nhw i mewn i'r tŷ *drwy* °dorri un o ffenestri'r °gegin

They got into the house *by* breaking one of the kitchen windows

°Dorres i ⁿnghoes *wrth* chwarae pêldroed wythnos .diwetha

I broke my leg play*ing* football last week

All the above reflect general use except **dan°**, which is in practice restricted to certain phrases.

200 Form of the verbal noun

The VN can either be a basic form of the verb (i.e. a word not obviously derived from another one), or it can be a form derived from another part of speech, usually a noun or adjective. In the latter case, it is usually formed by adding an ending to the original word. Another way of looking at this is to say that non-derived VNs have no endings, while derived VNs do.

Examples of non-derived VNs: **dal** *catch*, **siarad** *speak*, **gwrthod** *refuse*, **darllen** *read*, **cadw** *keep*

Examples of derived VNs **talu** *pay* (from noun **tâl** *pay*), **pleidleisio** *vote* (from noun **pleidlais** *vote*), **ffeindio** *find* (from English *find*), **rhewi** *freeze* (from noun **rhew** *frost*), **rhyddhau** *free, liberate* (from adjective **rhydd** *free*).

Quite often, as can be seen from some of the examples above, English makes no distinction between, say, a noun and a verb derived from it (*pay, vote*), but the distinction is made in Welsh. This can pose problems in finding the right option in a dictionary, since the English word may be the same in both cases. Good dictionaries will indicate whether the Welsh word is a noun (**e.** for **enw** noun) or a VN (**be.** for **berfenw**). It is a good rule of thumb that entries ending in -u, -o, -io, -i, -a and -au are almost certainly VNs.

201 Determination of final vowel in verbal nouns

As regards vowel-endings used to make VNs, some general rules do apply. In many cases the preceding vowel is the determining factor:

  -u is used where the preceding vowel is **-a-, -ae-, -e-** or **-y-: crafu** *scratch*, **saethu** *shoot*, **denu** *attract*, **llyfu** *lick*

  -o is used where the preceding vowel is **-i-, -u-, -eu-** or **-wy-: rhifo** *count*, **rhuthro** *rush*, **goleuo** *light*, **twyllo** *cheat*

  -i is used where the preceding vowel is **-o-** or **-oe-: torri** *cut*, break **cyhoeddi** *publish*. Also with a preceding consonantal **-w: berwi** *boil*

It should be borne in mind that the rules given above are general only, and exceptions will be encountered. It is best simply to learn these rather than try to fit them into a system. Examples of exceptions: **gwrando** *hear*, **mynegi** *express*.

202 -io **ending in verbal nouns**

The preceding vowel is irrelevant with **-io**, a very common VN ending used particularly to make VNs from nouns – indeed, the original vowel may often change:

> **teithio** *travel* (from **taith** *journey*)
>
> **llywio** *steer* (from **llyw** *helm*)

-io is also very productive in forming VNs from English loan-words:

> **parcio, mapio, stopio**

Many S dialects use **-o** widely for **-io**, especially with loan-words: **parco**, etc. The reverse, however, is not normally the case, i.e. VNs ending in **-o** do not become **-io** in the N: there is no N counterpart *twyllio for **twyllo**. Dictionaries always make the distinction between true **-o** VNs and **-io** types.

Whether non-derived or derived, the VN is always the form listed in the dictionary, and as VNs they all behave in the same way.

203 **Miscellaneous VN endings**

Other than the endings detailed in §§200–202 above, there are others that are found much less frequently, though among commonly used verbs.

-ed:	**cerdded** *walk*; **ystyried** *consider*; **dynwared** *imitate*; **clywed** *hear*; **ymddiried** *trust*; **yfed** *drink*; and the obsolete **gweled** (see – now **gweld**) and **myned** (*go* – now **mynd**)
-eg:	**rhedeg** *run*
-yd:	**cymryd** *take* (but stem **cymer-**); **dychwelyd** *return*; **ymyrryd** *interfere*
-an:	**boddran** *bother*; **loetran** *loiter*
-ian:	**hongian** *hang* (picture, etc.); **cloncian** *chatter, gossip*

The last two, **-an** and **-ian** are more widespread in some dialects than in the standard language, and are common in (early) loan-words from English.

Since it is not really a verb, the VN cannot on its own do the job of a verb in a sentence. If it is to be used verbally it needs to have a true verb to hang on to – and in the vast majority of cases this will be either **bod** *be*, or an auxiliary verb such as **gwneud** *do*. The principles of verbal auxiliaries are dealt with in §215, but here are some typical sentences involving auxiliary + VN:

Mae [aux] **Elwyn yn canu** [VN] **heno**

Elwyn's singing tonight

Naeth [aux] **y llestri syrthio** [VN] **oddiar y bwrdd**

The dishes fell off the table

°Fedrwch [aux] **chi °alw** [VN] **heibio yfory?**

Can you call round tomorrow?

When the auxiliary is **bod**, a linking element (usually **yn**) is required between this and the VN, as in the first example above.

When used as a true noun, it behaves essentially as any other noun. It can be used:

with adjectives:	**gyrru peryglus**	dangerous driving
	yfed cymedrol	moderate drinking
with possessive	**ei nofio**	his/her swimming
adjectives:	**dy °ddarllen**	your reading
with prepositions:	**wrth °fynd**	while going
	heb edrych	without looking
as an adjective itself:	**dillad garddio**	gardening clothes
	sbectol darllen	reading glasses

As a noun, the VN is very often translated as *-ing*. But sometimes the best English translation is a related noun:

Mae'n amlwg °fod *gweithredu* uniongyrchol weithiau yn angenrheidiol

It's clear that direct *action* is sometimes necessary [**gweithredu** – *act*]

Byddwch yn °barod â'ch papurau cofestru os gwelwch yn °dda

Please have your registration papers ready [**cofrestru** – *register*]

205 Verb-stem formation

The verb-stem is formed from the VN, and is used where inflected forms of the verb are required, i.e. when endings have to be added to the verb. Sometimes the stem is the same as the VN, but often it involves some kind of change. Many of these changes are predictable, but some are not and simply have to be learnt. For predictable formations, we start with the VN. The preterite and imperative endings (§§293, 377) are used in the examples of usage in this section.

206 Stems of VNs ending in a vowel

VNs ending in a vowel generally drop this vowel to make the verb-stem:

talu *pay* – stem: **tal-**   **torri** *cut* – stem: **torr-**

anafu *injure* – stem: **anaf-**   **rhuthro** *rush* – stem: **rhuthr-**

VNs ending in -io (a very common type) conform to the above rule in dropping the final vowel, i.e. their stems end in -i-:

teithio *travel* – stem: **teithi-**   **stopio** *stop* – stem: **stopi-**

°**Deithies i ar hyd a lled Cymru**
I travelled the length and breadth of Wales

Stopiwch nhw rhag dod i mewn!
Stop them from coming in!

207 Stems of VNs ending in -au

VNs ending in -au change this to -eu for the verb-stem:

dechrau *begin* – stem: **dechreu-**   **maddau** *forgive* – stem: **maddeu-**

Dechreuwch y gwaith yfory
Begin the work tomorrow

Maddeuwch i mi am anghofio'ch penblwydd eto
Forgive me for forgetting your birthday again

An apparent exception to this is **cau** *close*, whose stem is **cae-**:

Caewch y giât!   Close the gate!

Stems of VNs ending in a consonant

Many of these require no change – the verb-stem is the same as the VN:

atal *prevent* – stem: **atal-**   gwrthod *refuse* – stem: **gwrthod-**

eistedd *sit* – stem: **eistedd-**   danfon *send* – stem: **danfon-**

cadw *keep* – stem: **cadw-**   galw *call* – stem: **galw-**

These are the endingless VNs mentioned in §200. Note that **cadw** and **galw** belong here, since the -w ending is a consonant (see §1(c)).

Some endingless VNs, especially if they contain an -n- or an -r-, add an -h, or replace -nn- and -rr- by -nh- and -rh- respectively. This is by no means a hard-and-fast rule, however, and it is probably simpler just to learn these as they come up:

cyrraedd *arrive* – stem: **cyrhaedd-**   **cynnwys** *include* – stem: **cynhwys -**

aros *wait* – stem: **arhos -**

°Gyrhaeddoch chi mewn da °bryd?

Did you arrive in good time?

Cynhwyswch °bopeth sydd angen

Include everything necessary

Arhoswch fan'na eiliad!

Wait there a moment!

VNs ending in -ed drop this to form the stem. For all practical purposes this involves **clywed** *hear*, **yfed** *drink*, **cerdded** *walk* and **ystyried** *consider*. **Gweld** *see*, formerly **gweled**, also comes under this rule.

Common verbs with unpredictable stems

A complete list would be impractical, but the following constitute the most commonly encountered unpredictable verb-stems:

addo *promise* (**addaw-**)	**gadael** *let, leave* (**gadaw-**)
amau *doubt* (**amheu-**)	**gollwng** *drop* (**gollyng-**)
annog *urge, encourage* (**anog-**)	**gorchymyn** *order* (**gorchmyn-**)
cymryd *take* (**cymer-**)	**gwrando** *listen* (**gwrandaw-**)
cynnal *hold* (*meeting*) (**cynhali-**)	**meddwl** *think* (**meddyli-**)
cynnig *offer* (**cynigi-**)	**rhedeg** *run* (**rhed-**)
derbyn *receive, accept* (**derbyni-**)	**rhoi** or **rhoid** *give, put*
	(**rho- rhoi-** or **rhodd-**)
dianc *escape* (**dihang-**)	**troi** *turn* (**tro-** or **trodd-**)
ennill *win* (**enill-**)	

210–217 THE TENSE SYSTEM OF THE WELSH VERB

General principles

As has been outlined above (§198), the basic form of the verb in Welsh is the VN, which is technically not a verb at all. To make it act as a verb, there are two main options in Welsh: the periphrastic method, and the inflected method. These may be defined as follows:

The periphrastic method involves using another (auxiliary) verb (usually, though not necessarily, **bod** *be*) in conjunction with the VN to form a compound tense. In this way, the VN carries the meaning of the action described, while the auxiliary verb does the work of specifying time, person etc.

The inflection method involves converting the VN to a verb stem (§§205–209) and then adding endings. In this way, the verb stem carries the meaning of the action, and the endings attached to it carry the information on time, person etc.

The structural difference between the two systems can be illustrated by a simple comparison of present and preterite sentences:

[Periphrastic]:

present   **Mae'r hen °ddyn yn *llosgi* sbwriel yn yr °ardd**

              The old man is *burning* rubbish in the garden

[Inflected]:

preterite   **Llosgodd yr hen °ddyn y sbwriel yn yr °ardd**

              The old man *burnt* the rubbish in the garden

These two examples show a parallel situation in English, which also uses auxiliary (in this instance *is*) and VN (*burning*) to express an action taking place at the time of speaking, while using the main verb on its own with endings to express an event that has already happened. On the other hand, the English system is more complex in this regard than the Welsh, and such exact parallels are not necessarily the rule.

211   Comparison of Welsh and English tense systems

Broadly speaking, Welsh has a verbal tense system very similar to that of English. Not only does it have more or less the same complement of tenses, but also their meanings and usage coincide to a very great extent. There are exceptions, and these will be noted where appropriate.

Though it is misleading and sometimes counterproductive to explain the workings of a system in one language by referring to its counterpart in another, a broad overview of the tense systems in Welsh and English is useful. Here, the permutations of the verb **prynu** *buy* in the 3rd pers. sing. AFF only, with rough English equivalents, show not only the essential similarity of the systems in Welsh and English, but also the main points of divergence. The tenses are given their traditional names, as throughout this grammar, for the sake of convenience:

present	**mae hi'n prynu**	she buys/she is buying
imperfect	**oedd hi'n prynu**	she was buying
perfect	**mae hi wedi prynu**	she has bought
pluperfect	**oedd hi wedi prynu**	she had bought
preterite/past	(I) **°brynodd hi**	she bought/she did buy
	(II) **naeth hi °brynu**	
	(III) **ddaru hi °brynu**	

future	(I) °**brynith hi**	she will buy
	(II) **bydd hi'n prynu**	
	(III) **neith hi °brynu**	
future perfect	**bydd hi wedi prynu**	she will have bought
conditional	**basai hi'n prynu**	she would buy
	byddai hi'n prynu	
	prynai hi	
conditional perfect	**basai hi wedi prynu**	she would have bought
	byddai hi wedi prynu	

The above is a simplified overall view of the Welsh tense system, and does not take into account predictable dialect variants. These, along with other points of detail, will be dealt with under the fuller tense-by-tense treatment below. Three very general points, however, are worth noting straight away from the above comparison:

(a) that one single present tense in Welsh corresponds to two possible alternatives in English (see §**264**)

(b) that there are three (more or less interchangeable) ways of expressing the preterite (simple past) tense in Welsh (see §**292**)

(c) that the inflected formation (see §**290**) is represented in the above overview by only three tenses: one of the preterite variants – °**brynodd e**; one of the future variants – °**brynith e**; and one of the conditional variants – **prynai fe**. All other tenses are periphrastic in that they use the VN **prynu** in conjunction with an auxiliary verb, either some part of **bod** *be* (here **mae, oedd, bydd** or **basai**), or with **naeth** or **ddaru** (both preterites), or **neith** (a future). The parts of **bod** *be* need also **yn** or **wedi**, but **naeth, ddaru** and **neith** need nothing else.

212   3rd pers. pl. forms of verbs

It is a fundamental rule with verbs in Welsh that 3rd pers. pl. forms are only used where the corresponding pronoun **nhw** *they* is explicitly stated. In all other cases where the subject is 3rd pers. pl., the 3rd pers. sing. form must be used. Compare:

*Maen nhw***'n siarad Cymraeg** [pl. verb]

They speak Welsh

but: *Mae* **Elin a Meinir yn siarad Cymraeg** [sing. verb]

Elin and Meinir speak Welsh

°*Gân nhw* ailwneud y gwaith 'ma yfory [pl. verb]

They can redo this work tomorrow

but: **°*Geith* y myfyrwyr ailwneud y gwaith 'ma yfory** [sing. verb]

The students can redo this work tomorrow

This rule holds for identification sentences (see §§220, 223) as well:

Prif °ddiddordeb Julie *yw* paentio

Julie's main interest *is* painting

Prif °ddiddordebau Kat *yw* yfed coffi a darllen Baudelaire

Kat's main interests *are* drinking coffee and reading Baudelaire

213   Affirmative markers mi°, fe°

A characteristic of spoken Welsh is the affirmative marker **mi°** or **fe°** which can be placed before AFF verbs with endings (including future, preterite and conditional of **bod**) to indicate that a statement is being made (rather than a question or negative). Both particles cause SM, and are optional:

(Fe) °glywes i'r newyddion ar y radio bore 'ma

I heard the news on the radio this morning

(Mi) agora i'r drws i ti

I'll open the door for you

(Fe) °fyddwn ni gartre erbyn naw

We'll be home by nine

These particles (which, by the way, are not 'meaningless' as some authorities claim) are used irrespective of whether it is *he*, *I*, *you* or anyone else who is the subject: **Mi agora i, mi agorwn ni, mi agorwch chi** etc. Where an affirmative particle is used, geographical location tends to determine whether one hears **fe°** or **mi°**. **Fe°** does appear to be a predominantly S form, very unusual in the N except in a few set phrases, while **mi°** is more widespread in the N though not unheard of in some S areas. Then again, insofar as there are regions where affirmative particles do not seem to be used much at all, they may be regarded as entirely optional.

Affirmative marker mi° **with present and imperfect of** bod

Mi° (but not **fe°**) is sometimes heard as an intensifier before imperfect forms of **bod**, and also occasionally before the present tense:

Mi oedd 'na °gyfarfod yno neithiwr

There *was* a meeting there last night

Mi ydw i'n mynd

I *am* going

It is, however, not always easy to identify any strong sense of emphasis in this usage.

Difference between bod **and other periphrastic auxiliaries**

As is clear from the table in §211, most verb tenses in Welsh make use of **bod** *be* as an auxiliary in conjunction with the VN. Whenever this is the case, a further linking element is also needed to join the two together.

Usually this is the predicative particle **yn**, but in some cases (involving completed action) it is **wedi**. One of these must be present, and it is wrong to say, for example **Mae Elwyn mynd for *Elwyn goes/is going*. The **yn** is an integral part of the present tense.

Other verbs used as auxiliaries (and not just **naeth** and **ddaru** seen above) do not have a linking element of any kind, and it is wrong to put one in: **Naeth Elwyn yn prynu is a serious and basic mistake.

The rule, therefore, for periphrastic tenses is:

linking element with **bod**, otherwise not

And there is a supplementary rule for non-**bod** auxiliaries:

SM of VN after all auxiliaries except **bod**

This is really the consequence of a basic mutation rule (see §14) that the grammatical subject, whether expressed or understood, is followed by SM. The only reason that there is no SM of the VN where **bod** is the auxiliary is that the linking **yn** blocks it. With other auxiliaries, there is no **yn** (or other element) to block SM, because this linking element is used only with **bod**. Compare the following, where Elwyn is the subject in both sentences:

Mae Elwyn° yn *mynd*   Elwyn is going

Naeth Elwyn° *fynd*   Elwyn went

216 Difference between tense systems in spoken and literary Welsh

It is in the tense system of the verb that the literary language most obviously and radically differs from the spoken. Verb forms are predominantly what cause problems to native speakers in reading literary Welsh, because much of the inherent structure of the system is so alien to spoken usage anywhere. It is a language almost entirely confined to the printed word, and never heard on anyone's lips except in the most formal and unnatural situations.

What relevance the literary language does have for the learner of spoken Welsh lies in the fact that, once competence in basic sentence patterns has been achieved, reading is the best and quickest way to acquire more vocabulary, and it is here that the literary construct will be encountered. A passive knowledge of literary Welsh, then, is worth acquiring for a variety of reasons.

The most fundamental difference between spoken and literary Welsh in the tense systems is the rather wider use of inflected tenses in literary Welsh, and differing uses for some tenses. Four main areas can be identified:

(a)   literary Welsh has an inflected pluperfect which has no counterpart in spoken Welsh, e.g. **prynasai** instead of spoken **oedd e wedi prynu**

(b)   the inflected future does the job of the present in literary Welsh where an idea of continuity or state is involved. This occasionally happens in spoken Welsh (see §**217**), but is the norm in the literary language

(c)   literary Welsh has a subjunctive which has all but died out in the spoken language (see §**388**)

(d)   the inflected conditional of spoken Welsh functions as an inflected imperfect in the literary language: broadly speaking, **prynai (fe)** means *he would buy* in spoken Welsh but *he used to buy* in literary Welsh. This imperfect meaning is occasionally found in spoken Welsh with verbs describing a state rather than an action (see §**320**).

Three main differences can be identified as regards verb-endings:

(a)   the spoken 1st pers. pl. preterite (past) ending **-on (ni)**, and 1st pers. pl. conditional ending **-en (ni)** are **-om** and **-em** respectively in literary Welsh

(b)   the 3rd pers. pl. of all inflected tenses in literary Welsh ends in **-nt**, a feature abandoned by the spoken language hundreds of years ago.

(c)   the personal pronouns are much less commonly used with verbs in literary Welsh – **prynaf**, for instance, would mean *I buy* and **prynasech** would mean *you had bought*, without any need for **i** *I* or **chi** *you*.

A few examples of equivalents in the two types of Welsh may help to give some idea of the gap that can exist:

Literary	Spoken	
saif	**mae'n sefyll**	he/she stands
canent	**gadewch iddyn nhw °ganu**	let them sing
gadawsit	**o't ti wedi gadael**	you had left
na ʰthaflwch!	**peidiwch taflu!**	don't throw!

217   Inflected present (future with present meaning) in proverbial expressions

This is the one instance where a characteristically literary usage is heard in natural speech, since proverbs and other set expressions by their nature tend to preserve older forms of the language. What is now the short-form (inflected) future – with certain alterations – was in the older language the present tense. It differs mainly from the modern inflected future in that the 3rd pers. sing. lacks an ending (-ith/-iff in the future – see §304) and sometimes undergoes a change of vowel. The details of this particular verb-form are not of strict relevance to a grammar of the spoken language, but they may be seen in the fair number of examples of this usage that still survive in the spoken language in folk-sayings and proverbial expressions:

Mawrth a °ladd, Ebrill a °fling   (lladd, blingo)
March slays, April flays

Nid yn hir y ceidw'r diawl ei °was   (cadw)
Not for long does the Devil keep his servant

Dyfal donc a °dyrr y °garreg (torri)

Persistent hammering breaks the stone (i.e. perseverance will pay off)

Gwyn y gwêl y °frân ei ʰchyw (gweld)

The crow sees her chick as white (i.e. mothers all see the best in their children)

Yr hen a °ŵyr a'r ieuanc a °dybia (gwybod, tybio)

The old know and the young think they know

Am °gwymp hen y chwardd ieuanc (chwerthin)

The young laugh when the old fall

The inflected present is an aspect of Welsh usage where the dialects quite often show variation from the norm, however, and blunt assertions about the limitations of this verb-form in speech are almost bound to be contradicted by experience sooner or later. By and large, though, apart from the usage outlined above, it belongs unambiguously to the written language, with very occasional appearances in the media. But see §328 for modal presents.

218–259 BOD – 'BE'

218 Bod

The verb **bod** is in many ways the linchpin of the verb system in Welsh, more so than in other languages. This is because, in addition to being a verb in its own right, it performs an important, and indeed central, secondary function as an auxiliary in forming most of the periphrastic tenses (see §262), which in Welsh constitute the overwhelming majority.

Bod is a verb like any other except in the following characteristics:

(a)   it has inflected forms not only for future and conditional, but also for present and imperfect

(b)   the present, and to some extent the imperfect, have different forms for use in statements (affirmative – AFF), questions (interrogative – INT) and negatives (NEG)

(c)   the 3rd pers. sing. present appears in varying forms to convey three distinct fields of meaning (see §223)

(d)   while it does have an inflected preterite, this is much less frequently used than with other verbs

(e)   it has two verb stems: **bydd-** and **bu-**

(f)   some of its inflected forms cannot be used with the affirmative particles **fe°/mi°** (see §§213, 214).

Some tenses of **bod**, particularly the present and imperfect, show not only considerable regional variation, but also drastic divergence (in many cases simplification) from the 'underlying forms' (see Glossary). The most useful approach in these circumstances is to present all inflected forms of **bod** together as a system, using the underlying forms for the present and imperfect for the sake of simplicity. Variations for these two tenses will then be dealt with in their own sections.

219   Bod **(meanings and definitions)**

There are three main fields of meaning to **bod**:

(a)   identification

(b)   existential

(c)   descriptive

English makes no distinction between (**a**) and (**c**), but does have a special form for (**b**). Welsh distinguishes all three from each other, but only in 3rd pers. sing. present. Definitions of these three meanings will be made with reference to English in the first instance, and then to Welsh.

220   **Identification sentences**

Identification covers those uses of *to be* asking or answering a question beginning *Who is/are . . .?* or *What is/are . . .?*, where a simple identification is the only information required. The following are all identification questions and answers in English:

What is that?

That's a pencil

Who is that man over there?

That's Charlie's psychiatrist

What is the capital of Scotland?

The capital of Scotland is Edinburgh

In all these examples (and in the Welsh versions), an important character-istic is that both elements or phrases on either side of the verb *to be* refer to the same person or thing. This is the acid test for identification sentences, and so the following, though apparently of the same structure, are *not* iden-tification sentences:

Who is there?

[*who* and *there* do not refer to the same thing]

What is crawling up your leg?

[*what* and *crawling up your leg* do not refer to the same thing]

This makes no difference in English, where *is* (or *are* for plural) is used in either case. But in Welsh, as noted, the 3rd pers. sing. distinguishes these meanings. Compare:

Pwy ydy hwnna?	Who is that?
Pwy sy 'na?	Who is there?
Beth ydy hwn?	What is this?
Beth sy'n cropian ar dy °goes?	What is crawling up your leg?

221   Existential sentences

Existential corresponds to English *There is/are . . .*, *There was/were . . .* etc. in all main tenses. This is the meaning of *be* that is distinct also in English (by the presence of a dummy or 'empty' *there* as part of the verb), and so is easy for English speakers to spot. Examples of existential sentences:

There is a giraffe in the garden

Will there be buns for tea, mother?

Have there been any calls?

There is no excuse for this

All the above have *there* as an integral part of the sentence (i.e. they sound wrong without it, and even those that can be rearranged to do without it still sound odd). The question of existential sentences and their implications in Welsh are dealt with fully under §**251**.

Descriptive sentences

Descriptive covers all uses of *be* not covered by identification and existential uses mentioned above. This includes all uses of **bod** *be* as an auxiliary (in other words, where another verb appears further on in the clause, see §262), and all instances where the element following **bod** *be* is an adjective or adverb. Examples with *is*:

Who is going on the trip?	[verb *going* follows *is*]
This apple is sour	[adjective *sour* follows *is*]
The cat is outside	[adverb of position *outside* follows *is*]

223 **Distinctions in 3rd pers. sing. present**

With the definitions of these three fields of meaning established, it is worth seeing how they are distinguished in the 3rd pers. sing. present in Welsh in affirmative (AFF), interrogative (INT) and negative (NEG) sentences:

	AFF	INT	NEG
identification	. . . **ydy** . . .	. . . **ydy** . . .?	**Dim** . . . **ydy** . . .
existential	**Mae** . . .	**Oes** . . .?	**Does dim** . . .
descriptive	**Mae** . . . (. . . **sy** . . .)	**Ydy** . . .?	**Dydy** . . . °**ddim**

The S variants of **ydy** (**yw**: found in all identification uses and in INT descriptive in some areas as well) and of **dydy** (**dyw**) have been omitted from the above to make the 3 x 3 arrangement clearer. There is also a very common N variant of **dydy** – **tydy** or **tydi** – which is likewise omitted above.

Notes:

(a) Identification sentences involve abnormal (for Welsh) word order, since the verb **ydy** never appears at the front of the sentence (note that the INT descriptive **Ydy** always does, however)

(b) Existential and descriptive **bod**, on the other hand, come at the start of the main sentence in the usual way

(c) The appearance of **dim** in the NEG column is distinctive for each type: it is the first element with identification; it is permanently attached to **does** with existential use; and it follows the subject phrase in descriptive use, receiving SM because of this (see §14)

(d) AFF descriptive also has a special relative form **sy** (§**229**) which, however, can appear in certain types of question. This is dealt with fully under §**230**

224 Examples of all nine 3rd pers. sing. base forms

AFF ident:	**Crys Sioned ydy hwnna**	That is Sioned's shirt
INT ident:	**Crys Sioned ydy hwnna?**	Is that Sioned's shirt?
NEG ident:	**Dim crys Sioned ydy hwnna**	That isn't Sioned's shirt
AFF exist:	**Mae llaeth yn yr oergell**	There is milk in the fridge
INT exist:	**Oes llaeth yn yr oergell?**	Is there milk in the fridge?
NEG exist:	**Does dim llaeth yn yr oergell**	There is no milk in the fridge
AFF descr:	**Mae'r cwrw 'ma'n °gryf**	This beer is strong
INT descr:	**Ydy'r cwrw 'ma'n °gryf?**	Is this beer strong?
NEG descr:	**Dydy'r cwrw 'ma °ddim yn °gryf**	This beer is not strong

Notes:

(a) In each of these triads, the basic word-order remains the same for AFF, INT and NEG

(b) In identification, the only difference between AFF, INT and NEG at all is the addition of **dim** to the front of the NEG sentence

(c) A more literary alternative **nid** is sometimes found in speech for **dim** in NEG identification only: **Nid crys Sioned ydy hwnna**

(d) In existential and descriptive, there are differing forms of the verb for each of AFF, INT and NEG

225 Notes on other tenses

In practice, the only other tenses in which the identification verb is likely to be found are the imperfect **oedd** and the future °**fydd**.

Siarl V oedd Brenin yr Iseldiroedd adeg hynny

Charles V was King of the Netherlands at that time.

Pwy °fydd y canfed ymwelydd, tybed?

Who will be the hundredth visitor, I wonder?

Existential is the same as 3rd pers. sing. descriptive in all other tenses, except for **dim** instead of °**ddim** in NEG, as above for the present (see §223(c)). The existential verb is treated separately under its own sections (see §§251–256) after all aspects of descriptive **bod** have been examined.

226   Partially simplified overview of inflected forms of bod

		Present	*Imperfect*	*Preterite*
Sing.	1st	**dw i**	**roeddwn i**	**bues i**
	2nd	**(r)wyt ti**	**roeddet ti**	**buest ti**
	3rd	**mae e/hi**	**roedd e/hi**	**buodd e/hi**
Pl.	1st	**dyn ni**	**roedden ni**	**buon ni**
	2nd	**dych chi**	**roeddech chi**	**buoch chi**
	3rd	**maen nhw**	**roedden nhw**	**buon nhw**

		Future	*Conditional*
Sing.	1st	**bydda i**	**byddwn/baswn i**
	2nd	**byddi di**	**byddet/baset ti**
	3rd	**bydd e/hi**	**byddai/basai fe/hi**
Pl.	1st	**byddwn ni**	**bydden/basen ni**
	2nd	**byddwch chi**	**byddech/basech chi**
	3rd	**byddan nhw**	**bydden/basen nhw**

It will be noted from the table above that the verb-stem **bydd-** is used for both the future and one of the conditionals, while the other verb-stem **bu** is used for the preterite (it also underlies the other conditional, though this is not of direct relevance to the spoken language). The present and imperfect are not formed from either verb-stem.

The usual periphrastic **wedi**-tenses (see §262) are also available, using the required inflected form of **bod** with **wedi bod**, for example:

°**Fyddan nhw wedi bod**	They will have been
Roedd hi wedi bod	She had been
°**Fasen ni wedi bod**	We would have been

227 **Present tense of** bod

It was mentioned in the general remarks on **bod** (see §218) that the present tense has different sets of forms depending on whether the speaker is making a statement, asking a question, or making a negative statement. A further complication is that there is a distinct North/South divide in the forms of this tense. In the table following, therefore, AFF, INT and NEG forms are given first for Northern speech areas, and then again for Southern.

NORTH:

		AFF	*INT*	*NEG*
Sing.	1st	dw i	ydw i?	(dy)dw i ddim
	2nd	ti	wyt ti?	dwyt ti ddim
	3rd	mae o/hi	ydy o/hi?	dydy o/hi ddim
Pl.	1st	dan ni	ydan ni?	(dy)dan ni ddim
	2nd	dach chi	(y)dach chi?	(dy)dach chi ddim
	3rd	maen nhw	ydyn nhw?	dydyn nhw ddim

SOUTH:

		AFF	*INT*	*NEG*
Sing.	1st	rw i, wi	ydw i?	(d)wi ddim
	2nd	ti	wyt ti?	ti ddim
	3rd	mae e/hi, (ma' fe)	ydy/yw e/hi?	dyw e/hi ddim
Pl.	1st	(ŷn) ni	ŷn ni?	ŷn ni ddim
	2nd	ych chi	ych chi?	(ych) chi ddim
	3rd	maen nhw	ŷn nhw?	ŷn nhw ddim

Notes:

(a)   Many parts of the S have special NEG forms based on **sa-/so-**:

sa i	I'm not	**so ni**	we're not
so ti	you're not	**so chi**	you're not
so fe	he's not	**so nhw**	they're not
so hi	she's not		

From these come the typically S expressions **sa i'n gwybod** *I don't know* (= N **dwn i °ddim**; see §322), **sa i'n credu** *I don't think (so)* (= **dw i °ddim yn meddwl**).

Certain parts of the S have **smo** for all persons:

smo fi	I'm not	**smo ni**	we're not
smo ti	you're not	**smo chi**	you're not
smo fe	he's not	**smo nhw**	they're not
smo hi	she's not		

Other less common variants are also found.

(b)   AFF forms for 2nd pers. sing. in both North and South are most frequently heard as the pronoun **ti** alone, and this is often true also of the INT forms:

Ti'n edrych yn union fel dy °dad

You look just like your father

Ti wedi siarad â nhw'n °barod?

Have you spoken to them already?

Ti °ddim wedi arwyddo eto, nag wyt?

You haven't signed yet, have you?

Where the verb is heard, it is usually **(r)wyt**, (perhaps the only **r-** form of the verb that truly is part of the spoken language; cf. note **(g)** below)

(c)   All elements enclosed in brackets in the tables are optional, and may or may not be heard depending on the style or speed of conversation. In these cases it is impossible to state baldly that one variant is more 'correct' than another

(d)   3rd pers. sing. INT in the South can be either **Ydy . . .?** or **Yw . . .?**:

Ydy Gwenllian yn moyn dod draw i warae? (S)

or: **Yw Gwenllian yn moyn dod draw i warae?** (S)

Does Gwenllian want to come round and play?

(e) **Ydy** can be, and is often, written **ydi**, and the same is sometimes true of **dydy**

(f) NEG forms in many parts of the North are heard with a **t-** instead of **d-**. This is very common and might almost be regarded as the norm. Examples:

> **Tydi hi °ddim yn rhy hwyr i ffonio, 'sti** (N)
>
> It's not too late to phone, you know
>
> **Tydan nhw °ddim yn dŵad rŵan, mae arna i ofn** (N)
>
> They're not coming now, I'm afraid

The same is also true of the existential present (see §252)

> **Toes 'na °ddim**   There isn't/aren't

(g) 'Normalized' and therefore essentially inauthentic AFF forms beginning with **ry-**, although often encountered in textbooks for learners, have never reflected general spoken usage. Most sound affected, some are simply wrong. The most common are ***Rydw i**, ***Rydyn ni** and ***Rydych chi**, for *I am*, *we are* and *you are* respectively.

228 Yes/no answers for present tense of bod

If a *yes/no* question is phrased in Welsh with the verb as first element of the question, then the answer *yes* is expressed by restating the verb, unless the preterite (and sometimes the perfect) tense is involved. This is dealt with fully under Function section XLI. For the present tense of **bod**, special answering forms exist for North and South, with some Northern forms showing a certain amount of variation.

		North	South
Sing.	1st	**(y)(n)dw**	**ydw/odw**
	2nd	**wyt**	**wyt**
	3rd	**(y)(n)dy**	**ydy/ody**
Pl.	1st	**(y)(n)dan**	**ydyn/odyn**
	2nd	**(y)(n)dach**	**ydych/odych**
	3rd	**(y)(n)dyn**	**ydyn/odyn**

Examples:

> **Ti'n dŵad i'r cyfarfod heno? – Ndw** (N)
>
> Are you coming to the meeting tonight? – Yes (I am)

Ŷn ni'n mynd i edrych o °gwmpas yr amgueddfa? – Odyn (S)

Are we going to look round the museum? – Yes (we are)

To answer *No* **Nag** (usually written: **Nac**) is prefixed to all these forms, except that Northern variants with -n- (e.g. **yndw**) drop this. So **Yndw** *Yes* (*I am*) becomes **Nag ydw** *No* (*I'm not*). Sometimes **Na** is found instead of **Nag** (**Nadw** for **Nag ydw**), or else the all-purpose **Na** *No* is used without any repetition of the verb at all:

Ydw i i °fod i aros amdano fo? – Nag wyt

Am I supposed to wait for him? – No (you're not)

Ydych chi'n dal i °weithio yn y °dre? – Nadw/Nag ydw

Are you still working in town? – No (I'm not)

Ydy'r plant eisiau dod 'da fi i'r siop? – Nadyn/Nag ydyn

Do the children want to come to the shop with me? – No

Note in the last example that the general rule (see §212) that all 3rd pers. pl. subjects take a 3rd pers. sing. verb except where the word **nhw** *they* is actually used does not apply to *yes/no* answers: **Ydy** (3rd pers. sing.) 'r plant . . .? but **Nag ydyn** (3rd pers. pl.).

229   Present relative sy(dd)

The verb **bod** has – in the present tense only – a special relative form **sy** or **sydd**. This underlying form **sydd**, though common in even informal writing, is the less frequent in the modern spoken language, though it will be heard in more careful speech, and in one particular sentence pattern where it appears, unusually, at the end of the sentence (see §235).

The basic meaning of **sy** in this context is *which/who* (*is/are*) . . . . It therefore corresponds to **mae**, but with the additional relative element *which/that* or *who* included as part of its meaning. This relative element must be the subject of the verb. Examples:

Drychwch ar y llanast *sy* fan hyn!

Look at the mess (*which is*) here!

Dewch â'r llythyron 'na *sy* ar y bwrdd

Bring those letters (*which are*) on the table

Y peth sy'n iawn sy'n iawn

What's right is right [lit. '(It is) the thing which is right (which) is right']

The subject of a construction like this does not necessarily have to be a noun:

Sy °ddim ('which/who is/are not')

Felly sy isio gwneud

This is how it needs to be done [lit. 'Thus (which) needs (to) do']

Relative sentences, including those with **sy**, are explained in §§479–485.

230 Sy **after** Pwy?, Beth?, Faint?, P'un?

When the question-words **Pwy?** *Who?*, **Beth?** *What?*, **Faint?** *How many?*, **P'un?** *Which (one)?* or **Pa rai?** *Which (ones)?* appear as the subject of the present tense of **bod**, it is the relative form **sy** that is required:

Pwy sy 'na?

Who's there?

Pwy sy'n dod heno?

Who's coming tonight?

Beth sy 'da chi fan'na?

What have you got there? [lit. What is with you . . .?]

P'un sy'n perthyn i ti?

Which (one) belongs to you?

Pa rai sy'n dŵad hefo fi?

Which (ones) are coming with me?

Faint onoch chi sy eisiau tanysgrifio drwy °ddebyd uniongyrchol?

How many of you want to subscribe by direct debit?

A full explanation of the difference between **sy**, **mae** and **ydy/yw** after these interrogatives may be found in §140.

231 Sy °ddim ('which/who is/are not')

The negative of **sy** is **sy °ddim**:

Dw i'n nabod rhywun *sy °ddim* yn talu ei °drethi

I know someone *who doesn't* pay his taxes

Dw i °ddim yn licio pobl *sy °ddim* yn °garedig i anifeiliaid

I don't like people *who aren't* kind to animals

This usage is not so frequent in the written language, where alternative constructions **nad ydy e/hi** or **nad yw e/hi** (sing.) and **nad ydyn nhw** (pl.) are favoured, with optional °ddim:

Rhywun nad ydy e'n talu ei °drethi

Someone who doesn't pay his taxes

Pobl nad ydyn nhw (°ddim) yn °garedig i anifeiliaid

People who aren't kind to animals

See also §479.

232 Relative of bod in other tenses

No corresponding special forms exist for the other primary tenses – *which was/were . . ., who will be . . .*, etc. For these, the ordinary 3rd pers. sing. is used, with SM where possible.

°Welson ni'r dyn 'na *oedd* ar y teledu wythnos diwetha

We saw that man *who was* on the TV last week

Dw i'n gwerthu popeth °*fyddai*'n atgoffa fi ono fe

I'm selling everything *that would* remind me of him

Dw i angen gliniadur °*fydd* yn rhedeg Photoshop

I need a laptop *that will* run Photoshop

Hoffwn °ddiolch i'r staff i gyd °*fuodd* efo ni eleni

I would like to thank all the staff *who have been* with us this year

233 Idioms with sy

Several common idioms involve **Beth sy(dd)** *What is . . .?*:

Beth sy(dd)?	What's up?
Beth sy'n bod?	What's up? What's the matter?
Beth sy arnat ti?	What's wrong/the matter with you?
Beth sy arnoch chi?	

234 **Sy after** fel – *as is* . . .

The relative **sy** is used for the 3rd pers. sing. present tense of **bod** after the
conjunction **fel** *as, like* in certain phrases:

Oedd 'na °wrthwynebiadau, fel sy'n digwydd yn aml iawn

There were objections, as very often happens

**'Chydig iawn o °bobol °ddaeth yn y diwedd, fel sy'n arferol adeg
'ma o'r °flwyddyn**

Very few people came in the end, which is usual at this time of year

Note also the set expression **fel *mae*'n digwydd** *as it happens*:

Fel mae'n digwydd, mae ffurflen °danysgrifio 'da fi fan hyn

As it happens, I've got a subscription form here

235 **Existential use of** sy(dd)

Sy can also carry existential meaning (see §**251**), and in this sense translates
the English *which there is/are*. In this usage it can appear at the end of a
sentence, and when it does the full form **sydd** is common.

Dyna'r cwbl sydd

That's all there is [lit. . . . which there is]

Faint onoch chi sydd?

How many of you are there?

Dan ni °ddim eisiau diweithdra fel sy yn y dinasoedd mawr

We don't want unemployment like (that) which there is in the big cities

236 **Use of** sy **in focused sentences**

(See also §**19**.) The initial position or 'slot' in the sentence is used for giving
focus or emphasis to a particular word or idea. Normally, of course, the
verb occupies this position, and usually a simple switching of the verb to
second position is sufficient to emphasize the word which then occupies
first place.

[neutral] **Oedd Geraint yn chwarae pnawn ddoe**

Geraint was playing yesterday afternoon

[focus] **Geraint oedd yn chwarae pnawn ddoe**

It was Geraint who was playing yesterday afternoon

[neutral] **Wedodd Sioned hynny wrtha i gynnau**

Sioned told me that just now

[focus] **Sioned wedodd hynny wrtha i**

It was Sioned who told me that

But where the neutral sentence uses **mae**, and the emphasized element is the subject, **sy** must replace it in the altered word-order:

[neutral] **Mae'r plant yn diodde**

The children are suffering

[focus] **Y plant sy'n diodde**

It's the children who are suffering

But with **plant** as the object, it is simply moved to the front of the sentence with no other changes made:

[neutral] **Mae'r °Groes °Goch eisiau helpu'r plant °gynta**

The Red Cross want to help the children first

[focus] **Y plant mae'r °Groes °Goch eisiau helpu °gynta**

It's the children the Red Cross want to help first

The general principles of focused sentences are dealt with fully in §§17–21.

237   Command forms of bod

The 2nd pers. sing. command form of **bod** is either **bydda** or, much more often in speech, **bydd**. The 2nd pers. pl. is always **byddwch**.

Bydd yn °ofalus gyda'r °badell 'na!

(Be) careful with that bowl!

Byddwch yma am naw neu mi awn ni hebddoch chi

Be here at nine or we'll go without you

Negative **bod** commands are done in the usual way with **paid/peidiwch** (see §383):

Paid bod mor °bigog – 'mond gofyn nes i

Don't be so touchy – I only asked

Mi na i ⁿgorau, ond peidiwch bod yn rhy °obeithiol

I'll do my best, but don't be too hopeful

238 Imperfect tense of bod (underlying forms)

The same three-way system exists for the imperfect of **bod** as outlined for the present (see §227), but in this case there is much less regional and stylistic variation. It is possible to give generalized underlying forms for AFF, INT and NEG imperfect as follows:

		AFF	INT	NEG
Sing.	1st	roeddwn i	oeddwn i?	doeddwn i °ddim
	2nd	roeddet ti	oeddet ti?	doeddet ti °ddim
	3rd	roedd e/hi	oedd e/hi?	doedd e/hi °ddim
Pl.	1st	roedden ni	oedden ni?	doedden ni °ddim
	2nd	roeddech chi	oeddech chi?	doeddech chi °ddim
	3rd	roedden nhw	oedden nhw?	doedden nhw °ddim

Notes:

(a) This tense corresponds usually to English *was/were* etc. So **roeddwn i** – *I was*, **oeddwn i?** – *was I?*, **doeddwn i °ddim** – *I wasn't*, and so on

(b) The basic forms are seen in the INT set; addition of prefixed **r-** gives the AFF set, while addition of prefixed **d-** and following **°ddim** gives the NEG set

(c) These underlying forms are valid for both North and South, though some N dialects have **-a-** in final syllables instead of **-e-**, as would be expected (see §2(b)) – **roeddach chi**, etc.

(d) The system of the underlying forms of the imperfect is much favoured in textbooks for its neatness. In fact, however, the spoken system (see §239 below) is even neater, because it is simpler.

239 **Imperfect of bod (spoken variants)**

The underlying forms of this tense of **bod** have been simplified in the spoken language in two ways:

(a) The **-edd-** element, (and often the following vowel as well), usually disappears in all persons AFF, INT and NEG except 3rd pers. sing. (where it is final)

(b) The distinction **r-, -, d-** for AFF, INT and NEG respectively, noted in §238 note (b) above, has been largely abandoned in all but careful or formal speech, and the INT base-forms adopted for all three sets (though the NEG set still requires, of course, the **°ddim**).

This leaves a radically simplified system that, in rapid speech, is sometimes hard to identify with the underlying forms detailed in §238:

		AFF	*INT*	*NEG*
Sing.	1st	o'n i	o'n i?	o'n i °ddim
	2nd	o't ti	o't ti?	o't ti °ddim
	3rd	oedd/o'dd e/hi	oedd/o'dd e/hi?	oedd/o'dd e/hi °ddim
Pl.	1st	o'n ni	o'n ni?	o'n ni °ddim
	2nd	o'ch chi	o'ch chi?	o'ch chi °ddim
	3rd	o'n nhw	o'n nhw?	o'n nhw °ddim

Notes:

(a) In this system there is no difference between AFF and INT except for intonation

(b) 3rd pers. sing. **o'dd** is a very frequent alternative to **oedd** in speech

(c) The NEG set also appears with the prefixed **d-** retained, so **do'n i °ddim** appears for **o'n i °ddim** *I wasn't*, etc. The versions without **d-**, however, are very common

(d) These simplifications are applied with varying degrees of consistency. For example, while the intial **r-** of the statement forms is regularly and widely ignored, the **-edd-** element is often heard, particularly in the question forms, and generally in the N

(e) The full forms of the INT set are retained (without the pronouns) as answer-words to yes/no questions:

> **O't ti'n helpu gyda'r bwyd neithiwr? – Oeddwn.**
> Were you helping with the food last night? – Yes (I was)

?8
bs

Imperfect of
bod with verbs
of mental state

O'n i'n anghwrtais *iawn* **iddi? – Oeddet**

Was I *very* rude to her? – Yes (you were).

Though even here the short forms are hardly unheard of or in any way remarkable.

O't ti yn y dosbarth ddoe? - O'n.

Were you in class yesterday? - Yes (I was)

But with *no*-answers, the reduced forms can be used after **Nag**:

O'n nhw'n °falch o'ch gweld chi? – Nag o'n (nhw)

Were they pleased to see you? – No (they weren't)

In this case, the pronoun is optionally reinstated.

(f)   The affirmative particles **fe°/mi°** are not normally found with the imperfect, except that **mi°** is occasionally used in the North in a vaguely emphatic sense: **Mi oeddwn i yno** *I was there.*

Overall, the diversity of the imperfect of **bod** makes it difficult to suggest options other than on grounds of local usage, and even here two parallel variants can sometimes be heard from the same speaker in the same sentence. For that matter, the underlying forms are by no means unheard of in natural speech (particularly 3rd pers. sing.).

240   Imperfect of bod **with verbs of mental state**

Verbs expressing a continued mental or physical state – such as **gwybod** *know* (*a fact*), **nabod** *know* (*a person*), **meddwl** *think*, **gobeithio** *hope*, **perthyn** *belong* – form their past tense in Welsh with the imperfect of **bod**. That is, where in English we can say *I knew, thought, hoped*, Welsh prefers *I was knowing, thinking, hoping*, since the past tense is more closely associated in Welsh with completed action than is the case in English.

O'n i °ddim yn gwybod 'ny

I didn't know that

O'n i'n meddwl mai ti oedd biau fo (N)

I thought it was yours

Oedd y tŷ'n perthyn i'w °fam-yng-nghyfraith °bryd hynny

The house belonged to his mother-in-law at the time

Doedd neb yn nabod y teulu drws nesa'n °dda o °gwbl

Nobody knew the family next door well at all

See also §303.

241 Imperfect of bod with arfer . . . *used to*

I used to . . ., you used to . . ., etc. are usually expressed in Welsh by using the imperfect of **bod** + yn arfer:

O'n i'n arfer mynd i'r ysgol tua chwarter i naw

I used to go to school at about a quarter to nine

Do'n nhw °ddim yn arfer ffeindio'r °fath °bethau fan hyn

They didn't used to find things like that here

For a different method of expressing past habitual action, see §278.

242 Other inflected tenses of bod

Apart from the present and imperfect, the inflected tenses of **bod** behave much as those of any other verb:

(a)   They have the same basic forms, regardless of whether they occur in statements, questions or negative statements

(b)   There is initial SM in questions, and in negatives (+ **°ddim**)

(c)   SM is commonly used in speech with ordinary statements as well

(d)   The tenses are produced using the same endings as with other verbs – but the verb-stem (uniquely to **bod**) has differing forms for different tenses: preterite – stem **bu-**, future – stem **bydd-** and conditional – stem **bydd-** or **bas-**

(e)   The affirmative particles **fe°/mi°** can be used with them in statements.

243 Preterite tense of bod – forms

As mentioned in §242(d), the preterite tense of **bod** uses its own verb-stem **bu-** with the normal endings for the past tense. The forms without initial mutation, then, are as follows:

	Singular	*Plural*
1st	**bues i**	**buon ni**
2nd	**buest ti**	**buoch chi**
3rd	**buodd e/hi**	**buon nhw**

(a)   The 1st pers. sing. (as in preterite tense generally in many areas) often has a -*sh*- pronunciation for the **-s-**; so '*beeshi*' [biʃi] or, with SM, '*veeshi*' [viʃi] is heard

(b)   3rd pers. sing. **buodd** sometimes occurs in speech as **buo**. There is also an alternative form comprising the stem only – **bu**. This is dealt with separately below (see §245)

(c)   2nd pers. sing. **buest** is sometimes **buost**

244 Meaning and uses of preterite tense of bod

In English, where *be* has only one simple past tense, no distinction can be made between the imperfect and preterite, so **bues i**, like **roeddwn i/o'n i**, can be translated as *I was*, and the question therefore arises as to what difference there is between the imperfect and preterite tenses of **bod**.

In practice, the preterite tense is much more restricted in use than the imperfect, and **o'n i** forms predominate overwhelmingly both in speech and writing for this reason.

The preterite tense in Welsh tends to be more definitely associated with completed action in Welsh than the all-purpose English counterpart. This factor is common to most uses of **bues i**, and accounts for its relative infrequency compared with **roeddwn i**, because the verb **bod** is by its nature normally a verb indicating existence or continued, non-completed state. **Bues i** is found, then, on those relatively rare occasions where the idea of being coincides with some sense of a completed state of affairs. Probably the most common use in speech is in asking someone if they have been somewhere:

°Fuoch chi erioed yn yr Unol °Daleithiau?

Have you ever been to the United States?

°Fues i erioed yno, ond °fuon ni yng ⁿNghanada llynedd

I've never been there, but we went to Canada last year

Note how, in the above examples, English copes with this specialized use of *be* in two different ways – first, by using the perfect *have been* form of the verb (governing the preposition *to* in this restricted sense), and later by switching a verb more easily associated with completion of action (*go*) where the time expression *last year* precludes the use of *have been*.

The usual translation of **bues i**, etc., then, is *have/has been* etc. rather than *was/were*, etc. (though the latter is possible in certain types of English). In its use in *Have you been to . . .?*, it carries the implication that the person has since come back, while the **roeddwn i** imperfect forms would carry no such connotation. Compare:

°Fuodd 'n chwaer i yn Ffrainc

My sister has been to France   (she is not there now)

Oedd 'n chwaer i yn Ffrainc pan °laniodd dyn ar y lleuad

My sister was in France when man landed on the moon

Of course, the sister may no longer be in France in the second example – but imperfect **oedd** is used here as the neutral past-tense choice for **bod** because in this case the important thing is that at the time that man landed on the moon, she was in France and nowhere else. Whether or not she left subsequently is of no relevance to her circumstances at the time of the first moon-landing. The first example, on the other hand, requires **fuodd** because we are specifying that the sister not only went to France, but some time later returned – after all, if she had not returned we would be saying **Mae 'n chwaer i yn Ffrainc** *My sister is in France*.

Also in other senses corresponding to the English perfect 'have/has been':

Lle buest ti?

Where have you been?

And in the same sense, but as an auxiliary with a VN:

°Fuoch chi i gyd yn helpu Mr Williams, gobeithio

I hope you've all been helping Mr Williams

Dyna lle buon nhw'n palu trwy'r bore

That's where they've been digging all morning

Short form 3rd pers. sing. preterite – bu

Of even more restricted use is **bu,** an alternative to **buodd** (3rd pers. sing. preterite). This is simply the special preterite-tense stem of **bod** with no ending, and is used nowadays in certain well-defined circumstances only:

(a)   **bu farw** *has died/is dead.* See defective verbs (see §**395**)

(b)   as a past tense of the existential verb (see §**251**) where very recent time is indicated, and translating English *There has/have been . . . .* This usage is perhaps most commonly, though not exclusively, encountered in the media:

   Bu trafodaethau heddiw rhwng yr undebau a'r cyflogwyr

   There have been discussions today between unions and employers

   Bu cystadlu brwd unwaith eto eleni

   There has been fierce competition once again this year

(c)   a similar recent past connotation is sometimes expressed with **bu** (**hi**) when talking about the weather:

   Mae'n brafiach nag y bu trwy'r dydd

   It's nicer (now) than it has been all day

Future of bod

The radical forms for statements are as follows, with no appreciable dialect variation:

	Singular	*Plural*
1st	**bydda i**	**byddwn ni**
2nd	**byddi di**	**byddwch chi**
3rd	**bydd e/hi**	**byddan nhw**

Notes:

(a)   The mutated forms °**fydda i** etc. are more common in speech, even for statements

(b)   Affirmative particles **fe°/mi°** can be used with this tense

(c)   INT forms (*will I be?* etc.) are °**fydda i?** etc. with obligatory SM; the NEG forms (*I won't be*) simply add °**ddim** to INT: °**fydda i** °**ddim,** etc.

(d)   Ist pers. sing. is frequently shortened in speech to **'dda i: 'Dda i'n ôl mewn munud** *I'll be back in a minute*

247   **'Answer-words' for future of** bod

The *yes* answer-words are the appropriate non-mutated forms as above, but with the following pronouns usually omitted:

°Fydd y rheolwr i mewn bore fory? – Bydd.

Will the manager be in tomorrow morning? – Yes [he will]

°Fyddwch chi'n dal fan hyn pan °ddo i yn ôl? – Byddwn.

Will you still be here when I get back? – Yes [we will]

°Fyddi di'n aros tu allan? – Byddaf.

Will you be waiting outside? Yes [I will]

Note in the last example that the original final -f, now hardly ever heard in spoken Welsh, is optionally restored in this instance, where the following pronoun is dropped in answer words.

'No' answers use **Na°: Na °fyddaf** *No, I won't (be),* **Na °fydd** *No, he/she won't (be),* etc.

°Fyddan nhw'n mynd i ffwrdd eleni? – Na °fyddan.

Will they be going away this year? – No [they won't]

For the secondary use of **bydda i** etc. as a habitual present tense, see §313.

248   **Conditional of** bod

This tense of **bod** appears in two forms in Welsh, one with the stem **bydd-** and the other with the stem **bas-**. The unreality endings (see §291) are used in either case. Radical forms:

	Singular	Plural	Singular	Plural
Ist	byddwn i	bydden ni	baswn i	basen ni
2nd	byddet ti	byddech chi	baset ti	basech chi
3rd	byddai fe/hi	bydden nhw	basai fe/hi	basen nhw

Notes:

(a)   Like the future (see §246), the conditional of **bod** generally appears with initial SM in statements: **°Fyddwn i** *I would be,* etc.

(b) The affirmative particles **fe°/mi°** can optionally be used with this tense.

(c) In accordance with pronunciation variations explained in §2(a), 3rd pers. sing. **byddai/basai** sounds as **bydde/base** in S areas, and as **bydda/basa** in N areas. These forms are often so spelt.

(d) In accordance with a general rule of N pronunciation (see §2(b)), all non-reality endings with **-e-** in the final syllable (2nd pers. sing., 1st, 2nd, 3rd pers. pl.) are pronounced with **-a-** in many parts of the N and these days often so written.

> **Mi °fasan nhw'n °ormod iddo fo, dw i'n meddwl**
>
> I think they would be too much for him

(e) The **baswn i** forms are frequently shortened in speech to **swn i** etc.:

> **Se fe'n gorfod esbonio ei °benderfyniadau**
>
> He would have to explain his decisions
>
> **Sa hynny'n neis iawn, on' basa?**
>
> That would be very nice, wouldn't it?
>
> **Sach chi wedi meddwl fel arall, on' basach?**
>
> You would have thought otherwise, wouldn't you?

Hypothetical conditions involving the use of the conditional of **bod** in constructions **pe byddwn** and (**pe**) **taswn** are dealt with in detail in §280.

The same principles apply for *yes/no* answers in the conditional as in the future (see §247). **Baswn** etc. forms do not drop the **ba-** in these circumstances:

> **°Fyddech chi'n °fodlon i °lofnodi'r °ddeiseb 'ma? – Byddwn**
>
> Would you be willing to sign this petition? – Yes [I would]
>
> **Sa dy °fam yn °fodlon gofalu am y plant? – Basai**
>
> Would your mother be willing to look after the children? – Yes [she would]

For the secondary use of **byddwn i** (but not **baswn i**) as a habitual past tense, see §319(b).

---

249 **Tag elements for bod after affirmative statements**

Tag elements (e.g. English *aren't they?, isn't she?, wouldn't you?*) are added to a statement by way of seeking confirmation from the other speaker that what has just been said is true. They anticipate the answer *Yes*. Where **bod** is involved in the original statement, the tag element is arrived at by prefixing **on'd** or **on'** to the appropriate question form. Examples in different tenses of 3rd pers. sing. will serve to illustrate:

. . ., **on'd ydy?**	. . ., isn't it?
. . ., **on'd oes?**	. . ., isn't/aren't there?
. . ., **on'd oedd?**	. . ., wasn't it?
. . ., **on'(d) °fydd?**	. . ., won't it (be)?
. . ., **on'(d) °fyddai?**	. . ., wouldn't it (be)?
. . ., **on'(d) °fasai?**	

The radical is also often heard after **on'**(d) in the future and conditional: **on' bydd?**, **on' base?** etc.

In the 3rd pers. sing., there is often no following pronoun; in other persons, the pronoun is more frequently included. Further examples:

°Fyddan nhw'n °ddigon diogel yn yr °ardd, on' °fyddan nhw?

They'll be safe enough in the garden, won't they?

Dan ni'n hwyr unwaith eto, on'd ydan ni? (N)

We're late again, aren't we?

San ni o fewn ein hawliau i °wneud 'ny, on' basan? (N)

We'd be within our rights to do that, wouldn't we?

O'ch chi yn llygad eich lle, on'd oeddech chi?

You were dead right, weren't you?

Note in the last example that the full underlying form of the verb tends to be restored in these circumstances (**oeddech chi** instead of **o'ch chi**), and this would be especially true if the pronoun was omitted.

This **on'd/on'** tag is in origin the LW particle **onid/oni**, used at the start of the sentence, usually but not necessarily before verbs, to combine INT + NEG, and still encountered in perhaps more formal styles:

Onid yw'n °bryd inni ailystyried y mater?

Isn't it time we reconsidered the matter?

Onid dyna yw llywodraeth agored?

Isn't that what open government is?

Onid yw Llydaw yn °wlad °Geltaidd?

Is Brittany not a Celtic country?

Oni °wyddoch chi'r ateb?

Don't you know the answer?

Oni °ddylen ni hyrwyddo'r cynllun hwn?

Shouldn't we promote this scheme?

Oni °ddaethon nhw gyda'i gilydd?

Didn't they come together?

Oni ʰchytunwch chi?

Don't you agree?

250   Tag elements for bod after negative statements

These tags anticipate the answer *No*. The same principle applies as in §249, except that **na°** (nag before vowels) is used in place of **on'd**, and the translation will be *is it?, was it?* etc. SM is used with the future and conditional. 3rd pers. sing. examples:

. . ., **nag ydy?**	. . ., is it?
. . ., **nag oes?**	. . ., is/are there?
. . ., **nag oedd?**	. . ., was it?
. . ., **na °fydd?**	. . ., will it (be)?
. . ., **na °fyddai?**	. . ., would it (be)?
. . ., **na °fasai?**	

Naturally, these and related elements are tagged onto negative statements.

Ond °fyddwn i °ddim yn gwybod lle i °ddechrau, na °fyddwn?

But I wouldn't know where to begin, would I?

O'n nhw °ddim yn °gyfeillgar iawn, nag oedden nhw?

They weren't very friendly, were they?

Yffach, ti °ddim yn siarad Llydaweg hefyd, nag wyt?

Goodness, you don't speak Breton as well, do you?

°Fyddan nhw °ddim yn cyrraedd yr °orsaf mewn pryd, na °fyddan?

They won't get to the station in time, will they?

251 The existential verb – principles and definitions

In English, Welsh and other languages, the verb *be* has two broadly separate uses: an existential use, and a non-existential use. Existential statements simply introduce information about the existence of something, while non-existential statements introduce information about something whose existence we are already aware of. For example, in English we can say *The tiger is in the garden*. This is a simple statement telling us where the tiger is – it answers a notional question *Where is the tiger?* so we must already know about the tiger, because the question contains the definite article *the*. Or, to look at it another way, the tiger cannot be the new information, because it appears both in the question and the answer.

But there is a corresponding existential question *What is in the garden?* to which the answer might be *A tiger is in the garden* or, more naturally in English: *There is a tiger in the garden*. Here, the very existence of the tiger is the new information – while what we already knew about (the garden) appears in both question and response. Note that in this type of English sentence, *there* has nothing to do with location (*in the garden* does that), but is present merely to signal that this is an existential use of *be*. See also §256.

Generally, existential sentences in English can be identified by the presence of *There . . .* without its literal location meaning.

252 The existential verb – ('there is/are', etc.)

In Welsh the existential forms of **bod** *be* are 3rd pers. sing. only, and the *is/ are, was/were* etc. distinction between singular and plural in English is not reflected in Welsh. The underlying forms for all tenses in use are best presented as a table:

	AFF	INT	NEG
Present	mae	oes?	does dim
Imperfect	roedd	oedd?	doedd dim
Future	bydd	°fydd?	°fydd dim
Conditional	byddai	°fyddai?	°fyddai dim
	basal	°fasai?	°fasai dim

Wedi-tenses are also possible with the existential verb, of which by far the most common is the perfect:

Dim – ('not any') in existential sentences

Examples of usage:

Mae gormod o °bobol fan hyn – awn ni i °rywle arall

There are too many people here – let's go somewhere else

Oes digon o °de ar ôl ar °gyfer y lleill? – *Oes*, dw i'n meddwl

Is there enough tea left for the others? – Yes, I think so

Does dim llawer o °ddisgyblaeth yn yr ysgol 'ma, nag oes?

There isn't much discipline in this school, is there?

Mae creulondeb ofnadwy yn y byd, on'd oes?

There is terrible cruelty in the world, isn't there?

Mae tipyn go lew o °law *wedi bod* yn y nos

There's been quite a bit of rain during the night

Note that the *yes*-answer for questions beginning **Oes . . .?** is, as we might expect (see XLI), **Oes.**

The tag elements for the present existential (. . ., *isn't/aren't there? . . . is/are there?*) *are* . . ., **on'd oes?** and . . ., **nag oes?** Tag elements for other tenses are as for **bod** generally (see XLI).

253   Dim – ('not any') in existential sentences

Note that **dim** is always non-mutated with the existential verb, since it always directly follows the verb itself, instead of waiting until after the subject as would otherwise be the case (except in the special circumstance detailed in §256). It always comes before the noun in existential sentences, and corresponds in this use only to *not any*, *not . . . a* or *no . . .* in English. Compare:

Dydy'r to °ddim yn °ddiogel

The roof isn't safe

Does dim to ar y tŷ

The house has no roof [lit. There is no roof on . . .]

°Fydd y geiriadur °ddim yn °gostus

The dictionary won't be expensive

°Fydd dim geiriadur 'da chi, cofiwch

You won't have a dictionary, mind [lit. There will be no dictionary . . .]

In existential sentences, **dim** can precede both sing. and pl. nouns:

°Fydd dim geiriaduron 'da chi

You won't have (any) dictionaries

If a negative sentence in English can be expressed with *not* (. . .) *any* and make sense, even clumsily, then the existential **dim** is required in Welsh. Applying this test to the above examples, the existential meanings are clearly identifiable:

There is *not any* roof on the house;

There will *not* be *any* dictionary with you;

but: *The roof is *not any* safe;

*The dictionary will *not* be *any* expensive.

Dim may also appear as the first element in focused sentences (see §157(b)).

254 Variant spoken forms of the existential verb

In normal speech, **sdim** is much more commonly heard than the full version does dim.

Mae'n °ddrwg gen i – sdim bara 'da ni ar ôl

Sorry – we haven't got any bread left

Sdim (byd) o'i °le fan hyn, nag oes?

There's nothing wrong here, is there?

Note in the second example that, although the usual expression for *nothing* is dim byd (see §153), in colloquial usage the phrase *There is nothing* can be conveyed by **sdim** alone, optionally dropping the **byd**.

Just as in non-existential uses of **bod**, AFF imperfect roedd . . . is often heard as oedd . . ., making it sound exactly like the INT-form (intonation and context serve to avoid ambiguity in speech). And AFF present mae . . . is just as frequently heard as ma' . . . .

**Differences between existential and
non-existential** bod

To return to our English examples from §251, in Welsh the two sentences
are as follows:

Mae'r teigr yn yr °ardd

Mae teigr yn yr °ardd

with the indefiniteness of the second expressed in Welsh by absence of an
article (see §22). The same is true of plural nouns, which require a different
structure in English (*The children are in the garden/There are children in
the garden*), but not in Welsh:

Mae'r plant yn yr °ardd

Mae plant yn yr °ardd

In each of these two Welsh pairs, the first sentence contains a non-existential form of **bod**, while the second is existential. This is not immediately
apparent in the statement (in the verb-form at least), but is clear if we turn
them into questions, because the present tense 3rd pers. sing. INT forms of
bod differ as to whether or not the use is existential (see §223).

Ydy'r teigr yn yr °ardd?	*Is* the tiger in the garden?
Oes teigr yn yr °ardd?	Is *there* a tiger in the garden?
Ydy'r plant yn yr °ardd?	Are the children in the garden?
Oes plant yn yr °ardd?	Are *there* children in the garden?

The negative versions would also show the distinction:

Dydy'r plant °ddim yn yr °ardd

The children are not in the garden

Does dim plant yn yr °ardd

There are no children in the garden

All of the above applies also to the less common perfect tense of the existential verb, since in Welsh the perfect is nothing more than the present +
wedi (see §268):

Ydy'r tywydd garw wedi bod yn °broblem i chi?

Has the bad weather been a problem for you?

Oes tywydd garw wedi bod fan hyn yn °ddiweddar, 'te?

Have you had bad weather here lately, then? [lit. Has there been . . .]

Dydy'r tywydd garw °ddim wedi bod yn °broblem inni

The bad weather has not been a problem for us

Does dim tywydd garw wedi bod ers misoedd

There's been no bad weather for months

Again, the statement forms of the above examples would both start with **Mae . . .**, which does not in itself distinguish existential from other use.

The verb-forms for other tenses of the existential verbs are not exclusively existential in the way that, for example, **oes?** and **sdim** are, except that **dim** is non-mutated (see §253). The inherent difference in sentence structure, however, remains true for all tenses. Further examples:

Doedd y plant °ddim yn yr ysgol ddoe

The children weren't in school yesterday

Doedd dim plant yn yr ysgol ddoe

There were no children in school yesterday

Mi °fyddai'r adroddiad yn °barod o °fewn wythnos

The report would be ready within a week

Mi °fyddai adroddiad ar ei desg erbyn diwedd y dydd

There would be a report on her desk by the end of the day

Fe °fydd y lluniaeth ar °gael o unarddeg o'r °gloch

The refreshments will be available from 11 o'clock

Fe °fydd lluniaeth ar °gael o unarddeg o'r °gloch

There will be refreshments available from 11 o'clock

Note in the last example that the rules for use or non-use of the affirmative particles **fe°/mi°** with **bod** (see §§213, 214) are unaffected by the existential/non-existential distinction.

256 Optional use of 'na°

English usually marks an existential sentence by using *there* as an adjunct to the verb *be* (see §251), and this construction has been transferred into Welsh, with the adverbial **'na°** *there* being added to existential forms of **bod**. This represents a closer and more literal translation of the English pattern. But while the *there* element is virtually obligatory in English, it is entirely optional in Welsh.

Mae dyn yn y stafell aros

Mae 'na °ddyn yn y stafell aros

There's a man in the waiting room

°Fydd dim dosbarth Cymraeg wythnos nesa

°Fydd 'na °ddim dosbarth Cymraeg wythnos nesa

There'll be no Welsh class next week

257 Oes **or** Ydy?; Does dim **or** Dydy . . . °ddim?

Deciding whether to start an *Is/Are. . .?* question in Welsh with **Oes . . .?** or **Ydy . . .?** is simply a matter of determining whether it is an existential question or not. **Oes** is required if *there* comes as second word in the English sentence, or if it does so in the literal rendering of the English sentence. This last point takes into account patterns where English does not use the existential verb but Welsh does, e.g. to express possession (see XXXVIII).

Exactly the same criteria apply for deciding between **Dydy . . . °ddim** and **Does dim . . . .**

258 **Use of the existential verb with other verbs**

Where an indefinite subject is involved, the existential verb can be used in conjuction with other verbs in much the same way as **bod** generally

Mae 'na °ddyn yn chwilio amdanat ti yn y pentre

There's a man looking for you in the village

Oes rhywun wedi gadael neges i mi bore 'ma?

Has anyone left me a message this morning?

[lit. Is there someone (who) has left me a message . . .]

Does neb yma'n gwybod dim am y peth

No-one here knows anything about it

[lit. There is no-one here (who) knows . . .]

259   **Special uses of the existential verb**

There are two main circumstances where Welsh uses the existential verb and English does not:

(a)   to express possession – because the Welsh phrasing of *I've got a new car* is lit. '*There is* a new car with me'. This is dealt with in full in **XXXVIII**.

(b)   with modal expressions using **rhaid** or **rhaid**-type constructions – because expressions such as *I must* . . . are phrased in Welsh as (literally) '*There is* a necessity for me to . . . .' See §**349**.

260   Gwneud **as an auxiliary**

This common verb meaning *do* is used as an auxiliary (i.e. with another verb) in the following instances:

(a)   to form a past tense (Preterite II – see §**298**)

(b)   to form a future tense (Future III – see §**306**)

(c)   in certain set constructions:

> **Nei di°** . . .**?/Newch chi°** . . .**?** *Will you* . . .*?* (see §**382**)
> **Nawn ni°** . . . *Let's* . . . (see §**307**)

261   Ddaru **auxiliary**

This auxiliary verb is found only in the N and is used solely for forming a past tense (Preterite III – see §**301**).

262–289 PERIPHRASTIC TENSES

262   **Periphrastic tenses – general remarks**

The broad principles of periphrastic tenses in Welsh are outlined in §**210**, as are their syntactic implications in opposition to inflected tenses. For an overview of the tense-system in Welsh showing the relationship and inter-action between periphrastic and influenced tenses, see §**211**.

Most of the periphrastic tenses in Welsh use **bod** *be* as the auxiliary verb and it is these that will be dealt with below. **Gwneud** *do* is used as an auxiliary for alternative periphrastic formations of the preterite and future, and **ddaru** is used in the N for an alternative (and very common) periphrastic preterite. These non-**bod** periphrastic tenses are examined under the inflected preterite (§§298, 301) and the inflected future (§306).

Using traditional terminology, and with possible rough 1st pers. sing. English correspondences given for each, the periphrastic tenses may be grouped into four pairs as follows:

present (with **yn**) (see §263)	(I do, am doing)
perfect (with **wedi**) (see §268)	(I have done)
imperfect (with **yn**) (see §270)	(I was doing)
pluperfect (with **wedi**) (see §273)	(I had done)
future (with **yn**) (see §274)	(I will do)
future perfect (with **wedi**) (see §276)	(I will have done)
conditional (with **yn**) (see §278)	(I would do)
conditional perfect (with **wedi**) (see §288)	(I would have done)

In each pair, both tenses are formally identical in Welsh except that the first uses **yn** to link the auxiliary **bod** to the VN, while the second uses **wedi**. VNs are not mutated after **yn** or **wedi**.

It should be borne in mind here that the above translations are for guidance only. The actual correspondences between Welsh and English tenses are more complex than might be inferred from the above, and are explained separately for each tense below.

The above tenses can be formed with all VNs.

263 Formation of the present tense

This is formed with the present tense of **bod** (see §227) + **yn** + VN of the verb in question. Examples:

Dach chi'n darllen y papur newydd 'na?

Are you reading that paper?

Ydy dy ffrind yn dod 'da ni hefyd?

Is your friend coming with us as well?

Dw i °ddim yn siarad Cymraeg yn rhugl, ond mae ⁿnghymydog i'n helpu fi

I don't speak Welsh fluently, but my neighbour is helping me

Mae tad Ioan yn cystadlu yn y treialon cŵn defaid eleni

Ioan's father is competing in the sheepdog trials this year

Maen nhw'n mynd i Tenerife am °ddeufis

They're going to Tenerife for two months

264 Present tense with present meaning

The most important thing to remember about the Welsh present tense is that it does the job of two distinct tenses in English. These are: *I (do)* and *I am (doing)*. These mean different things in English (the first has a habitual or 'repeated action' sense, while the second has an 'immediate' sense) and are not interchangeable. In Welsh no distinction is made – there is only one form. (In theory, though not so frequently in practice as with the present, this is equally true of all periphrastic tenses). Therefore a present tense sentence can have two translations:

Mae'r dyn 'na'n darllen y Daily Telegraph

(a) That man is reading the *Daily Telegraph*

(b) That man reads the *Daily Telegraph*

The meanings of (a) and (b) are quite distinct in English: (a) describes what the man is doing at the moment, while (b) states a more general fact and implies habitual action with no particular reference to the present (indeed, he might not be reading it at the moment). In this sense, then, the Welsh sentence as it stands is ambiguous (though context or additional words nearly always remove the uncertainty). The difference in the English sentences is even more apparent in the question forms, where again Welsh makes no distinction:

Ydy'r dyn 'na'n darllen y Daily Telegraph?

(a) Is that man reading the *Daily Telegraph*?

(b) Does that man read the *Daily Telegraph*?

Similarly, then, some of the examples in §263 above could have alternative translations, e.g. *Do you read that paper*? (instead of *Are you reading . . .?*). Note that the fourth example has its ambiguity removed by the time-word eleni *this year*, and that not all the examples are capable of alternative translations.

265 Present tense with future meaning

The final example in §263 – Maen nhw'n mynd i Tenerife am °ddeufis – is a case where there can be no present tense ambiguity because the meaning is not present but future (they have not yet gone to Tenerife). This usage is common in English also, and in this case, unusually, the *-ing* form of the present alone is acceptable – i.e. not *They go to Tenerife for two months* – because present time is not involved. The situation is simpler in Welsh, where **Maen nhw'n mynd** can mean (according to context):

	They go	[habitual]
	They are going	[action happening now]
or	*They are going*	[sometime in the future]

266 Present tense with ers *since*

Where a situation is described which began in the past and is still going on now, as in *We've lived in this area for three years* [and we're still here], the conjunction **ers** *since* is used, generally with the present.

Dan ni'n byw yn yr ardal 'ma ers tair blynedd

We've lived in this area for three years [lit. We are living . . . since . . .]

Influence of English, however, makes the perfect an acceptable alternative in this construction in many areas:

Dan ni wedi byw yn yr ardal 'ma ers tair blynedd

The present with **ers** can also correspond to a progressive in English, in which case the alternative will include **wedi bod** (see §289):

Mae Tony'n dysgu Hebraeg °fodern ers blwyddyn

or **Mae Tony wedi bod yn dysgu Hebraeg °fodern ers blwyddyn**

Tony has been learning Modern Hebrew for a year

Asking *How long . . .?* a situation has existed up till now involves **Ers pryd . . .?** (*Since when . . .?*), again with present or perfect alternatives:

	Ers pryd mae Maggie'n gweithio fan hyn?	[pres.]
or	**Ers pryd mae Maggie wedi gweithio fan hyn?**	[perf.]
	How long has Maggie worked here?	

	Ers pryd dych chi i gyd yn aros fan hyn, 'te?	[pres.]
or:	**Ers pryd dych chi i gyd wedi bod yn aros fan hyn, 'te?**	[perf.]
	How long have you all been waiting here, then?	

	Ers pryd mae Elen yn llysieuwraig?	[pres.]
or:	**Ers pryd mae Elen wedi bod yn llysieuwraig?**	[perf.]
	How long has Elen been a vegetarian?	

267   Habitual present

Where a repeated or habitual action, or continuous state, is referred to, Welsh uses the future of **bod**, rather than the present, + **yn** + VN:

'Dda i'n cysgu'n ysgafnach yn yr Ha

I'm a lighter sleeper in the summer

Lle bynnag bydda i bydd y ci

Wherever I am, the dog is

Note in the first example above the common spoken contraction **'dda i** from **bydda i**.

See further §313 for this special use.

268   Formation of the perfect tense

This is formed exactly as the present (see §263), except that **wedi** is used to link **bod** to the VN instead of **yn**. Compare:

Mae'n cymydog *yn gwerthu* ei °dŷ

Our neighbour is selling his house

Mae'n cymydog *wedi gwerthu* ei °dŷ

Our neighbour has sold his house

Dw i'*n hala* llythyr atat ti

I'm sending you a letter

Dw i *wedi hala* llythyr atat ti

I've sent you a letter

Ydyn nhw'*n chwilio* am fflat yn y °dre?

Are they looking for a flat in town?

Ydyn nhw *wedi chwilio* am fflat yn y °dre?

Have they looked for a flat in town?

Dyw Sioned °ddim *yn astudio* llenyddiaeth o °gwbwl

Sioned isn't studying literature at all

Dyw Sioned °ddim *wedi astudio* llenyddiaeth o °gwbwl

Sioned hasn't studied literature at all

It is important to note that the formal difference between the present and perfect in English is much greater than in Welsh – English uses different auxiliaries (and sometimes no auxiliary at all in the present), and also changes the form of the other verb to a participle for the perfect. Welsh always uses **bod** as auxiliary in both tenses, and leaves the VN unchanged. In fact, the only difference between the two in Welsh at all is the choice of **yn** or **wedi**.

The distribution of the perfect in Welsh is almost identical to that of English, with the exception of **ers** explained above (see §266).

269   **Heb° ('without') for °ddim wedi**

The preposition **heb°** *without* is used as an alternative to °**ddim wedi**, especially in the perfect – *He has not bought the tickets* is phrased as *He is without buying the tickets*. This rephrasing requires two changes:

(a)   removing the NEG form of **bod** that would have gone with the °**ddim** and substituting the AFF equivalent (this does not hold true for all speakers, however)

(b)   converting to the SM form of the VN (after **heb°**):

       (Dyw e °ddim wedi prynu'r tocynnau)

       Mae e heb °brynu'r tocynnau

       (some speakers: **Dyw e heb °brynu . . .**)

Further examples:

Dan ni °ddim wedi cysylltu â'r swyddfa 'to

Dan ni heb °gysylltu â'r swyddfa 'to

We haven't got in touch with the office yet

Dyw'r rhan °fwya o'r ymwelwyr °ddim wedi cyrraedd

Mae'r rhan °fwya o'r ymwelwyr heb °gyrraedd

Most of the visitors haven't got here

Stopiwch nhw – dydyn nhw °ddim wedi talu

Stopiwch nhw – maen nhw heb °dalu

Stop them – they haven't paid

This use of **heb°** is also possible with the other **wedi** tenses, for example pluperfect:

Doedden nhw ddim wedi ystyried y goblygiadau

Oedden nhw heb ystyried y goblygiadau

They had not considered the implications

270   Formation of the imperfect tense

This is formed using the imperfect of **bod** (see §§238, 239) + **yn** + VN. It normally corresponds in meaning to the English continuous past *I was . . . -ing* etc. Examples:

O'n i'n cerdded heibio i'r swyddfa °bost pan °weles i fe

I was walking past the post-office when I saw him

Oedd ⁿmrawd i'n sôn am hyn wrthot ti neithiwr?

Was my brother talking to you about this last night?

Doedd y planhigion °ddim yn edrych yn rhy iach

The plants weren't looking too healthy

Sometimes the English simple past is the more appropriate translation, especially where the verb in question is stative rather than dynamic (see Glossary).

O'n i'n meddwl byddai fe'n dweud hynny

I thought he'd say that [rather than: *I was thinking . . .*]

Doedd y tŷ °ddim yn perthyn iddi °bryd hynny

The house didn't belong to her then

[not: *. . . wasn't belonging . . .*]

O't ti'n gwybod °fod Dafydd wedi'i °daro'n sâl?

Did you know that Dafydd had been taken ill?

[not: *Were you knowing . . .?*]

See also §303.

Pan° and the
imperfect
tense

271   Ers **and the imperfect tense**

In sentences with **ers** *since*, the imperfect is often found where a pluperfect would be used in English:

Oedd y teulu'n byw yno ers deng ⁿmlynedd

The family had lived there for ten years

The imperfect with **ers** can also correspond to a progressive in English, in which case the alternative will include **wedi bod** (see §289):

     Roedd y °ddwy'n byw yno ers ugain ⁿmlynedd

or **Roedd y °ddwy wedi bod yn byw yno ers ugain ⁿmlynedd**

     The two of them had been living there for twenty years

Compare §266. See also §503 for **ers**.

272   Pan° **and the imperfect tense**

As I was . . . -ing etc. can be translated using **pan** *when* + the imperfect:

Pan o'n i'n mynd i'r gwely, °ges i °ganiad ffôn gynno fo

As I was going to bed, I got a phone-call from him

For an alternative construction for *as I was . . . -ing* with **wrth°**, see §503.

273   Formation of the pluperfect tense

This is formed exactly as the imperfect (see §270), except that **wedi** is used to link **bod** to the VN instead of **yn**. Compare:

O'n i'n *siarad* ag e y diwrnod o'r blaen

I was speaking to him the day before

O'n i *wedi siarad* ag e y diwrnod o'r blaen

I had spoken to him the day before

Doedd hi °ddim *yn gofalu*'n iawn am yr anifeiliaid

She wasn't looking after the animals properly

Doedd hi °ddim *wedi gofalu*'n iawn am yr anifeiliaid

She hadn't looked after the animals properly

O'ch chi'n *sgrifennu* ati hi'n rheolaidd?

Were you writing to her regularly?

O'ch chi *wedi sgrifennu* ati hi'n rheolaidd?

Had you written to her regularly?

274   **Formation of the future tense**

The periphrastic future (Future II) is formed with the future of **bod** (see §246) + **yn** + VN. Examples:

Bydd y gweddill yn cysgu yn y pebyll

The rest will sleep in the tents

°Fydd Sioned °ddim yn mynd i'r °Ŵyl eleni

Sioned won't be going to the Festival this year

Fe °fyddwch chi'n gweld ar unwaith beth maen nhw wedi °wneud i'r lolfa

You'll see at once what they've done to the lounge

Mi °fyddwn ni'n trafod hyn oll gyda'n cyfreithwyr yfory

We'll discuss all this with our lawyers tomorrow

Byddan nhw'n dod â'r dogfenni angenrheidiol yfory

They'll bring the necessary documents tomorrow

Note that there is the same ambiguity of translation (between continuous and non-continuous) with Future II as with the present: **Bydd y gweddill yn cysgu** . . . can mean either *The rest will sleep* . . . or *The rest will be sleeping* . . ., and similarly for most instances of Future II.

This periphrastic tense is also used as a habitual present – **Bydda i'n mynd yno °bob wythnos** *I go there every week*. See §313.

For Future I (inflected), see §304.

275 **'Will you . . .?'**

It is worth remembering with the future that some sentences beginning *Will you . . .?* in English are ambiguous: *Will you call round tomorrow?*' can be (a) a simple question about a future event, or (b) a polite request (since the formula for these in English uses *Will you . . .?*' with no particular sense of future). There are two possible translations for this in Welsh, then, depending on the sense:

(a)   **°Fyddwch chi'n galw draw yfory?**

(b)   **Newch chi °alw draw yfory?**

(and similarly for **ti** modes of address – **°Fyddi di'n . . .?; Nei di° . . .?**) Polite requests with **Nei di°/Newch chi°** are dealt with under §382.

276 **Formation of the future perfect**

This is formed in exactly the same way as Future II (see §274), except that **wedi** is used to link **bydda i** etc. to the VN instead of **yn**. Compare:

Bydda i'n *gadael* cyn i ti °gyrraedd, mae'n °debyg

I'll probably leave before you arrive

Bydda i *wedi gadael* erbyn i ti °gyrraedd, mae'n °debyg

I'll probably have left by the time you arrive

Further examples of the future perfect:

°Fydd Caryl wedi ffonio drwodd erbyn hyn?

Will Caryl have phoned through by now?

Trwy ennill yr hawl, fe °fydd y cwmni wedi cyflymu'r °broses o °werthu soseri lloeren

In winning the right, the company will have speeded up the process of selling satellite dishes

°Fyddan nhw °ddim wedi cael cyfle i °ddadlwytho 'to

They won't have had a chance to unload yet

Mi °fyddwch chi i gyd wedi derbyn copïau o'r adroddiad erbyn hyn

You will all have received copies of the report by now

277   The conditional tense

While the conditional (*would* . . .) is usually formed with the conditional of **bod** (see §248) + yn + VN, on the same principles as the other periphrastic tenses preceding, its status is rather more complex for the following reasons:

(a)   There are two sets of conditional forms of **bod** (see §248) To some extent they are interchangeable, but there are some important differences in usage. This is also true, therefore, for verbs using them as auxiliaries.

(b)   An inflected conditional does exist in Welsh, and is given preference in certain well-defined circumstances. It is dealt with under inflected tenses (see §§314–319).

(c)   *If*-sentences sometimes require a conditional, and sometimes not. For convenience, the problems this question presents for the English speaker, and their solutions, are discussed under the conditional (see §279ff. below).

278   Formation and meaning of the conditional tense

As explained above, the principles of the periphrastic conditional are the same as for other periphrastic tenses: **byddwn i** etc. or **baswn i** etc. (see §248) are used with yn + VN. Examples:

Mi °fyddech chi'n aros amdano fe trwy'r dydd, credwch chi fi!

You'd be waiting for him all day, believe me!

°Fasai'r °ddau °ddyn draw fan 'na'n helpu ni, tybed?

I wonder would those two men over there help us?

°Fyddai neb yn rhoi °fawr o °goel ar hynny

Nobody would give much credence to that

Sometimes the conditional translates English *should* – see §339.

The **byddwn** conditional (but not the **baswn**) is also used to describe a habitual action in the past – byddwn i'n mynd yno °bob wythnos *I used to go there every week*. See also §319.

279 'If-sentences': conditional or not?

All *if*-sentences by definition imply conditions, but these conditions fall into two broad types:

(a) 'open' conditions – where the condition may possibly be fulfilled;

(b) 'closed' or 'unreal' conditions – where the condition is regarded as unlikely or impossible to fulfil.

These two types may be illustrated in English as follows:

(a) *If Freddie comes to the party tonight, I'll tell him.*

(b) *If Freddie came* [or *were coming*] *to the party tonight, I'd tell him.*

The sense difference between the two is that:

(a) implies that Freddie may well be coming, even though the speaker doesn't yet know one way of the other, while

(b) implies that Freddie definitely isn't coming – the speaker would tell him, but he can't.

The difference in form is best seen in the part of the sentence without *if*:

(a) has a future – *I'll tell him*, while

(b) has a conditional – *I'd tell him*.

The *if*-clauses in these sentences, however, are misleading because English does not use the same tense in both clauses – i.e. we do not say in English 'If Freddie will come to the party, I will tell him', nor do we say (at least in British English) 'If Freddie would come to the party, I would tell him'. But since all *if*-sentences have an accompanying second non-*if* clause (giving details of what will or would happen on the condition stated), this non-*if* test in English is sufficient in itself to determine whether a conditional is required in Welsh, because whatever is used here in English is used in both

217

if and non-*if* parts in Welsh. Generally the relationship between *if*-sentences in the two languages is as follows:

open conditions:	(E) if + present, future in other clause
	(W) if + future, future in other clause
closed conditions:	(E) if + past, conditional in other clause
	(W) if + conditional, conditional in other clause

Note, incidentally, that the order of the 'if-' and 'non-if' clauses can be reversed with no change of sense: *If we're late, they'll be cross* or *They'll be cross if we're late.* This is as true in Welsh as in English.

Welsh, then, has the option of *if* + future (for neutral conditions) or *if* + conditional (for hypothetical conditions); but it draws an even sharper distinction between the two than does English, because the word 'if' itself is different in each case: **os** (open) and **pe** (closed). In other words, the choice in Welsh is **os** + future or **pe** + conditional.

The example open sentence above is therefore:

> **Os daw Freddie i'r parti, weda i wrtho**

or   **Os bydd Freddie'n dod i'r parti, bydda i'n deud wrtho**

depending on whether Future I or II is chosen (any combination in either or both parts is in fact possible).

The closed *if*-sentence, however, cannot be attempted until the mechanics of **pe** have been investigated.

280   Pe ('if') in closed conditions

Pe is used not only with both forms of the conditional of **bod** listed in §248 (**baswn i** etc.), but also with a number of variations on the theme. For example, *if I were* can appear in spoken Welsh not only as

> **pe byddwn i**

and   **pe baswn i**

but also as:

> **pe bawn i**
>
> **pe tawn i**

and   **pe taswn i**

Note that all these have the same unreality ending -wn i (see §§290–1), and are conjugated exactly the same way as **byddwn/baswn**; but **pe bawn i** and **pe tawn i** lose the -a- before 3rd pers. sing. ending -ai, i.e not *pe baai but **pe bai**.

The alternative forms including t- are distinctive enough without the **pe** for *it* to be omitted in normal speech, so **tawn i** and **taswn i** are heard for *if I were*.

Pe byddwn i and (**pe**) **taswn i** are promoted in schools and officially, but all variants are likely to be encountered in one part of Wales or another.

The closed condition example sentence, therefore, might read:

>**Pe byddai Freddie'n dod i'r parti, byddwn i'n deud wrtho**

or

>**Tasai Freddie'n dod i'r parti, swn** (= baswn, see §248(e)) **i'n deud wrtho**

with other versions possible. Note also that there is nothing to stop, say, **byddwn** appearing in one half of the sentence and (**pe**) **taswn** in the other, though learners are generally advised to use either both -dd- forms or both -s- forms in the one sentence.

Further examples:

>**Byddai Eleri'n pasio'i ʰphrawf pe bai ychydig mwy o hyder 'da hi**
>Eleri would pass her test if she had a bit more confidence

>**Basai fo'n mynd o'i °go tasai fo'n clywed 'ny** (N)
>He'd go mad if he heard that

>**Pe bawn i'n rhoid yr arian i ti, °fyddet ti'n prynu fe drosta i?**
>If I gave you the money, would you buy it for me?

>**Se fe °ddim yn ymddwyn fel 'na tasai ei °gariad yn y stafell**
>He wouldn't behave like that if his girlfriend was in the room

>**Taswn i yn dy °le di, swn i °ddim yn cymryd hwnna'n °ganiataol**
>I wouldn't take that for granted if I were you [lit. if I were in your place]

281 Non-use of periphrastic conditional

The modals **gallu/medru** (see §329) and **hoffi/leicio/caru** (see §341) although they can be used with **byddwn/baswn**, are more likely to be found with unreality endings (see §§290, 291): **gallwn i** rather than **byddwn i'n gallu**. Both are heard, however.

The four irregular verbs **mynd, dod, gwneud** and **cael** have special conditional forms (see §§315–317) (some of them restricted to certain dialect areas), which are often heard instead of periphrastic constructions – **Nelwn i mo hynny** *I wouldn't do that* as well as **Swn i ddim yn gwneud hynny**. Again, both are current usage.

Otherwise, the inflected conditional (see §314) is something of a rarity in the modern language, except in certain constructions with more common verbs. These days °**Fyddwn i °ddim yn byta hynny** is more likely than °**Fytwn i mo hynny** for *I wouldn't eat that*. But see §319 for details and exceptions.

282 Os ('if') in open conditions

As explained in §279, open conditions are generally expressed with **os** + future. This can be Future I (inflected) or II (periphrastic), but Future I is neater and is often preferred, at least in the *if*-clause – if anything, Future II is more likely in the non-*if* clause. But all this is a matter more of frequency than correctness. Examples:

Os °gymeri di'r pecynnau 'ma, byddwn ni'n rhoi'r lleill yn ôl yn y car

If you take these packages, we'll put the others back in the car

Os dewch chi'n °gynnar, bydd digon o °fwyd i °bawb, mae'n °debyg

If you come early there'll probably be enough food for everyone

Os galwi di draw bore fory, bydd y pethau 'da fi yn °barod i ti

If you call round tomorrow morning I'll have the things ready for you

Note: the **gwneud**-future (**na i°** etc. – see §306) is also possible, especially in the non-*if* clause where intention is implied:

Os digwyddith hyn 'to, na i °roi gwybod i chi ar unwaith

If this happens again I'll let you know at once

283 Os **and tenses other than future**

The inherent impossibility of closed conditions makes time an irrelevant factor for them (for this reason they always occur with unreality verbs and endings). Open conditions, on the other hand, can refer to events that:

will happen (*if he comes tomorrow*)

are happening (*if he is still looking at me*)

have happened (*if she has already arrived*)

For this reason, **os** is more versatile with regard to tenses used after it than pe.

284 Os **and the present tense**

While the future is very common in open *if*-clauses (because they often refer to events that have not yet happened), the present is by no means excluded if the sense demands it. Note that, in this case, 3rd pers. sing. is **ydy/yw** and not **mae**; and 3rd pers. pl. is **ydyn**, not **maen**.

Os yw Gwenith yn sâl heddiw, nawn ni °ohirio popeth tan yfory

If Gwenith is ill today, we'll put everything off till tomorrow

In this example, the implication is clearly that Gwenith is ill at the time of speaking, and so the present is appropriate in the *if*-clause. Further examples:

Chi sy ar °fai os dyn ni ar y ffordd anghywir

It's your fault if we're on the wrong road

Os dw i'n cofio'n iawn, yn y stryd nesa rhywle maen nhw'n byw

If I remember rightly, they live somewhere on the next street

285 Os **and the perfect tense**

The perfect is also used after **os** if the sense requires:

Os ydyn nhw wedi camddeall rhywbeth, esbonia fe 'to iddyn nhw

If they have misunderstood something, explain it to them again

Os ydw i wedi camddeall eich dadl fan'na, dwedwch os gwelwch yn °dda

If I have misunderstood your argument there, please tell me

221

Os ydy hi wedi cyrraedd yn °barod, fe °welwch chi ei ʰchar tu allan

If she's already arrived, you'll see her car outside

286 Os and the future perfect tense

The future perfect can appear after os where a perfect tense event is viewed in advance:

Os bydd hi wedi ailfeddwl pan ffoniwch chi heno, rhowch °wybod i mi

If she's had second thoughts when you phone tonight, let me know

Here the event of the subject changing her mind is not perceived as having happened at the time of speaking (therefore **bydd**), but is anticipated perhaps to have happened (**wedi**) by the time the phone call is made.

287 Os na° . . . – negative open conditions

Negative open conditions use **os na°** (or MM) (**nad** before radical vowels) with optional °**ddim** after the verb:

Os na °driwch chi nawr, °gewch chi °ddim cyfle eto

If you don't try now, you won't get another chance

Os nad yw'ch ffrind yn °fodlon helpu, pam °fod e fan 'ma?

If your friend isn't willing to help, why is he here?

Os na °ddôn nhw cyn hir mi °fydd hi'n rhy hwyr

If they don't come soon it'll be too late

288 Formation of the conditional perfect tense

The conditional perfect (*would have* . . .) is formed in exactly the same way as the conditional (see §278) except that **wedi** is used to link **byddwn/ baswn**, etc. to the VN instead of **yn**. Compare:

°Fasai hi °ddim *yn caniatáu*'r °fath °bethau

She wouldn't allow such things

°Fasai hi °ddim *wedi caniatáu*'r °fath °bethau

She wouldn't have allowed such things

Further examples:

Byddai'n gweithwyr ni wedi gwneud y jobyn yn °wahanol

Our workers would have done the job differently

°Fyddet ti wedi derbyn y cynnig?

Would you have accepted the offer?

**Wedes i wrtho fo y baswn i wedi trefnu'r °daith 'n hun taswn i
wedi gwybod amdani**

I told him I would have organized the trip myself if I had known about it

In the last example, an *if*-clause appears with **wedi** – compare the following:

Taswn i/Pe byddwn i/Pe bawn i, etc. **'n gwybod**	*If I knew*
Taswn i/Pe byddwn i/Pe bawn i, etc. **wedi gwybod**	*If I had known*

Os cannot be used with the conditional perfect, any more than it can with the conditional (see §279).

Further examples of conditional perfect *if*-clauses:

Sen ni wedi llwyddo pe byddai'r glaw wedi peidio am awr neu °ddwy

We would have managed it if the rain had stopped for an hour or two

**Fe °fyddai'r °dre 'ma wedi edrych yn °dra gwahanol pe byddai'r
ffatri °ddim wedi'i sefydlu ochor draw i'r afon**

This town would have looked quite different if the factory hadn't been set
up on the other side of the river

289 ... wedi bod yn ... – perfect continuous tenses

The addition of **bod yn** in **wedi**-tenses gives them a continuous sense, corresponding to English *have been ... -ing, had been ... -ing* etc. Apart from this additional element, they work in exactly the same way as ordinary **wedi**-tenses. Compare:

Mae'r °bobol 'na wedi dysgu Cymraeg

Those people have learnt Welsh

Mae'r °bobol 'na wedi bod yn dysgu Cymraeg

Those people have been learning Welsh

Dan ni wedi aros yn °ddigon hir rŵan

We've waited long enough now

Dan ni wedi bod yn aros am oriau

We've been waiting for hours

Oedd e wedi darllen y llyfr o'r blaen

He had read the book before

Oedd e wedi bod yn darllen y llyfr drwy'r bore

He had been reading the book all morning

Other tenses are possible, though less common:

Byddwn ni wedi siarad ag e . . .

We will have spoken to him . . .

Byddwn ni wedi bod yn siarad ag e . . .

We will have been speaking to him . . .

Sa fo wedi galw . . . (N)

He would have called . . .

Sa fo wedi bod yn galw . . . (N)

He would have been calling . . .

Pe byddet ti wedi teithio . . .

If you had travelled . . .

Pe byddet ti wedi bod yn teithio . . .

If you had been travelling . . .

290–347 INFLECTED TENSES

290 Inflected tenses – general remarks

There are three sets of endings or inflections for the verb in spoken Welsh. All are added to the verb-stem (see §§205–9) in the same way, and the verb-stem does not change, except for **bod** *be*, which can use two distinct stems (see §218(e)), and, on the periphery of the system (for the spoken language, at least), the non-past impersonal/autonomous **-ir**, which sometimes alters a vowel in the stem (see §370(b)). Each set of inflections comprises six distinctive forms, corresponding to 1st, 2nd and 3rd persons sing. and pl. The personal pronouns follow immediately on the inflections, and are omitted only in certain restricted circumstances (see §293(b)).

Different time/aspect profiles are conveyed by the different sets of inflections:

(a) NON-PAST time

(b) PAST time

(c) UNREALITY

Non-past may be taken to mean present/future, though to all intents and purposes the predominant sense in which these inflections are used nowadays is the future. Some instances of these endings with present meaning will be pointed out.

Past carries the sense not only of time, but also of completion of the action.

Unreality is used in hypothetical situations, or where the action is thought unlikely to happen, or is impossible.

291 Inflections for non-past, past and unreality

		Non-past	Past	Unreality
Sing.	1st	-a	-es	-wn
	2nd	-i	-est	-et
	3rd	-ith(/iff)	-odd	-ai
Pl.	1st	-wn	-on	-en
	2nd	-wch	-och	-ech
	3rd	-an	-on	-en

The past and unreality sets are subject to a certain degree of phonetic variation in the spoken language. This aspect will be treated in the relevant sections.

292–303 THE PRETERITE TENSE

292 General remarks

The preterite is the only tense of the verb in Welsh which makes no use of bod (the future uses bod as an option – see §274). In meaning, it generally corresponds to the simple past tense in English, but with the added connotation – not necessarily true in the English tense – of completed action. It has already been mentioned (see §211) that the use and distribution of tenses in Welsh and English is broadly parallel. In particular it should be noted that the relationship between the preterite and perfect (see §268) in Welsh is almost exactly the same as that between the *saw* – *has seen* alternatives in English (with a very few exceptions – see §266). In practical terms, then, one can be fairly sure that if the simple past (*saw*) option is used in English then the corresponding Welsh usage will be the preterite.

The preterite appears in Welsh, however, in three different guises, with little to choose between them (except that one is restricted to N dialects).

293   Inflected preterite (Preterite I)

The standard colloquial language and the media favour an inflected form – that is, endings added to the verb-stem (see §205–9). Except for the four irregulars **cael, mynd, dod** and **gwneud** (see §296), and **bod** (see §243), these endings are the same for all verbs:

	Singular	Plural
1st	**-es (i)**	**-on (ni)**
2nd	**-est (ti)**	**-och (chi)**
3rd	**-odd (e/hi)**	**-on (nhw)**

Notes:

(a)   1st pers. sing. and 2nd pers. sing. are often spelt **-ais** and **-aist** respectively. In general this does not reflect modern pronunciation.

(b)   In spoken language, the personal pronouns following the verb are nearly always retained, though the 3rd pers. sg. **-odd** is sometimes used on its own if the subject has already been previously stated and is therefore clear from context, e.g.:

> **Ond beth am Dewi? - Fe °gyrhaeddodd yn °gynnar.**
> But what about Dewi? - (He) arrived early.

In writing, particularly in 'elevated' style, all pronouns are very frequently omitted, giving for example **torrais** for **torres i** *I cut.*

(c)   In some parts of Wales, an **-s-** is sometimes inserted between the stem and the ending in the plural forms, e.g. **gwelson ni** *we saw* for **gwelon ni; °glywsoch chi?** *did you hear?* for **°glywoch chi?**

(d)   In some parts of SE Wales, **-ws** is heard instead of 3rd pers. sing. **-odd: Fe atebws e** *he answered* (= **Fe atebodd e**).

294   Questions with inflected past tense

Questions in the past (beginning with *Did . . .?* in English) are expressed
simply using SM on the verb:

Gweles i	I saw
°Weles i?	Did I see?
Collodd e'r arian	He lost the money
°Gollodd e'r arian?	Did he lose the money?

But in practice this distinction seems to have been long disregarded in
natural speech, with the SM being used increasingly with all verb-forms
carrying endings (except perhaps the imperative), so one is quite likely to
hear °**Weles i ti ddoe** *I saw you yesterday* as often, if not more often, than
Gweles i ti ddoe.

A similar uncertainty exists with the negative. Officially, one is supposed to
use AM where possible, but otherwise SM. This is the so-called Mixed
Mutation. So *I didn't lose anything* would be ʰ**Cholles i °ddim byd** (AM
possible with **C**), while *I didn't see anything* would be °**Weles i °ddim byd**
(no AM possible with **G**, so SM, which is possible). But so many native
speakers use °**Golles i °ddim byd** here that it is clear that SM is gaining
ground in all situations. The media tend to follow the more complex
pattern, though erratically.

All of the above applies equally to the other inflected tense, the Future I (see
§304).

295   Mo **with direct objects**

'Specific' direct objects (see §35 for definition of 'specific' in this context) of
negative inflected verbs – either preterite or future – require **mo**, a contraction
of **dim o** (*nothing of*), by a rule of Welsh which does not allow **dim** to be
directly followed by a 'specific' noun or pronoun:

> °**Welson ni °ddim + y °ddamwain**

becomes   °**Welson ni *mo*'r °ddamwain**

We didn't see the accident

°**Dalodd e** °**ddim + y bil**

becomes   °**Dalodd e *mo'r* bil**

He didn't pay the bill

With pronouns, **mo** combines to give the following forms:

Singular	*Plural*
mo(ho)no (f)i	**mo(ho)non ni**
mo(ho)not ti	**mo(ho)noch chi**
mo(ho)no fo	**mo(ho)nyn nhw**
mo(ho)ni hi	
°**Welsoch chi mono fo?**	Didn't you see him?
Helpodd Sian mono fi	Sian didn't help me

Sometimes the longer forms **mohono i, mohonot ti** etc. (cf. **o**, §462) are heard.

296   **Irregular preterites** – mynd, gwneud, dod **and** cael

These four irregular verbs are best approached initially as sharing the same basic pattern. In fact, regional variation complicates the picture somewhat, but this is a matter for the individual and depends on local usage. The simplest pattern is as follows (non-mutated forms for **dod** and **cael**):

		mynd	*gwneud*	*dod*	*cael*
Sing.	1st	**es i** (I went)	**nes i** (I did)	**des i** (I came)	**ces i** (I got)
	2nd	**est ti**	**nest ti**	**dest ti**	**cest ti**
	3rd	**aeth e/hi**	**naeth e/hi**	**daeth e/hi**	**caeth e/hi**
Pl.	1st	**aethon ni**	**naethon ni**	**daethon ni**	**caethon ni**
	2nd	**aethoch chi**	**naethoch chi**	**daethoch chi**	**caethoch chi**
	3rd	**aethon nhw**	**naethon nhw**	**daethon nhw**	**caethon nhw**

Notes:

(a)   In some parts of Wales, **cael** does not go like the other three: 3rd pers. sing. **cafodd**, 1st pers. pl. **cafon** or **cawson**, 2nd pers. pl. **cafoch** or **cawsoch**, 3rd pers. pl. **cafon** or **cawson**; **cafodd, cawsoch** and **cawson** are generally promoted as standard these days.

(b) Both **dod** and particularly **cael** are very frequently heard with SM in virtually all circumstances, reflecting general practice with inflected verbs (see §11(d)): °**ddes i** *I came,* °**ges i** *I got.*

(c) Inflected forms of **gwneud** nearly always drop both the **g-** and the following **-w-**. Quite often the VN does the same (**neud**).

(d) Many regions have **ddôth e/hi** for **ddaeth e/hi** *he/she came.*

(e) Many regions replace **-th-** in the pl. with **-s-**: **(a)eson nhw** *they went* instead of **aethon nhw**; **pryd d(a)esoch chi?** *when did you come?* etc.

(f) The preterite of **gwneud** is itself used to form an alternative preterite for other verbs (see §298).

Examples of the irregular preterites:

Pryd °gaeth e'r neges?

When did he get the message?

Be' °gest ti i 'Dolig eleni?

What did you get for Christmas this year?

Fe aethon ni mas am awr neu °ddwy, ac wedyn dod yn ôl

We went out for an hour or two, and then came back

Dw i'n eitha siwr na °ddôth neb draw wrth i mi °fod 'ma

I am fairly sure no-one came round while I was here

Pwy naeth y coffi 'ma? Mae'n erchyll!

Who made this coffee? It's horrible!

Mi °gawson ni amser hyfryd iawn yn yr °Ŵyl

We had a lovely time at the Festival

Be' naethoch chi ar ôl graddio?

What did you do after you got your degree?

297 Alternative (periphrastic) formations of the preterite

There are two alternative methods of forming the preterite in spoken Welsh – one using **gwneud** *do* as an auxiliary (Preterite II), and the other using **ddaru**. It is fair to say that, though they are hardly ever encountered in more formal situations, they are every bit as common in speech as the inflected described in §293. They have three distinct advantages, incidentally, for the learner: (a) they avoid the use of the verb-stem, which in many verbs has to be learnt and remembered; (b) they obviate the need for the particle **mo**, for reasons outlined below; (c) the uncertainty over mutations which is undeniably part and parcel of the Preterite I (see §294) does not arise with auxiliaries (see below).

298   Preterite with gwneud (Preterite II)

For this method we require the preterite of **gwneud** itself *(I did, you did, etc.)*

	Singular	*Plural*
1st	**nes i**	**naethon ni**
2nd	**nest ti**	**naethoch chi**
3rd	**naeth o/hi**	**naethon nhw**

Note in passing the fixed SM, and that, in speech, not only the **g-** but also the **-w-** are dropped from this very common verb. Spellings such as **wnes i** reflect what would be a distinctly stilted and over-careful pronunciation.

From here, the process is completed by adding the appropriate verb in its dictionary (VN) form, but with SM after the preceding pronoun subjects (there is no **'n** to block it, because **nes i** etc. is not part of the verb **bod** – see §§15, 215). In effect, this construction turns *I paid* (°**dales i**) into *I did pay* (**nes i** °**dalu**) with no difference in meaning. Note that there is a difference between the two in English, with *I did pay* serving as an emphatic. There is generally no such connotation in Welsh, and by and large the two methods are interchangeable. See further §300.

The affirmative particles **fe°/mi°** are not normally used with the **gwneud** preterite unless particular emphasis is intended:

   Nes i °dalu *I paid*, **Mi nes i °dalu** *I (really) did pay*.

Therefore, instead of °**weles i** etc. as above (§§293–294), we have instead:

	Singular	*Plural*
1st	**nes i °weld**	**naethon ni °weld**
2nd	**nest ti °weld**	**naethoch chi °weld**
3rd	**naeth o/hi °weld**	**naethon nhw °weld**

The question forms are exactly the same except for the question-mark at the end, and differing intonation: **Naethoch chi °weld . . .?** – *Did you see . . .?*

The negative forms simply require **°ddim** after the pronoun, which blocks the SM to the following VN: **Nes i °ddim talu** *I didn't pay.* And because in this construction the **°ddim** finds itself between the auxiliary verb and the VN, it cannot immediately precede a specified direct object, and so no use of **mo** is required. Compare:

°Welson ni *mo'*<u>r ffilm</u> ar y teledu neithiwr

Naethon ni *°ddim* gweld <u>y ffilm</u> ar y teledu neithiwr

We didn't see the film on TV last night

299   Gwneud-**preterite used for focus**

This auxiliary preterite usage involves, as has been seen, the free-standing VN of the main verb, and therefore also allows the position in the sentence of this main verb to be altered. This is a technique most often associated in Welsh with focus (see §17 for a more general discussion). Compare the following:

Naeth o °wrthod

He refused [normal word-order – neutral statement]

Gwrthod naeth o

He *refused* [focused element placed in initial position]

A wider idea can be focused in this way, by placing several elements in the focus position:

Gwrthod y cynnig naeth o	He *refused the offer*
Gwrthod y cynnig yn llwyr naeth o	He *completely refused the offer*
Dim ond gofyn nes i	I *only asked!* (**dim ond** – only)

This useful technique, which is also possible, though less common, with the **gwneud**-future (see §306), and with periphrastic tenses using **bod**, is unavailable with inflected tenses.

It should be noted that Welsh and English share a dual (inflected v. periphrastic) system of forming the preterite:

[I – inflected]	**agores i**	*I opened*	[AFF]
	agores i?	**opened I?*	[INT]
	agores i °ddim	**I opened not*	[NEG]
[II – periphrastic]	**nes i agor**	*(I did open)*	[AFF]
	nes i agor?	*did I open?*	[INT]
	nes i °ddim agor	*I did not open*	[NEG]

Where the two languages part on this, however, is that in spoken Welsh the two types are, to all intents and purposes, entirely interchangeable. All six Welsh forms given above as examples are perfectly normal, and comprise mutually equivalent pairs for AFF, INT and NEG. Modern English, on the other hand, uses only a partial combination of the two systems to fill out the minimum requirement of AFF, INT and NEG, discarding two others (*) and reserving *I did open* for a special use (emphasis).

In practice, this means that any English sentence involving a preterite can be translated in two ways in Welsh – either by the inflected method or the periphrastic:

AFF   Fiona bought a new car for her sister last week

[infl.]   **°Brynodd Fiona °gar newydd i'w chwaer wythnos diwetha**

[peri.]   **Naeth Fiona °brynu car newydd i'w chwaer wythnos diwetha**

INT   Did you see a man go past just now?

[infl.]   **°Welsoch chi °ddyn yn mynd heibio gynnau?**

[peri.]   **Naethoch chi °weld dyn yn mynd heibio gynnau?**

NEG   I didn't agree to the conditions in the end

[infl.]   **°Gytunes i °ddim i'r amodau yn y diwedd**

[peri.]   **Nes i °ddim cytuno i'r amodau yn y diwedd**

Since both types are interchangeable in Welsh, with **Agores i** and **Nes i agor,** for example, both translating *I opened,* the distinction expressed in English between *I opened* and *I did open* is lost. The emphatic sense of *I did open* must be conveyed by use of the affirmative particle **fe°/mi°** (see §213).

Preterite with ddaru

Ddaru (fixed SM) is another auxiliary, originally with the meaning *happened*. It is used widely in N regions to form the preterite, and has the virtue of greater simplicity even than the **gwneud** method outlined in §298.

	Singular	*Plural*
1st	**ddaru mi °weld**	**ddaru ni °weld**
2nd	**ddaru ti °weld**	**ddaru chi °weld**
3rd	**ddaru o/hi °weld**	**ddaru nhw °weld**

Ddaru, therefore, does not change throughout, but simply adds the pronoun (or other subject, of course) and then the VN with SM. Questions and negatives are done in the same way as with **gwneud**:

Ddaru chi °weld . . .? (N)

Did you see . . .?

Ddaru ni °ddim gweld y ffilm neithiwr (N)

We didn't see the film last night

Sometimes it is found on its own, where the VN is understood:

Dwn 'im ddaru hi neu °beidio (N)

I don't know if she did or not

An important point to remember with these two auxiliary constructions is that the VN must have SM in the statement and question patterns because it follows the subject:

Naeth Sioned °dalu'r bil trydan o'r diwedd p'nawn 'ma

Sioned paid the electricity bill at last this afternoon

Naeth Sioned °dalu'r bil?

Did Sioned pay the bill?

Ddaru'r un ola °ddiffodd y golau wrth °fynd allan (N)

The last one switched the light off as he went out

Ddaru'r un ola °ddiffodd y golau? (N)

Did the last one switch the light off?

'Yes/no' answers to preterite questions

If a *yes/no* question is phrased using the preterite in Welsh, by whichever method, the answer *yes* will be **do**, and the answer *no* **naddo**, regardless of person:

Wedsoch chi wrthyn nhw bod ni'n dod? – Do
Did you tell them we were coming? – Yes

Nest ti °basio dy °brawf gyrru, 'te? – Do
Did you pass your driving test, then? – Yes

Ddaru nhw °fynd i Iwerddon yn y diwedd? – Naddo (N)
Did they go to Ireland in the end? – No

For *yes/no* answers generally, see XLI–XLIII.

303   Limitations on use of preterite

With certain types of verb the preterite is not normally used. These are mostly stative verbs expressing mental or physical states or other circumstances that cannot be thought of as actions – they use the imperfect (see §270) instead. This is unlike the English usage, where such criteria make no difference in the past tense: *He ran* (action) and *He knew* (mental state) are both correct, but in Welsh they are rendered as follows:

°Redodd e
Naeth e °redeg
Ddaru o °redeg (N)
He ran

Oedd e'n gwybod
He knew [lit. He *was knowing*]

Other common stative verbs are **nabod** *know* (*a person*) (but not the related verb **adnabod** which means *recognize* and is therefore an action), **perthyn** *belong*, **meddwl** or **credu** *think*, **hoffi** and **leicio** *like*, **ofni** *fear* and **poeni** *worry*.

Oedd y tŷ 'ma'n perthyn i'w °deulu am °flynyddoedd °lawer
His house belonged to his family for many years

O'n i'n meddwl byddai rhaid aros tan y Gwanwyn
I thought we would have to wait till spring

This is often not such a hard-and-fast rule, however, and the influence of English usage sometimes makes itself felt – **meddwl** in particular is not infrequently heard in the preterite – **meddylies i** instead of **o'n i'n meddwl**; on the other hand **hoffes i / leicies i** *I liked* (for **o'n i'n hoffi / o'n i'n leicio**) sounds distinctly odd (not to say wrong) to many speakers, and should probably not be imitated.

304–313 THE FUTURE TENSE

304 Inflected future (Future I)

The same general principles apply here as for Preterite I (see §293), but with different endings to add to the stem:

	Singular	Plural
1st	**-a (i)**	**-wn (ni)**
2nd	**-i (di)**	**-wch (chi)**
3rd	**-ith (e/hi)**	**-an (nhw)**

Notes:

(a)   The 2nd pers. sing. pronoun is **di** rather than **ti** in the future.

(b)   For the 3rd pers. sing. there is an alternative, though considerably less common, form in **-iff**. This is mainly confined to areas in the S though it can crop up elsewhere.

(c)   The affirmative particles **fe°** and **mi°** can optionally be used with the inflected future: **Mi °wela i chi** *I'll see you*; **Fe ffoniwn ni ti** *We'll phone you*.

305 **Irregular futures** – mynd, gwneud, dod **and** cael

As in the preterite (see §296), these four verbs show a broadly similar pattern, but in the future **dod** deviates in most areas. Standardized forms (non-mutated for **dod** and **cael**) are as follows:

		mynd	*gwneud*	*dod*	*cael*
Sing.	1st	**a i** (I'll go)	**na i** (I'll do)	**do i** (I'll come)	**ca i** (I'll get)
	2nd	**ei di**	**nei di**	**doi di**	**cei di**
	3rd	**eith e/hi**	**neith e/hi**	**daw e/hi**	**ceith e/hi**
Pl.	1st	**awn ni**	**nawn ni**	**down ni**	**cawn ni**
	2nd	**ewch chi**	**newch chi**	**dewch chi**	**cewch chi**
	3rd	**ân nhw**	**nân nhw**	**dôn nhw**	**cân nhw**

Notes:

(a)   In some parts of Wales, **dod** goes like the other three: **da i, dei di, deith e** etc.

(b)   Both **dod** and particularly **cael** are very frequently heard with SM in virtually all circumstances, reflecting general practice with inflected verbs (see §11(d)): **°ddo i** *I'll come*, **os °ga i . . .** *if I (will) get . . .*

(c)   Inflected forms of **gwneud** nearly always drop both the **g-** and the following **-w-**. Quite often the VN does the same (**neud**).

(d)   Many regions have **cewn ni** for **cawn ni: os °gewn ni °ragor** *if we (will) get any more*, and similar variants with **-e-** are heard for **awn, nawn** and **down**.

(e)   In some S areas **aiff** = **eith, naiff** = **neith** and **caiff** = **ceith**. In fact, these S forms tend to be the standard in written colloquial language, but in speech the **-ith** versions are by far the more widespread in Wales as a whole.

(f)   The future of **gwneud** is itself used to form an alternative future (Future III) for other verbs (see §306).

Examples of the irregular futures:

Mi °ddo i hefo chdi rŵan (N)

I'll come (along) with you now

Os na °gewch chi °gyfle i siarad ag e fory, bydd hi'n rhy hwyr

If you don't get a chance to speak to him tomorrow, it'll be too late

Eith hi °ddim hebddat ti

She won't go without you

Be' nei di os eith pethau'n chwith eto?

What'll you do if things [will] go wrong again?

Gobeithio °gei di °deisen °flasus

I hope you (will) get a tasty cake

Mi °ddaw yn °fuan, siwr iawn

(I'm) sure she'll be along soon

Dyna pryd awn ni

That's when we'll go

Nân nhw mo hynny 'to

They won't do that again

Gwneud-
future
(Future III)

306   Gwneud-**future (Future III)**

Just as the preterite of **gwneud** (**nes i** etc. – see §296) can be used as an auxiliary to form the preterite of other verbs (Preterite II: **nes i °weld** *I saw* – see §298), so the inflected future of **gwneud** (**na i** etc. – see §305) can be used to make a future tense of other verbs. But while the **gwneud** preterite can be used in almost all circumstances, the **gwneud** future is more restricted in use.

Future III of **darllen** *read*, then, is:

	Singular	Plural
1st	**na i °ddarllen**	**nawn ni °ddarllen**
2nd	**nei di °ddarllen**	**newch chi °ddarllen**
3rd	**neith e/hi °ddarllen**	**nân nhw °ddarllen**

INT forms are the same, except for intonation. The 2nd pers. sing. and pl. forms **Nei di° . . .?** and **Newch chi° . . .?** are the usual way of phrasing polite requests in Welsh (see §382).

NEG forms simply add **°ddim** after the subject: **na i °ddarllen** *I'll read*, **na i °ddim darllen** *I won't read*. SM is of course transferred from the VN to the **°ddim**, since this now directly follows the subject.

The 1st pers. sing. AFF **Na i° . . .** is particularly common in expressing a definite intention or decision – in this use it exactly mirrors Future I

237

(inflected); and indeed the Future III is best thought of as an alternative to Future I. The **bod** future (Future II) differs from I and III in several important respects – see §§309–313.

307 Future I 1st pers. sing. and pl. used to express intention

Where the use of the future involves some sense of intention on the part of the speaker, the inflected future is more normally the choice than the periphrastic construction with **bod**.

Ffoniwn ni nhw ar ôl cinio	Let's phone them after dinner (or: We'll phone them . . .)
Ffonia i chi o °Gaerdydd	I'll phone you from Cardiff
Awn ni gyda'n gilydd	Let's go together

Another way of expressing this is with the 1st pers. sing. or 1st pers. pl. Future III – Na i° . . ., Nawn ni° . . .

Na i hala'r manylion atoch chi bore 'fory

I'll send you the details in the morning

Nawn ni siarad â fo nes ymlaen

Let's speak to him later (or simply: We'll speak to him later)

See also §§384, 385.

308 Use of mo with negative Future I

As with the inflected preterite, the inflected future in the negative requires **mo** to precede a definite direct object. The reasons for this are the same as for the preterite (see §295), and in the same way **mo** is not needed with auxiliary or periphrastic futures:

Dw i'n teimlo fel rhoi'r gorau i'r swydd! – Ond nei di *mo* hynny, na nei?

I feel like packing the job in! – But you won't do that, will you?

Enillwch chi *mo*'r gêm fel 'ny, °wyddoch chi

You won't win the game like that, you know

but:

Newch chi °*ddim* ennill y gêm . . .

309–313 FUTURE TENSE: INFLECTED (I) OR PERIPHRASTIC (II)?

Note: while the inflected future and the future with **bod** are often used apparently interchangeably, and while the whole question of which to use frequently seems to depend on where you are in Wales, there are certain types of sentence where one or other is more likely.

309   Future i with os . . . and os na° . . .

The inflected future is very common after **os** *if* (open – see §282), although the alternative constructions with **bod** (or **gwneud**) could hardly be considered wrong:

°Fyddwn ni'n iawn os *daw*'r bws yn °brydlon

We'll be OK if the bus comes on time

Os *collwch* chi'r °dderbynneb, °alla i mo'ch helpu chi

If you lose the receipt, I can't help you

Os *eith* hi hebddat ti, rho °wybod i mi

If she goes without you, let me know

Similarly with **os na°** *if . . . not*:

°Ddo i hefo chdi os na °*ga* i °gynnig gwell (N)

I'll come with you if I don't get a better offer

Os na °*fydd* digon o arian 'da ni, bydd rhaid inni ailfeddwl

If we haven't got enough money, we'll have to rethink (lit. 'If there will not be . . .')

Na° . . . in this construction and in **Pam na°** . . .? below is followed by SM, or optionally MM.

The future, rather than the present tense of English, is to be expected after **os**, because most *if . . .* phrases do refer to things that have not yet happened. But the English usage of present with future meaning is common enough these days, and any of the above examples might be heard with the present after **os** (**os** *dych chi'n colli*'r °dderbynneb . . ., **os na** *dw i'n cael* cynnig **gwell**). The inflected future option, however, is neater and somehow more Welsh. There are, of course, cases where an *if . . .* clause does refer to present time, and here the Welsh present would be expected. Compare:

Os ydy Islwyn yn sâl, na i °adael y peth tan yfory

If Islwyn is ill [at the moment], I'll leave it till tomorrow

Os bydd Islwyn yn sâl yfory, rhowch °wybod i mi ar unwaith

If Islwyn is ill tomorrow, let me know at once

Os ydyn nhw i gyd yn °barod, gadewch inni °ddechrau

If all of them are ready, let's begin

Os byddan nhw i gyd yn °barod erbyn tri o'r gloch, byddwn ni'n
gallu dechrau

If all of them are ready by three o'clock, we will be able to begin

310   Future I with pan° . . .

As with **os** *if* above, **pan°** . . . *when* . . . can refer to a future event. In this case English requires a 'present with future meaning', while Welsh generally prefers the future – usually Future I:

Gwenwch i gyd pan °*dynnith* hi'r llun

All smile when she takes the picture

Dw i eisiau i ti ffonio pan °*gyrhaeddi* di yno

I want you to phone when you get there

The present and preterite are, of course, also found after **pan°** . . . where the sense requires it. The additional consideration with the future, however, is that the inflected version is perhaps more common than the periphrastic (and this is usually also true of the preterite with **pan°**).

311   Future I with pam na° . . .?

This is mostly used with the 2nd pers. sing. and 2nd pers. pl. to translate *Why don't you . . .?*:

Pam na °*ddewch* chi draw ar ôl y cyfarfod pwyllgor?

Why don't you come round after the committee meeting?

Pam na °*fwci* di ymlaen llaw a talu wedyn?

Why don't you book in advance and pay later?

Other persons are also possible:

Pam na °ddaw hi'n ôl nes ymlaen?

Why doesn't she come back a bit later on?

312 Future I with present meaning (stative verbs)

With a few verbs expressing state rather than action, the Future I retains its old sense of the present. The most common instance of this in the spoken language is **gweld** *see*:

Gwela i	I see [confirmation of understanding]
°Welwch chi'r dyn acw?	Do you see that man over there?

Note also °Greda i!/ °Goelia i! *I (can) believe it!*:

Dan ni wedi bod wrthi trwy'r nos hefo'r gwaith papur 'ma. - °Greda i!

We've been at this paperwork all night. – I can believe it!

313 Future II used with habitual present sense

The English usage *Every Sunday I will go for a walk on the beach* – meaning not something that you intend to do from now on but rather that you are in the habit of doing, has its counterpart in Welsh, and in this usage the **bod** future (Future II) must be used:

°Fydda i'n mynd am °dro ar y traeth °bob Dydd Sul

Further examples:

Tua hanner awr wedi chwech °fydda i'n codi yn y bore

I get up around half past six in the morning

°Fydda i byth yn sâl

I'm never ill

This last is a particularly good illustration that °**fydda i** etc. need not necessarily have anything to do with the future – the period that the speaker is actually talking about is, if anything, the past, and on the basis of this he is making a general statement. And for this reason the **bod** future is often found in proverbs:

Fel y °fam °fydd y °ferch

The daughter is like the mother (i.e. Like father, like son)

314–320 THE CONDITIONAL TENSE

314 Inflected conditional

This is formed by adding the unreality endings (see §291) to the stem of the verb. However, unlike Preterite I and Future I, the inflected conditional is much more restricted in use in spoken Welsh. By far its most common occurrences are with various forms of the modals (**gallwn i, leiciwn i** etc. see §§329, 341), and in the conditional of **bod** (**byddwn/baswn i**, see §248), itself used for the periphrastic conditional (see §277).

Other than with modals and **bod**, unreality endings are not unusual with the four irregular verbs **mynd, dod, gwneud** and **cael** (though even here they are for the most part an optional alternative to the periphrastic with **byddwn/baswn i**). There are a considerable number of variant forms in the conditional for all these verbs (see §§315–317).

With verbs other than the above, the periphrastic conditional is by and large far more frequent in speech, with the inflected method reserved for certain specific uses (see §319).

315 Inflected conditional – mynd, dod, gwneud **and** cael

It is impractical to go into the bewildering variety of formations of this tense for the four irregulars. Instead we may confine ourselves to two sets of related forms, the first common over a wide area of N and central Wales, and the second perhaps more closely associated with the S.

316 Forms of the inflected conditional of the four irregular verbs (N)

In N and central Wales the following system is the norm:

		mynd	*gwneud*	*cael*	*dod*
Sing.	1st	awn i	nawn i	cawn i	down i
	2nd	aet ti	naet ti	caet ti	doet ti
	3rd	âi fe/hi	nâi fe/hi	câi fe/hi	dôi fe/hi
Pl.	1st	aen ni	naen ni	caen ni	doen ni
	2nd	aech chi	naech chi	caech chi	doech chi
	3rd	aen nhw	naen nhw	caen nhw	doen nhw

Notes:

(a) The unreality endings are added to **a-**, **na-**, **ca-** and **do-**, with 3rd pers. sing. **-ai** ending merging with final **-a-** to give **-âi** (but **dôi** for **dod**).

(b) The **gwneud** forms, as with most other inflected parts of this verb, are rarely heard with **gw-**.

(c) The **dod** and particularly **cael** forms are very frequently heard with SM in most circumstances in speech.

317 Forms of the inflected conditional of the four irregular verbs (S)

An alternative arrangement operates in many parts of the S:

		mynd	*gwneud*	*cael*	*dod*
Sing.	1st	**elwn i**	**nelwn i**	**celwn i**	**delwn i**
	2nd	**elet ti**	**nelet ti**	**celet ti**	**delet ti**
	3rd	**elai fe/hi**	**nelai fe/hi**	**celai fe/hi**	**delai fe/hi**
Pl.	1st	**elen ni**	**nelen ni**	**celen ni**	**delen ni**
	2nd	**elech chi**	**nelech chi**	**celech chi**	**delech chi**
	3rd	**elen nhw**	**nelen nhw**	**celen nhw**	**delen nhw**

Notes:

(a) In this system, all four irregulars, including **dod**, go the same way.

(b) An **-l-** element is infixed in all forms, and the unreality endings are added unchanged, including 3rd pers. sing.

318 Inflected conditional – ordinary verbs

The same principle of adding endings to the verb-stem is followed for the inflected conditional as for Preterite I and Future I, but with unreality endings. A further complication is that an infixed -s- is often added between the stem and the endings, with no apparent alteration in meaning or use. The inflected conditional of **agor** *open*, therefore, can be either of the following:

Sing.	1st	**agorwn i**	**agorswn i**
	2nd	**agoret ti**	**agorset ti**
	3rd	**agorai fe/hi**	**agorsai fe/hi**
Pl.	1st	**agoren ni**	**agorsen ni**
	2nd	**agorech chi**	**agorsech chi**
	3rd	**agoren nhw**	**agorsen nhw**

319   Uses of the inflected conditional

There are several possible uses of the inflected conditional, some of which can (and usually do) substitute the periphrastic formation with **byddwn/baswn**, and others which cannot. Those which must use the inflected conditional are so noted below:

(a)   closed conditional statements after **pe**

(b)   habitual event in the past (**byddwn** possible, but not **baswn** – see §278)

(c)   future in the past in reported speech

(d)   volition in the past (**byddwn/baswn** not possible)

Examples:

(a)   closed conditional statements:

> **Gallwn i °weld yn °well *pe symudai*'r °ddynes 'na**
>
> I could see better if that woman *moved*
>
> [or: . . . **pe byddai/tasai'r °ddynes 'na'n symud**]

(b)   habitual event in the past:

> **Fe °*alwai* 'yn chwaer i heibio °bob Dydd Llun**
>
> My sister *would call* round every Monday
>
> [or: **Byddai 'yn chwaer yn galw . . .**]

(c)   future event related in the past (reported speech):

> **Wedodd hi na °*gâi* hi byth swydd eto**
>
> She said she *would* never *get* another job
>
> [or: . . . **na °fyddai/°fasai hi'n cael . . .**]

(d) volition in the past:

> ***Agorsai* fe mo'r drws i mi**
>
> He *wouldn't open* the door for me [i.e. was unwilling to]

Further examples:

Nelwn i mo hynny yn dy °le di

I wouldn't do that if I were you

Awn i °ddim mor °bell â honni °fod 'na °ddim byd o'i °le

I wouldn't go so far as to claim that nothing was wrong

°Drion ni °gysylltu â nhw, ond atebsen nhw mo'r ffôn

We tried to contact them, but they wouldn't answer the phone

Wedodd y rheolwr wrtha i na °ddigwyddai'r °fath °gamgymeriad eto

The manager told me such a mistake would not happen again

Pe °welset ti'r lle nawr, fe °gaet ti syndod

If you saw the place now, you'd get a surprise

320 Inflected conditional with imperfect

Stative verbs (see Glossary) sometimes appear with unreality endings where the meaning is that of the imperfect (i.e. **o'n i'n . . .** etc.) rather than the conditional. Examples:

Pan °fedrwn i °weld eto, oedd hi wedi nosi'n °barod

When I could [= was able to] see again, night had already fallen

Y cwbwl °welai fe oedd llwybyr cul tywyll o'i °flaen

All he saw [was seeing] was a dark narrow path ahead of him

This meaning of what we have called the inflected conditional is usually clear from context.

321 Inflected tenses of gwybod – 'to know'

This anomalous verb (VN usually pronounced **gwbod**), which means *know* (*a fact*) and so corresponds to French *savoir*, German *wissen*, is unusual in having an inflected present and imperfect. These are both optional alternatives to the normal periphrastic formations (**dw i'n gwybod** etc. and **o'n i'n gwybod** etc.), though in certain circumstances they are preferred.

322 Inflected present of gwybod

	Singular	Plural
1st	**gwn i** I know	**gwyddon ni** we know
2nd	**gwyddost ti** you know	**gwyddoch chi** you know
3rd	**gŵyr e/hi** he/she knows	**gwyddon nhw** or
		gwyddan nhw they know

This is used in a number of set expressions:

dwn i °ddim, dwn i'm	I don't know
pwy a °ŵyr?	who knows?
Duw a °ŵyr	God knows
am °wn i	for all I know
hyd y gwn i	as far as I know

Note also the N parenthetical expressions °**wyddost ti** and °**wyddoch chi** *y'know*, often heard simply as **'sti** and **'ddchi** in natural speech. These are not heard in the S, where **timod** and **chimod** are the norm.

Mi °wn is used with the meaning *I suppose* or *I dare say*:

Naeth o °gyrraedd yn y diwedd, mi °wn
I dare say he got there in the end

'Sgwn i (for **os gwn i**) is used in the N for *I wonder . . .*

'Sgwn i ydi o'n bwriadu dŵad?
I wonder if he's intending to come?

'Sa hynny'n iawn, 'sgwn i?
I wonder if that would be alright?

(In the S **tybed** is used instead: **Tybed ydy e'n bwriadu dod?**)

323 Inflected imperfect of gwybod

The imperfect of **gwybod** is the most common example of a stative verb using unreality endings with past meaning (see §320). In effect it is the inflected conditional, and can be so used, but it frequently appears with an imperfect sense, in which case it is almost always interchangeable with the periphrastic **o'n i'n gwybod** etc.

	Singular	Plural
1st	**gwyddwn i** I knew	**gwydden ni** we knew
2nd	**gwyddet ti** you knew	**gwyddech chi** you knew
3rd	**gwyddai fe/hi** he/she knew	**gwydden nhw** they knew

Examples:

[imperfect]

> **Gwyddwn i na °faset ti'n °fodlon neud 'ny**

or: **O'n i'n gwybod na °faset ti'n °fodlon neud 'ny**

> I knew you wouldn't be willing to do that

> **°Wyddet ti °fod Gethin wedi'i °daro'n °wael?**

or: **O't ti'n gwybod °fod Gethin wedi'i °daro'n °wael?**

> Did you know that Gethin had been taken ill?

[conditional]

> **Pe °wyddai fo hynny, mi âi o'i °go**

> If he knew that, he'd go mad

324   Inflected forms of other compounds of bod

Other compounds of **bod** behave more regularly, and usually have stems in -**bydd-**/-**bu-**: **adnabod** (*recognize*), 3rd pers. sing. Future I **adnabyddith**; **darganfod** (*discover*), past autonomous **darganfuwyd**, non-past autonomous **darganfyddir** (both primarily media Welsh). There is considerable uncertainty about these among native speakers, and periphrastic forms are often preferred in speech.

325   VN instead of second inflected verb in sequence

Where a sentence begins with an inflected verb (usually Preterite I or Future I), and another verb follows *with the same subject*, the ordinary VN is used instead. The endings of the first (inflected) verb give all the required information on time and person, so there is no need to repeat this in the second verb where none of these factors have changed. This device, strange though it appears to an English speaker, is consistent with the principle of economy of expression that permeates the internal logic of Welsh.

247

Rhedodd y plant i mewn ac *eistedd* wrth y bwrdd

The children ran in and *sat down* at the table

°Godes i'n °gynnar a *mynd* am °dro

I got up early and *went* for a walk

Where the inflected verb is future, however, the translation difference is not so marked, because English has no inflected future, and therefore simply allows the auxiliary *will* to refer to the second infinitive as well as the first. In Welsh, the principle remains the same:

Os awn ni yno a *cwyno*, efallai y byddan nhw'n gwrando

If we go there and *complain*, perhaps they'll listen

°Werthwn ni'r hen °dŷ 'ma a ʰ*chodi* un newydd yn y cae wrth ymyl

We'll sell this old house and *build* another one in the next field

This construction is especially to be preferred when an object pronoun is also repeated:

°Olches i'r ceir i gyd a'*u sgleinio* o °fewn pedair awr

I washed the cars and *polished them* all in four hours

[rather than: °Olches i'r ceir i gyd a *sgleinies i nhw* . . ., which, while not exactly wrong, sounds unwieldy by comparison and reminiscent of English sentence structure].

326–360 MODALS

326   Verbal modals

Verbal modals in English, Welsh and other languages convey ideas such as *can, ought to, may, should, will, must*, etc. They are (almost all) used in conjunction with other verbs, and in this sense act very like auxiliaries (see Glossary). They are often referred to as modal auxiliaries for this reason but in Welsh the situation is slightly more complex than in many other European languages, for not all the modals are verbal in form or use. Nonverbal modals are dealt with in §§348–360.

As in English, one of the striking things about verbal modals in Welsh is that, though they are clearly verbs, they do not have the range of tenses possible with ordinary verbs. In English we can say *I trust* (present) and also *I trusted* (past), but *I must* cannot be turned into **I musted* in the past

– to do this we have to have recourse to *to have to* and say *I had to*. The situation is similar, though by no means parallel, in Welsh.

As with other non-**bod** auxiliaries, there is no mutation-blocking **yn** to link them to the following verb, and this verb will consequently have SM except in the negative, where °**ddim** has it instead.

327 Gallu/medru **('can', 'be able')**

For most uses of *can* these two verbs are interchangeable (for exceptions see §331), with **medru** having a distinctly N feel to it. Both are found with non-past (-**a i**, etc.) and unreality (-**wn i**, etc.) endings. The past endings (-**es i**, etc.) are sometimes encountered also, but many speakers do not regard them as acceptable.

328 **Non-past of** gallu/medru

With these verbs the non-past inflection conveys present tense (and not future as is the case with ordinary verbs). So **galla i** means *I can*, not *I will be able*, which must be expressed periphrastically with **bod** – **bydda i'n gallu**, etc.). Radical forms are as follows:

Sing.	1st	**galla i** (I can)	**medra i** (I can)
	2nd	**galli/gelli di**	**medri di**
	3rd	**gall e/hi**	**medr e/hi**
Pl.	1st	**gallwn ni**	**medrwn ni**
	2nd	**gallwch/gellwch chi**	**medrwch chi**
	3rd	**gallan nhw**	**medran nhw**

It will be noticed that 2nd pers. sing. and 2nd pers. pl. of **gallu** have alternative forms with vowel **a** or **e**. There seems little to choose between them, though **gelli di** may have the edge on **galli di** in many areas.

SM is very frequently used in all inflected forms of **gallu** and **medru** – including statements, whether particles **fe°/mi°** are used or not.

Examples of non-past gallu/medru:

°**Alla i °ddallt dy safbwynt, ond mae rhaid i mi anghytuno**

I can see your point of view, but I have to disagree

°**Fedrwch chi °dorri'r rhain i mi?**

Can you cut these for me?

Mi °ellwch chi °weld y ffin rhwng Cymru a Lloegr o fan hyn

You can see the border between Wales and England from here

°**Fedra i °ddim siarad °gystal â chi**

I can't speak as well as you

The 'standard' -ith ending of the non-past 3rd pers. sing. is occasionally found with **gallu: gallith/gellith** besides **gall**. Its use is more restricted however. °**Ellith °fod** (*it*) *can be* is often heard as an answer *Maybe*:

Ydy Dwynwen wedi cyrraedd yn ôl 'to? – Dwn 'im, °ellith °fod

Has Dwynwen got back yet? – I don't know, maybe

329 Unreality gallu/medru

The same general principles apply as for non-past above, but with the unreality endings. Where **galla i** means *I can*, **gallwn i** means *I could* (= *I would be able*). Therefore radical forms are as follows:

Sing.	1st	**gallwn i** (I could)	**medrwn i** (I could)
	2nd	**gallet ti**	**medret di**
	3rd	**gallai fe/hi**	**medrai fe/hi**
Pl.	1st	**gallen ni**	**medren ni**
	2nd	**gallech chi**	**medrech chi**
	3rd	**gallen nhw**	**medren nhw**

Examples:

°**Fedrwn i °ddim cymryd pres gynnoch chi am hwnna**

I couldn't take any money off you for that

Fe °allai Dylan °fynd i nôl y bwyd wedyn

Dylan could go and get the food later

°**Fedren ni °ddim llofnodi onibai bod chi'n llofnodi hefyd**

We couldn't sign unless you did too

°**Fedret ti °roi'r rheina yng ⁿghefn y car?**

Could you put those in the back of the car?

Gallen nhw lawrlwytho'r app 'na eu hunain, on' gallen?

They could download that app themselves, couldn't they?

Notes:

(a) Both **gallu** and **medru** frequently insert an **-s-** before the unreality endings, causing some alteration in form: **gallswn i, llaswn i; medswn i**

Examples:

°Biti na °fedsa'r °freuddwyd yma °bara am byth   [medrsai]

A pity that this dream could not last forever

Dw i °ddim yn ama na °lasa fo   [(ga)llasai]

I don't doubt that he could

(b) In both non-past and unreality 3rd pers. sing. (**gall/medr** and **gallai/ medrai**) the pronouns **fe/fo** and **hi** can be omitted if the sense is clear without them:

°Allai °fod yn iawn fel 'ny, timod

It could be alright like that, you know

330   Periphrastic tenses of gallu/medru

The present, imperfect and future of **bod** can all be used with **gallu/medru**:

Dw i'n gallu

I can (virtually synonymous with **galla i**)

O'n i'n gallu

I could (not necessarily synonymous with **gallwn i** – see §335)

Bydda i'n gallu

I will be able

The periphrastic present **Dw i'n gallu**, etc. is a very common alternative to the inflected non-past **Galla i** in many areas. In addition, the periphrastic conditional **Byddwn/Baswn i'n gallu** is sometimes heard for *I would be able*, i.e. as a synonym of **gallwn i**.

In these periphrastic uses, **gallu** and **medru** act just as any other verb.

331   Gallu **or** medru?

These two words are interchangeable, with **medru** clearly preferred in N areas, where *can* implies:

(a)   ability

Mi °all/°fedr Sioned °yrru car

Sioned can drive a car

(b)   physical possibility

°Ellwch/°Fedrwch chi °ddim gyrru i °Fethesda heno

You can't drive to Bethesda tonight

(c)   disposition

°Elli/°Fedri di °yrru fi adre?

Can you drive me home?

Sense (**a**) entails mental or physical ability on the part of the subject. Originally, these two abilities were distinguished in Welsh, as in other languages, with **gallu** meaning physical ability, and **medru** mental. But the distinction has been all but lost (with certain exceptions detailed below), and the choice is a purely dialectal one.

Sense (**b**) implies that, though the subject can drive, he will be physically prevented by other factors, e.g. weather.

Sense (**c**) uses **gallu/medru** to ask not whether someone is able to do something, but whether they feel disposed to do it. The same usage is found in English.

But **gallu** alone is used, in N and S areas alike, where *can* means *have permission*:

Galli di °fenthyg y llyfr 'ma ar ôl i mi °ddefnyddio fe

You can borrow the book after I've used it

In this case, *Medri di . . . would sound inappropriate to many speakers, since its rather narrower range of meaning does not include permission.

Medru alone can be used in the sense of *knowing a subject* or *having command of a subject* – this is an extension of its original sense of mental ability:

Mae'r °ddynes 'na'n medru Cymraeg yn iawn

That woman knows Welsh well/knows a lot of Welsh

Efallai °fod e'n °ddrud, ond mae'n medru'i °Gyfraith

He may be expensive, but he knows his Law [i.e. knows his subject]

332 Methu/ffili ('cannot')

These two verbs mean fail or be unable, with **ffili** (often spelt **ffaelu** but almost invariably pronounced **ffili** nevertheless) confined to S areas and **methu** more widespread. They are used colloquially to negate *can* (either **gallu** or **medru**) where the implication is ability or physical possibility (see §331 above).

Dw i'n methu gweld y teledu o fan hyn

I can't see the TV from here

O'n i'n ffili deall beth oedd e'n moyn weud (S)

I couldn't understand what he was trying to say

Wi'n ffili siarad gair o Ffrangeg (S)

I can't speak a word of French

Dan ni wedi methu cael gafael arno hyd yn hyn

We haven't been able to get hold of him so far

The normal NEG forms for **gallu** and **medru** would be possible alternatives in all these cases except perhaps the last, where the presence of **wedi** sits a little awkwardly with a modal. So:

°Fedra i °ddim gweld y teledu o fan hyn

O'n i °ddim yn gallu deall beth oedd e'n moyn weud

°Alla i °ddim siarad gair o Ffrangeg

but some speakers do not like:

Dan ni °ddim wedi medru cael gafael arno hyd yn hyn

333 Gallu + (fod) wedi ('may have'; 'could/might have')

Although **gallu**, like **medru**, is generally followed by the VN – Galla i nofio *I can swim* – it can also, unlike medru, be followed by °fod wedi + VN. Used with non-past endings, this construction translates . . . *may have* . . .

Fe °all y lladron °fod wedi dianc yn °barod

The thieves may already have escaped

°Elli di °fod wedi mynd yn rhy °bell tro 'ma

You may have gone too far this time

Pobol sy'n meddwl y gallan nhw °fod wedi cael eu rhoi mewn peryg

People who think that they may have been put in danger

The same technique with unreality endings translates . . . *could have* . . . or . . . *might have* . . .

Mi °allai fo °fod wedi dianc drwy'r ffenest °gefn

He could have escaped through the back window

Dydyn nhw chwaith °ddim yn medru hawlio budd-dal y gallan nhw °fod wedi cael pe bydden nhw wedi aros yn y gwaith

Nor are they able to claim benefits that they might have received had they stayed in work

Gallet ti °fod wedi'n lladd i!

You could have killed me!

There is a tendency in the spoken language to omit °fod in constructions of the type above: **Gallet ti wedi'n lladd i**, etc.

May and *might* are usually paraphrased with **efallai/hwyrach** *perhaps*. See §436.

334 Autonomous/impersonal forms gellir, gellid

These correspond roughly to *one can* . . . (**gellir**) and *one could* . . . (**gellid**). Like nearly all autonomous/impersonal verb-forms (see §367), they are more a feature of written Welsh than the spoken language, but are fairly commonplace in newspapers, on the media and in official documents:

Fe °ellir en plannu rhwng Mawrth a Mehefin

They can be planted between March and June

Gellir talu biliau trydan drwy °ddebyd uniongyrchol

Electricity bills can be paid by direct debit

Gellid datrys y °broblem 'ma gydag ychydig mwy o amser

With a bit more time, this problem could be solved

Fe °ellid dweud mai gorymateb ydy hwn

It could be said that this is an over-reaction

Note that the most natural translation in English is often a *can/could be . . .* passive, to avoid the stilted-sounding one.

Interrogative forms for **gellir** and **gellid** are a °**ellir?** and a °**ellid?**, and the negatives are **ni** °**ellir** and **ni** °**ellid**. These are even less common in speech than the affirmatives:

A °ellir honni, yn y byd cyfoes, °fod y °dreth hon yn un °gyfiawn?

Can it be claimed, in the modern world, that this tax is a fair one?

Ni °ellir mynd â llyfrau o'r llyfrgell dros nos

Books may not be taken from the library overnight

Ni °ellid byth darparu sicrwydd mor absoliwt, °waeth pa mor °drylwyr y caiff safle ei °lanhau a'i °fonitro

Such absolute certainty could never be provided, however thoroughly a site might be cleaned and monitored

335   Translation problems ('could')

Could is ambiguous in English – it means either (a) *was able*, or (b) *would be able*:

(a)   All I could see through the mist was the church spire

(b)   I could see better if this woman took off her hat

Was able is the past tense of *can*, and this is usually expressed in Welsh by the periphrastic imperfect, i.e. imperfect of **bod** + **gallu/medru** + VN. Sentence (a) above therefore would be:

Y cwbwl o'n i'n medru °weld drwy'r niwl oedd pigdwr yr eglwys

Would be able is the unreality form of *can*, and this is expressed simply by **gallwn/medrwn i** etc. Sentence (b) in Welsh reads:

°Fedrwn i °weld yn °well tasai'r °ddynes 'ma'n tynnu'i het

But in many parts of Wales, verbs denoting state (like **medru/gallu** *can*) do (optionally) use the unreality endings with past meaning (see §320), and so **Y cwbwl/fedrwn i °weld** would be possible in sentence (a) above.

336 Dylwn i ('I ought/should')

This verb appears only with unreality (**-wn i**) endings, because actions that ought to be done are not yet a fact, and may never be.

An optional **-s-** can appear in all forms, with no apparent difference in meaning.

Sing.	1st	**dyl(s)wn i**	(I ought)
	2nd	**dyl(s)et ti**	
	3rd	**dyl(s)ai fe/hi**	
Pl.	1st	**dyl(s)en ni**	
	2nd	**dyl(s)ech chi**	
	3rd	**dyl(s)en nhw**	

°Ddylwn i °fynd nawr, ond wi'n moyn aros tan y diwedd

I ought to go now, but I want to stay till the end

°Ddylen ni weud rhywbeth wrtho fe, neu °adael i'w °frawd °wneud e?

Should we say something to him, or let his brother do it?

°Ddylsai fo °ddim talu cyn gweld ansawdd y nwyddau

He shouldn't pay before he's seen the quality of the goods

Dylset ti °fod yn gwneud rhywbeth arall

You should be doing something else

As with **gallu/medru** (see §329(b)), the 3rd pers. sing. **dylai** is often used without the pronoun **fe/fo** or **hi** when the meaning is clear enough without:

Dyna fel y dylai °fod

That's how it should be

Dyma Siôn rŵan – mi °ddylai °gychwyn neu mi eith yn nos arno (N)

Here's Siôn now – he ought to get started or it'll be getting dark

Sometimes an **-i-** is heard inserted in all forms, with no change of meaning: **dyliwn i, dyliai fe,** etc.

Mae'n °debyg y dyliwn i °ofyn am °ganiatâd cyn defnyddio'r llun 'ma

I probably ought to ask permission before using this picture

337   Dylwn + °fod wedi – ('should/ought to have')

Dylwn is followed by either °VN, as above, to mean *ought to* (*do*), or by
°fod wedi + VN, to mean *ought to have* (*done*).

°Ddylai'r myfyrwyr °fod wedi gweithio'n °galetach

The students should have worked harder

°Ddylsech chi °ddim °fod wedi gweiddi fel 'ny

You shouldn't have shouted like that

Hwyrach y dylsen ni °fod wedi rhagweld hyn

Perhaps we should have anticipated this

Note: as with **gallu/medru**, there is a tendency in the spoken language to
omit °fod in this type of construction. So °Ddylai'r myfyrwyr wedi
gweithio'n °galetach is heard.

For general discussion of translation problems with *should*, see §339.

338   Autonomous/impersonal form dylid

Like **gellir** and **gellid** above (see §334), this useful word is confined largely
to writing. The force of it is *one ought to . . .*, and it is found particularly
where written instructions are involved. The question form is **a °ddylid?**,
and the negative is **ni °ddylid**, often used as a slightly less direct way of
saying **peidiwch** *don't*:

Dylid cadw'r label hon yn °ddiogel er gwybodaeth

This label should be retained for information

A °ddylid erlyn achosion hanesyddol?

Should historical cases be prosecuted?

Ni °ddylid ysgrifennu o dan y llinell hon

Do not write below this line

339   Translation problems – ('should')

Should has a number of different senses in English, of which the most
common are:

(a)   *ought to* – You should ask Helen about that

(b) formal 1st pers. sing. and 1st pers. pl. of *would* – We should be grateful if you could reply within a week

(c) *supposed to* in questions – How should I know?

(d) as an alternative to *if* in hypothetical situations – Should anyone call, tell them I'll be back soon

Examples:

(a) requires **dylwn i**: **°Ddylset ti °ofyn i Helen am hynny**

(b) is simply the conditional tense using **bod** (see §277): **Fe °fydden ni'n °ddiolchgar pe gallech chi ateb o °fewn wythnos**

(c) *supposed to* is **i °fod i°**: **Sut ydw i i °fod i °wybod?**, although the less cumbersome translation from the English – **Sut dylwn i °wybod?** – is common enough as well

(d) requires **os** + future: **Os bydd unrhywun yn galw, dwedwch y bydda i'n ôl toc**

340 Modal use of cael ('be allowed to')

One specialized meaning of **cael** may be said to be modal – that of *having permission*. American English uses *get* in the same way: *Do we get to see the late film tonight?* (i.e. *are we allowed?*). In Welsh this is expressed in an exactly parallel way, using either periphrastic present (**a**) or non-past endings (**b**):

(a) **Ydan ni'n cael gweld y ffilm hwyr heno?**

(b) **Gawn ni °weld y ffilm hwyr heno?**

But **cael** differs from true modals like **gallu** and **dylwn i** in that:

(a) the whole range of tenses, both periphrastic and inflected, are possible, as the sense requires. Examples:

°Gaeth y °ddau °frawd eistedd gyda'i gilydd [preterite]

The two brothers were allowed to sit next to each other

O'n nhw wedi cael mynd i °gyfarfodydd ar eu pennau eu hun [pluperfect]

They had been allowed to go to meetings on their own

°Fyddwn innau'n cael cyfrannu hefyd?   [conditional]

Would I be allowed to contribute as well?

Pe caet ti °fynd yn °gynnar, mi °faswn innau am °fynd hefyd
[conditional]

If you were allowed to go early, I'd want to go too

(b)   the unreality endings (**-wn i**) are not an obligatory or intrinsic part of the modality of this verb. Unreality endings are possible with modal **cael** – see last example in note (a) above – but only in the same way as they are technically possible with any other verb. **Dylwn i**, on the other hand, is a true modal and is by its very meaning inseparably bound to unreality endings (to the extent that it does not even exist in VN form).

341   **Modal use of** hoffi/leicio/caru **('like')**

In that modals usually view an action from the subjective standpoint of the speaker, one particular use of **hoffi/leicio/caru** *like* may be included here. With unreality endings, these verbs convey *... would like (to) ...*. There is little difference between the three, except that **caru** is predominantly a S usage, **leicio** (almost invariably pronounced **licio**) more widespread, and **hoffi** increasingly promoted in the schools and media. They differ from true modals, however, in one respect: they can be followed not only by a VN, but also by a noun to indicate the thing desired, whereas **gallu** and **dylwn i** are always linked to another verb.

Hoffech chi °baned arall o °goffi cyn mynd?

Would you like another cup of coffee before you go?

A be' °garet tithau weud ar y pwnc 'ma, 'te? (S)

And what would *you* like to say on this subject, then?

Leiciai'r °ddwy sy gen ti °ddŵad hefo ni hefyd? (N)

Would your two like to come with us as well?

Fe °garwn i °wylio'r rhaglen 'ma os yw hynny'n iawn 'da chi i gyd (S)

I'd like to watch this programme if that's all right with you lot

Notes:

(a)   **Leicio**, in this modal use, can have **-s-** optionally inserted: **Leicsiwn i °wybod, Leicsiech chi °ddod?** etc.

(b) **Leicio** alone of the three can also take non-past endings, at least in 2nd pers. sing. and 2nd pers. pl., where the meaning is not *would like*, but simply *like*:

> **Cymer faint leici di**
>
> Take as many as you like
>
> **°Ellwch chi aros hyd leiciwch chi**
>
> You can stay as long as you like
>
> **°Gewch chi °wneud be' leiciwch chi**
>
> You can do what you like

342 Hoffi/leicio/caru – modal v. non-modal use

It is important to distinguish modal from non-modal uses with these verbs. In English it is the difference between:

(a) I'd like an apple   [I feel like having one now]

(b) I like apples   [generally, though I may not want one now]

Modal use (a) uses the unreality endings as explained in §291:

> **Hoffwn i afal**

while non-modal use (b) simply involves **hoffi** etc. being used as an ordinary VN:

> **Dw i'n hoffi afalau**

In practice the distinction is easy to recognize in English, since the modal use of *like* (for which the unreality endings will be required in Welsh) always contains *would* or *'d*.

343–347 UNREALITY ENDINGS WITH OTHER VERBS

Note: these are mainly idiomatic phrases, and are probably best learnt as such. Most involve subjective judgment and are therefore most usefully classified under modals.

343   Synnwn i °ddim (**'I shouldn't wonder'; 'I dare say'**)

**Wedwn i
(dwedwn i,
°ddwedwn i)**
('I should say'
'I suppose/
guess')

°Fydd e'n hwyr eto, synnwn i °ddim

He'll be late again, I shouldn't wonder.

Synnwn i °ddim tasai'ch gŵr yn pleidleisio yn erbyn

I dare say your husband will vote against

[lit. I shouldn't be surprised if . . . were to vote . . .]

The AFF equivalent **synnwn i** is also found, if less frequently:

Fe synnwn i pe bai'r lleill °ddim yn teimlo'r un °fath

I would be surprised if the others didn't feel the same way

The periphrastic version – using the conditional of **bod** + VN **synnu** – is also common:

'Swn i ddim yn synnu tasai'ch gŵr yn pleidleisio yn erbyn

'Swn i'n synnu pe bai'r lleill °ddim yn teimlo'r un °fath

344   °Dybiwn i (**'I should think', I suppose', 'I guess'**)

'Se hwnnw'n costio mwy nag sy 'da ni, °dybiwn i

That'd cost more than we've got, I should think

Ni °fydd yn gorfod talu yn y diwedd, °dybiwn i

I suppose it'll be us who'll end up paying

345   Wedwn i (dwedwn i, °ddwedwn i) (**'I should say'
'I suppose/guess'**)

Faint o °daflenni °fydd angen, tybed? – Tua pum mil, wedwn i

I wonder how many leaflets will be needed? I should say about 5,000

Pryd bydd hyn oll yn °barod inni? – Erbyn diwedd y mis, wedwn i

When will it all be ready for us? I guess by the end of the month

This is also used in NEG to mean *I wouldn't say* . . .

Wedwn i °ddim byd yn ei herbyn yn °bersonol, ond mae'n gorfod mynd

I wouldn't say anything against her personally, but she's got to go

Ydy hi'n swil? Wedwn i mo hynny, ond mae hi yn °dawel weithiau

Is she shy? I wouldn't say that, but she is quiet sometimes

The 1st pers. pl. **weden ni** is used for *say* or *let's say* where an estimation or an example is being given:

Beth am inni °adael am, weden ni, naw o'r °gloch, 'te?

How about if we left at, say, nine o'clock, then?

. . . ond yn ⁿNe Ffrainc, weden ni, mae'r sefyllfa'n °gwbwl °wahanol

. . . but the situation's quite different in, say, the South of France

346 °Feiddiwn i °ddim ('I wouldn't dare')

°Feiddiwn i °ddim rhoi'n enw i o dan °rywbeth felly

I wouldn't dare put my name to [under] something like that

Also:

°Feiddiet ti °ddim!	You wouldn't dare!
°Feiddiech chi °ddim!	You wouldn't dare!
°Feiddiai fo °ddim	He wouldn't dare etc.

Note also **Paid ti â meiddio!** Don't you dare!

And indeed, the VN **meiddio** is in common enough use:

Mae 'na agwedd arall nad oes neb fan hyn wedi meiddio sôn amdani hyd yn hyn

There is another aspect that so far nobody here has dared to mention

347 °Goeliet/ʰchoeliet ti °ddim, °goeliech/ʰchoeliech chi °ddim ('you wouldn't believe it')

°Goeliech chi °ddim faint o °bobol oedd 'na

You wouldn't believe how many people were there

°Goeliet ti °ddim °gymaint mae wedi newid

You wouldn't believe how much he/she's changed

Coelio is also used with non-past endings in the expressions **Coeliwch chi fi** *believe you me* or *take it from me* and **Coeliwch neu °beidio** *believe it or not*:

Mi °fasai'r goblygiadau ariannol yn °ddifrifol, coeliwch chi fi

The financial implications would be serious, believe you me

Coeliwch neu °beidio, dyma'r tro cynta i mi °glywed hynna erioed

Believe it or not, that's the first time I've ever heard that

Credwch neu °beidio is a common alternative for **Coeliwch neu °beidio**.

348–360 NON-VERBAL MODALS

348 **Non-verbal modals – general remarks**

All of these operate on the same sentence structure: modal word – i – [perceived or notional] subject° – VN.

For example, using **°Well** *had better . . .*: *Siân had better hurry* (**brysio**) is rearranged according to the pattern above to give:

°Well i	**Siân**	**°frysio**
modal	perceived/notional subject°	VN

Where the subject is a pronoun, the personal forms of **i** (see §460) are needed:

°Well iddi (hi) °frysio

She'd better hurry

The VN in all these expressions immediately follows the subject, and so appears with SM.

The non-verbal models are all either nouns or adjectives originally, and view the action of the verb from some subjective viewpoint of the speaker:

rhaid must	**°well** had better
°waeth might as well	**°wiw** dare not
man a man might as well	**(hen) °bryd** (high) time

Of these, **rhaid** can be used in all tenses, and in AFF, INT and NEG forms. The others are much more restricted, at least in practice.

263

349   Rhaid ('must', 'have to')

Rhaid is a noun meaning *necessity*, so that *I must go now* is phrased (*There is*) *necessity for me to go*. This means that there is an underlying existential verb (§252) involved which, however, is frequently omitted in the present AFF:

Rhaid i mi °fynd nawr   [for: **Mae rhaid i mi °fynd nawr**]

But the existential verb reappears in INT and NEG:

Oes rhaid i mi °fynd?   Must I go? [lit. Is there need . . .?]

Does dim rhaid i mi °fynd   I needn't go [lit. There's no need]

Note: *I must not* is dealt with separately (see §350).

Other tenses of rhaid are then simply constructed using the appropriate AFF, INT or NEG forms of the existential verb (§252):

Roedd rhaid i mi °fynd	I had to go
Oedd rhaid i mi °fynd?	Did I have to go?
Doedd dim rhaid i mi °fynd	I didn't have to go
Bydd rhaid i mi °fynd	I'll have to go
°Fydd rhaid i mi °fynd?	Will I have to go?
°Fydd dim rhaid i mi °fynd	I won't have to go
Basai/Byddai rhaid i mi °fynd	I would have to go
°Fasai/°Fyddai rhaid i mi °fynd?	Would I have to go?
°Fasai/°Fyddai dim rhaid i mi °fynd	I wouldn't have to go

Wedi-tenses, though possible with rhaid, are usually expressed by substituting the verb gorfod (see §352).

Rhaid constructions can be impersonalised by simply removing the [i + subject] component. Compare:

Rhaid i Julie °ddychwelyd y llyfrau erbyn diwedd y mis

Julie must return the books by the end of the month

Rhaid dychwelyd y llyfrau erbyn diwedd y mis

The books must be returned by the end of the month

Note in the second example that:

1   the SM of the VN (**dychwelyd**) is removed, because the notional subject (**Julie**) that had caused it has itself been removed

2   removal of the subject results in a switch from active to passive in the natural English translation, because of the rule in English requiring a subject to be stated in all sentences.

Further **rhaid** examples without subject:

Rhaid cofio hynny

That must be remembered

Rhaid gweithredu'n °gadarnhaol

Positive action must be taken

Two useful expressions using impersonal **rhaid** are **rhaid dweud** *it must be said* and **rhaid cyfadde** *it must be admitted* or *admittedly*:

Rhaid dweud fod Huw wedi achosi niwed parhaol i'w perthynas

It must be said that Huw has permanently damaged their relationship

350   *Must not* and *need not*

It must be borne in mind at the outset that **rhaid** is *not* a verb meaning *must*, but a noun meaning *necessity* or *need*. This difference between English and Welsh becomes apparent in the negative:

AFF	**(Mae) rhaid i ti °fynd**	You must go
		[lit. There is need for you to go]
NEG	**Does dim rhaid i ti °fynd**	You needn't go
		[lit. There is no need for you to go]

The point here is that *necessity* and *must* are fairly close in meaning in AFF statements, but they diverge in the NEG:

	AFF	NEG
English:	You must	You must not
Welsh:	There is need	There is no need

The true negative of *you must* in Welsh, then, is *you needn't* – a very different thing from *you mustn't*. The relationship between *you must* and *you mustn't* in Welsh is that both are commands – one telling you to do something, and the other telling you not to. Both, therefore, will begin with rhaid in Welsh:

Rhaid i ti °fynd	You must go
	[Necessity for you to go]
Rhaid i ti °beidio mynd	You must not go
	[Necessity for you not to go]

In all *must not* phrases, the word immediately following the subject is peidio *not to* (*do*), and this takes the SM that otherwise falls on the VN. Further examples:

Rhaid inni °beidio sôn nes bod ni'n siwr

We mustn't talk about this until we're certain

Rhaid i mi °beidio anghofio ⁿngherdyn credyd i tro 'ma

I mustn't forget my credit card this time

Sometimes English has difficulty translating the wide range of tenses available with rhaid . . . °beidio – *have to not . . .* is usually the only way out short of a rephrasing:

Bydd rhaid i Gwilym °beidio siarad â hi o hyn ymlaen

Gwilym will have to not talk to her from now on

Byddai rhaid iddyn nhw °beidio cytuno i hynny

They would have to not agree to that/have to withhold their consent

351 'Must' (supposition)

Must in English can be used not only for 'obligation', but also for 'supposition'. Compare:

(a) Elen must be in town by ten o'clock
     [because she's got a meeting]

(b) Elen must be in town
     [because she isn't here, so where else could she be?]

Rhaid is used for both meanings in Welsh, but because the 'supposition' meaning is not modal, a different construction is used, with rhaid used on its own and a following clause with bod/°fod:

(a)   *Rhaid* i Elen °fod yn y °dre (erbyn deg o'r °gloch)

(b)   *Rhaid* °fod Elen yn y °dre

Further examples of supposition rhaid:

Rhaid bod nhw o'u co

They must be mad

Rhaid bod y plant wedi mynd â'u harian cinio wedi'r cwbwl

The children must have taken their dinner money after all

Rhaid bod hi'n bwriadu sgrifennu ar ôl Nadolig

She must be intending to write after Christmas

It is easy to distinguish the two uses in Welsh – when it means *obligation*, rhaid is immediately followed by i°; when it means *supposition*, rhaid is immediately followed by bod/°fod.

The NEG supposition **Does dim rhaid bod . . .** means *It is not necessarily the case that . . . , . . . may/need not (be) . . .* , and with following **wedi . . .** *needn't necessarily have . . .* :

Does dim rhaid bod Medi yn gweld rhywun arall

It's not necessarily so that Medi is seeing someone else

Does dim rhaid bod nhw wedi gadael y maes awyr 'to

They may not (necessarily) have left the airport yet

All 'supposition' rhaid sentences can substitute the emphatic **mai** (S **taw**) (see §492) for **bod/°fod** where a 'focused' element (see §17) is required:

Rhaid mai gwario'r arian naeth e yn lle ei °gadw'n °ddiogel

He must have spent the money instead of keeping it safe

Does dim rhaid mai dy °frawd naeth hyn

It needn't be your brother that did this

[lit. It need not be that (it was) your brother (who) did this]

(Focused sentences are dealt with in detail in §§17–21.)

352   Gorfod

Gorfod (**goffod** in many areas) is a verb meaning *must, have to*. It is synonymous with rhaid but, being a true verb (**rhaid** is a noun), works differently. Compare:

| **Rhaid i mi °fynd i'r °dre** | I must go to town |
| **Dw i'n gorfod mynd i'r °dre** | I must go to town |

Note that **gorfod** operates like any other VN, and uses **bod** as an auxiliary. (The preterite, however, is not used because the sense of completed action associated with this tense is inconsistent with **gorfod**'s modal or stative meaning.) Generally, **rhaid** is the more common option for *must/have to*, though it is hard to find instances where **gorfod** would not be just as good.

With **wedi** tenses, however, there *is* a preference for **gorfod** because the corresponding **rhaid** construction is unwieldy:

Mae'r pwyllgor wedi gorfod ailystyried y mater

The committee has had to reconsider the matter

Dan ni wedi gorfod gohirio'r trafodaethau oherwydd salwch

We have had to postpone the talks because of illness

The above examples using **rhaid** would be:

Mae wedi bod yn rhaid i'r pwyllgor ailystyried y mater

Mae wedi bod yn rhaid inni °ohirio'r trafodaethau oherwydd salwch

or, possibly, **Bu rhaid . . .,** though this is not very common in speech.

Gorfod *have to* should not be confused with **gorfodi** *force, compel*. Note particularly that the preterite **gorfododd** etc. is not ambiguous as might be thought, but can only be from **gorfodi**, because **gorfod**, being stative, cannot form a preterite (see §303).

Gorfod cannot be used for 'supposition', in the same way that *to have to* cannot be so used in (British) English.

353 °Well i . . . ('had better')

In the present AFF this works exactly like **rhaid** (see §349), so:

°Well i mi °brynu'r bwyd bore 'ma

I'd better buy the food this morning

Compare:

Rhaid i mi °brynu'r bwyd bore 'ma

I must buy the food this morning

And, also like **rhaid**, **peidio** is added to render the NEG *had better not*:

> **°Well i ti °beidio deud hynny wrth ei gŵr hi**
>
> You'd better not tell her husband that

Compare:

> **Rhaid i ti °beidio deud hynny wrth ei gŵr hi**
>
> You mustn't tell her husband that

But the INT form *Had I better . . .?* etc. is done not with **Oes . . .?** (there is no existential sense to **°Well i . . .**, not least because **gwell** is an adjective, not a noun), but with **°Fyddai/°Fasai'n . . .?**:

> **°Fyddai'n °well inni °droi'r teledu i lawr ychydig?**
>
> Had we better turn the TV down a bit?

though **°ddylwn i**, etc. (see §336) is often used for this meaning, since *Ought we . . .?* and *Had we better . . .?* amount virtually to the same thing:

> **°Ddylen ni °droi'r teledu i lawr ychydig?**

Other tenses are theoretically possible, but rare.

354 'Prefer'

°Well used with **gan°/gyda** instead of **i°** means *prefer*:

> **°Well *i mi* siarad Cymraeg yn y °dafarn 'ma**
>
> I'd better speak Welsh in this pub

> **Well *'da fi* siarad Cymraeg yn y °dafarn 'ma**
>
> I prefer to speak Welsh in this pub

Note the expressions:

P'un sy °well 'da ti? (S)	Which do you prefer?
P'un sy °well 'da chi? (S)	
P'un sy °well gen ti? (N)	
P'un sy °well gynnoch chi? (N)	
P'un sy °orau 'da ti? (S)	Which do you most prefer/like best?
P'un sy °orau 'da chi? (S)	
P'un sy °orau gen ti? (N)	
P'un sy °orau gynnoch chi? (N)	

355 °Waeth i° . . . 'might as well . . .'

This modal works in exactly the same way as °Well i . . . (see §354) for AFF and NEG. INT is not used.

°Waeth i ti °drial

You might as well try

°Waeth iddyn nhw °gyfadde popeth nawr

They might as well own up to everything now

°Waeth i mi °beidio deud dim am y tro

I might as well say nothing for the moment

356 °Waeth i . . . heb na or heb °ddim

Sometimes **heb na** or **heb °ddim** is inserted between the person and the VN. This does not alter the meaning:

°Waeth i ti heb na trial

°Waeth i ti heb °ddim trial

You might as well try

357 Gwaeth **with future of** bod

An alternative construction uses the radical **gwaeth** with the future of **bod**:

°Fyddi di °ddim gwaeth na trial (= °Waeth i ti °drial)

You might as well try

358 Man a man i° . . . 'might as well . . .'

In some areas, **Man a man** takes the place of °**Waeth** with no difference in meaning:

Man a man i chi aros fan hyn am sbel a ʰchael panaid

You might as well wait here for a bit and have a cup of tea

Man a man inni °fod wedi aros gartre

We might as well have stayed at home

359 °Wiw(/fiw)i° . . . ('dare not'; 'no use')

This modal (very often **fiw** in speech) is altogether rarer than the preceding ones, but may be encountered from time to time. Its original meaning of *It is no use* . . . now co-exists with a more common secondary development as *dare not*. The context often serves to distinguish them, but some sentences are ambiguous, at least as they stand:

°Wiw i chi °fynd

You daren't go

or: It's no use you going

°Wiw i mi °ddeud y °drefn wrtho o °flaen y lleill

I daren't tell him off in front of the others

or: It's no use my telling him off in front of the others

Other tenses are possible with °**wiw**, e.g.:

Doedd fiw i mi °wrthod o

I didn't dare refuse him

360 (Hen) °bryd i° . . . '(High) time that . . .'

This expression may conveniently be included among the modals because it uses the same sentence pattern, and does imply subjective judgment of the action. **Mae'n** precedes where °**bryd** alone is used; with **Hen °bryd** it is often omitted:

Mae'n °bryd inni edrych yn °fanwl ar y ffeithiau

It's time we examined the facts

Mae'n °bryd i ti °fod yn y gwely

It's time you were in bed

Hen °bryd i ti ymddeol a gadael i'r plant °ofalu am y busnes

It's high time you retired and let the children look after the business

Hen °bryd i chi'ch dau °fynd adre

It's high time you two went home

Note that in these expressions the apparent English past tense is actually the unreality form of English verbs (identical with the past), and is logically translated by the tenseless VN in Welsh. Further discussion on this function of the VN will be found under the time expressions **ar ôl i°** . . ., **cyn i°** . . . etc. (§501).

361–376 PASSIVE

361 Passive constructions

Note: while *Iwan built the house* is an active construction, changing it to *The house was built by Iwan*, makes it passive. The object of the original sentence thus becomes the subject, and the original subject becomes the agent.

There are two basic ways of forming passive sentences in spoken Welsh:

(a) using **cael** *get* in a periphrastic construction;

(b) using special autonomous/impersonal forms in a non-periphrastic construction.

In the spoken language, method (a) is by far the more common, while in media Welsh, and particularly news reports, method (b) is almost as frequent.

362 Cael-passive – basic principles

In English, we can turn a sentence like *A dog bit my brother* into a passive in two ways:

My brother was bitten by a dog

My brother got bitten by a dog

Sometimes the *got* version is acceptable (especially when there is a sense of suddenness or immediacy in the event), but sometimes *was* sounds better – *My ticket was checked at the door.*

The point here is that, in dynamic sentences where there is a clear sense of action, no such distinction exists in Welsh. In this type of construction, **cael** *get* is the only option available, and it is wrong to use **bod**.

The structures of passive sentences in English and Welsh are broadly parallel:

Terry	got/was	hit	by	a snowball
subj.	verb	participle	preposition	agent

°Gafodd	Terry	ei	°daro	gan	°bêl eira
verb	subj.	poss.	VN	preposition	agent
[lit. Got	Terry	his	hit(ting)	by	a snowball]

From this it is clear that the only essential difference between the two constructions is that English uses a special form of the main action verb (the participle), while Welsh uses the simple VN with a possessive adjective (see §109). This possessive adjective 'echoes' the subject of the sentence, so that 'I was hit' is rendered literally 'I got my hit(ting)', 'You were hit' is 'You got your hit(ting)', and so on. Many of these possessive adjectives cause mutations, so the VN taro *hit(ting)* can appear in a variety of forms, depending on the person:

°Ges i ⁿharo	I was hit
°Gest ti dy °daro	you were hit
°Gafodd e ei °daro	he was hit
°Gafodd hi ei ʰtharo	she was hit
°Gawson ni'n taro	we were hit
°Gawsoch chi'ch taro	you were hit
°Gawson nhw eu taro	they were hit

The mutation patterns on the VN are exactly as would be the case with an ordinary noun following the possessive adjectives (see §109). But with VNs there is one small difference – the 'echoing' pronoun often used with possessives (e.g. ei °dad (e), ei ʰthad (hi) *his father, her father*) is not used after VNs: °Gafodd e ei °daro, not: *°Gafodd e ei °daro fe.

363 Cael-**passive – tenses**

The **cael**-passive uses the various tenses of **cael** just as English uses *be* or *get*. Examples in 3rd pers. sing. (using **codi** *build*):

[pres.]	***Mae'r tŷ yn cael* ei °godi**
	The house *is being/is* built
[impf]	***Oedd y tŷ yn cael* ei °godi**
	The house *was being* built
[fut.]	***Bydd y tŷ yn cael* ei °godi**
	***°Geith* y tŷ ei °godi**
	The house *will be* built
[condt]	***Basai/Byddai'r* tŷ yn cael ei °godi**
	The house *would be* built
[pret.]	***°Gafodd* y tŷ ei °godi**
	The house *was* built
[perfect]	***Mae'r tŷ wedi cael* ei °godi**
	The house *has been* built
[pluperf.]	***Oedd y tŷ wedi cael* ei °godi**
	The house *had been* built

The other **wedi**-tenses (see §262) are available in the same way.

364 **Stative passives – omission of** cael **after** wedi, newydd, heb

Consider the following two sentences in English:

(a) The door was opened

(b) The door was open

In (a) there is a dynamic sense, in that we have a mental picture of the action of someone opening the door, while in (b) there is more a sense of the result of the action – we have a picture of an open door, and it may have been like that for hours. This second example is a stative passive, and is distinguished from dynamic passives in Welsh by the absence of **cael** from the passive construction. In practice, this usually leaves a pattern of the type **wedi** + [poss. adj.] + VN. Compare the Welsh versions of the English examples above:

(a) °Gafodd y drws ei agor

(b) Oedd y drws wedi'i agor

Note that a possible alternative English version for (b) would be *The door had been opened*. This corresponds to the cael-passive **Oedd y drws wedi [cael] ei agor**, with the **cael** removed to indicate state rather than action.

Students of other European languages will recognize the difference between the **cael** and **cael**-less passives in Welsh as being essentially the same as that between *werden-* and *sein*-passives in German, and *ser-* and *estar*-passives in Spanish. English can make the same distinction – either by using an obviously stative adjective *open* (not usually an option), or by changing the action/state *was* to the (slightly) less ambiguous . . . *has been* . . . *-ed* to emphasize state. More often than not, however, the ambiguity stands, with *The door was closed* implying action or state. The English-speaking student must make a decision in these cases before translating into Welsh.

Cael can also be removed, for the same reason, from passive constructions where **newydd°** and **heb°** are in place of **wedi**:

Mae'r stafell 'ma newydd [°gael] ei glanhau

This room has (only) just been cleaned

Dan ni heb [°gael] ein talu

We haven't been paid

365 **Further omission of** cael

A similar construction with cael removed, uses i + poss. adj. + VN, with a future sense, often corresponding to *to be* . . . *-ed* in English:

Manylion pellach i'w cyhoeddi yfory

Further details to be announced tomorrow

Mae'r dirprwy i'w °benodi yn ystod y gwyliau

The deputy is to be appointed during the holidays

In this case, note that possessive adjectives ei and eu change as normal to 'w after the preposition i (see §112). That is, when the underlying i [°gael] eu cyhoeddi, i [°gael] ei °benodi have their cael removed, this leaves the i and the following ei/eu adjacent, thus converting to i'w.

366   **Adjectival sense of constructions without** cael

All these **cael**-less constructions can be used in a purely adjectival sense. Note particularly that **wedi** + poss. adj. + VN corresponds to the English past participle, while the same construction with **heb** is used for *un-* . . . *-ed*:

Arlywydd wedi'i ailethol	A re-elected president
Siec wedi'i llofnodi	A signed cheque
Siop newydd ei hagor	A shop just opened
Siec heb ei llofnodi	An unsigned cheque
Llythyr heb ei °orffen	An unfinished letter
Bygythiad i'w °wrthwynebu	A threat to be resisted

367   **Autonomous/impersonal forms** -ir **and** -wyd – **general principles**

These forms, which it is important to know at least for recognition purposes, are found primarily in newspapers and in the media. However, they are not unknown in ordinary speech, and reports of their demise – especially -**wyd** – are, certainly for many dialects, premature.

This method avoids any use of **cael**, and involves adding endings to the verb, therefore the verb-stem (see §205–209) is required for this. In the modern language only non-past (-**ir**) and past (-**wyd**) are available, so any other tenses have to be formed using **cael** anyway.

Although sometimes listed as 'passives', these two forms are properly referred to as autonomous or impersonal, since they are not strictly speaking passive in sense (note that they can be formed for all verbs, including intransitives like *come* and *go* that have no passive). They convey the idea of the general action of the verb without specifying who or what is doing it. English has no exact equivalent of these, and must resort to slightly awkward paraphrases with *one* if a close translation is sought: (non-past) **siaredir** *one speaks/will speak*; (past) **siaradwyd** *one spoke*. But in practice the English passives *is/will be* . . . *-ed* and *was/has been* . . . *-ed* are usually the closest natural equivalent – **Siaredir Cymraeg fan hyn** *Welsh (is) spoken here.*

Personal pronouns or nouns can be used with these autonomous forms, which themselves do not vary. It is quite possible to use them without, however – see examples below. The preverbal affirmative particles **fe°/mi°** can also be used.

368 Other particles with autonomous/impersonal forms

Being essentially part of the written or formal register of the language, autonomous/impersonal forms prefix a° for INT and ni (MM) for NEG:

Cynhelir cyfarfod	A meeting will be held
A °gynhelir cyfarfod?	Will a meeting be held?
Ni ʰchynhelir cyfarfod	No meeting will be held
	(A meeting will not be held)

369 Absence of SM following autonomous forms

Note that, as no subject is stated or implied in the autonomous forms, there is no SM following. Compare:

Fe °drefnodd °gyfarfod	S/he organized a meeting
Fe °drefnwyd cyfarfod	A meeting was organized

370 Non-past autonomous/impersonal -ir

This inflection is added to the verb-stem (see §205–209), but two points must be noted:

(a) verb-stems ending in **-i** drop this before adding **-ir**, i.e. **cynnig** *offer* (**cynigi-**) gives not *****cynigiir** but **cynigir**; **gwthio** *push* (**gwthi-**) gives not *****gwthiir** but **gwthir**

(b) unusually, the verb-stem itself, normally invariable, is altered if the vowel before the last consonant of the stem is **-a-**: this is changed to **-e-** before **-ir** is added:

(talu)	**tal-**	**telir**
(cynnal)	**cynhali-**	**cynhelir**

no other **a** in the stem is affected:

(siarad) siarad-		**siaredir**

Examples:

(darparu)	**Darperir lluniaeth ysgafn**
	Light refreshments (will be) provided
(talu)	**Telir eich cyflog yn °fisol**
	Your salary will be paid monthly
(cadw)	**Cedwir pob hawl**
	All rights reserved
(awgrymu)	**Awgrymir i chi °wneud apwyntiad arall**
	It is suggested that you make another appointment

371 ## Verbs with irregular -ir forms

A few verbs have irregular -ir forms:

cael – ceir **gwneud – gwneir** **mynd – eir**

Ceir dewis helaeth o °gylchgronau perthnasol yn llyfrgell y coleg

A wide selection of relevant magazines is available in the college library

Eir yno yn °gyson dros y Nadolig

People often go there over Christmas

The more literal – but painfully ungrammatical and unnatural in English – sense of the neat forms **ceir** and **eir** is something like 'there is a getting' (i.e. *there is available*), 'there is a going' (i.e. *people go*).

372 ## Past autonomous/impersonal -wyd

This inflection is simply added to the verb-stem, and generally corresponds to the past or perfect passive: *was/were . . . ed* or *has/have been . . . ed.*

VN	*verb-stem*	*past autonomous*
taflu (throw)	**tafl-**	**taflwyd** (was/were thrown)
dangos (show)	**dangos-**	**dangoswyd** (was/were shown)
cynnig (offer)	**cynigi-**	**cynigiwyd** (was/were offered)
dechrau (begin)	**dechreu-**	**dechreuwyd** (was/were begun)
cau (close)	**cae-**	**caewyd** (was/were closed)

Often the object and the agent of the action (with **gan°**) are stated:

Fe °lansiwyd y llong ar y pumed o Ebrill llynedd

The ship was launched on the 5th of April last year

Ataliwyd dwsin o °geir gan yr heddlu yn y Bala neithiwr

A dozen cars were stopped by the police last night in Bala

But the autonomous form can be used on its own:

Dechreuwyd yn °gynnar ar y gwaith

An early start was made on the work

This is the one autonomous/impersonal that is occasionally encountered in speech in some areas – usually pronounced -wd:

Fe °gollwd y cwbwl

The whole (lot) was lost

373 Irregular -wyd forms

dod – daethpwyd	cael – cafwyd
mynd – aethpwyd, aed	geni – ganwyd, ganed
gwneud – gwnaethpwyd, gwnaed	

Gwnaed yng ⁿNghymru

Made in Wales

Daethpwyd o hyd i'w °gorff nes ymlaen y diwrnod hwnnw

His body was found later on that day   [**dod o hyd i** *find*]

Aethpwyd (or **Aed**) **â tri o °ddynion i'r ysbyty**

Three men were taken to hospital   [**mynd â** *take*]

Ganed (or **Ganwyd**) **Enid Williams ym ⁿMhorthaethwy ar °droad y °ganrif**

Enid Williams was born in Porthaethwy at the turn of the century

Cafwyd noson °ddiddorol a bywiog gan °bawb

An interesting and lively evening was had by all

374 Non-past autonomous form -er

Occasionally another non-past autonomous form **-er** is encountered in public notices and official documents. This is added to the verb-stem in the normal way, and means roughly *Let one . . .* It is used as a neat if formal polite request:

| (gwthio) | Gwthier i agor | Please push to open |
| (gweld) | Gweler isod | See below |

The NEG is **Na** (MM) (**Nac** before radical vowels):

Nac ysgrifenner o dan y llinell hon

Please do not write below this line

See §334 for autonomous forms **gellir**, **gellid** and §338 for **dylid**.

375 Cases where an English passive cannot be translated by either of the Welsh passives

Consider the following correct sentences in English:

(**1a**) Freddie *was helped* by Bert

(**1b**) The book *was given* to Freddie by Bert

(**1c**) Freddie *was given* the book by Bert

If we rearrange them to make Bert the subject, the relationship between them is made clear:

(**2a**) Bert helped Freddie

(**2b**) Bert gave the book to Freddie

(**2c**) Bert gave the book to Freddie

Sentences (**b**) and (**c**), then, mean the same thing. The point is that it was the book that was given, not Freddie – *Freddie was given* really means *to Freddie was given* (*the book*), but we drop the *to* in English, just as we can say *I gave Freddie the book* for *I gave the book to Freddie*. The word order difference allows the *to* to be understood. In Welsh we cannot use word order to make this kind of distinction, and so the idea of *to* (**i**) cannot be left unexpressed. Sentences (**2a**) and (**2b/c**) above in Welsh are:

Helpodd Bert Freddie

Rhoddodd Bert y llyfr i Freddie

Then the passive constructions in (la) and (1b/c) will be:

°**Gafodd Freddie ei helpu gan Bert**

°**Gafodd y llyfr ei °roi i Freddie gan Bert**

In other words, there is no equivalent translation for (1c) 'Freddie was given the book', because this really means 'the book was given to Freddie' (1b).

This 'false' passive arises where in English the verb takes an indirect object, whether or not the word *to* is actually expressed. This type can be identified by the fact that an extra item is always present in English immediately after the verb. Compare:

I	2	3	
The house	was built	by my brother	

I	2	3	4
The house	was given	new windows	by my brother

°**Gafodd y tŷ ei °godi gan ⁿmrawd**

°**Gafodd ffenestri newydd eu rhoi i'r tŷ gan ⁿmrawd**

Sometimes these constructions can be so awkward with the **cael**-passive that the **-ir/-wyd** autonomous forms are preferred. Further examples:

The visitors were shown the new leisure centre

°**Gafodd y °ganolfan hamdden newydd ei dangos i'r ymwelwyr**

or: **Dangoswyd y °ganolfan hamdden newydd i'r ymwelwyr**

We were taught the literary language instead of spoken Welsh

Dysgwyd yr iaith °lenyddol inni yn lle Cymraeg llafar

All students will be given a season ticket

Rhoddir tocyn tymor i °bob myfyriwr

376   Alternatives to the passive

Sometimes a passive is rather cumbersome in Welsh (often in cases of the 'false' passive described above), and a rephrasing of the sentence is more natural:

We were offered a trip to Fiji as compensation

°**Gawson ni °gynnig o °daith i Fiji fel iawndâl**

[lit. We got the offer of . . .]

We were told that the ship had already sailed

Wedson nhw wrthon ni °fod y llong wedi ymadael

[lit. They told us . . .]

Pryce will be expected to pay for what he did

Bydd disgwyl i Pryce °dalu am yr hyn naeth e

[lit. There will be (an) expectation . . .]

377–387 IMPERATIVE

377 Imperative (command forms)

The imperative of the verb, used for giving commands, appears in two forms – one (singular) for use where the pronoun **ti** is indicated, and the other (plural/formal) for **chi**. The imperative is arrived at by adding endings to the verb-stem (see §205–209), -a for singular and -wch for plural. Examples:

VN	verb-stem	sing. command	pl. command
taflu (throw)	**tafl-**	**tafla**	**taflwch**
ffonio (phone)	**ffoni-**	**ffonia**	**ffoniwch**
dechrau (start)	**dechreu-**	**dechreua**	**dechreuwch**
aros (wait)	**arhos-**	**arhosa**	**arhoswch**
meddwl (think)	**meddyli-**	**meddylia**	**meddyliwch**

378 Alternative formation of the sing. (ti) command form

There is an increasing tendency with VNs ending in a consonant to use the VN on its own as the **ti** command form. So, for example, besides **arhosa!** and **meddylia!** above, one is likely also to hear **aros!** and **meddwl!**:

Aros fan hyn eiliad	Wait here a moment
Meddwl am yr hyn wedes i	Think about what I said

Dechrau, although it is not a consonant-ending VN, can also be included here.

There is no comparable alternative for the **chi**-command form.

Both **ti** and **chi** commands can be reinforced by adding the pronouns **di** (note mutation) and **chi** immediately after, much as in English we can say *Wait here!* or *You wait here!*

Dechrau di, Elfyn, tra bo fi'n gwneud y coffi

You start, Elfyn, while I make the coffee

Darllenwch chi'r nodiadau, ac fe °fydda innau'n dosbarthu'r cwestiynau

You read the notes, and I'll give out the questions

Sometimes, again as in English, this 'echoing' pronoun not so much reinforces as softens the tone of the command. In this use it is frequent when addressing small children.

Chwilia di am dy °dedi, 'te

You look for your teddy, then

Agor di'r cwpwrdd, ac mi °rodda i nhw i mewn

You open the cupboard, and I'll put them in

380   **Mutations with command forms**

The command forms themselves are *not* mutated – as forms with endings they are exceptions in this regard. Note also that they *cannot* be used with the preverbal affirmative particles **fe°/mi°** (because they are not statements). There is SM after all command forms, because of the understood subject **ti/di** or **chi**. Sometimes, of course, this subject is actually present as an 'echoing' pronoun (see §379).

Rhowch °wybod i mi pan °gyrhaeddwch chi

Let me know when you get there   [**rhoi gwybod** *let know*]

Rho °ddarn o °bapur oddi dano

Put a piece of paper under it

381   **Irregular command forms**

These are relatively few in number, and must simply be learnt. Those for **edrych** and **mwynhau** listed below are widely used spoken variants not generally seen in writing. The rest are established in all forms of the language.

VN	sing. command	pl. command
dod (come)	tyrd (N) / dere (S)	dewch
mynd (go)	dos (N) / cer (S)	ewch/cerwch (S)
bod (be)	bydd	byddwch
gadael (let/leave)	gad	gadewch
edrych (look)	drycha	drychwch
mwynhau (enjoy)	mwynha	mwynhewch

The command forms of **gwneud** *do/make* – **gwna** and **gwnewch** – are, apart from the VN itself, one of the few instances in spoken Welsh where the initial **gw-** is widely retained.

Gwna dy °orau/Gwnewch eich gorau   Do your best

Imperative forms for **cael** are rarely encountered – rephrasings are more common; so, for example, the imperative forms of **cymryd** *take* (**cymer**, **cymerwch**) sometimes correspond to *have*:

Cymerwch °banaid o °de   Have a cup of tea

Occasionally imperative *have* in English corresponds to a rephrasing using **bod**:

Bydd yn °ddewr   Have courage (literally: Be courageous)

As for imperative *get*, this usually means *go and fetch*, and is so rephrased in Welsh:

Dos i nôl y papurau   Get the papers

382   Alternatives to command forms – polite requests

In practice, command forms are rather restricted in their use for the purposes of everyday conversation. Most situations require polite requests rather than orders. There are three main methods of forming requests for someone else to do something, with little difference in meaning between them.

Nei di° . . .?, Newch chi° . . .? *Will you . . .?*:

Newch chi °roid hwn iddo pan °welwch chi fe, os gwelwch yn °dda?
Will you give him this when you see him, please?

Nei di °gadw'r peth 'ma'n °ddiogel i mi tan yfory?

Will you keep this safe for me till tomorrow?

°Alli/°Elli di° . . .?, °Allwch/°Ellwch chi° . . .? *Can you . . .?*

°Elli di helpu fi gyda'r holl °fagiau 'ma?

Can you help me with all these bags?

°Allwch chi °ddeud wrtha i lle mae'r swyddfa °bost o fan hyn?

Can you tell me where the post office is from here?

°Fedri di° and °Fedrwch chi° are common alternatives for *Can you . . .?*, especially in N areas.

°Allet ti° . . .?, °Allech chi° . . .? *Could you . . .?*

°Allet ti °gyfieithu hyn inni °rywbryd?

Could you translate this for us sometime?

°Allech chi siarad °dipyn yn uwch inni yn y cefn?

Could you speak up a bit for us at the back?

The relationship between these three methods is the same as between their English equivalents: *Can you . . .?* and *Could you . . .?* are virtually interchangeable as slightly less direct alternatives to *Will you . . .?*

383 Prohibitives ('don't . . .')

To tell someone not to do something, we use **Paid** (ti-form) and **Peidiwch**, followed either by the verb alone, or by âʰ (ag before vowels) + VN:

Paid mynd yn rhy °bell, mae cinio bron yn °barod

Don't go too far, lunch is nearly ready

Peidiwch gweiddi arna i fel 'ny!

Don't shout at me like that!

As far as use or non-use of âʰ is concerned, the above examples would sound equally natural with an âʰ included, but nowadays its inclusion is entirely optional except in a few set phrases (e.g. **Paid â malu** *Don't talk (such) nonsense*), and it is perhaps on the decline. If it is used, then the AM required in the written language is likewise optional. So there are three possible ways of saying, for example, *Don't lose that money*:

Paid colli'r arian 'na

Paid â colli'r arian 'na

Paid â ʰcholli'r arian 'na

and there are the same options, of course, with **Peidiwch**. There is no appreciable difference between them, except that â + AM, being closest to the literary usage, is perhaps slightly more frequent in formal situations and in the media.

For prohibitives using **Na** + command or autonomous forms of the verb, occasionally encountered on official forms, see §374.

Note that the 'reinforcing' pronoun (see §379) with **paid** is not **di** but radical **ti**, and that the use of **âʰ** is much more likely with the reinforced forms:

Paid ti â chwerthin, achan!	Don't you laugh, my lad!
Peidiwch chi ag anghofio, nawr!	Don't you forget, now!

---

384 **1st pers. pl. imperative:** gad/gadewch inni° **('let's . . .')**

Although not strictly speaking a command-form, it is convenient to deal with *Let's* . . . here, as it involves the command-forms of **gadael** *let* (**gad** and **gadewch**). These are used with **inni**, followed by SM:

Gadewch inni °fynd	Let's go
Gad inni °ddadlwytho'r car wedyn	Let's unload the car later

Use of the sing. form **gad** (as opposed to pl. **gadewch**) **inni** of course presupposes a conversation between two people only.

---

385 **1st pers. pl. imperative alternatives –** -wn ni, nawn ni° . . .

The 1st pers. pl. inflected future of the verb (see §304) can be used to express *Let's* . . ., especially with commonly used verbs:

Awn ni!	Let's go!
	[lit. We will go!]
°Ddown ni'n ôl yfory!	Let's come back tomorrow!
	[lit. We will come . . .]

But lesser used verbs like, for example, **dadlwytho** would probably not be heard as °**Ddadlwythwn ni** in this context, even though there is nothing technically wrong with it.

Because this is simply the future tense, and not a true command-form, initial SM is possible here.

The **gwneud**-future (see §306) can also be used in this sense, in its 1st pers. pl. form **nawn ni°**:

Nawn ni °brynu'r bwyd ar y ffordd adre

Let's buy [or: We'll buy] the food on the way home

Nawn ni °ddadlwytho'r car wedyn

Let's unload [or: We'll unload] the car later

The ambiguity of these future-tense forms (*We will* . . . v. *Let's* . . .) is nearly always resolved by context, intonation etc. **Gad/gadewch inni°** is, of course, unambiguous.

386   'Let me' . . . ; 'Let him/her/them . . .'

These are expressed using **gad/gadewch** + **i** in the same way as *Let's* . . . above, again with SM of the VN:

Gadewch i mi °feddwl, rŵan

Let me think, now

Gad iddo °ddod pan °fydd e'n °barod

Let him come when he's ready

Gadewch iddyn nhw °dalu am yr hyn naethon nhw

Let them pay for what they did

Mae Sioned yn bwriadu galw'r cyfreithwyr i mewn. – Gad iddi . . . dim ots gen i.

Sioned's intending to call the solicitors in. – Let her . . . I don't care.

387 Idioms with command forms

A number of common idiomatic expressions use command forms:

Cer/Cerwch o 'ma!	Get lost!
Dos o "ngolwg i!	Get out of my sight!
Ewch amdani!	Go for it!
Ewch ati!	Go to it!
Daliwch ati!	Stick at it!
Gad °lonydd iddo!	Leave him alone!
Gad °lonydd iddi!	Leave her alone!
Gad fe'n llonydd!	Leave him alone!
Gad hi'n llonydd!	Leave her alone!
Gad iddo fe!	Leave him alone!
Gad iddi hi!	Leave her alone!
Gwna fel y mynni di	Do as you please
Gwnewch fel y mynnoch (chi)	Do as you please

388 Subjunctive

Although grammars of the literary language show a fairly well-developed subjunctive, the spoken language has long abandoned this particular verbal category except for its retention in a few set phrases. The status of the subjunctive in Welsh almost exactly parallels the subjunctive in English, though written Welsh makes a slightly wider use of it, and biblical Welsh even more so.

A full treatment of the forms of the subjunctive, therefore, can be found in grammars of the literary language. For the spoken language, we need only concern ourselves with identifying those few forms and constructions that are likely to be met in everyday speech. Mostly they express the idea of uncertainty, or unfulfilled wish, and they may be classified as either parts of **bod** (the more frequent), or of other verbs (in a very few set phrases).

Da *boch* **chi!**	Goodbye! (slightly formal)
Hidiwch be' °*fo*!	Never mind!
Lle *bo* **angen**	Where need be
Pan °*fo* (or: *bo*) **angen**	(As and) when needed
Lle bynnag y *bo*	Wherever it (may) be
Pryd bynnag y *bo*	Whenever it (may) be
A °*fo* °**ben, bid** °**bont**	He who would be a leader, let him be a bridge (proverb)

The subjunctive form **bo** is sometimes found after the conjunction tra *while*, where some sense of the indefinite future is implied:

Mi °**fydd Cantre'r Gwaelod yn parhau am byth tra bo'r muriau'n** °**gadarn, y drysau ynghau a Seithennyn ar y tŵr**

Cantre'r Gwaelod will last forever while the walls are firm, the doors closed and Seithennyn on the tower

390   **Subjunctive forms of other verbs**

[dod]	**Doed a** °*ddelo*	Come what may
[gwneud]	**Does a (**°*w*)*nelo* . . .	. . . nothing to do with
	(see below)	
[helpu]	**Duw a'n** *helpo*!	God help us!
[mynnu]	**Gwnewch fel y mynnoch chi**	Do as you please

Note the sentence structure with Does a °wnelo:

Does a (°**w)nelo cwestiynau moesoldeb** °**ddim â hi**

Questions of morality have nothing to do with it

Other persons are possible as well:

Does 'na ddim neloch chi â fi

You have nothing to do with me

Other instances of the subjunctive, nearly all of them proverbial or biblical expressions, or oaths, are of less frequent occurrence, though they are certainly still alive among native speakers of the older generation.

391 Defective verbs

Definition: these are verbs used only in some of their forms. Their uses are very restricted, and consequently they are not found with the full range of endings that ordinary verbs are allowed.

392 Defective verbs meddai **and** ebe

Meddai, with its virtually defunct synonym **ebe,** is a quotative verb – that is, it is used with the meaning *says/said* after words quoted. In practice, this means that, like its exact counterpart in archaic English *quoth,* and the charming and increasingly popular modern quotative *like,* it is found only after quotation marks, or where quotation marks are understood. It cannot be used before quotations marks (except perhaps in poetical language), and it cannot be used where reported speech (see §§495, 496) is used instead of quotation marks, in which case **dweud** is the most likely option. Examples with **meddai:**

> **'Cerwch o 'ma', meddai nhw wrtho fo**
>
> 'Get lost' they said to him

> **'°Wyddost ti be?', meddai hi. – 'Be'?' meddai fo**
>
> 'Do you know what?', she said. – 'What?', he said

> **'Be' ti'n °feddwl?' meddai fi. 'Be' ti'n °feddwl bo fi'n meddwl?' meddai hi.**
>
> I'm like, 'What do you mean?', and she's like, 'What do you think I mean?'

Examples of differing treatment of the same reported speech:

> **'°Ddylset ti °fod wedi codi'n °gynharach',** *meddai fi*
>
> 'You should have got up earlier', I said

> **Wedes i y dylai fo °fod wedi codi'n °gynharach**
>
> I said he ought to have got up earlier

As is clear from the above examples, **meddai** can be used with all persons (and with names as well – '. . .', **meddai Rhys**), and although some grammars give differing forms for different persons, the all-purpose **meddai** does seem to be well-established.

Three other forms, however, must be noted as being part of the living language: **meddwn i** (*I said*), **medden nhw** (*they said*) and **medd** (*says . . .*). In practice, **meddai** is quite sufficient for all quotative situations.

Ebe is encountered frequently enough in writing in place of **meddai**, but is virtually unheard of in speech. Even its colloquial counterpart **ebra** seems rare.

In N dialects there is also a non-verbal quotative particle **chadal** (from **chwedl** *story*): . . ., chadal nhwthau . . . (*so*) *they say*; . . ., chadal Lowri . . ., (*so*) *Lowri says*.

393 **Defective verb** biau

Biau (usually fixed mutation, though sometimes non-mutated **piau** is heard, especially in dialect speech), has the basic meaning of *own, possess*. It is not a VN, and does not use **bod** in the present:

Pwy biau'r llyfr 'ma? – Fi biau fo

Whose book is this? – It's mine

But the relative form of **bod** (**sy**) is sometimes used in the above pattern:

Pwy sy biau'r llyfr 'ma? – Fi sy biau fo

Both variants are acceptable to native speakers

In the past tense (imperfect), **oedd** must be used, but note that, because **biau** is not a VN, no linking **yn** is required:

Pwy oedd biau'r llyfr? – Siân oedd biau fo

Whose book was it? – It was Siân's

Because it is essentially about *identification* (i.e. asking who owns something), the subject of **biau** always precedes it (see §223(a) for word-order rule in identification sentences), and so reported speech will require the special conjunction **mai** (or **taw**). Note that any present/past distinction lapses in these cases:

O'n i'n meddwl mai ti biau hwn

I thought this was yours

[lit. 'I thought that (it was) you (who) own this']

Wyt ti'n siwr mai Elfed biau hwnna?

Are you sure that's Elfed's?

[lit. 'Are you sure that (it is) Elfed (who) owns that?']

394 **Defective verb** geni

Geni *be born* occurs only as a VN and in the past tense autonomous/ impersonal forms **ganwyd** and **ganed**, which are interchangeable in speech.

Lle a pryd °gaethoch chi'ch geni, 'te?
When and where were you born, then?

°Ges i ⁿngeni yn Llanfairfechan ym mil naw dim wyth
I was born in Llanfairfechan in 1908

Ganwyd (Ganed) fi yn ystod yr Ail °Ryfel Byd
I was born during the Second World War

The first two examples above show that the VN is used in a passive construction with **cael**. The cael and autonomous form constructions are themselves interchangeable (e.g. **ganwyd chi** is a perfectly good, though less frequent, alternative to °**gaethoch chi'ch geni**, and so on). The VN is also used for birth: **dyddiad geni** *date of birth*, **man geni** *place of birth*, although in the sense of a 'happy event' the related noun **genedigaeth** is preferred – **Llongyfarchiadau ar °enedigaeth eich merch °fach** *Congratulations on the birth of your daughter. Birthday*, however, is **penblwydd**.

395 **Defective verb** marw

Marw *die* as a VN is mostly found in the phrase **bu °farw** *has died/is dead*, and in various combinations of **wedi marw** with related meanings:

Bu °farw Cadeirydd y Bwrdd ar ôl gwaeledd estynedig
The chairman of the board has died after a protracted illness

°Drion ni helpu'r anifail °druan, ond oedd e wedi marw
We tried to help the poor animal, but it was dead/had died

Broadly speaking, the usage with **bu** is more 'dynamic' – it focuses attention more on the occurrence of death, while the **wedi** usage is concerned more with the fact or state of death or being dead. Note that **bu °farw** serves as the preterite for this verb. A true preterite **marwodd** is sometimes heard, but is unusual.

Sometimes a future for this verb is done with **gwneud** (i.e. Future III):

Neith o °farw?
Will he die?

The plural of **bu °farw, buon nhw °farw**, is also theoretically possible, though not encountered as much in practice.

> **Buon nhw °farw bron â bod ar yr un pryd**
>
> They died virtually at the same time

Where the sense requires a continuous or habitual meaning, **marw** can be used with **yn**:

> **Mae cannoedd yn marw °bob dydd yn Ethiopia tra bod gwledydd y Gorllewin yn gwneud y peth nesa i °ddim**
>
> Hundreds are dying every day in Ethiopia while the West does next to nothing

396   Pseudo-verbs – eisiau and angen

Eisiau *want* and angen *need*, although used as verbs and corresponding to verbs in English, are not VNs but nouns. They have no stem-form, and they cannot take endings, therefore they have to rely on **bod** when used as verbs. Even here they differ from VNs, in that they do not take the linking particles **yn** or **wedi**, and this means that only **yn**-tenses of **bod** (leaving out the **yn**) can be used with them:

[present]	**Dw i eisiau gweld y llythyr cyn penderfynu**
	I want to see the letter before deciding
	Wyt ti angen y papur 'ma bellach?
	Do you need this paper any more?
[imperfect]	**Doedd o °ddim eisiau tâl am y gwaith**
	He didn't want pay(ing) for the work
	O'n i angen y peth 'na ddoe – lle °ddest ti o hyd iddo?
	I needed that thing yesterday – where did you find it?
[future]	**°Fydda i eisiau trafod hyn oll gyda chi pnawn 'ma**
	I'll want to discuss all this with you this afternoon
	°Fyddan nhw angen y car wedyn, mae'n °debyg
	They'll probably need the car later
[conditional]	**'Swn i °ddim eisiau treulio wythnos °gyfan yno**
	I wouldn't want to spend a whole week there
	Basai hi angen mwy o °bres i °fedru gwneud hynny (N)
	She'd need more money to be able to do that

Both these pseudo-verbs can be followed not only by persons and objects, but also by verbs (. . . *want to discuss* . . . etc.).

The original status of these words as nouns can be seen in the frequent use of **Oes** for *Yes* in answer to questions of the type *Do you want . . .?, Does he need . . .?*, where the phrasing of the question might suggest **Ydw/Ydy** etc.

Dach chi eisiau hwn?	Do you want this?
Oes	Yes
Ydy Gwilym angen y car?	Does Gwilym need the car?
Oes	Yes

(This is especially characteristic of the N, although even here **Ydw/Ydy**, etc. is gaining ground in many areas.)

Notes:

(a) There is one circumstance where **eisiau** is used with **yn**. In classified and job advertisements in the newspapers, **yn eisiau** is always used for 'wanted' – this is a set phrase and is found only in this situation.

> **YN EISIAU: TEIPYDD RHAN-AMSER**
> WANTED: PART-TIME TYPIST

(b) **Eisiau** is usually so spelt, but is heard in an alarming variety of differing pronunciations, largely dependent on area; **isie, ise** and **isio** are all very common.

(c) An alternative to **eisiau** in its verbal use is **moyn** or **mofyn** (both S), which is, however, a true VN and requires **yn** with **bod**. The following pairs, then, are synonymous:

> **Faint ohonoch chi sy eisiau talu nawr?**
> **Faint ohonoch chi sy'n moyn talu nawr?**
> How many of you want to pay now?
>
> **Mae Dafydd eisiau gwylio'r canlyniadau pêl-droed**
> **Mae Dafydd yn moyn gwylio'r canlyniadau pêl-droed**
> Dafydd wants to watch the football results

397 Use of eisiau and angen as nouns

As true nouns, these words work in a similar way to a small number of other nouns used as stative expressions, i.e. to denote temporary states of mind or bodily conditions. These others are dealt with below (see §398), but eisiau and angen are slightly more versatile and must be looked at separately.

As nouns, they are used impersonally (i.e. *there is a need* . . . rather than *I need* . . . etc.) with the existential forms of **bod** (see §252), and with the person (if any) specified later in the sentence using **ar** *on*. Examples will help clarify the structure required:

Mae angen dwy °bunt arna i	I need two pounds
Hwyrach mai eisiau bwyd sy arni	Perhaps she needs something to eat
Faint °fydd eisiau arnoch chi?	How many will you need?
Cyffuriau – does mo'u hangen!	Drugs – who needs them!
	[lit. Drugs – there is not their need]

Note that, in this usage, eisiau has a sense of *need* rather than *want*, and therefore comes much closer in meaning to **angen**. But unlike the statives detailed in §398, eisiau and angen, because of their meaning, do not necessarily require a person to be specified – in other words, one can say simply *There is a (general) need to (do something)* without referring to anyone in particular. This often sounds awkward in English, where we have a virtual obligation to state a subject of some sort, but there is no such rule restricting Welsh here, and the following examples without specified subjects are by far the most natural way of expressing general need or requirement:

Mae eisiau dweud wrthyn nhw be' 'dy be', on'd oes?

They need telling what's what, don't they?

[lit. There is a need to tell them . . ., isn't there?]

Oes angen aros am y lleill?

Do (we) need to wait for the others?

[lit. Is there a need to . . .?]

Oedd angen dweud rhywbeth yn y diwedd

In the end, something had to be said

[lit. There was a need to say something . . .]

Note in the past example that the English version manages to convey the general, non-person-specific sense of the Welsh by turning the sentence into a passive and thereby filling the 'subject' slot with what is in effect the object – this is similar to what happens with impersonal **rhaid** (see §349). But Welsh does not need to resort to this rephrasing, and there is no passive construction in the Welsh version, as the literal translation makes clear.

398 **Noun constructions with** ar **expressing temporary state**

Temporary states of mind or body are generally expressed with existential **bod** and ar *on* + person, phrasing *I've got a cold* as *There is a cold on me*. Because temporary conditions like this constitute a departure from the norm, it is not surprising that the states of mind using this construction tend to be unpleasant or unwelcome, while the physical states tend to be illnesses or diseases. Nouns used in this construction are:

Mind: **cywilydd** *shame*; **hiraeth** *longing, homesickness*; **ofn** *fear.*

Body: **annwyd** *(a) cold*; **y °ddanno(e)dd** *toothache*; **eisiau bwyd**
          hunger; **y °frech °goch** *measles*; **y ffliw** *flu*; **peswch** *a cough*;
          syched *thirst*; diseases generally

°Alla i °ddim dod heno – mae annwyd trwm arna i

I can't come tonight – I've got a heavy cold

Ers pryd mae'r °ddannodd arnoch chi bellach?

How long is it now that you've had toothache?

Bydd syched arnon ni erbyn diwedd y °gystadleuaeth 'ma

We'll be thirsty by the time this competition's over

Cywilydd arnat ti!

Shame on you!

Oes eisiau bwyd ar y plant, tybed? – Oes, mae'n °debyg.

I wonder if the children are hungry? – Yes, probably

Exceptions to this construction are names for bodily aches and pains incorporating **tost** *sore, ill*. These use **(gy)da** *with* instead of ar:

Mae pen tost ofnadwy 'da fi ar hyn o °bryd

I've got a terrible headache at the moment

Oedd stumog °dost 'da "mrawd ar ôl y dathlu neithiwr

My brother had stomach ache after the celebrations last night

This usage has spread to the ar-words listed above as well in parts of Wales, helped by the influence of English, and it is not uncommon to hear, for example, **Mae annwyd 'da fi** in some areas.

Cur *pain* is used with **gan°** *with* (N) in phrases such as:

'S gen ti °gur (yn) dy °ben di?

Have you got a headache?

Adverbs and adverbials

399 Definitions

Adverbs are a large class of words that supply additional information, generally regarding the manner (see §401), time (see §§402–414) or place (see §§415–424) of an action. Examples in English would be *quietly, carefully, fast* (all manner), *yesterday, last year, now* (all time), and *here, inside, away* (all place). These three types constitute the vast majority of **adverbs** in Welsh, as in English.

Some adverbs do not come under the three main types, and will be dealt with separately as follows:

adverbs of degree (see §425)

adverbs of state (see §426)

miscellaneous adverbs (see §§427–440)

interrogative adverbs (see §441)

Finally, comparison of adverbs is dealt with under §442.

400 Form of adverbs

As far as form is concerned, Welsh adverbs fall into two broad classes: either they are derived from other words (in much the same way as *carefully* is derived from *careful* in English), or they are primary words or phrases in their own right. Note that it does not necessarily follow that, say, a primary adverb in English will also be primary in Welsh – *soon*, for example, is primary in English but derived (**yn °fuan**, from **buan**) in Welsh. The principles of deriving adverbs using **yn°** will be discussed in the context of adverbs of manner (see §401), nearly all of which are formed in this way.

Other types of adverb, both primary and derived, will then be dealt with by meaning, as listed above.

Sometimes whole phrases are used as adverbs, and these are referred to in this grammar as adverbials where a distinction is needed: for example, *always* is an adverb in English because it is a single word, while *last year* and *at the moment* are adverbials. In spoken Welsh, the single word **llynedd** *last year* is an adverb, while the phrase **trwy'r amser** *always* is an adverbial. But note that adverbials are simply a type of adverb, and when reference is made in this grammar to 'adverbs', this includes adverbials unless specifically stated otherwise.

401   Derived adverbs with yn°

These constitute a very large class of words, and include virtually all manner adverbs – that is, adverbs which answer the question *how?* or *in what way/ manner?* They are formed from adjectives by placing **yn°** (but with no mutation of ll- or rh-, see §9) in front. This often, but not always, corresponds to adding -*ly* to the English adjective. Examples:

cyflym	quick	**yn °gyflym**	quickly/fast
gofalus	careful	**yn °ofalus**	carefully
cyhoeddus	public	**yn °gyhoeddus**	publicly
prydlon	punctual, prompt	**yn °brydlon**	punctually, promptly
araf	slow	**yn araf**	slowly

Cofiwch °ddarllen y cyfarwyddiadau'n °ofalus cyn cychwyn y peiriant

Remember to read the instructions *carefully* before starting the machine

Mae'r pwyllgor llywio wedi ymateb yn °brydlon i'r sefyllfa

The steering committee has responded *promptly* to the situation

Mae'r bws 'ma'n mynd yn °gyflym, on'd ydy?

This bus is going *fast*, isn't it?

Rhaid cydnabod yn °gyhoeddus y camgymeriad difrifol a °wnaethpwyd ddoe

The serious error made yesterday must be *publicly* acknowledged

Siaradwch yn araf os gwelwch yn °dda

Speak *slowly* please

It is worth bearing in mind that this **yn°** is an integral part of the adverb, and should not be confused with the identical **yn°** used to link the verb **bod** to be with a following noun or adjective (see §15). Compare:

(a)   **Darllenwch y llyfryn yn °ofalus**   Read the booklet carefully

(b)   **Rhaid i chi °fod yn °ofalus**   You must be careful

In (a), the **yn°** is present to turn **gofalus** *careful* into *carefully*; in (b), **yn°** does not alter the meaning of **gofalus** (*careful*) at all, but is simply required as a link element after a part of **bod** (here the mutated VN, but equally necessary with any other part – **mae, ydy, basai** etc.). Looking at it another way, we have the adverb **yn °ofalus** in (a), and **yn°** + the adjective **gofalus** in (b).

English has a small number of adjectives which do not add *-ly* to form the adverb, notably *straight, fast* and the irregular *well* (instead of **goodly*). But in Welsh the corresponding adjectives will still need **yn°** if the adverb is intended – **yn syth, yn °gyflym, yn °dda**.

Miscellaneous derived adverbs (i.e. not of manner) are noted under the appropriate primary adverb sections below.

402   Adverbs of time

This is a much smaller class than manner, but extremely important if any degree of fluency is to be achieved and sustained. It includes a large number of adverbials, many of them idiomatic, and a smaller number of primary adverbs and derived adverbs with **yn°**. They answer questions like *When?*, *How often?* or *For how long?* As many of the following as possible should be committed to memory. Those requiring more detailed explanation as to use or construction are indicated by separate section numbers. (**Wythnos**) (*week*) indicates that other time periods (e.g. **mis, blwyddyn, dydd Llun**) can be substituted as required.

adeg y . . .	at the time of . . .
ambellwaith	sometimes, occasionally
am byth	for ever
am faint?	for how long?
am hir	for long
am °gyfnod	for a period
am sbel(en)	for a period

am (wythnos)	for a (week)
amser maith yn ôl	a long time ago
am y tro	for now/for the time being
ar adegau	at times
ar °brydiau	at times
ar hyn o °bryd	at the moment
ar ôl hynny	afterwards
ar unwaith	at once, immediately
ar y °foment	at the moment
ar y pryd	at the time
ar yr un pryd	at the same time
bellach	now (see §407)
°bob amser	always; every time
°bob blwyddyn	every year
°bob dydd	every day
°bob mis	every month
°bob tro	always; every time
°bob wythnos	every week
bore fory	tomorrow morning
°bryd hynny	at that time, then (see §408)
byth	ever; never (see §§409–413)
byth a beunydd	for ever and a day
byth bythoedd	for ever and ever
byth eto	never again
cyn (bo) hir	before long
(wythnos) diwetha	last (week)
°drannoeth (or trannoeth)	the next day
°droeon	several times
(y) dyddiau'ma	these days; nowadays
°ddim eto	not yet; not again
ddoe	yesterday
echdoe	the day before yesterday
echnos	the night before last

eisoes	already	Adverbs of time
eleni	this year	
erbyn hyn	by now; now	
erbyn hynny	by then; then	
erioed	ever; never (see §§409–413)	
ers hynny	since then	
(er)s °lawer dydd	in/for (i.e. since) many a day	
(er)s meitin	in/for (i.e. since) quite a time	
(er)s talwm	in/for (i.e. since) a long time	
ers tro	for (i.e. since) a long time	
ers (wythnos)	for (i.e. since) (a week)	
eto	yet	
gydag amser	in (the fullness of) time	
gyda'r nos	at night, by night	
gynnau	just now (see §407)	
heddi(w)	today	
heno ('ma)	tonight	
hyd yma	till now	
hyd yn °ddiweddar	till recently	
hyd yn hyn	till now	
i °ddechrau	at first	
(y) llynedd	last year	
maes o °law	later on; presently	
mewn da °bryd	in good time	
mewn pryd	in time (i.e. not late)	
nawr	now (S) (see §407)	
neithiwr	last night	
nes ymlaen	later on; presently	
(wythnos) nesa	next (week)	
nos yfory	tomorrow night	
o °bryd i'w gilydd	from time to time	
o hyn ymlaen	from now on	
o'r blaen	before (i.e. previously)	

o'r diwedd	at last
°rywbryd	some time
°rywdro	some time
rŵan, wan	now (N) (see §407)
sawlgwaith	more than once; several times
tan hynny	till then
tan yn °ddiweddar	till recently
toc	soon; shortly
trannoeth (°drannoeth)	the next day
trwy'r amser	all the time; always
unrhywbryd	any time
unrhywdro	any time
wastad	always
wedyn	then; after(wards); later on (see §408)
weithiau	sometimes
yfory	tomorrow
yma ac yn y man	now and again
ymhen (wythnos)	in a week (week's time)
ymlaen llaw	beforehand; in advance
yn achlysurol	occasionally
yn aml	often
yn anaml	seldom
yn °barod	already
yn °ddibaid	constantly; continuously
yn °ddiderfyn	ceaselessly; continuously
yn °ddiweddar	recently
yn °feunyddiol	daily
yn °fisol	every month
yn °flynyddol	annually, every year
yn °fuan	soon
yn °fynych	frequently
yn ôl	ago (see §414)
yn syth	straight away

yn wythnosol	every week	
yn y cyfamser	in the meantime; meanwhile	
yn y dechrau	at first; to begin with	
yn y diwedd	finally; in the end	
yn y man	later on; in a bit	
yn ystod y dydd	during the day; by day	
y tro diwetha	last time	
y tro 'ma	this time	
y tro nesa	next time	

403   SM of time adverbs

Time adverbs – primarily those which indicate 'when', 'how often' or (sometimes) 'for how long' an action or event takes place – undergo SM. This is the reason that many of the single-word time adverbs in the list appear with fixed or near-fixed SM. Examples:

°Fydda i'n mynd yno °bob mis

I go there *every month*   [time how often]

°Welwn ni chi i gyd °ddydd Mawrth!

We'll see you all *on Tuesday*!   [time when]

Fe °gyhoeddwyd °drannoeth °fod y penderfyniad wedi'i °ohirio

It was announced the next day that the decision had been postponed
   [time when]

Naethon ni symud fan hyn °ddwy °flynedd yn ôl

We moved here *two years ago*   [time when]

°Fis a hanner o'n i yn yr Eidal yn y diwedd

In the end I was in Italy *for a month and a half*   [time how long]

This is a fundamental and consistently applied mutation rule, and it extends to simple adverbs as well, so that several of these appear always with a fixed mutation – *yesterday* is always °**ddoe** (despite the fact that many dictionaries give only the radical **doe**, which is to all intents and purposes nonexistent except in the compound **echdoe** *the day before yesterday*). °**Bellach** *now* (see §407), °**bryd hynny** *at that time*, and a number of others are similar. Apparent exceptions to the rule are **llynedd** *last year*, which is really y llynedd, and **byth** *ever, never* which resists mutation in this sense because °**fyth** has a different meaning (see §104(c)).

404 'Today', 'tomorrow', etc.

The following grid of nine expressions should be memorized:

	yesterday	*today*	*tomorrow*
morning	**bore ddoe**	**bore 'ma**	**bore 'fory**
(day)	**ddoe**	**heddiw**	**yfory**
night	**neithiwr**	**heno ('ma)**	**nos yfory**

Notes:

(a) **heddiw** *today* is often pronounced **heddi** in many parts of Wales

(b) although **heno** on its own means *tonight*, a reinforcing **'ma** is often heard, especially where immediacy or urgency is intended: **heno 'ma**

(c) expressions for . . . *afternoon* use **pnawn** (written: **prynhawn**) in place of **bore** in the first line: e.g. **pnawn ddoe** *yesterday afternoon*

405 Special adverbials with time units

Special adverbials can be used with the time-units *day, week, month* and *year*. With **mis** *month* as example:

o fewn mis	within a month
°**ddechrau'r mis**	at the beginning of the month
°**ganol y mis**	in the middle of the month
°**ddiwedd y mis**	at the end of the month
ymhen mis	in a month (month's time)
trwy gydol y mis	throughout the month; all month

All but **o fewn** and **ymhen** can also be used with the names of days and months, and the seasons, e.g. °**ddechrau Medi** *at the beginning of September,* °**ganol yr hydre** *in the middle of autumn,* etc.

How to translate 'time'

There are no fewer than seven words in Welsh corresponding to the all-purpose English word *time*: ADEG, AMSER, CYFNOD, GWAITH, OES, PRYD, TRO. In some cases, there is overlapping of meaning, while others are used in quite specific circumstances. They are dealt with here in alphabetical order.

ADEG means *period of time* rather than a point in time, and as such is very close in meaning to **pryd** (see below). Indeed, in some phrases the two are interchangeable, e.g. °**bryd/adeg hynny** *at that time*, **ar adegau/°brydiau** *at times*. This interchangeability is probably more general in the colloquial language than in the standard – **mae'n adeg inni °fynd** *it's time for us to go* is a common alternative in many parts of Wales to the more standard **mae'n °bryd inni °fynd**. Used on its own with events, it has acquired the adverbial meaning *at the time of . . .*: **adeg y rhyfel** *at the time of* (i.e. *during*) *the war*, **adeg yr arholiadau** *at exam time*. No preposition is used in these phrases:

°Fues i yn Llundain adeg y Streic °Gyffredinol

I was in London at the time of the General Strike

Certain set phrases must simply be learnt as encountered, e.g. **ar adeg °gyfleus** *at a convenient time*.

AMSER is the word for *time* in its most general sense, as a commodity or concept:

Oes amser 'da chi?	Have you got time?
Mae amser yn °brin ('da ni)	(We're) pushed for time
Bydd hyn yn arbed amser	This will save time

In colloquial usage, **Mae'n amser i°** is a common alternative for **Mae'n °bryd i°** *It's time to . . .*, perhaps by analogy with English:

Mae'n amser inni °fynd

or **Mae'n °bryd inni °fynd**

It's time for us to go

Note also **rhan-amser** *part-time* and **llawn amser** *full-time*:

Dan ni'n gweithio'n rhan-amser tan y Dolig

We're working part-time till Christmas

CYFNOD means *period* or *term*, i.e. a stretch of time with a clearly perceived beginning and end, so it is the normal word in historical contexts – **cyfnod y Dadeni** *the time of the Renaissance*, **cyfnod Owain Glyndŵr** *the time of Owain Glyndŵr.*

Note the adjectival expressions **cyfnod hir** *long-term* and **cyfnod byr** *short-term*:

Be' °fydd *effeithiau cyfnod hir* y penderfyniad 'ma, tybed?

What will be the *long-term effects* of this decision, I wonder?

GWAITH is a feminine noun meaning *time* where the number of times is being stated. It is used with cardinal numerals (see §183), e.g. °**ddwywaith** *twice*, and in certain other related expressions, most notably °**weithiau** *sometimes*. See also **tro** below.

OES is very similar in meaning to **cyfnod**, and again implies *period of time*, but generally a longer period than **cyfnod**. It often corresponds to English *age*: **Y Canol Oesoedd** *The Middle Ages*; **Oes yr Iâ** *The Ice Age*, **Oes yr Efydd yng °Nghymru** *The Bronze Age in Wales*.

It has a secondary meaning of *lifetime*: **am °weddill ei oes** *for the rest of his life*; **carchar am oes** *life imprisonment*; **ar hyd ei hoes** *all her life*; **Hir oes i'r iaith!** *Long live the language!*

PRYD, apart from its use as the interrogative *when?* (**pryd?** – see §441), is very similar in range and meaning to **adeg**, see above. It is found mainly in idiomatic expressions as listed in §402. Most of these are very common and should be learnt for active use, particularly **ar hyn o °bryd** *at the moment*, **o °bryd i'w gilydd** *now and again*, **ar y pryd** *at the time*, **ar yr un pryd** *at the same time* (also **ar yr un adeg**), and **mewn pryd** *in time*. Note also the adjective **prydlon** *punctual, prompt*.

TRO is used with ordinal numbers as **gwaith** (see above) is used with cardinals, and corresponds to *the . . . -th time*: **yr ail °dro** *the second time*, **am y canfed tro** *for the hundredth time*, **am y tro cynta erioed** *for the first time ever/for the first ever time*. Further details are under §184.

Note also **y tro ola** *the last time* (in a series) vs. **y tro diwetha** *the last time* (most recent) – see also §172.

The idea of successive times is also found in some idioms, and these also require **tro**: °**dro ar ôl tro** *time and again*; °**bob tro** *every time*. The mutated pl. °**droeon** is sometimes found meaning *several times*.

Telling the time in Welsh is explained under numerals (see §173).

Rŵan (often **wan** in speech) in the N and **nawr** in the S are simply regional alternatives for the general word *now*. The variant **yn awr** sometimes encountered in writing, and often given instead of **nawr** even in modern dictionaries, sounds stilted in speech.

Bellach means *now* with a particular connotation: it is used where there is some sense of a change of situation or circumstance, with an implied contrast between *now* and *then*. Examples:

Oedd hi'n byw wrth ei hun °bryd hynny, ond mae hi'n °briod bellach

She lived on her own then, but she's married now

Heddwas o'n i, ond diffoddwr tân ydw i bellach

I used to be a policeman, but now I'm a firefighter

Mae hyn bellach wedi'i °gywiro

This has now been corrected

Mae'r awdurdodau bellach yn gwadu °fod unrhywbeth o'i °le

The authorities now deny that anything is wrong

Note the implication in the last example that, at some time previously, they had not been denying it. This is the element of change that is central to the meaning of **bellach**.

This connotation of change means that, in NEG sentences, **bellach** corresponds to (*not*) *any more*:

Dw i °ddim yn tanysgrifio bellach

I don't subscribe any more (or now)

Does neb yn byw yno bellach

No-one lives there any more

Nid tedi bach cyffredin mohono bellach

(He's) not an ordinary little teddy any more

Mwyach is sometimes heard as an alternative to **bellach** in negative (*not*) *any more* sentences:

Dyw hi °ddim yn mynychu'r ysgol 'na mwyach

She doesn't go to that school any more

Gynnau (pronounced as -a/-e) means *just now*, referring to events that happened a very short time ago:

Be' wedodd e gynnau?

What did he just say?   [i.e. What did he say just now?]

Rhaid i mi °gytuno â'r sylwad naethoch chi gynnau

I have to agree with the point you made just now

It is an adverb, and comes at the end of the sentence, like the English *just now*. For newydd° + VN (*have*) *just . . .*, see XL

408   Translation problems ('then')

This one word has several meanings in English, for which different Welsh equivalents are required.

WEDYN means *then* in the sense of *subsequently*. *And then . . .* is ac wedyn (not *a wedyn), and this is commonly pronounced chwedyn in speech.

Aethon ni i'r °dre, ac wedyn i'r traeth

We went to town, and then to the beach

Tacluswch eich stafelloedd, ac wedyn gellwch chi °wylio'r teledu

Tidy your rooms, and then you can watch TV

Colloquially, wedyn is frequently used for *later on*.

YNA (*there*) can be used as an alternative to wedyn, especially when a sequence of events is being narrated:

Eisteddodd o °flaen y tân. Yna daeth Elen i mewn.

He sat down in front of the fire. Then Elen came in.

°**BRYD HYNNY**(or **ADEG HYNNY**) means *then* in the sense of *at that time*:

Doedd dim bananas i'w cael o °gwbwl °bryd hynny

You couldn't get bananas at all then   [i.e. at some time in the past]

Sut °olwg oedd ar y pentre °bryd hynny?

What did the village look like then?

Compare:

Sut oedd eu tŷ nhw'n edrych °bryd hynny?

What did their house look like then? [i.e. at that time in the past we are talking about]

Sut oedd eu tŷ nhw'n edrych wedyn?

What did their house look like then? [i.e. after they'd done the renovations]

FELLY – in sentences where *then* means *so* or *therefore* (i.e. used to seek confirmation), **felly** is used in Welsh:

Ti'n dod gyda ni wedi'r cwbwl, felly?

You're coming with us after all, then?

Felly mae'r gêm wedi dechrau'n °barod?

Then the game has started already?

In its use at the end of a sentence (but not at the start), **felly** can be substituted with **'te** (see below): **Ti'n dod gyda ni wedi'r cwbwl, 'te?**

'TE   The parenthetical . . ., *then* is rendered in Welsh by **'te** (**'ta** in N):

Be' sy wedi bod yn digwydd fan hyn, 'te?

What's been going on here, then?

Rŵan 'ta, gadewch inni °weld be' sy gynnon ni (N)

Now then, let's see what we've got

Pwy sy am °gael ychydig rhagor o °gyw iâr, 'te?

Who wants to have a little bit more chicken, then?

409   Byth ('ever', 'never'); erioed ('ever', 'never')

These words mean the same in English, but are used in different circumstances and are <u>not</u> interchangeable.

English makes a formal distinction between *ever* and *never*, but Welsh, like French (*jamais*), does not; both **byth** and **erioed** mean either *ever* or *never*. From the English-speaking student's point of view, context always makes clear which translation from the Welsh is appropriate – only one of the two choices will ever sound right in English. The problem for non-native users is whether to use **byth** or **erioed**. The difference is best explained by taking **erioed** first.

410 Erioed

Erioed *ever*, *never* refers to past time (with one apparent exception explained below under **byth**) or completed action. It is used in conjunction with:

(a) all **wedi**-tenses (see §262)

(b) the preterite (see §292)

Examples:

Dw i erioed wedi clywed am y °fath °beth

I've never heard of such a thing

Sa 'n chwaer i erioed wedi cytuno i'r amodau 'na

My sister would never have agreed to those conditions

Weles i 'rioed gymaint o °bobol mewn un stafell   [pret.]

I never saw so many people in one room

Y menyn gorau nes i °flasu erioed

The best butter I ever tasted

411 Byth

Byth (fixed non-mutation) *ever*, *never* refers to non-past time or ongoing action and is used with all other tenses including the imperfect:

Cymru am byth!   [fut. understood]

Wales for ever!

Byth a hefyd   [fut. understood]

For ever and a day

Dw i byth yn talu â siec fan hyn   [pres.]

I never pay by cheque here

°Fydda i byth yn dod fan hyn 'to   [fut. II]

I'll never come here again

°Ddo i byth 'to   [fut. I]

I'll never come again

Swn i byth yn gadael iddyn nhw °fynd ar eu pennau eu hunain   [condt]

I would never let them go on their own

O'n i byth yn darllen nofelau °bryd hynny [impf]

I never read (or: used to read) novels then

412 Byth **and the imperfect**

The use of **byth** with the imperfect, as in the last example above, demon-strates that the nature of the action (i.e. completed or ongoing) is ultimately the deciding factor with **byth** and **erioed**. The imperfect clearly refers, of course, to past time, but in saying *I never used to read novels . . .*, we are describing a habitual or ongoing situation. Put another way, the important thing about the imperfect is that it is an **yn**-tense (even if it does refer to the past), and **yn**-tenses imply ongoing or habitual action as opposed to completion. All simple **yn**-tenses will use **byth**, just as all **wedi**-tenses will use **erioed**. As for the inflected tenses, note that the only one that cannot be done alternatively with **yn** (the preterite – §292) takes **erioed**, while the inflected future and (rarer) conditional (which do have periphrastic alterna-tives with **yn**) take **byth**.

413 Byth, erioed **and** °ddim

Note that **byth** and **erioed** do not need °**ddim** to convey the meaning of *never*, though it is sometimes heard before **erioed**: Dw i (°ddim) erioed wedi bod . . . *I've never been . . . .* This usage (with °ddim) is regarded by many speakers as sub-standard.

Byth and **erioed** are used on their own as answer-words to mean *Never*:

°Fuoch chi yn yr Unol °Daleithiau? – Erioed

Have you been to the United States? – Never

Wyt ti'n gweld hi o °gwbwl dyddiau 'ma? – Byth

Do you see her at all these days? – Never

They can combine with **bron** *almost* to mean *Hardly ever*:

Pa mor aml dych chi'n gwylio'r teledu? – Bron byth

How often do you watch television? – Hardly ever

Where **byth** occurs in set phrases such as **byth eto** *never again*, the completed/ongoing criterion does not apply: °**Weles i mono fo byth eto** *I never saw him again*, but note that in this type of example, the word **byth** is not in its

311

usual place (after the subject) anyway, and is associated much more closely with the **eto** than with the preterite verb °**weles**.

414   Yn ôl ('ago')

Like its English equivalent, **yn ôl** follows the time expression, which itself undergoes SM because of the 'time when' principle (see §403). Examples:

> **Wedes i'r un peth wrtho °ddwy °flynedd yn ôl**
>
> I told him the same thing two years ago

> **°Ddaethon ni i'r casgliad 'na °dair wythnos yn ôl**
>
> We came to that conclusion three weeks ago

> **Fe symudodd y cwmni i °Ogledd Llundain chwe mis yn ôl**
>
> The company moved to North London six months ago

Care must be taken with **yn ôl** generally, as it has two other meanings in common use: *back* (**Dewch yn ôl!** *Come back!*) and *according to* (**Yn ôl yr adroddiadau diweddara** . . . *according to (the) latest reports* . . .). Context always makes clear which is the appropriate translation.

415   Adverbs of place

Adverbs of place are the smallest of the three main classes, and include both location in a place, and direction/motion towards (or away from) a place. Therefore they answer the questions *Where?*, *(To) where?* and *From where?*

416   Words for 'where'

Although **ble?** is almost universally recommended in textbooks for *where?*, **lle?** (fixed non-mutation, or °**le?** in some areas) is probably more usual in native speech overall. **Lle** (pl. **llefydd, lleoedd**) is also a noun meaning *place*, but in practice there is no ambiguity in context, and most speakers neither make, nor feel it necessary to make, such a distinction. Extended variants **yn lle?** (*in where?*) and **ymhle?** are occasionally heard as well.

(To) where? uses **i(°)** optionally:

> **Lle dach chi'n mynd?**
>
> **I lle dach chi'n mynd?**

I °le dach chi'n mynd?

Where are you going (to)?

From where? is O lle? or O °le?:

O lle dach chi'n dod yn °wreiddiol?

O °le dach chi'n dod yn °wreiddiol?

Where do you come from originally?

417   'Here', 'there', etc.

Welsh has a three-level system of expressing location relative to the speaker, while English has only two (*here and there*). In Welsh, as in some other European languages (notably Spanish), a distinction is made between *there* (close to the speaker) and *there* (further away from the speaker). In addition, Welsh has yet another word for *there* when the place is not in sight of the speaker.

A further complication here is that each of the three basic place-words (set I below) has one or more alternative forms with **fan** (set II below). In expressing location sets I and II are to all intents and purposes interchangeable, but they behave differently when expressing motion. The basic forms are as follows:

	here	*there (close by)*	*there (further away)*
(I)	**yma**	**yna**	**acw**
(II)	**fan hyn** **fan'ma** **famma**	**fan'na**	**fan'cw** **nacw**

There is a special set I form **yno** which is dealt with in §419.

For location – set I forms are used as they stand; set II forms are used with optional prefix **yn (y)** (except **nacw**): e.g. **fan hyn** or **yn (y) fan hyn** *here*, etc.

Eisteddwch yma

Eisteddwch fan hyn

Eisteddwch yn fan hyn

Sit here

Note that the set II forms, though rarely mentioned in textbooks, are much more frequent in speech in many areas than the 'standard' set I forms; and

313

that shortened versions of set I have developed an adjectival use as *this* . . ., *that* . . . etc. (see §117).

For motion towards – set I forms are used as they stand; set II forms are used with optional prefix **i ('r)** (except **nacw**): e.g. **fan hyn** or **i ('r) fan hyn** (*to*) *here.*

> **Ewch yn ôl yna**
>
> **Ewch yn ôl fan'na**
>
> **Ewch yn ôl i fan'na**
>
> Go back there

For motion from – both sets require **o**. Set I forms: **yma** and **yna** usually drop the initial **y-**:

> **Cer o 'ma!** (pl. **Cerwch o 'ma!**)
>
> Get lost!   [lit. Go from here]

> **Tyrd o 'na!**
>
> Get away from there!   [lit. Come from there]

Note that **acw** is rarely heard with **o** (set II forms **o fan'cw** or **o nacw** are used instead).

Set II (except **nacw**) optionally uses **'r** after **o**:

> **Sut mae cyrraedd yr °orsaf o ('r) fan'ma?**
>
> How do I get to the station from here?

418   Dyma°, dyna°, dacw°

These are special extended set I forms (see §417) used for pointing out or drawing attention to something. They correspond to French *voici*, *voilà* and to various English phrasings: *Here is/are* . . ., *There is/are* . . ., *This is. . . / These are* . . . etc. All are followed by SM, and **dyna°** particularly is often shortened to **'na°**.

> **Dyma newyddion Radio Cymru**
>
> Here is the Radio Cymru news

> **Dyma'ch stafell am y °ddwy °flynedd nesa**
>
> This is your room for the next two years

Dyma lle byddwch chi'n gweithio o hyn ymlaen

[fixed non-mutation of adverb lle – §416]

This is where you'll be working from now on

(Dy)na °gar mawr sy 'da ti!

That's a big car you've got!

Yn anffodus, dyna yw arholiad

Unfortunately, that's (what) an exam is

[i.e. what exams are all about]

Lle mae Dafydd?	– **Dacw fo, yn dŵad lawr y stryd** (N)
Where's Dafydd?	– There he is, coming down the street

'Co, a variant of (da)cw, is very common in some S areas for *There . . .* regardless of distance from the speaker: '**Co fe, ar y llawr** *There it is, on the floor.*

'Na is used with the pronouns to indicate agreement on something, or confirmation of something the other speaker said. It often corresponds to *Right . . .* in English and obviously underlies Welsh English phrasings of the type *There we are, (then)*, *There you are, (then)*:

Awn ni eto yfory, 'te.	**'Na ni**
We'll go again tomorrow, then.	There we are [i.e. OK, then]
Ydw i'n sgwennu fe fel hyn?	**'Na fe**
Do I write it like this?	That's it [i.e. That's right]
A i â hwn nawr, iawn?	**'Na ti, 'te**
I'll take this now, OK?	There you are, then
	[i.e. Right you are, then]

'Na fe/fo in particular can occur repeatedly as a periodic response, with no more significance than to confirm to the other speaker that everything is being understood and/or agreed with.

Felly mae'r peth 'ma'n mynd i mewn fan hyn?	– **'Na fe**
So this thing goes in here?	– That's it

419 Yno ('there')

This special set I form (see §417), with no corresponding set II or d-variants, is used where *there* indicates a place not in sight (usually because it is too far away from the speaker). **Yma**, **yna** and **acw** can all be pointed at – **yno** cannot:

Mae teulu 'da fi yn Efrog Newydd, ond °fues i erioed yno

I've got family in New York, but I've never been there

Os ei di rŵan, mi °fyddi di yno erbyn amser cinio yfory

If you go now, you'll be there by lunchtime tomorrow

Ti °ddim wedi mynd i'r gwely, 'ta? – Nadw, ond mi a i yno toc (N)

You haven't gone to bed then?   – No, but I'll go (there) soon

420 **'Somewhere', 'nowhere'/'(not) anywhere',
'everywhere'**

The basic forms in speech are **rhywle**, **nunlle** (or **nunman**) and **°bobman** respectively, but care should be taken with the differing ways in which they operate, and with the numerous slight variants encountered in speech.

location	motion to	motion from
(yn) rhywle, r(h)ywle	**i °rywle**	**o °rywle**
nunlle	**(i) nunlle**	**o nunlle**
	i'r unlle	**o'r unlle**
ymhobman	**i °bobman**	**o °bobman**

Examples:

°Adawes i 'n sgidiau fi °rywle fan hyn, dw i'n siwr

I'm sure I left my shoes somewhere here

Mae'r rheiny'n dod o °rywle yn y Gogledd

Those come from somewhere in the North

°Weles i nhw nunlle

I didn't see them anywhere

Doedd dim pobol nunman

There were no people anywhere

Y cwbwl oedd i'w °weld oedd ceir ymhobman

All you could see was cars everywhere

Dan ni'n °barod i °fynd i °bobman i °ddatrys y °broblem 'ma

We are ready to go anywhere [= to all places] to solve this problem

°Fydd cantorion yn dod fan hyn o °bobman

Singers will be coming here from all over

Note also (yn) rhywle arall *somewhere else.*

421   Other adverbs of place and direction

(i) fyny (N)	up, upwards	**ffordd hyn**	this way
lan (S)	up, upwards	**ffordd 'na**	that way
(i) lawr	down, downwards	**adre**	home (direction) – see Notes
(i) ffwrdd (N)	away, off	**ga(r)tre**	home (location) – see Notes
bant (S)	away, off	**drws nesa**	next door
ar y °dde	on the right	**fyny ('r) grisiau**	upstairs
ar y chwith	on the left	**lan y grisiau**	upstairs
i'r °dde	to the right – see Notes	**fyny staer**	upstairs
i'r chwith	to the left – see Notes	**lan staer**	upstairs
ymlaen	ahead; on	**lan llofft**	upstairs
yn ôl	back	**lawr y grisiau**	downstairs
drwodd	through – see Notes	**lawr staer**	downstairs
drosodd	over – see Notes		

Notes:

(a)   **i fyny** and **lan** are interchangeable regional variants as indicated

(b)   although officially **adre** and **ga(r)tre** have the distinct meanings of *home-wards* and *at home*, this distinction is increasingly blurred in modern usage, partly at least through the influence of English, where *home* encompasses both meanings. Certainly it is not unusual to hear **Ydy Siôn adre?** for *Is Siôn (at) home?*, and **Awn ni gatre** for *Let's go home*

317

(c) all five variants for *upstairs* are in common use – note particularly that **lan llofft** does not normally mean *in the loft*

(d) °**dde** *right* has a fixed mutation – see also §**423**

(e) **mynd yn chwith** is a common idiomatic expression for *go wrong*: **Aeth popeth yn chwith bore 'ma** *Everything went wrong this morning*

(f) **drwodd** and **drosodd** are adverbial forms of the prepositions **trwy°/ drwy°** *through* and **dros°** *over*. Compare:

   Aeth y bws drwy'r °dre heb stopio   [prep. + noun]
   The bus went through the town without stopping

  but: **Aeth y bws drwodd heb stopio**   [adverb]
   The bus went through without stopping

   Mae'r atebion i gyd dros y °dudalen
   All the answers are over the page

  but: **Trowch y peth drosodd i °weld be' sy odano**
   Turn the thing over to see what's underneath (it)

422   Tu-**adverbials**

In addition to the list above, Welsh has several common direction/place adverbials using **tu**, an element meaning *-side* (the normal independent word for *side* is **ochor**):

tu allan (tu fas – S)	outside
tu °fewn (or **tu mewn**)	inside; within
tu cefn	behind
tu ôl	behind
tu draw	beyond; over there
tu hwnt	beyond

and also sometimes heard:

tu °flaen	in front

Notes:

(a) **tu hwnt** is also an adverb of degree meaning *extremely* (see §**425**)

(b) do not confuse **tu °fewn** *within* (place) with **o °fewn** *within* (time) (see §**405**)

(c)   mutation variants such as **tu mewn/°fewn** are interchangeable, though
     the mutated versions are probably somewhat more common in speech

On their own, the **tu**-adverbials indicate location:

Maen nhw i gyd tu °fewn yn gwylio'r teledu

They're all inside watching TV

Gad fe tu allan am °funud

Leave it outside a minute

Rho fe tu ôl, nei di?

Put it behind (there), will you?

Where further specification (e.g. *inside where?*) is needed, **i°** is added.
Compare:

tu °fewn inside	**tu fewn i'r adeilad** inside the building
tu cefn behind/round the back	**tu cefn i'r bar** behind the bar

Motion uses **i'r** before the **tu**-adverbial, though this seems optional with
many speakers:

Ewch chi i gyd (i'r) tu allan!

All of you go outside!

423   Points of the compass

The cardinal points are: **gogledd** *north*, **de** *south*, **dwyrain** *east* and **gorllewin**
west, all masculine. Intermediate points are formed as in English, but with
SM of second element, e.g. **gogledd-°orllewin** *north-west*, **de-°ddwyrain**
southeast.

Location is expressed with **yn y**: **yn y Gogledd** *in the North*, or **yn** + place
name: **Yng ⁿNgogledd Cymru** *in North Wales*, **yn ⁿNe-Ddwyrain Lloegr** *in
South-East England*. The NM is fairly common in speech with the points of
the compass. *To the north of* . . . is **i'r gogledd o°**: **Mae'r ffatri wedi'i lleoli
i'r dwyrain o'r °dre ei hun** *The factory has been situated to the east of the
town itself*.

Motion uses **i'r**: **i'r gogledd** *to the north, north(wards)*, etc. **Dan ni'n
bwriadu mynd ymlaen i'r gogledd ar ôl cinio** *We're planning to go on north
after lunch*. Sometimes **tua** is heard for this instead: **troi tua'r de-°ddwyrain**
turning south-east(wards).

Note the distinction between **i'r de** *to the south* and **i'r °dde** *to the right* (see §421).

Adjectives are: **gogleddol** *northern* (or *northerly*), **deheuol** *southern*, **dwyreiniol** *eastern* and **gorllewinol** *western*, but they are less frequently used than their English equivalents – **acen gogleddol** *a northern accent*, but **Gogledd Lloegr** *Northern England* (lit. *the North of England*), **gwynt o'r Gogledd** *a northerly wind*.

424   Syntax of place adverbs when used with bod

Adverbs of place are, by their nature, frequently used with **bod** *be*, and it is important to note that the predicative or 'linking' **yn** (see §15) is <u>not</u> used in these circumstances. Compare:

Mae ei °frawd yn °beiriannydd	[**bod** + noun]
His brother is an engineer	
Mae ei °frawd yn sâl ar hyn o °bryd	[**bod** + adjective]
His brother is ill at the moment	
but: **Mae ei °frawd fan hyn**	[**bod** + adverb of place]
His brother is here	
Mi °fydd Jimbo tu ôl i'r bar trwy gydol y noswaith	[**bod** + **tu**-adverbial]
Jimbo will be behind the bar all evening	

425   Adverbs of degree

These are used to modify adjectives. Examples in English are *very big, rather difficult, extremely boring, awfully expensive*. There are two main types in Welsh:

(a)   a limited number of primary adverbs such as **iawn** *very*, **rhy°** *too*. These are listed under adjective modifiers (see §95), together with notes on position relative to the adjective. To these can be added the place adverbial **tu hwnt** (*beyond* – see also §422), used idiomatically after an adjective to mean *extremely*: **Oedd y °ddarlith yn °ddiflas tu hwnt** *the lecture was extremely boring* (cf. some types of Welsh English *boring beyond*). Also the more literary alternative **i'r eitha**, used in the same way: **diflas i'r eitha** *extremely boring*.

(b) adjectives used adverbially, much as in English *completely exhausted, horribly vain*. While this technique is theoretically possible with almost any adjective, in Welsh as in English, its use in normal conversation is confined to a relatively small number of words. Most of these usually precede the main adjective, but are linked by an intervening **o°**:

arbennig o °dda	especially good
hynod o °ddiddorol	extraordinarily interesting
ofnadwy o °ddrud	awfully expensive
andros o °drwm (N)	awfully heavy

though **hollol** *complete(ly)* and **gwir** *real(ly)* are used without the **o°**:

Oedd y ffilm yn hollol annealladwy

The film was completely unintelligible

Mae'r °bobol 'ma'n °wir °dlawd

These people are really poor

Some can alternatively be used like **iawn**, i.e. immediately after the adjective:

Mae'r sgidiau 'ma'n ofnadwy o °ddrud

or: **Mae'r sgidiau 'ma'n °ddrud ofnadwy**

These shoes are awfully expensive

This is an option possible only with certain adjectives, and the construction with **o°** is the safer when in doubt.

426 Stative adverbs with ar°

All of these involve **ar°** + noun or verb, and express mostly physical states. It is simplest just to learn them as one-off items:

ar agor	open	**ar °gael**	available
ar °ben	finished, done with	**ar °gau**	closed, shut
ar °dân	on fire	**ar °glo**	locked
ar °ddihun	awake	**ar °goll**	lost
ar °fai	to blame, at fault	**ar °wahân**	separate, apart
ar °frys	in a hurry	**ar °werth**	on/for sale
ar °gadw	put away, tidied away		

The stative meaning is particularly clear with the verbs; compare:

Bydd y llyfrgell yn cau am hanner awr wedi pump heno

The library will close at half past five tonight

Bydd y llyfrgell ar °gau am °weddill yr wythnos

The library will be closed for the rest of the week

Note that no 'linking' **yn** is used when these appear after **bod**. Further examples:

Mae hi ar °ben 'da ni nawr

We're finished (done for) now   [lit. 'It is finished with us now']

Chi sy ar °fai am hyn oll!

This is all your fault!   [lit. You are to blame for all this]

Brechdanau ffres ar °gael yma °bob bore

Fresh sandwiches available here every morning

Dw i'n meddwl bod ni ar °goll erbyn hyn

I think we're lost now (or: . . . we've got ourselves lost)

Teganau i gyd ar °gadw nawr, °blantos!

All toys put away now, children!

Cadwch nhw ar °wahân am y tro

Keep them apart for now

427 Miscellaneous adverbs

These include a number of words indicating probability of varying degrees, and others difficult to classify. They are all treated together here, and are all in common use. Peculiarities of construction with some of them are dealt with in more detail after the main listing, as indicated. Certain adverbs, marked here with an asterisk, modify whole sentences – see §428 for general remarks on these.

ar °gyfartal	on average
bron	almost (see §429)
chwaith	either (with preceding NEG) (see §430)
dim ond	only (see §435)
efallai*	perhaps (see §436)

eto	(in speech often **'to**) again	Miscellaneous adverbs
eto i gyd	(but) then again . . .	
ac eto	and then (again) . . .	
fel arall	otherwise	
fel arfer	as usual; usually (see §431)	
fel rheol	as a rule	
felly	so; thus (see §432)	
gan amla	mostly (i.e. most often)	
gan °fwya	[written: . . . **mwya**] mostly	
gobeithio*	hopefully (see §433)	
gwaetha'r modd	unfortunately, regrettably	
heb os nac onibai	without a doubt	
hefyd	also	
hwyrach*	perhaps (see §436)	
mae'n °debyg*	probably	
mae'n ymddangos*	apparently	
o °bosib	possibly	
o °gwbwl	at all (see §434)	
o'r herwydd	for that reason	
prin	hardly, scarcely (see §437)	
serch hynny	despite that; all the same [rather literary]	
siwr o °fod	certainly; very likely	
ta beth	anyway; in any case (see §438)	
ta °waeth	anyway; in any case (see §438)	
wrth °gwrs*	of course	
wrth °reswm*	of course; naturally	
yn anffodus	unfortunately	
yn arbennig	especially	
yn °bendant	definitely	
yn °ddi-os	without a doubt	
yn hytrach (na[h])	rather (than)	
yn ogystal (â[h])	as well (as)	
yn ôl pob tebyg	in all likelihood	

yn unig	only (see §435)
(yn) °wir	indeed (see §439)
yn yr un modd	in the same way
ysywaeth	alas, regrettably

428 Adverbs modifying a whole sentence

Those adverbs asterisked above have in common the fact that they modify
the whole sentence. As such, they tend to appear either as first element
(followed by a *that* clause – §486), or as a final 'afterthought' element,
tagged on after a comma. For example, *Perhaps he is ill* could be either:

Efallai °fod e'n sâl

or **Mae'n sâl, efallai**

Similarly, *They are apparently denying everything* could be either:

Mae'n ymddangos bod nhw'n gwadu popeth

or **Maen nhw'n gwadu popeth, mae'n ymddangos**

Particular care should be taken in this regard with **mae'n °debyg**, since the
English equivalent *probably* nearly always comes somewhere in the middle
of the sentence, before the verb or after an auxiliary. Compare:

Bydd e'n hwyr eto bore 'ma, *mae'n °debyg*

or ***Mae'n °debyg* (y) bydd e'n hwyr eto bore 'ma**

He'll *probably* be late again this morning

Note that as an answer-word, **mae'n °debyg** is interchangeable with **tebyg**
(or °**debyg**) **iawn**:

Ti'n mynd i °wylio'r gêm °fawr heno?   **– °Debyg iawn.**

Are you going to watch the big match tonight?   – Probably

429 Bron ('almost')

Note that, like **braidd** *rather* (see §95) but unlike most similar modifying words (**eitha, rhy°**), **bron** precedes the 'linking' **yn°**. Compare:

Oedd y sylwad 'na'n eitha *sarhaus*

That remark was rather insulting

Oedd y sylwad 'na bron *yn sarhaus*

That remark was almost insulting

When **bron** modifies a verb, it may either follow on its own, or precede with an intervening **â** (note that with this second option the **â** replaces the linking **yn**):

Mae'r crwt bach *yn* cysgu *bron*

or **Mae'r crwt bach *bron â* cysgu**

The little lad's almost asleep

Constructions of the type *almost . . .* (+ past tense) usually use **oedd** and **i**:

Oedd bron i mi °gwympo

I almost fell

Oedd bron (iawn) i'r Sacsoniaid ennill y dydd

The Saxons (very) nearly won the day

An expanded variant **bron â bod** is particularly common where *almost* is used as a response:

Ti 'di gorffen sgwennu'r gwahoddiadau 'to? **– Bron â bod.**

Have you finished writing [out] the invitations yet? – Almost

430 Chwaith ('either')

This is used only after NEG verbs or expressions – in other words, it must always be thought of as following on from a *not*.

Dyw Sioned °ddim yn dod chwaith

Sioned's not coming either

Dw i °ddim yn mynd allan yn aml. **– Na finnau chwaith**

I don't go out often. – Me neither [lit. 'nor me either']

For *either . . . or . . .* (conjunction), see §512.

431 Fel arfer

This adverbial is potentially ambiguous, since it is used for both *as usual* and *usually*. Context usually makes it clear, but examples such as the following are difficult to resolve as they stand:

Fel arfer, mae hi'n hwyr

She's late as usual

or: She is usually late

In these cases, **fel rheol** as a rule can be used as an unambiguous synonym for *usually*. Otherwise, the only clue for the listener is perhaps a difference in intonation.

432 Felly

This word means both *so* (i.e. *therefore*) and *in this/that way*:

Felly °fyddi di'n galw heibio wedyn?

°Fyddi di'n galw heibio wedyn, felly?

So you'll be along later?

°Well inni °wneud e felly

We'd better do it this way

Felly oedd e'n dweud

So he said

Felly y digwyddodd

That's how it happened

Note the idioms **pethau felly** *such things*, and a ʰ**phelly** (for a ʰ**phethau felly**) *and suchlike*:

Hogia'n crwydro'r strydoedd a gweiddi a ʰphelly

Young lads roaming the streets and shouting and suchlike

433 Gobeithio **('hope')**

This is technically a VN, and can be used as such, though its stative meaning (see Glossary) rules out the preterite and for that matter any other inflected tense. So, *I hoped* is not ***gobeithies i** but **o'n i'n gobeithio** – §303).

But unusually, **gobeithio**, in the spoken language at least, has acquired a ‘Only’ secondary status as an adverb, and this use is probably more common nowadays than the original VN. As an adverb, it corresponds exactly to German *hoffentlich*, on which the English *hopefully* has been modelled. Like all the asterisked adverbs in the list above (in §427), it is confined (in its adverbial use) to either the beginning or the end of the sentence (see §428).

> **Gobeithio bydd hi'n °well yfory**
>
> or: **Bydd hi'n °well yfory, gobeithio**
>
> I hope she'll be better tomorrow

> **Gobeithio y parith o dros Dolig** (N)
>
> or: **Mi °barith o dros Dolig, gobeithio** (N)
>
> I hope it will last over Christmas

434 O °gwbwl ('at all')

Like its English equivalent, this adverbial has essentially negative connotations, and is used in conjunction with NEG verbs and particles:

> **Dw i heb °weld hi o °gwbwl ers y Dolig**
>
> I haven't seen her at all since Christmas

> **'Sdim byd o °gwbwl ar ôl**
>
> There's nothing left at all

> **Doedd e °ddim yn ei gwerthfawrogi hi o °gwbwl**
>
> He didn't appreciate her at all

It occurs also in INT sentences, sometimes in conjunction with **unrhyw°** *any* (see §115):

> **Oes gin yr un onoch chi unrhyw syniad o °gwbwl lle gallen nhw °fod?**
>
> Have any of you got any idea at all where they might be?

435 'Only'

Dim ond (often **'mond** in speech) and **yn unig** can mostly be used interchangeably, but their positions in the sentence are different: **dim ond** precedes what it modifies, while **yn unig** generally follows:

Dim ond hanner dwsin o °bobl sy wedi cyrraedd hyd yn hyn

Hanner dwsin o °bobl yn unig sy wedi cyrraedd hyd yn hyn

Only half a dozen people have arrived so far

But **dim ond** is definitely more common where the modified element is a verb:

'Sdim eisiau i ti °wylltio – dim ond gofyn o'n i

There's no need to get angry – I was only asking

In practice, because all instances of *only* + verb involve focusing (see §17) of the verb, it will always be in the VN form with a following auxiliary, even in the preterite:

Dim ond gofyn nes i

I only asked

Dim ond cannot modify an inflected verb, so to use the inflected preterite in the above example would theoretically require **yn unig**. This in turn is impossible in Welsh because **yn unig** has to immediately follow what it modifies (here: *ask*), but this position is occupied by the subject **i** *I* – so we cannot say ***Gofynnes yn unig i,** and even if we could, we would still not have succeeded in focusing on the idea of **gofyn**, because **gofynnes** would still be in the normal, neutral position for an inflected verb. The construction **dim ond** + VN + auxiliary is both the neatest and the most faithful to the principles of Welsh sentence structure. Focused sentences are dealt with at length in §§**17–21.**

436 'Perhaps'

Efallai (often **falle** in speech, and also **ella** in the N) is the standard word for *perhaps* or *maybe*. In the N an alternative, and in many areas far more common, word is **hwyrach** (often **hwrach** or even **wrach** with stressed **w-** in speech). Either word requires a following *that*-clause (see §486) when it starts a sentence. For example, not:

*Efallai mae Iestyn wedi mynd hebddon ni

but: **Efallai °fod Iestyn wedi mynd hebddon ni**

Perhaps Iestyn has gone without us

Similarly, focused sentences starting with **efallai** or **hwyrach** require **mai** (or **na** or **taw**) (see §492):

Ella mai yn y stafell °gefn mae o (N)

Perhaps it's in the back room

Hwrach na breuddwydio o't ti (N)

Perhaps you were dreaming

All these examples could equally be done with **efallai/hwyrach** tagged on the end, and therefore with no need for a *that*-clause:

Mae Iestyn wedi mynd hebddon ni, efallai

Yn y stafell gefn mae o, ella

Breuddwydio o't ti, hwrach

In addition, **efallai/hwyrach** is used in paraphrases of English modal verbs for which Welsh has no equivalent, notably *may* and *might*:

Efallai y bydda i'n ffonio wedyn os bydd amser

I might phone later if I have time   [lit. 'Perhaps (that) I will phone . . .']

Efallai ⁿmod i wedi camddeall

I may have misunderstood   [lit. 'Perhaps (that) I have misunderstood']

Hwyrach fod hynny'n °wir, ond . . .

That may be true, but . . .   [lit. 'Perhaps (that) that is true . . .']

437   Prin

This word is an adjective meaning *scarce*: **mae'r amser yn °brin 'da ni** *we're short of time, time is against us*. But it also has the negatively connoted adverbial use of *hardly* or *scarcely*, and generally comes at the start of the sentence in this use:

Prin dw i'n cofio'r un peth amdano fo

I hardly remember anything about him

Prin y gallet ti °gyfiawnhau'r °fath ymddygiad dyddiau 'ma

You could hardly justify such behaviour these days

Prin °fod y syniad 'na'n un gwreiddiol

That idea is scarcely original

Prin y gellir credu hynny

That is scarcely believable   [lit. 'Scarcely (that) one can believe that']

438   Ta beth, ta °waeth

These are colloquial expressions meaning *whatever*, *anyway* or *all the same*. They often imply an action will be proceeded with despite what has just been said. They seem to be synonymous, and generally appear where the standard language would have **beth bynnag** (see §149).

Na i hela'r llythyr ta beth
I'll send the letter anyway

Ta beth mae pobol wedi °ddeud 'that ti, mae'r sefyllfa'n un °ddifrifol
Whatever you've been told, the situation is serious

Gorliwiad efallai, ond ta waeth, mae'n dangos cymeriad y dyn
An exaggeration perhaps, but all the same it shows the character of the man

But unlike **beth bynnag** they sometimes correspond to *never mind*:

Dan ni'n rhy hwyr erbyn hyn, mae'n °debyg, ond ta °waeth
We're probably too late by now, but never mind
[i.e. what the hell, we'll do it anyway]

For ta meaning *or*, see §512.

439   (Yn) °wir ('indeed', 'honest(ly)')

Usually the **yn** is dropped when the emphatic sense of *indeed* is intended. A common construction in speech is to tag °**wir** either to the start or the end of a statement and reinforce it with **i ti/chi** (to the speaker):

Oedd 'na dros °fil o °bobol yno, °wir i chi
I'm telling you, there were more than a thousand people there

Un o °luniau gorau Elin i mi eu gweld erioed, wir i chi!
One of the best pictures of Elin that I've ever seen, honest!

On its own, or sometimes with **ie** or **nage**, **wir** can express surprise or disbelief:

Mae'r °bunt i lawr eto bore 'ma.	– °**Wir?**
The pound's down again this morning.	– Really?
Mae hi wedi ailbriodi.	– **Nage, °wir!**
She's remarried.	– You don't say!

As a tag after a verb, °wir reinforces the statement:

°Ga i °fenthyg dy °feic modur newydd?   – Na °gei °wir!

Can I borrow your new motorbike?   – No you (jolly well) can't

Note also the common combinations efallai °wir *quite likely, . . . may well be . . .* and felly °wir *just so, just as I said*:

Efallai °wir mai 'na be' °fydd isio yn y diwedd

That is what may well be needed in the end

Felly °wir, 'na sut oedd hi

It really was just the way I'm telling you

440   Miscellaneous adverbs

Examples of other adverbs on the list (see §427):

Dw i'n teimlo drosto; *eto i gyd,* **mi °ddylai fo wedi gwybod yn °well**

I feel for him; *then again*, he should have known better

Dyna be' mae hithau'n °ddeud, ond dw innau'n meddwl *fel arall*

That's what she says, but I think *otherwise*

Dyna be' °glywch chi *gan amla* **ffor' [ffordd] 'ma**

That's what you hear *mostly* round here

Mae pethau'n edrych felly, *gwaetha'r modd*

That's the way things look, *unfortunately*

Mae hynny'n °beryglus ac, o °bosib, yn anghyfreithlon

That is dangerous and *possibly* illegal

***Serch hynny,* mi °fyddai hi'n °gyfle delfrydol**

All the same, it would be an ideal opportunity

***Wrth °gwrs* bod hi'n dod, ond dan ninnau'n dod hefyd**

Of course she's coming, but we're coming too

Mae'r pentre'n °dawel, *yn arbennig* **gyda'r nos**

The village is quiet, *especially* at night

Hon yn °ddi-os yw'r rhaglen °deledu °foreol °waetha erioed

This is *without a doubt* the worst morning TV programme ever

Mi °ddylen ni anelu at °gyfaddawdu *yn hytrach na* gwrthdaro

We should aim for compromise *rather than* confrontation

°Fedr hi °ddarllen Iseldireg *yn ogystal ag* Almaeneg

She can read Dutch *as well as* German   [i.e. in addition to]

441 Interrogative adverbs

lle?	where?
pryd?	when?
ers pryd?	since when?
ers faint?	since when?; for how long (up till now)?
tan pryd?	till when?
am faint?	for how long (in the future)?
pa mor°?	how . . .? (+ adjective)
sut?	how?
pam?	why?

Lle? has variants °Le? and Ble? These and compound terms for motion to and from are all dealt with in §416.

Pryd? strictly speaking is confined to questions and indirect questions, while pan° *when* (often pronounced pen° in many N areas) is a conjunction and not a question-word. Compare:

Pryd mae'r canlyniadau'n cael eu cyhoeddi?

When are the results being given?

Dw i °ddim yn siwr pryd mae'r trên nesa i'w °ddisgwyl

I'm not sure when the next train is due   [indirect question]

Pan °ddes i adre, dyma fi wedi anghofio 'n allwedd i

When I got home, I found I'd forgotten my key   [conjunction]

Some areas extend the use of pryd to cover pan° as well, however, and pryd des i adre, though not standard, is quite common especially in the S.

Ers pryd? and ers faint? are virtually synonymous. Both are used to ask how long a situation has existed, or an action has been going on. But ers pryd? expects a specific time or date as an answer, while ers faint? expects a period of time:

Ers pryd dych chi'n sefyll tu allan fan hyn?	**– Ers chwech o'r gloch**
How long have you been standing out here?	– Since six o'clock
Ers faint dych chi'n sefyll tu allan fan hyn?	**– Ers dwy awr**
How long have you been standing out here?	– Two hours

Tan pryd? and **Am faint?**, on the other hand, ask similarly related questions about the future:

Tan pryd °fyddi di yma?	**– Tan wyth**
How long will you be here (till)?	– Till eight
Am faint dych chi'n mynd i Ffrainc?	**– Am °bythefnos**
How long are you going to France for?	– For a fortnight

Pa mor° . . .? (see also §105(c)) means *how* in the sense of *to what extent*. It is always used with a following adjective:

Pa mor °fawr yw'r stafelloedd yn eich tŷ newydd?

How big are the rooms in your new house?

Sut? is the general word for *how?* in the sense of *in what way?*:

Sut daethoch chi fan hyn yn y diwedd?

How did you get here in the end?

Dw i °ddim yn gwybod sut i °ddatrys y °broblem 'ma

I don't know how to solve this problem

Note that **Sut° . . .?** is an interrogative adjective meaning *what kind of . . .?*: **Sut °dre yw hi?** *What kind of town is it?*.

Pam? *why?* is generally followed by a *that* construction – **pam °fod e yma?** *why is he here?* It has a literary variant **paham?** which must be avoided in speech; even in writing its use is indicative of a very affected style.

442   Comparison of adverbs

Turning *quickly* into *more quickly* and *most quickly* is a simple procedure in Welsh, depending as it does entirely on the comparative forms of the adjectives (see §§103, 106).

The comparative (*more . . . ly*) is formed by prefixing **yn°** to the comparative form of the adjective, whether this is with ending **-ach** or prefix **mwy**:

araf *slow*, **arafach** *slower* > **yn arafach** *more slowly* gofalus *careful*, mwy gofalus *more careful* > yn °fwy gofalus *more carefully*:

Bydd rhaid i chi °fynd trwy hyn yn arafach gyda fi

You'll have to go through this more slowly with me

Gwna dy °waith cartre'n °fwy gofalus tro nesa

Do your homework more carefully next time

The superlative (*most . . . ly*) is simply the mutated (SM) form of the superlative adjective, with no preceding yn°:

tawel *quiet*, tawela (*the*) *quietest* > °dawela (*the*) *most quietly*

effeithiol *effective*, mwya effeithiol (*the*) *most effective* > °fwya effeithiol (*the*) *most effectively*:

Y peiriant yma sy'n rhedeg °dawela

This machine runs the most quietly

Dyma'r polisi °fydd yn delio °fwya effeithiol â'r argyfwng

This is the policy which will deal most effectively with the crisis

It is worth remembering that some English adverbs do not end in *-ly*. They look like adjectives, but they are really adverbs, and will behave as such in Welsh:

Mae'r awyren 'ma'n hedfan yn °gyflym

This plane flies fast

Ond mae'r Saab yn hedfan yn °gyflymach

But the Saab flies faster

Y Sukhoi-27 sy'n hedfan °gyflyma (ohonyn nhw i gyd)

(It is) the Sukhoi-27 (that) flies fastest (of all)

Note that the equative of the adjective (*as . . .*) can be used unaltered as an adverb – da *good*, cystal *as good, as well*; cyflym *quick*, mor °gyflym *as quick(ly)*

Mae hi cystal â neb yma

She is *as good* as anyone here

Mae hi'n canu cystal â neb yma

She sings *as well* as anyone here

Does neb mor °gyflym ag e

Nobody is *as quick* as he is

Does neb yn rhedeg mor °gyflym ag e

Nobody runs *as quickly* as he does

Prepositions

443   Definitions

Prepositions are words like English *at, on, to, for*. They describe a relationship, often spatial, between objects or persons. For example, 'the book is *on* the table', 'the table is *by* the window', 'the car is *in front* of the house', etc.

Welsh prepositions come in two broad categories: simple prepositions (comprising single words – like English *on, at* etc.) and compound prepositions (comprising a simple preposition + some other element, usually a noun – like English *in front of*). The compound type is less frequent and operates in a different way from simple prepositions. It will be discussed separately in §§475–476.

444   Simple prepositions

There are about two dozen in common use. Meanings are given under the separate sections. While some have fairly clear-cut and consistent translations in English (e.g. **heb°** *without*), many of the very common ones correspond to different English prepositions depending on context. Idiomatic usage often prevails over logic with the prepositions of any language, and it is misleading and often counterproductive for the learner to think of, say, **am°** as meaning *for* – of course, it often does translate as *for*, but just as often it does not. The main prepositions in use in spoken Welsh are:

âʰ	iº
amº	mewn
arº	oº
atº	oddiarº (oddi arº)
cyn	oddiwrthº (oddi wrthº)
(o) danº	rhag
drosº (trosº)	rhwng
efo	tanº
ganº	trwyº
ger	(drwyº)
gydaʰ	tuaʰ
hebº	wrthº
hydº	ynⁿ

Most (not all) of these share the following characteristics:

(a)   they cause mutation of the following word (see §445 for further discussion)

(b)   they show verb-like inflections when used with pronouns (see §446)

(c)   they can be used with a following VN – see individual sections, and summary in §199

445   Mutations after prepositions

As is clear from the list above, by far the majority cause SM of a directly following word. Examples:

am ºddim	for nothing	ar ºfwrdd	on a table
dan ºofal	under care	heb ºfynd	without going
i ºGaerdydd	to Cardiff	o ºgaws	of cheese

Several (notably **rhag**, **rhwng** and **mewn**) do not cause any mutation, while â, **gyda** and **tua** technically cause AM. In practice, this puts them, for many speakers, in either the non-mutating class (except in set expressions), since AM is not and generally has not been an active feature of many varieties of spoken Welsh, or in a partially mutating class, since for many speakers AM of c- is normal while AM of p- and (particularly) t- is not. (See section on Aspirate Mutation in §9 for further discussion.)

Yn alone causes NM, which is also not as widespread as suggested by the literary standard, and for which a number of alternatives are found in speech. These will be explained in §472.

Note that as a general rule personal names are not mutated after prepositions: i °ferch to *a girl*, but i Mererid *to Mererid* (not *i °Fererid). This rule does not always apply in older forms of Welsh (i °Ddafydd for modern i Dafydd).

446   Principles of 'inflected' prepositions

When used with the pronouns (see §119), most prepositions insert a linking syllable before the pronoun. This syllable itself changes with each pronoun, and the result is an inflection pattern reminiscent of verbs. Compare a non-inflecting preposition (**gyda** *with*) with an inflecting one (**ar** *on*):

(with name)	**gyda Sioned**	**ar Sioned**
(with noun)	**gyda'r °ferch**	**ar y °ferch**
(with pronoun)	**gyda hi**	**arni hi**

The two prepositions work in exactly the same way when used with names or nouns, but diverge where a pronoun (**hi** *her*) follows: **gyda** simply adds the pronoun in the usual way (and just as in English – *with Sioned, with the girl, with her*), but **ar** has to insert **-ni** before the **hi**. In other words, one cannot simply follow the procedure with **gyda** and say *ar hi for *on her*.

This principle holds true for the majority of simple prepositions in Welsh, and because it is at such a basic level of language any serious learner must master the mechanics of the system. Fortunately, there is a perceptible pattern to inflected prepositions (**i°** is irregular, however), and in speech the pattern is if anything more regularized and consistent than the literary version. Broadly speaking, the endings (+ pronouns) are as follows:

	Singular	*Plural*
1st	**-a i**	**-on ni**
2nd	**-at ti**	**-och chi**
3rd	**-o fe/fo**	**-yn nhw**
	-i hi	

There is some dialect variation in these endings, particularly with 1st and 2nd pers. sing., which often have **-o i** and **-ot ti** (this is also the case with the standard language). Conversely, 2nd pers. pl. **-och chi** is often heard as **-ach** chi in many areas. Overall, the best approach is probably to follow natural local practice.

3rd pers. sing. and 3rd pers. pl. endings, on the other hand, are nearly always as shown, but with the complication that **fe/fo** and **hi** are often omitted in speech, leaving the ending alone to indicate the person:

Gad °lonydd *iddo*!   [for **Gad °lonydd iddo** *fe*]

Leave him alone!

Na i hala llythyr *ati* bore fory   [for . . . *ati hi* . . .]

I'll send her a letter tomorrow morning

Paid deud wrtho am y tro   [for . . . **wrtho** *fo* . . .]

Don't tell him for the time being

Note that 3rd pers. pl. **-yn nhw** is never shortened in this way.

The linking element between the preposition and the ending is more problematic, with different prepositions using different elements. For example, **am°** inserts **-dan-** before the endings (**amdana i, amdani hi** etc.), while **heb°** uses **-dd-** (**hebdda i, hebddi hi** etc.). **Rhwng** *between* changes its vowel as well as inserting **-dd-** (**rhyngddyn nhw**), and a few, like **at°** and **wrth°**, add the endings without any linking element – **ato fe, wrthyn nhw**. And of course we have seen that a few, like **gyda**, do not have inflected forms with pronouns at all.

447   Âh

Âh (**ag** before vowels) optionally causes AM, and basically means *with*. Note that there are three other equivalents of *with* in spoken Welsh (**efo**, **gan°** and **gydaʰ**). Use of **âʰ** is fairly restricted:

(a)   It indicates the means by which something is done, or the instrument of an action:

Nes i agor 'y ⁿmys i â ʰchyllell °fara

I cut [lit. opened] my finger with a breadknife

This use often involves *by* in English as an alternative to *with*:

°Gawn ni °dalu â siec fan hyn?

Can we pay by cheque here?

(b)   Where the relationship between two objects is regarded as a close and permanent association, **âʰ** is more common than **gydaʰ/efo**

(c) It means *as* with equative forms of adjectives (see §105):

Mor °ddu â'r °frân

As black as a crow

For the specific difference between âʰ and **gydaʰ/efo** as used with **mynd** and **dod**, see idioms below.

There are no inflected forms for âʰ: **â hi** *with her*, **â nhw** *with them*. Note that with him is **â fo** in the N, but either **â fe** or **ag e** in other regions.

Âʰ/ag is found with several common verbs:

siarad âʰ *speak/talk to* (cf. US English *talk with*):

Dim ond ddoe o'n i'n siarad ag e

It was only yesterday I was speaking to him

cwrdd âʰ *meet* (cf. US English *meet with*):

Lle °gwrddest ti â fe °gynta?

Where did you first meet him?

ymweld âʰ *visit* (cf. US English *visit with*):

Pa mor aml dach chi'n ymweld â'ch nain yn y Gogledd?

How often do you visit your grandmother up North?

Peidio (*stop, cease*), used to form NEG commands (see §383), is followed by âʰ in the standard language, but this use is optional at best in speech except in certain set phrases, e.g. **paid â malu** *stop talking nonsense*. In speech, both **paid â p(h)oeni** and **paid poeni** *don't worry* will be heard.

Methu *fail* is similarly followed optionally by âʰ, often by i° instead, or nothing:

°Fethes i'n llwyr â'u hargyhoeddi nhw

[or: . . . **i'w hargyhoeddi nhw** or: . . . **i argyhoeddi nhw**]

I completely failed to convince them

Dod âʰ (*come with*) and **mynd âʰ** (*go with*) are used for *bring* and *take* respectively. Welsh has no word in its own right for *bring*, while **cymryd** (*take*) strictly speaking implies the action of taking hold of, grabbing or seizing. For the other meaning of *take* in English (*accompany*), **mynd âʰ** is the logical choice. Compare:

Dewch â fo i lawr (N)

Bring it down

Cymerwch eich bagiau oddiar y bwrdd!

Take your bags off the table!

Ewch â'ch sbwriel adre!

Take your rubbish home!

Note that, in the senses of *bring* and *take*, the â^h is inseparable from the **dod** or **mynd**:

Es i â'r plant i Ffrainc

I took the children to France

Es i i Ffrainc â'r plant

I went to France with the children

and that, in the second example, **gyda**^h would be a possible alternative, whereas *take* in the first example requires the set phrase **mynd â**^h.

A few idioms involve â^h/ag, usually with a pronoun:

(i) ffwrdd â chi!	be off with you!
allan â hi!	out with it!
(i) ffwrdd â ni!	off we go!

In S regions, **bant** is usually heard in place of standard and N **i ffwrdd**.

448   Am°

Am° is a very common preposition with a range of English equivalents:

(a)   A common meaning of **am°** is *for*, when this means *in exchange for*; so with **talu am°** *pay for* (i.e. give money in exchange for): **°Dales i °bedair punt am y rhain** *I paid £4 for these*

(b)   In time expressions, **am°** means *at*:

°Ddo i 'n ôl am saith

I'll come back at seven

or it expresses duration of time (*for*):

°Fuon nhw yng ^nNgogledd yr Eidal am °fis

They were in Northern Italy for a month

(c) **Siarad** *speak, talk*, **sôn** *speak, talk* and **meddwl** *think* use **am°** to mean *about* in the sense of *concerning*:

> **Am beth dych chi'n sôn?**
>
> What are you talking about?
>
> **°Gawn ni °weld be' mae'n °feddwl am hynny**
>
> We'll see what s/he thinks about that

(d) Spatially, **am°** means *about* or *around*, where the sense is of something being actually enclosed or surrounded:

> **Rhowch °rwymyn am ei °ben o**
>
> Put a bandage round his head

Phrases like *around the town*, on the other hand, require a compound preposition like **o amgylch** or **o °gwmpas** (see §475)

(e) With a following VN it means . . . *want to* . . .

> **Wyt ti am °ddod 'da ni neu °beidio, 'te?**
>
> Do you want to come with us or not, then?
>
> **Dw i am siarad ag e cyn iddo °fynd**
>
> I want to speak to him before he goes

Inflected forms with pronouns are:

	Singular	*Plural*
1st	**amdana i**	**amdanon ni**
2nd	**amdanat ti**	**amdanoch chi**
3rd	**amdano fe/fo**	**amdanyn nhw**
	amdani hi	

Verbs of saying and thinking using **am°** (*about*) have been discussed above. With other verbs, **am°** usually corresponds to *for*: **chwilio am°** *look for*:

> **Dw i 'di bod yn chwilio amdanat ti ers awr**
>
> I've been looking for you for an hour

Some speakers use **edrych am°** for **chwilio am°** – this is a direct translation of the English phrase, but is accepted in many areas.

esgus am° *(an) excuse for*:

> **Does dim esgus am °fradychu ffrind, nag oes?**
>
> There's no excuse for betraying a friend, is there?

galw am° *call for*:

Os na °fydd y sefyllfa yn gwella, bydd rhaid galw am °gymorth

If the situation doesn't improve, we'll have to call for help

gobethio am° *hope for*:

Dan ni i gyd yn gobeithio am amodau tecach yn y dyfodol

We are all hoping for better conditions in the future

gofalu am° *look after, take care of*:

Pwy sy'n gofalu am y plant i ti heno?

Who's looking after the kids for you tonight?

Some speakers use **edrych ar ôl** for **gofalu am°** – this is a direct translation of the English phrase, but is accepted in many areas.

ysu am° *be itching/yearning to (do something)*:

Maen nhw'n ysu am °fynd

They're itching to go

Note also the important parallel constructions:

dweud wrth (°rywun) *am* °wneud (rhywbeth)

to tell (someone) to do (something)

gofyn i (°rywun) am °wneud (rhywbeth)

to ask (someone) to do (something)

For the conjunction am °fod *because, since*, see §504.

<h2>449   Ar°</h2>

Ar° has a number of meanings:

(a)   *on* in a purely spatial sense, whether with location or motion:

Mae'r llyfr ar y bwrdd	The book is on the table
Rho'r llyfr ar y bwrdd	Put the book on(to) the table

(b)   *about to* when followed by a VN:

Brysiwch, mae'r trên ar °fynd!

Hurry up, the train's about to go!

Mae teledu lloeren ar °ddod

Satellite TV is almost here [lit. about to come]

Pan o'n i ar °wneud hynny

When I was about to do that

(c)   with expressions of temporary physical and mental states (see §398), it often, but not necessarily, corresponds to *have*:

Mae'r °ddannodd arna i	I've got toothache
Roedd y ffliw arni	She had flu
Oes ofn arnat ti?	Are you afraid?

(d)   in stative expressions like **ar °gau** *closed* (see §426)

(e)   occasionally it means *of*, usually where there is some connotation of *part* or *sample*:

Dim ond rhyw °flas ges i arno fo

I only got a taste of it

(f)   with expressions involving time or the weather:

ar °Ddydd Llun	on (a) Monday, on Mondays
ar yr un adeg	at the same time
ar °dywydd poeth	in hot weather

Inflected forms with pronouns are:

	Singular	Plural
1st	**arna i**	**arnon ni**
2nd	**arnat ti**	**arnoch chi**
3rd	**arno fe/fo**	**arnyn nhw**
	arni hi	

Note that *listen to* and *look at* are **gwrando ar°** and **edrych ar°** respectively (not **i°** or **at°**):

Ar beth dych chi'n gwrando?   What are you listening to?

Other verbs using **ar** include:

cael gwared ar°	get rid of
cymryd ar°	pretend – usually in the construction **cymryd arno** + VN
manteisio ar°	take advantage of
sylwi ar°	notice

Important idioms:

Faint sy arna i i chi?	How much do I owe you?
Mae arnat ti ugain punt i mi	You owe me £20
Does dim dal ar° . . .	. . . cannot be depended on
Rhowch °gynnig arni!	Give it a try!

450 At°

At°, while sometimes corresponding to English *at*, has a wider field of meaning in Welsh:

(a) in particular it is used for *to* where this implies motion *up to* (but not into) a destination – *into* is covered by **i°**, and these two are often confused by speakers of English, where the distinction is not so clearly made. This explains why, for example, we must say **danfon llythyr *at* Sioned** *send a letter to Sioned*, but **danfon llythyr i °Lundain** *send a letter to London*. The same distinction is seen in: **mynd i'r °feddygfa** *go to the surgery* (i.e. *inside*, so **i**), but **mynd at y meddyg** *go to the doctor's*. Further examples:

Rhaid inni °fynd â ti at y deintydd bore fory

We must take you to the dentist's tomorrow morning

Lluchiwch y °bêl ata i!

Chuck the ball to me!

(b) **at°** means *for* in the sense of *for the benefit/good/purpose of*:

At beth mae hwnna i °fod?

What's that supposed to be for?

Mae'r arian i gyd yn mynd at achosion da

All the money is going to(wards) good causes

Tuag at is the normal expression in the spoken language for literary tua[h] **At°**
towards (tua[h] nowadays means *about* in time expressions – §175):

Rhedwch chi i gyd tuag ata i!

All of you run towards me!

Hyd at° is a variant of hyd° *up to* (see §459):

Dyma hi wedyn yn cochi hyd at ei [h]chlustiau

Then she blushed right up to her ears

Inflected forms with pronouns are:

	Singular	*Plural*
1st	**ata i**	**aton ni**
2nd	**atat ti**	**atoch chi**
3rd	**ato fe/fo**	**atyn nhw**
	ati hi	

Verbs using at include:

anelu at°	aim for/at
anfon/danfon at°	send to (a person)
cofio at°	remember (a person to another person)
cyfeirio at°	refer to
cyfrannu at°	contribute to
dychryn at°	be frightened at
edrych ymlaen at°	look forward to
hala at°	send to (a person)
paratoi at°	prepare for
(y)sgrifennu at°	write to (a person)
synnu at°	be surprised at, marvel at
ychwanegu at°	add to

Cofiwch fi at eich mam, newch chi?

Remember me to your mother, will you?

Mae'r canllawiau 'ma wedi'u hanelu'n °bennaf at °bobol ifanc

These guidelines are chiefly aimed at young people

Dywedodd ei °fod yn synnu at sylwadau diweddar arweinydd y °blaid

He said he was amazed at the party leader's recent remarks

Ŷn ni i gyd yn edrych ymlaen at y gwyliau, siwr iawn

I'm sure we're all looking forward to the holidays

Nawn ni hala'r manylion atoch chi bore fory

We'll send you the details tomorrow morning

Idioms with at mostly involve the 3rd pers. sing. fem. **ati**:

Ewch ati!	Get to it! [i.e. start on the job]
Daliwch ati!	Stick at it! Keep going!
Dal ati!	
. . ., ac ati	. . ., and so on/forth

451   Cyn

Cyn means *before* in time expressions only: **cyn y Rhyfel** *before the War*, **cyn deg o'r °gloch** *before 10 o'clock*. As such it is also used as a conjunction (see §503).

Mi °ddaw hi'n ôl cyn hynny

She'll come back before that

Gadewch inni °orffen hwn cyn y bore

Let's get this finished before morning

It is important for non-native speakers to understand the difference between **cyn** and the compound preposition **o °flaen** *in front of* (see §475). They are not interchangeable, even though *in front of* can sometimes be replaced by *before* in English, e.g. *to stand before the class*. Compare:

Na i °gwrdd â chi cyn y cyngerdd

I'll meet you before the concert

Na i °gwrdd â chi o °flaen Canolfan y Celfyddydau

I'll meet you in front of the Arts Centre

As an adjective (but always attached to the following noun), **cyn-°** means *ex-* or *former* (see §96).

452 Dan°

Dan°, alternatively sometimes **o dan°**, means *under*: **dan y dŵr** *under the water*, **dan °ddylanwad ei °rieni** *under the influence of his parents*. Inflected forms with pronouns are:

	Singular	Plural
1st	**dana i**	**danon ni**
2nd	**danat ti**	**danoch chi**
3rd	**dano fe/fo**	**danyn nhw**
	dani hi	

Note the related preposition **oddidan°** (also **odditan°**) *from under*.

Dan °ofal (abbreviated **d/o**) is the usual term for *care of* when addressing letters.

By far the most important idiom with **dan** is **dan ei sang** *full to bursting, packed*, used of rooms, buildings etc, and **dan haul** *under (the) sun*:

Mae'r lle 'ma dan ei sang heno, on'd ydy?

This place is packed tonight, isn't it?

Mi °ddylai addysg go iawn °gynnwys popeth dan haul

A proper education should include everything under the sun

The unmutated variant **tan°** is now to all intents and purposes obsolete in this meaning, and has in effect become a separate preposition with the meaning *until* – see §467.

453 Dros°

Dros°, with its variants **tros°** (rather literary these days) and **drost°** (very common in speech in many areas), means:

(a) *over* in a purely spatial sense – **dros y °bont** *over the bridge*, **edrych dros y clawdd** *to look over the hedge*

Mae caneuon Meinir Gwilym yn °boblogaidd dros °Gymru °gyfan

Meinir Gwilym's songs are popular all over Wales

(b) *over* in the sense of *more than* (as in English):

Mae dros °fil o °bobol yn y neuadd yn °barod

There are over a thousand people in the hall already

(c) *for* in the sense of *on behalf of*:

Nei di °fynd lawr i'r siop drosta i?

Will you go down to the shop for me?

Dan ni i gyd yn teimlo drostat ti

We all feel for you

(d) *for* after words like **rheswm** *reason* and **esgus** *excuse*, usually with a VN:

°Alla i'm gweld unrhyw °reswm dros ymddwyn fel 'ny

I can see no reason for behaving like that

Barn Huw ydy °fod 'na °ddim esgus dros °ragrith

Huw is of the opinion that there is no excuse for hypocrisy

Inflected forms with pronouns are:

	Singular	Plural
1st	**drosta i**	**droston ni**
2nd	**drostat ti**	**drostoch chi**
3rd	**drosto fe/fo**	**drostyn nhw**
	drosti hi	

Idioms are mostly adverbial, including the phrase **dros °ben llestri** *over the top*, and the very common and useful adjective modifier **dros °ben** *exceedingly*:

'Sdim eisiau mynd dros °ben llestri, nag oes?

There's no need to go over the top, is there?

Mae'r sefyllfa yn un °ddifrifol dros °ben

The situation is (an) exceedingly serious (one)

454   Efo

Efo (in some areas **hefo**) is the general word for *with* in the N. In the S it is always replaced by **gyda**, a word which, in turn, is virtually unknown in the N (except in certain set phrases, notably **gyda'r nos** *in the evening*). The two words are not, however, exactly complementary – **gyda** (or **'da**) is also used in the S to express possession (see **XXXVIII**), but for this function the N uses not efo but gan° (see §455). Examples:

Dan ni'n mynd i'r Swisdir efo'r Jonesiaid eleni (N)

We're going to Switzerland with the Joneses this year

Hefo pwy dach chi'n rhannu tro 'ma, 'ta? (N)

Who are you sharing with this time, then?

Mi °ddo i hefo chdi rŵan (N)

I'll come with you now

Rhaid i chi °gael sgwrs hefo fo (N)

You must have a chat with him

Dwn 'im be' °ddyliwn i °wneud efo nhw (N)

I don't know what I should do with them

For efo'i gilydd *together*, see §147.

455 Gan°

Gan°, very often gyn° in speech, is used in the N to express possession: **Mae gyn Mrs Williams °gath °fawr** *Mrs Williams has a large cat*. In this use it clearly means *with*, and corresponds to S gyda (see §457). Note however, that the constructions differ slightly:

(N) *Oes gen ti °ddigon o arian?*

(S) *Oes digon o arian 'da ti?*

Have you got enough money?

Expressing possession is dealt with fully in **XXXVIII**.

Main uses not involving possession (and therefore common to both N and S) are:

(a)   *by* in passive sentences (see §**362**):

Fe °geith copïau o'r llyfr eu harwyddo gan yr awdur bore fory

Copies of the book will be signed by the author tomorrow morning

°Ges i ⁿmrathu gan °gi ar y ffordd adre

I got bitten by a dog on the way home

By extension, it is also used to denote writers or authors of works:

'Nineteen Eighty-Four' gan George Orwell

(b) *from* or *off* where something has been handed over or transmitted from one person to another:

°Ges i °bunt gynno fo

I got a pound off him

Pa newyddion °gaethon nhw gynni hi?

What news did they get from her?

Gyn °bwy °gest ti °fenthyg ono fo?

Who did you borrow it from?

In this sense, compare **oddiwrth°** (see §464).

(c) with VNs, **gan°** sometimes implies simultaneous action:

Aethon nhw lawr y stryd gan °guro ar y drysiau i gyd

They went down the street banging on all the doors

Gan °feddwl, dw i °ddim yn siwr °fyddai hynny'n syniad da

Thinking about it, I'm not sure (if) that would be a good idea

In this sense, the usual pronunciation is **gan°** and not **gyn°**.

The inflected forms of **gan°** for pronouns show a number of variant forms. Basic colloquial versions are:

	Singular	*Plural*
1st	**gyn i, gen i**	**gynnon ni**
2nd	**gyn ti, gen ti**	**gynnoch chi**
3rd	**gynno fo**	**gynnyn nhw**
	gynni hi	

In writing, and sometimes in speech, **gynn-** is found as **gandd-** (from which it may originally have developed), and 2nd pers. pl. is often seen as **gennych (chi)**.

Idioms with **gan** include **gan °bwyll!** *steady on!, easy does it!*, and a number of expressions of personal feeling:

mae'n °ddrwg gen i	I'm sorry
(mae'n) °well gen i	I prefer (cf. **°well i mi** . . . I'd better . . . **§353**)
mae'n °dda gen i °gwrdd â chi	I'm pleased to meet you

For the conjunction **gan °fod** *since, as*, see §504.

---

456   Ger

Ger is used with geographical locations, usually names of towns, to mean *near, in the vicinity of*:

Ger Barcelona mae Mark a'i °deulu'n byw bellach

Mark and his family live near Barcelona now

Dan ni'n byw mewn pentre bach ger Harlech

We live in a little village near Harlech

Note the related term **gerbron**, meaning *before* in the sense of *into the presence of* or *for the attention of*, and mostly found with words like **llys** *court*, **bwrdd** *board*:

Daethpwyd â chwe achos gerbron y llys bore 'ma   [formal]

Six cases were brought before the court this morning

Bydd y bwrdd yn rhoi ystyriaeth °fanwl i'r holl °dystiolaeth a °roddwyd gerbron yr wythnos hon   [formal]

The board will carefully consider all the evidence that has been presented this week

---

457   Gyda^h

Gyda^h (**gydag** before vowels) is the general term in the S for 'with' (cf. **efo** in the N – §454). Except for in idioms (below), it is usually heard as **'da** in speech.

Oes amser 'da chi i °brynu'r tocynnau?

Have you got time to buy the tickets?

Bydd rhaid i ti °rannu fe 'da hi

You'll have to share it with her

It is used in the S to express possession (see **XXXVIII**), as **gan°** is used in the N, but with a differing sentence structure:

(S) *Oes digon o °fwyd 'da ti?*

(N) *Oes gen ti °ddigon o °fwyd?*

Unlike **gan**, **(gy)da**[h] does not have special inflected forms for use with pronouns: **gyda fi, gyda ni** etc. But note that *with him* can be either **(gy)da fe** or **(gy)dag e**.

There are two important idioms with **gyda**[h]:

gyda llaw	by the way
gyda'r nos	in the evening

For **gyda'i gilydd** *together*, see §147.

458   Heb°

Heb°, in its primary meaning of *without*, is straightforward: **heb arian** *without money*; **peidiwch mynd hebdda i!** *don't go without me!*

It is used with a VN as an alternative NEG construction in the perfect (see §269), equivalent to **°ddim wedi: Dan ni heb °benderfynu** *We haven't decided* (= **Dan ni °ddim wedi penderfynu**); **Mae o heb °fynd eto** *He hasn't gone yet* (= **Tydy o °ddim wedi mynd eto**).

Heb° + possessive adj. + VN corresponds to . . . *which/who has/have not been . . .*, or simply an adjectival *un- . . . -ed*: **pobl heb eu cofrestru** *people who have not been registered*; **pryd o °fwyd heb ei °fwyta** *an uneaten meal*; **papur newydd heb ei agor** *an unopened newspaper*. (See also §366.)

Inflected forms with pronouns are:

	Singular	Plural
1st	**hebdda i**	**hebddon ni**
2nd	**hebddat ti**	**hebddoch chi**
3rd	**hebddo fe/fo**	**hebddyn nhw**
	hebddi hi	

Idioms:

heb ei ail (f heb ei hail) *second-to-none, first-rate*:

Dyma °bortread heb ei ail o °fywyd y glowyr yn y tridegau

This is a first-rate portrayal of miners' lives in the thirties

yn amlach (or yn °fwy) na heb *more often than not*:

Yn amlach na heb, mae'r °fath ymddygiad yn arwain at °drychineb

More often than not, this kind of behaviour leads to disaster

459　Hyd°

Hyd° means:

(a)　*up* to in the sense of *until*:

Mae'r cyrsiau'n para hyd °ddiwedd mis Mehefin

The courses go on until the end of June

In this sense it is often interchangeable with **tan°** (see §**467**).

(b)　*up to* in a spatial sense – here it is often expanded to **hyd at°**:

Oedd e hyd at ei °wddw yn y dŵr

He was up to his neck in the water

Wedson nhw 'tha i am °dalu hyd at ugain punt a dim mwy

I was told to pay up to twenty pounds and no more

The pronouns are not normally used with this preposition.

All of the following are common idioms with **hyd°**, though it is not strictly a preposition in all cases:

cael hyd i° *find*

°Gest ti hyd iddo?

Did you find it?

dod o hyd i° *find*

Daethpwyd o hyd i °gorff

A body has been found [formal]

hyd yn oed *even*

Mae hyd yn oed Gareth wedi dod
Even Gareth has come

(but for *even . . . er*, see §104(c))

hyd yn hyn (or hyd yma) *so far, up till now*

'Sdim sôn am °fynd at y llysoedd hyd yn hyn
There's no talk of going to the courts so far

o hyd *still; all the time*

Dan ni yma o hyd
We're still here

Mae o'n siarad o hyd am ei ffôn symudol
He's always going on about his mobile phone

hyd y gwela i *as far as I can see*

°Fydd 'na °ddim problemau hyd y gwela i
There'll be no problems as far as I can see

hyd y gwn i *as far as I know*

Mae popeth wedi'i °drefnu, hyd y gwn i
Everything's set, as far as I know

This preposition also appears as a conjunction *until*, with a verb following:

Ewch ymlaen ffordd 'ma hyd gwelwch chi °faes chwarae ar y °dde
Go on this way until you see a playing field on the right

Note the compound preposition ar hyd *along, the length of . . .*, and with units of time *all . . . long*:

Ewch ar hyd y ffordd 'ma am °ddeng munud, yna trowch i'r °dde
Go along this road for ten minutes, then turn left

Ar hyd y nos
All night long

i° corresponds to English *to* in many of its senses:

(a) motion towards or into a place (cf. **at°** §450):

> **Dych chi'n mynd i'r °dre heddiw?**
>
> Are you going to town today?

It also expresses the indirect object (e.g. giving something to somebody), where it should incidentally be remembered that English often omits the *to* in this sense: *I gave the book to Fred* or *I gave Fred the book*. Welsh always requires the **i**:

> **°Roddes i'r llyfr i Fred**
>
> I gave the book to Fred
>
> **°Elli di °ddangos hwnna i mi am eiliad?**
>
> Can you show me that a moment?

(b) *purpose* (with following VN):

> **Fe °adawodd y °ddwy onyn nhw'n °gynnar i °ddal y bws**
>
> They both left early to catch the bus
>
> **°Ddaethon ni â'r pris lawr i °ddenu mwy o °bobol**
>
> We brought the price down to attract more people

In this sense, the compound preposition **er mwyn** *in order to* is a frequent alternative – . . . **er mwyn dal y bws**; . . . **er mwyn denu mwy o °bobol**, etc.

Other common uses do *not* correspond to *to*.

(c) *for*:

> **Mae gyn i °lythyron i chi**
>
> I've got some letters for you
>
> **Nes i'r holl °waith paratoi i ti bore 'ma**
>
> I did all the preparation for you this morning
>
> **Arhoswch °funud – na i llnau nhw i chi**
>
> Wait a minute – I'll clean them for you

(d) occasionally denoting possession, especially where the **gyda/gan°** construction is not possible because of the nature of the sentence:

Mae'r °bobol 'na'n ffrindiau i mi

Those people are friends of mine

(e) after verbs of *making* or *causing* etc.

Paid *gwneud i* Eleri chwerthin wrth iddi °fwyta

Don't make Eleri laugh while she's eating

Yr unig esboniad a °roddwyd oedd mai taro rhewfryn a *achosodd iddi* suddo

The only explanation given was that it was hitting an iceberg that caused her to sink

(f) after conjunctions (usually of time) to introduce the subject:

. . . cyn i mi °fynd   . . . before I go/went

. . . er mwyn iddo °ddeall   . . . so that he can/could understand

This use is dealt with fully in §**501**.

(g) *that* in past tense sentences + subject + VN:

Dw i'n eitha siwr iddi ffonio °rywbryd ddoe

I'm pretty sure (that) she phoned some time yesterday

This construction is dealt with in §**491**.

The inflected forms of **i°** with pronouns are irregular, with only 3rd pers. sing. and 3rd pers. pl. adding an internal syllable:

	Singular	Plural
1st	**i mi, i fi**	**inni, i ni**
2nd	**i ti**	**i chi**
3rd	**iddo fe/fo**	**iddyn nhw**
	iddi hi	

Notes:

(a) **i mi** and **i fi** are interchangeable, but **i fi** is much more likely in the S

(b) an old form of the 2nd pers. pl. **iwch** is still heard in the expression **Nos dawch!, 'sdawch!** *Good night!* (for **Nos da iwch** *Good night to you*) – primarily N colloquial

Most instances of i° used after verbs parallel English usage – except that, as noted above, the word *to* is often optionally omitted in English. But **gofyn** *ask* unexpectedly takes i°:

Gofynnwch iddo fo ydy o'n dŵad (N)

Ask him [lit. to him] if he is coming

Efallai y byddwch chi eisiau gofyn i'r plant am eu syniadau nhw

Perhaps you will want to ask the children for their ideas

The idiomatic expression **rhoi gwybod i°** means *inform* or *let . . . know*:

Rhowch °wybod i mi os °glywch chi °rywbeth

Let me know if you hear anything

Mae'n °bwysig eich bod yn rhoi gwybod i'r swyddfa am eich amgylchiadau

It is important that you let the office know about your circumstances

°Ellwch chi °roi gwybod inni'n syth?

Can you let us know straight away?

Yn dal i° is used before VNs to mean *still . . . ing*:

Mae Seren yn dal i °deimlo'n sâl

Seren is still feeling ill

Mae'n dal i °fwrw

It's still raining

°Fyddwch chi'n dal i °fyw fan hyn °flwyddyn nesa?

Will you still be living here next year?

Compare **(yn) dal** *yn°*+ adjective:

Mae hi ('n) dal yn rhy °wlyb i °fynd allan

It's still too wet to go out

Although i° on its own covers the meaning of *into*, by implication at least (**i'r tŷ** *into the house*, **i °Gymru** *(in)to Wales*), an expanded form **i mewn i°** (or **i °fewn i°** – less common) is available where this idea is central or emphasized:

Drychon ni o amgylch yr °ardd, wedyn mynd i mewn i'r tŷ ei hun

We had a look round the garden, then we went into the house itself

The second i° can be split off by an intervening element:

Fe °fyddwn ni'n edrych *i mewn* ar °frys *i*'r adroddiadau 'ma

We will be looking into these reports as a matter of urgency

Used as an adverb (i.e. with no following noun), this expression drops the final i (and often the first one as well) and corresponds to . . . *in*:

Dewch i mewn!	Come in!
Galwch (i) mewn °rywbryd!	Call in sometime!
(I) mewn â ni!	In we go!

461   Mewn

Mewn is different from **i mewn** (see §460). It means *in*, but is only used where the following noun is non-specific (see §35). Specific nouns require **yn** (see §471) instead. Compare:

Non-specific	Specific
mewn tŷ	**yn y tŷ**
in a house	in the house
mewn ardaloedd gwledig	**yn yr ardaloedd gwledig**
in rural areas	in the rural areas
mewn gwladwriaeth °ddemocrataidd	**yn Israel**
in a democratic state	in Israel
mewn gwlad estron	**yng ⁿNgwlad Pŵyl**
in a foreign country	in Poland

With a following singular noun, **mewn** usually corresponds to *in a*, but not always, as some singular non-specific nouns in English, particularly abstracts, do not use *a*: **byw mewn gobaith** *live in hope*. With a plural noun, **mewn** always means *in* (there is no plural indefinite article in English), while **yn** means either *in the* or *in* only (this second option with proper names, which are by definition specific – §35 – see last two examples above). See **yn** for further discussion.

O° means *from* or *of* but care should be taken with both.

(a)   It means *from* in most English senses, whether actual motion is implied or not:

Dw i'n dod o °Fangor yn °wreiddiol

I come originally from Bangor

O °Lanfairpwll ar Ynys Môn mae'r °gantores Elin Fflur yn dod

The singer Elin Fflur comes from Llanfairpwll on Anglesey

Mae ⁿmrawd i'n llogi tŷ yn ⁿNyfnaint o °fis Mehefin tan °fis Medi

My brother's renting a house in Devon from June to September

Diolch o °galon i ti

Thank you from [the bottom of] my heart

But **oddiwrth°** (see §464) is used where sending is involved, and **gan°** (see §455) where there is some sense of handing over.

(b)   o° means *of* usually with quantity expressions (see §185) or in circumstances where a 'part of' something is implied:

Wi'n moyn hanner pwys o °gaws a dwy °botel o °laeth (S)

I want half a pound of cheese and two bottles of milk

But **o°** in this sense is less frequent in Welsh than *of* in English, because genitive expressions (see §40) such as *the middle of the road*, which account for a large number of cases of *of* in English, use a different construction (**canol y ffordd**) in Welsh that does not use any word for *of*.

(c)   o° is sometimes used with VNs:

O ystyried mai dyma'r tro cynta iddo siarad yn °gyhoeddus, mae'n edrych yn hyderus iawn

Considering (or: When you consider . . .) that this is the first time he's spoken in public, he looks very confident [lit. 'From considering . . .']

O'n i'n mynd i °fod yn °grac, ond o siarad â nhw mae'n amlwg °fod 'na °ryw °gamddealltwriaeth wedi bod yn rhwyle

I was going to be cross, but (after) speaking to them it's clear that there's been some misunderstanding somewhere [lit. '. . ., but from speaking . . .']

Note the use with the possessive adjectives + VN **cymharu** compare: **o'i °gymharu â** *compared with* (m sing.), **o'i ʰchymharu â** (f sing.), **o'u cymharu â** (pl.).

> **Oedd y traethawd** (m) **'ma'n °wan o'i °gymharu â'r un diwetha nest ti**
>
> This essay was weak compared with the last one you did
>
> **Mae prisiau** (pl.) **fan hyn yn uchel o'u cymharu â Llundain**
>
> Prices here are high compared with London

(d) **o°** conveys adverbial *-ly* where this qualifies an adjective – **arbennig o °dda** *especially good*, **hynod o °galed** *extraordinarily difficult* (see §425(b))

Inflected forms with pronouns:

	Singular	*Plural*
1st	**ona i**	**onon ni**
2nd	**onat ti**	**onoch chi**
3rd	**ono fe/fo oni hi**	**onyn nhw**

Variants **ono i** and **onot ti** for 1st and 2nd sing. are quite common. Extended variants adding **-ho** – are also in use, but less frequent in rapid speech; so **ohonoch chi** = **onoch chi**. The same is true of the negative **mo** (see §295), a contraction of **dim o°**: **mohonoch chi** = **monoch chi**

Idioms with **o°**: **o'r gorau** *all right* (signifying agreement to something); **o'r diwedd** *at last* (cf. **yn y diwedd** *in the end, finally*); **o hyd** *still*; **o °ran** *as regards . . ., as far as . . . is concerned* (cf. **ar °ran** *on behalf of*); **o °blaid** *in favour* (of):

> **Nei di °roi gwybod i mi wedyn?**   **– O'r gorau**
>
> Will you let me know later?   – All right

> **O'r diwedd mae rhywbeth wedi'i °benderfynu'n °bendant!**
>
> At last a definite decision has been made!

> **Dan ni yma o hyd**
>
> We're still here

> **Mae lluniaeth wedi'i °drefnu, ond o °ran adloniant, well i ti °gysylltu â Siân**
>
> Food and drink has been arranged, but as regards entertainment, you'd better get in touch with Siân

Dych chi o °blaid datganoli neu yn erbyn?

Are you in favour of devolution or against?

Note also expressions of the type **peiriannydd o °Gymro** *a Welsh engineer*, **tafarnwr o Sais** *an English (pub-) landlord.*

463   Oddiar° (also oddi ar°)

Oddiar° is a compound of **ar°** (see §449), and inflects in the same way with pronouns, e.g. **oddiarno fo** etc. It describes motion in the reverse direction from **ar°**, and therefore means *off* in the narrow sense of *from upon*:

Cymer dy °bethau oddiar y bwrdd, nei di?

Take your things off the table, will you?

An object must already be **ar°** something for **oddiar°** to be used with it. Other instances of *off* in English are adverbial (*turn the TV off, buzz off*) and are translated by **(i) ffwrdd** or **(S) bant.**

464   Oddiwrth° (also oddi wrth°)

Oddiwrth° is a compound of **wrth°** (see §470), and inflects in the same way with pronouns, e.g. **oddiwrthi hi** etc. It means *from*, but is restricted to things or sentiments sent from one person to another – the reverse of **at°** (see §450) in this sense.

°Gaethon ni °ddim cerdyn oddiwrth dy °rieni eleni, naddo?

We didn't get a card from your parents this year, did we?

Penblwydd Hapus oddiwrth °bawb yn y swyddfa

Happy Birthday from everyone at the office

Where a verb of receiving like **cael** is actually stated, as in the first example above, **gan°** is a possible alternative to **oddiwrth°**.

465　Rhag

Rhag is a less commonly used preposition with very restricted meanings:

(a)　*from*, but only after verbs like **atal** *stop*, **rhwystro** *prevent*, **gwahardd** *forbid*, *prohibit*:

> **Bydd rhaid ceisio atal y °bobol 'ma rhag dod yn rhy agos**
>
> We'll have to try to stop these people from coming too close

> **Dw i am °rwystro chi rhag niweidio'ch hunan**
>
> I want to try to prevent you (from) hurting yourself

> **Fe °waharddwyd y teithwyr rhag mynd ymhellach**
>
> The travellers were forbidden to go any further

(b)　It is used as part of the conjunction **rhag ofn** *in case, for fear that*:

> **Dere di ag un yfory hefyd, rhag ofn i mi anghofio**
>
> You bring one tomorrow too, in case I forget

This usage is dealt with fully in **§508**.

(c)　It appears occasionally in set expressions like **rhag cywilydd!** *for shame!*, a less common alternative to **cywilydd arnat ti!** (or **arnoch chi!**) *shame on you!*

Inflected forms with pronouns are:

	Singular	Plural
1st	**rhagdda i**	**rhagddon ni**
2nd	**rhagddat ti**	**rhagddoch chi**
3rd	**rhagddo fe/fo** **rhagddi hi**	**rhagddyn nhw**

These are often pronounced rhactha i etc. in speech.

As a prefix, **rhag°**- usually corresponds to *pre-* or *fore-*: **rhagfarn** *prejudice*, **rhagweld** *foresee*.

466　Rhwng

Rhwng *between* is one of the few simple spatial prepositions in Welsh which does not cause SM. Its uses are much as in English.

Bydd y gêm rhwng Cymru a Lloegr yn cael ei haildrefnu

The game between Wales and England will be rescheduled

Dewch draw °rywbryd rhwng tri a pedwar

Come round some time between three and four

Inflected forms with pronouns are:

	Singular	*Plural*
1st	**rhyngdda i**	**rhyngddon ni**
2nd	**rhyngddat ti**	**rhyngddoch chi**
3rd	**rhyngddo fe/fo rhyngddi hi**	**rhyngddyn nhw**

These are often pronounced rhyngtha i etc. Variants with **rhwngdd-,** rhynth- and rhyng- are not uncommon.

Note Rhyngddat ti a fi, . . . or Rhyngddoch chi a fi, . . . *Between you and me*, ...

467   Tan°

Tan° means *until,* and is used with time expressions:

°Fyddwn ni ffwrdd tan °fis Tachwedd

We'll be away till November

'Dda i 'ma tan hanner awr wedi pedwar

I'll be here till half past four

It is used in taking leave of someone: **Tan yfory, 'te!** *Till tomorrow, then!,* **Tan hynny!** *Till then!,* **Tan y tro nesa!** *Till the next time!,* **Tan °Ddydd Llun!** *Till Monday!* etc.

Where *until* is a conjunction (i.e. followed by whole phrase with a verb in it), nes (see §503) is the usual translation. Compare:

Na i aros tan ar ôl cinio	I'll wait until after lunch
Na i aros nes iddo ffonio	I'll wait until he phones

But tan° is certainly used as a conjunction in some areas, so for example **Na i aros tan iddo ffonio.** Some speakers regard this as substandard, however.

468   Trwy°

Trwy° appears also as **trw°** and **drwy°**, and means *through* in the normal spatial sense – **mynd fel cyllell °boeth trwy °fenyn** *go like a hot knife through butter*, **edrych trwy'r twll** *look through the hole*.

With a following VN, it translates *by (means of) . . . ing*:

Ceisiwch ymlacio trwy anadlu'n °ddwfn am °funud neu °ddau
Try and relax by breathing deeply for a minute or two

°Fedrwn ni ennill trwy °ganolbwyntio'n °fwy ar °dactegau
We can win by concentrating more on tactics

With time expressions, **trwy°** means *all . . .* (not *every*, which is °**bob**):

trwy'r dydd	all day
(°**bob dydd**	every day)
trwy'r wythnos	all week
trwy'r °flwyddyn	all year

In this sense **gydol** is sometimes added – **trwy gydol y °flwyddyn**.

Inflected forms with pronouns are:

	Singular	*Plural*
1st	**trwydda i**	**trwyddon ni**
2nd	**trwyddat ti**	**trwyddoch chi**
3rd	**trwyddo fe/fo**	**trwyddyn nhw**
	trwyddi hi	

For related adverb **trwodd**, see §421(f).

469   Tua^h

Tua^h (**tuag** before vowels) in a spatial sense means *towards*, but in this meaning is nowadays combined with **at°** (see §450) except in set expressions like **tuag adre** *home(wards)*. Its main use in the modern spoken language is to convey approximation – i.e. *about* in both time and quantity expressions: **tua naw o'r °gloch** (*at*) *about nine o'clock*, **tua pum pwys o °datws** *about five pounds of potatoes*. With time expressions, the compound preposition **o °gwmpas** is sometimes heard instead – **o °gwmpas naw o'r gloch**.

Mae tua hanner y °boblogaeth °leol wedi ffoi

About half the local population have fled

Mae e tua'r un fath fel arfer

It's usually about the same

470 Wrth°

Wrth°, nearly always **wth°** in normal speech, has a variety of uses:

(a) in a purely spatial sense it means *by* or *at* where some sense of close proximity is indicated – **wrth y °ddesg** *by the desk*, **mae rhywun wrth y drws** *someone is at the door*. It also translates *by* after verbs of knowing or recognizing: **nes i adnabod ti wrth dy ffordd o °gerdded** *I recognized you by the way you walk*.

(b) *to* after **d(w)eud** *say, tell*, and similar verbs:

> **Beth yn union wedest ti wrth y °ferch °druan?**
>
> What exactly did you tell the poor girl?

(c) used with a VN, **wrth** means *while . . . ing*, and refers the action back to the subject:

> **Pwy °welson ni wrth °ddod allan o'r siop ond dy °gyn-wraig!**
>
> Who did we see (while) coming out of the shop but your ex!
>
> [i.e. we were the ones coming out]

cf. the following, with **yn**:

> **Pwy °welson ni yn dod allan o'r siop ond dy °gyn-wraig!**
>
> [i.e. it was your ex coming out of the shop]

(d) *for* after **rhaid** *need*. **Rhaid wrth°** . . . . . . *is needed*:

> **Rhaid wrth °gyfaddawdu mewn sefyllfaoedd felly**
>
> There is a need for compromise in such situations
>
> **Rhaid wrth °gefnogaeth**
>
> (We) need support; Support is needed

(e) **wrth (i)** is also a conjunction *as* . . . (see §**503**)

Inflected forms for pronouns are:

	Singular	Plural
1st	**wrtha i**	**wrthon ni**
2nd	**wrthat ti**	**wrthoch chi**
3rd	**wrtho fe/fo**	**wrthyn nhw**
	wrthi hi	

These inflected forms are routinely shortened to 'tha i, 'that ti etc. in speech everywhere, and especially after forms of d(w)eud say:

Mae isio deud 'thyn nhw be' 'dy be', on'd oes? (N)

They need telling what's what, don't they?

Be' wedodd hi 'thoch chi?

What did she say to you?

Several idiomatic phrases involve **wrth**: wrth °gwrs *of course*, wrth °reswm *of course, naturally*, wrth lwc *luckily* (also drwy lwc).

Wrth + possessive adjective + **bodd** means *delighted* or *in (one's) element*:

Dw i wrth 'y ⁿmodd   I'm as happy as can be

Mae e wrth ei °fodd   He's in his element

Similarly: wrth dy °fodd, wrth ei bodd, wrth ein bodd(au), wrth eich bodd(au), wrth eu bodd(au).

The 3rd pers. sing. f form **wrthi** is used with yn + VN to mean *busy . . . -ing*:

Mae'r plant i gyd wrthi'n codi castell tywod draw fan 'na

The kids are all busy building a sand castle over there

It can be used on its own where no action is specified:

Chi'n dal wrthi, 'te?   You're still at it, then?

Note also the compound preposition **wrth ymyl** *beside* (see §475).

471   Ynⁿ

Ynⁿ (but yn° in many spoken varieties) *in* is a true preposition, and should not be confused with the particle (complement-marker) yn°/yn (see §15). It is used only where a specific noun (see §35) follows, while **mewn** is used for the same meaning where a non-specific noun follows – yn yr °ardd *in the garden* but **mewn gardd** *in a garden*. This distinction is dealt with fully under **mewn** (see §461).

In more formal Welsh, **yn** not only causes NM – the only word to do so other than (f)y *my* (see §110) and occasionally certain numerals (see §176) – but itself undergoes a change in the process:

(Bangor)	*ym* ⁿ**Mangor**
(Ceredigion)	*yng* ⁿ**Ngheredigion**
(Dolgellau)	*yn* ⁿ**Nolgellau**
(Gogledd Cymru)	*yng* ⁿ**Ngogledd Cymru**
(Pwllheli)	*ym* ⁿ**Mhwllheli**
(Talybont)	*yn* ⁿ**Nhalybont**

In addition, radical **m-**, which is not susceptible to NM, nevertheless alters **yn** to **ym**: **ym Machynlleth**.

The examples above are all place names, but the same principle holds true for ordinary words, which usually appear after **yn** as the first element of a two-noun genitive expression of the type (*in*) *the . . . of the . . .*: **yng** ⁿ**nghanol y** °**dre** *in the middle of the town*. Note that **canol** here is specific in meaning, and therefore requires **yn**, even though the definite article has been removed in accordance with the genitive rule (see §40).

In the spoken language of many areas of Wales, the position of the NM is, as noted elsewhere (see §9), precarious at best. This is especially true after **ynⁿ** *in*, and particularly with place names, where, if any mutation at all is heard, it is usually the SM. So **yn** °**Fangor**, **yn** °**Geredigion**, **yn** °**Ddolgellau**, **yn** °**Bwllheli**, **yn** °**Dalybont** are heard. SM of names beginning G-, however, is resisted, and here the radical is substituted: **yn Gogledd Cymru**. The radical of all place names after **yn** is also common enough – **yn Bangor** etc. All these non-NM usages are regarded as dialectal at best – the formal written language does not allow them at all, and some speakers vehemently reject them. On the other hand, it must be said that NM of place names, and especially **yn** ⁿ**Nh** – and **ym** ⁿ**Mh-**, strikes other native speakers as affected, to say the least.

With names not of Welsh origin that happen to begin with sounds susceptible to mutation in Welsh, the situation is even more chaotic – if someone has a friend in, for example, the London Borough of Camden, then any of the following might be heard:

Mae gen i ffrind yng ⁿNghamden

Mae gen i ffrind yn °Gamden

Mae gen i ffrind yn Camden

I've got a friend in Camden

because in addition to the two mutations after **yn** (i.e. **ynⁿ** and **yn°**) already discussed above, there is the (official/standard) option of non-mutation of foreign names (see §12 (c)).

Application of NM on ordinary nouns in genitive constructions is perhaps more consistent, especially as many of these, like **yng ⁿnghanol y °dre**, are commonly used set phrases. But here again, **p-** and **t-** are likely to prove resistant to NM in natural speech. So **yn °babell ei °frawd** *in his brother's tent* showing SM instead of standard NM version: **ym ⁿmhabell ei °frawd.**

Note **yn °Gymraeg**, even in literary language, for *in Welsh* (rather than *yng ⁿNghymraeg). There is a 'lost' definite article here which blocks NM (i.e. originally it was **yn y °Gymraeg**: names of languages usually have the article).

Inflected forms with pronouns are:

	Singular	*Plural*
1st	**yndda i**	**ynddon ni**
2nd	**ynddat ti**	**ynddoch chi**
3rd	**ynddo fe/fo**	**ynddyn nhw**
	ynddi hi	

Variants with -d- instead of -dd- (**yndo fe** etc.) are often heard, as are variants with no linking element at all (**yno fe**, etc.).

Two common verbal phrases with **ynⁿ** are **cydio ynⁿ** and **gafael ynⁿ**, both meaning *catch/keep hold of*. Also **ymddiddori ynⁿ** *be interested in/take an interest in*. All these can also, of course, be followed instead by **mewn** if there is a non-specific noun involved. Another word with similar meaning, **cyffwrdd** *touch*, is also sometimes found with **ynⁿ**, though **aʰ** is perhaps more common.

Dim ond oedolion °ddylai °gynnau tân gwyllt a gafael ynddo

Only adults should light a firework and hold it

Peidiwch â gafael mewn mwy nag un ar y tro

Don't hold more than one at a time

Mae'n °wych gweld trigolion Abertawe'n ymddiddori yn hanes y °ddinas

It's great to see Swansea people taking an interest in the history of the city

Pan °fydd ffon °wreichion yn diffodd, peidiwch â ʰchyffwrdd ynddi

When a sparkler goes out, don't touch it

473 Meaning of yn

What is written **yn** in fact represents three different words – a preposition and two (related) particles.

The preposition **yn**ⁿ is the equivalent of English *in*, except that it can only be used with specific nouns (see §35). Nevertheless, it is in every sense a true preposition, and behaves like other Welsh prepositions in nearly all respects, and has inflected forms for use with pronouns. It is unusual only in that it is (optionally) followed by NM.

The two particles **yn** are really **yn°** and **yn**. **Yn°** is used before nouns and adjectives, while **yn** is used before VNs. Note that **yn°** does *not* cause mutation of words beginning with ll- and rh- – this is a rare instance in Welsh where SM is not applied consistently to all nine consonants generally susceptible to it (see also usage of **y°** and **un°** with feminines – §§28, 162). Both are markers of a following complement (see §15). In practice they draw attention to the subject of the sentence whenever the main verb of that sentence is **bod** *to be* (in any of its forms). As such, it is the counterpart of the 'grammatical' SM in non-**bod** sentences. Compare:

(a) **Mae Dilwyn *yn* darllen rhagolygon y tywydd ar y teledu °bob nos**

Dilwyn reads the weather forecast on TV every night

(b) **Mi °ddylai Dilwyn °ddarllen y newyddion hefyd**

Dilwyn ought to read the news as well

In the above examples, **Dilwyn** is the subject in both cases. The structural difference from the point of view of Welsh is that in (a) **darllen** *read* is in the present tense, and therefore needs **bod** as the main verb (here 3rd pers. sing. present **mae**), while in (b) there is a modal (see §326) *ought to* (3rd pers. sing. **dylai**) which obviates the need for **bod**; the same would be true with other modals, or for that matter with auxiliaries **gwneud** and **ddaru**. In (a), then, the subject is indicated by placing **yn** immediately after it, because it is a **bod**-sentence; in (b) the subject is indicated by SM immediately after it,

369

because it is not a **bod**-sentence. Once the choice of **yn** rather than SM has been made on these criteria, the question of SM or not after **yn** is a secondary matter depending on whether a verb or a noun/adjective follows.

Use of yn°/yn after the subject in a **bod**-sentence is a secondary modification of the fundamental grammatical mutation principle of SM after subject. This is discussed more fully in §14.

Note also the special use of yn° + adjective to make an adverb (see §401):

Dach chi'n gyrru'n rhy araf

You're driving too slowly

The first **'n** (yn) links subject **chi** to VN-phrase **gyrru'n rhy araf**, and within this VN-phrase the second **'n** (yn° – with obligatory non-mutation of following rh-, see above) turns **rhy araf** *too slow* into *too slowly*.

474   Yn **and** 'n

The true preposition **yn** *in* differs from all other instances of **yn** summarized above in one other respect: it cannot be shortened to **'n** after a vowel. Compare the following, with a vowel preceding the **yn** in each case:

°Fyddwn ni'*n* mynd i Aberystwyth yfory   [complement-marker + VN]

We'll be going to Aberystwyth tomorrow

°Fyddwn ni'*n* hwyr   [complement-marker + adj.]

We'll be late

but:

°Fyddwn ni *yn* Aberystwyth cyn hir   [preposition]

We'll be in Aberystwyth soon

475–476 COMPOUND PREPOSITIONS

475   General remarks

These consist of two elements – simple preposition + noun – and are like English compound prepositions of the type *in front of*, but with no equivalent for *of* (see §40). With a following noun (or VN) they present no problems, and do not cause mutation. They are relatively few in number:

ar °bwys	beside, near
ar °bwys y °ddesg	beside the desk
ar °draws	across
ar °draws y ffordd	across the road
ar °gyfer	for
ar °gyfer y rhieni	for the parents
ar ôl	after
ar ôl y rhyfel	after the war
ar ôl mynd	after going
er mwyn	for the sake of
er mwyn y plant	for the sake of the children
er mwyn mynd	in order to go
o amgylch	around
o amgylch y stafell	around the room
o °flaen	in front of
o °flaen y tŷ	in front of the house
o °gwmpas	around
o °gwmpas y cae	around the field
wrth ochor	beside
wrth ochor yr afon	beside the river
wrth ymyl	beside
wrth ymyl y palmant	beside the pavement
ymhlith	amongst (see §476(e))
ymhlith y °gynulleidfa	amongst the audience
ymysg	amongst (see §476(e))
ymysg y cystadleuwyr	amongst the competitors
yn lle	instead of
yn lle Gerwyn	instead of Gerwyn
yn lle mynd	instead of going

But when used with pronouns, they behave differently from English, using the corresponding possessive adjectives instead of the pronouns. For example, *in front of him* is o'i °flaen (e) (lit. 'in his front'), *in front of her* o'i blaen (hi) ('in her front'), *in front of you* o'ch blaen (chi) ('in your front') etc.

Possessive adjectives are explained fully in §§109–114, and they operate exactly the same way here.

476 Compound prepositions with pronouns

When using the compound prepositions with pronouns, it is important to understand their structure. The dictionary form of the expression is a phrase involving a simple preposition + noun-type element mutated as appropriate after it. So, for example, **o °flaen** is, structurally, **o°** + **blaen**; **ar °gyfer** is really **ar°** + **cyfer**, etc. We have **°flaen** and **°gyfer** simply because there is no blocking element to stop the mutation. But when pronouns are needed with these in English, the possessive adjectives will appear in Welsh, and will not only block the mutation after **o°**, **ar°**, etc., but may replace it with their own mutations (see §109). These will operate on the radical forms **blaen**, **cyfer** etc., as is always the case with initial mutations (see §5(c)).

Here are the pronoun forms for **ar °gyfer** by way of illustration – reference may be made to §109 (possessive adjectives) for comparison.

ar °gyfer *for* (radical **cyfer**):

		Singular		Plural	
1st		**ar 'y ⁿghyfer**	for me	**ar ein cyfer**	for us
2nd		**ar dy °gyfer**	for you	**ar eich cyfer**	for you
3rd	(m)	**ar ei °gyfer**	for him	**ar eu cyfer**	for them
3rd	(f)	**ar ei ʰchyfer**	for her		

Notes:

(a) 'echoing' pronouns are possible in all cases, as with the possessive adjectives generally – **ar ei ʰchyfer hi**, **ar ein cyfer ni** – and are more frequent in speech than in formal writing

(b) **(ar°) cyfer**, beginning as it does with **c-**, displays the fullest range of mutations, while **(o°) blaen** would, for example, remain unchanged in 3rd pers. sing. f, since **b-** is not susceptible to AM

(c) second elements beginning with a vowel (e.g. **ar ôl**, **wrth ymyl**) may (depending on region) prefix **h-** in 3rd pers. sing. f, 1st pers. pl. and 3rd pers. pl.: **wrth ein hymyl** *beside us*

(d) second elements **blaen** and **ôl** occasionally appear in plural form **olau** and **blaenau** after **ein**, **eich** and **eu**, e.g. **o'u blaenau** for **o'u blaen** *in front of them*

(e) **ymhlith** and (less commonly) **ymysg** *amongst*, though written as single words, represent **yn**[n] + **plith** and **yn**[n] + **mysg**. As such they behave as other compound prepositions, except that their meaning generally restricts them to the plural: **yn ein plith (ni)** *amongst us*.

Further examples of compound prepositions with pronouns:

Paid torri ar 'y [n]nhraws i o hyd!
Stop interrupting me all the time! [**torri ar °draws** *interrupt*]

Mae'n °ddrwg gen i °dorri ar eich traws chi eto
Sorry to interrupt you again

Rhedwch ar ei hôl hi!
Run after her!

'Sdim llaeth ar ôl, bydd rhaid inni °ddefnyddio dŵr yn ei °le
There's no milk left, we'll have to use water instead (of it)

Rhowch y byrddau yn y canol a'r cadeiriau i gyd o'u hamgylch
Put the tables in the middle and all the chairs around them

°Elli di eistedd ar 'y [n]mhwys i os ti isie
You can sit next to me if you want

Dyn ni wedi trefnu cyfweliad ar ei [h]chyfer
We have arranged an interview for her

Rwy'n mawr °obeithio y bydd y plant yn hapus iawn yn ein mysg
I very much hope that the children will be very happy amongst us

Gardd °fach gyda clawdd o'i [h]chwmpas
A little garden with a hedge round it

Mae angen llenwi'r meysydd sydd â seren (*) wrth eu hymyl
The fields with an asterisk (*) by their side must be filled in

Note finally that ar ôl, er mwyn and yn lle are also used with VNs:

ar ôl ffonio	after phoning
ar ôl dod yn ôl o'r gwaith	after coming home from work
er mwyn arbed arian	in order to save money
er mwyn sicrhau diogelwch	in order to ensure safety
yn lle cadw'n °dawel	instead of keeping quiet
yn lle bod yn rhagrithiol	instead of being hypocritical

Complex sentences

477 Definitions

These are sentences made up of two parts or clauses. Each clause has its own verb, and this is a good way of identifying a complex sentence. The second or subordinate clause is linked in some way to the first, or main clause. Complex sentences come in two types, depending on the nature of the subordinate clause, which can be either a relative clause or an indirect (or reported) speech clause. English examples, with clauses marked, are:

	[main]	[relative clause]
(a)	[This is the man]	[*who* phoned the fire brigade]
(b)	[I'll take the one]	[*which/that* weighs less]
	[main]	[indirect speech clause]
(c)	[Did you know]	[that his girlfriend had dumped him?]
(d)	[I'm not sure]	[*whether/if* he's coming]

These examples illustrate two types of complex sentence, identifiable by the linking word between the clauses. Type 1 (sentences (a) and (b)) uses *who/which/that* as the link, with the subordinate clause referring back to something in the main clause (*the man, the one*), while Type 2 (sentences (c) and (d)) uses *that* or *whether/if*. It is not necessary to go into the technical differences between Types 1 and 2, either in English or Welsh – it is enough to be able to tell them apart in English. This can be done by looking for the link-word, as explained above. There is one complication, however: *that* appears in both Type 1 (b) and Type 2 (c). How do we tell which Type a *that* . . . sentence is? A comparison of the two sentences gives us two foolproof ways of telling which is which:

[relative]	I'll take the one *that/which* weighs less
[indirect]	Did you know (*that*) his girlfriend had dumped him?

1) In a relative clause, *that* can be replaced by *which* with no difference in meaning; in an indirect clause, replacing optional *that* with *which* would not make sense. Or:

2) In an indirect clause we can remove the *that* altogether and still have a perfectly good sentence ('*Did you know his girlfriend had dumped him?*'), while removing the *that* from a relative clause leaves us with an incorrect and incomplete sentence (* '*I'll take the one weighs less*') .

Welsh also has both relative and indirect clauses, but a slightly more compli-cated procedure in both cases for joining them to the preceding main clause. There is a wider choice of linking words than in English. But the crucial thing to start with is to correctly identify relative or indirect, and this can be done from the English as explained above.

478   General principles for complex sentences in Welsh

The procedure for constructing any complex sentence in Welsh has two stages:

Stage 1:   identify the link-word joining the two clauses in English

Stage 2:   remove the link-word and make any slight changes necessary to arrive at two self-contained simple sentences (parts 1 and 2).

Once these stages have been carried out, the original sentence corresponding to the subordinate clause can be converted to Welsh (Stage 3), and the first element of this will indicate the way of linking the two clauses of the complex sentence in Welsh.

For example, taking a relative (*who/which*) complex sentence in English:

I know the man who works in the toy shop

Stage 1:   Link-word in English is *who*

Stage 2:   Remove *who* to isolate the two ideas

I know the man   works in the toy shop

and add *He* to make part 2 grammatical. This leaves us with two original sentences

I know the man

He works in the toy shop

375

Stage 3:   The second of these in Welsh is:

Mae o'n gweithio yn y siop °deganau

From here we can use the presence of **mae** at the front of this sentence to lead us to the right choice of linking construction (see §485).

Indirect complex sentences must be split in two in the same way. *That . . .* sentences simply involve the removal of *that*, while *if/whether* sentences usually require an alteration in word-order. For example:

Everyone knows that Bert has been ill lately

Stage 1:   Everyone knows Bert has been ill lately

Stage 2:   No alteration needed – both sentences are correct as they stand.

Stage 3:   Part 2 in Welsh: ***Mae* Bert wedi bod yn sâl yn °ddiweddar**

Go and ask him if he is coming with us

Stage 1:   Go and ask him He is coming with us

Stage 2:   Word order must be changed to keep the idea of a question:

Go and ask him   **Is he coming with us?**

Stage 3:   Part 2 in Welsh: ***Ydi* o'n dŵad hefo ni?**

Once the type of complex sentence has been established, and the first element of the original sentence underlying the subordinate clause (the subordinate original) in Welsh identified, simple procedures can be laid down for determining the appropriate linking construction.

The subordinate clause in relative (*who/which*) sentences can be either AFF or NEG; in indirect sentences it can be AFF, INT or NEG.

479–485 RELATIVE COMPLEX SENTENCES

As explained above, these will have *who* or *which/that* as the link-word between the two clauses. Once the original for the subordinate clause has been identified and translated into Welsh by the procedure described above, there are three possible options, dealt with below.

479   **Subordinate original beginning** mae: **option 1**

In this case the first element of the original sentence in part 2 is **mae**, and the noun (occasionally pronoun) at the end of part 1 is the subject of this verb:

This is the man who works in the toy shop

This is the man	He works in the toy shop
Dyma'r dyn	**Mae e'n gweithio yn y siop °deganau**

Here it is the man who is doing the working, so **dyn** *man* is the subject of **mae . . . 'n gweithio** *works*.

In this case, the original **mae** is replaced in the complex sentence by **sy(dd)** (the special present tense relative form of **bod** – see §229):

Dyma'r dyn *sy*'n gweithio yn y siop °deganau

If the subordinate clause is NEG ('the man who doesn't work . . .'), then the link will be **sy °ddim**, or less frequently **nad ydy/yw e/hi (°ddim)**:

Dyma'r dyn *sy °ddim* yn gweithio yn y siop °deganau

or: **Dyma'r dyn *nad ydy e* (°ddim) yn gweithio yn y siop °deganau**

This is the man who doesn't work in the toy shop

Note the fundamental point that **sy(dd)** can only be preceded by its own subject.

480   **Subordinate original beginning** mae: **option 2**

In this case the first element of the original sentence in part 2 is **mae**, and the noun (occasionally pronoun) at the end of part 1 is the object (direct or indirect) of this verb:

This is the man who(m)	Fred knows
This is the man	*Fred knows him*
Dyma'r dyn	**Mae Fred yn nabod e**

Here it is not the man who knows somebody, but Fred who knows the man – so **dyn** is the *object* of **mae (Fred) yn nabod . . . .**

In this case, in an AFF clause the **mae** is left unchanged, the object pronoun (**e**) is removed and a linking particle (**y**) – rarely heard in speech – is put between the two clauses:

Dyma'r dyn (y) *mae* Fred yn nabod

This is the man (whom) Fred knows

In a NEG clause, **mae** is replaced by **nad ydy/yw** with an optional °**ddim** following the subject:

Dyma'r dyn *nad ydy* Fred (°*ddim*) yn nabod

This is the man Fred doesn't know

481   Subordinate original beginning with verb-form other than mae

In this case the first element of the original sentence in part 2 is a verb-form other than **mae**.

This is the man who could do the work

This is the man   *He could do the work*

Dyma'r dyn   °**Allai fe °wneud y gwaith**

This is like the first **mae** option above, because it is the *man* (**dyn**) who could (°**allai**) do the work, so **dyn** is the subject of °**allai** – but the first element of part 2 is °**allai** and not **mae**. Note that optional affirmative markers **fe°/mi°** (see §213) should not be included when using this procedure.

In this instance the repeated pronoun (**fe** – referring back to **dyn**) is dropped, and the linking particle for an AFF subordinate clause is (**a**)°, with usually only the mutation heard in speech. In the spoken language, inflected verbs have initial SM in any case (see §11(d)), so the net effect is a simple joining of the two clauses, with deletion of redundant pronouns:

Dyma'r dyn (a) °allai °wneud y gwaith

Where the subordinate clause is NEG, the linking particle is **na°** (**nad** optionally before vowels and always before impf of **bod** – **oedd**, etc.):

Dyma'r dyn *na* °allai °wneud y gwaith

This is the man *who couldn't* do the work

Dyma'r dyn *nad oedd* yn °bresennol ddoe

This is the man *who was* not present yesterday

Sometimes an additional °ddim is added – **Dyma'r dyn na °allai °ddim gwneud y gwaith**; and sometimes the °ddim is used and the na not: **Dyma'r dyn °allai °ddim gwneud y gwaith.**

Note that the deletion of pronouns can lead to ambiguity in Welsh where the verb in part 2 is Preterite I or Future I - the inflected tenses that <u>don't</u> use an auxiliary (see §§293, 304):

This is the man who phoned Fred

This is the man	He phoned Fred
Dyma'r dyn	**Ffoniodd e Fred**
Dyma'r dyn ffoniodd Fred	

This is the man whom Fred phoned

This is the man	Fred phoned him
Dyma'r dyn	**Ffoniodd Fred e**
Dyma'r dyn ffoniodd Fred	

This is the man who will phone Fred

This is the man	He will phone Fred
Dyma'r dyn	**Ffonith e Fred**
Dyma'r dyn ffonith Fred	

This is the man whom Fred will phone

This is the man	Fred will phone him
Dyma'r dyn	**Ffonith Fred e**
Dyma'r dyn ffonith Fred	

In ambiguous cases like this, a solution is to use the auxiliary-type preterites and futures (Preterites II and III, Futures II and III) instead:

This is the man who phoned Fred	**Dyma'r dyn naeth ffonio Fred**	[Pret II]
	Dyma'r dyn ddaru ffonio Fred	[Pret III]
This is the man whom Fred phoned	**Dyma'r dyn naeth Fred ffonio**	[Pret II]
	Dyma'r dyn ddaru Fred ffonio	[Pret III]
This is the man who will phone Fred	**Dyma'r dyn °fydd yn ffonio Fred**	[Fut II]
	Dyma'r dyn neith ffonio Fred	[Fut III]
This is the man whom Fred will phone	**Dyma'r dyn bydd Fred yn ffonio**	[Fut II]
	Dyma'r dyn neith Fred ffonio	[Fut III]

482 'Whose'

There is no word for *whose* (i.e. *of whom*) in Welsh. Sentences like *This is the man whose son works with us* are done by the usual procedure of reverting to the two original simple sentences, the second of which, however, will have a possessive adjective (see §109):

This is the man whose son works with us

This is the man	His son works with us
Dyma'r dyn	**Mae ei °fab yn gweithio 'da ni**

Dyma'r dyn mae ei °fab yn gweithio 'da ni

I spoke to the man whose wife phoned us yesterday

I spoke to the man	His wife phoned us yesterday
°Ges i air â'r dyn	**Ffoniodd ei °wraig ni ddoe**

°Ges i air â'r dyn ffoniodd ei wraig ni ddoe

483   **Subordinate clauses with prepositions**

Where a preposition is involved in the subordinate clause, as in English 'This is the woman with whom I had lunch', 'This is the chair that you were sitting on', the same broad procedure is followed:

This is the woman	I had lunch with her
Dyma'r °ddynes	**°Ges i °ginio efo hi**

Dyma'r °ddynes °ges i °ginio efo hi

This is the chair	You were sitting on it
Dyma'r °gadair	**Oeddet ti'n eistedd arni hi**

Dyma'r °gadair oeddet ti'n eistedd arni

It is important to note here that the repeated pronoun **hi** (referring to **dynes**) after **efo** in the first example is retained – you really cannot end a sentence with a preposition in Welsh. But in the second example, **ar** is an inflecting preposition (see §446), and the repeated **hi** (referring to **cadair** f) can (and should be) dropped, because the extra syllable -ni is not strictly speaking the preposition, and so can end the sentence. This is also true for **-o fe/fo**:

Dyma'r dyn naethon nhw °roi'r °wobr iddo (for **iddo fe/fo**)

Here's the man they gave the prize to

But it is not the case with **-yn nhw**, which can never be shortened to **-yn** (see §446) under any circumstances:

Dyma'r °bobol naethon nhw °roi'r gwobrau iddyn nhw

Here are the people they gave the prizes to

Dyma'r cadeiriau oedden nhw'n eistedd arnyn nhw

These are the chairs they were sitting on

Principal non-inflecting prepositions are **â**, **efo**, and **(gy)da**.

484   **Further examples of relative complex sentences**

Dw i'n nabod rhywun sy'n medru siarad Hen Saesneg

I know someone who can speak Old English

Dim ond Kathryn na enillodd °wobr

It was only Kathryn who didn't win a prize

Dewiswch °rywbeth dach chi'n leicio

Choose something (that) you like

°Alla i °feddwl am °dri o °bobol na °fyddai'n rhy hapus

I can think of three people who wouldn't be too happy

Dyma'r llyfr o'n i'n siarad amdano

This is the book (that) I was talking about

Efrog Newydd yw'r °ddinas mae pobol yn meddwl °gynta amdani

New York is the city (that) people think of first

Es i i °weld y ffilm 'na naeth dy °frawd °gymeradwyo

I went to see that film your brother recommended

Ti yw'r unig un fan hyn na °ddaeth (°ddim) i'r parti neithiwr

You're the only one here who didn't come to the party last night

Mae 'na un peth bach na sonies i amdano ddoe

There's one little thing I didn't talk about yesterday

485 Summary of linking constructions for relative sentences

First element in subordinate original	AFF	NEG
mae (subj. is in main clause)	**sy(dd)**	**sy °ddim nad ydy**, etc.
mae (subj. is in subordinate clause)	**(y)**	**nad ydy** [subj.] **(°ddim)**
all other parts of **bod** and all other verbs	**(a)°**	**na(d)° . . . (°ddim)**

486–497 INDIRECT COMPLEX SENTENCES

486 Definitions

Indirect complex sentences involve what is often referred to as 'reported speech' – in other words, the subordinate clause represents a thought, statement or question in itself, introduced by main clause + (*that*):

(a)	Everybody knows	(that)	bananas are expensive
(b)	Go and ask	if/whether	they are coming
(c)	I am sure	(that)	we didn't agree to this

As with relative sentences above, the subordinate original holds the key to choosing the right link-word in Welsh. First we must decide what original statement or question the subordinate clause represents.

With (*that*) . . . sentences (a) and (c) above – AFF and NEG respectively – this is easy: *Bananas are expensive* and *We didn't agree to this*. No change at all is necessary. The only trap here is that, as mentioned earlier (see §477), it is common in English to omit *that* in indirect sentences. It is important to know where it belongs, even if it is not expressed, because its presence indicates the start of the all-important subordinate original that has to be translated into Welsh.

With *if/whether* . . . sentences ((b) above – INT) we need to convert the subordinate clause into a question: *Are they coming?* This is the unspoken thought or statement in *Go and ask them if they're coming*, even though English reverts to statement word-order after *if/whether*.

As with relative sentences, once the subordinate original has been identified, it must be translated into Welsh before the linking construction can be determined. With indirect speech, this is simply a case of imagining what was actually said. But because an indirect clause is simply reported speech, the original can be any type of sentence at all (the options for relative clauses are much more restricted). This means that the crucial first element can be either a verb (because the normal word-order in Welsh is VSO – see §13) or something that is not a verb (if there is focus of some kind – see §17). This has a bearing on link-words. Furthermore, the present tense of **bod** *to be* behaves differently in this regard from other verbs. So, beginning with two separate clauses that we are going to join, we have three things to look out for at the beginning of the second clause immediately after where the link-word will be going:

(a) part of the present of **bod**

(b) some other part of **bod**, or any other verb

(c) a word that is not a verb

and we must also consider whether the subordinate original is itself AFF, INT or NEG. This gives potentially 3 × 3 = 9 options – summarized under §495, but dealt with by first element (as above) in detail below.

487 Indirect sentences – present, perfect or imperfect of bod **starts subordinate original**

Here it is important to remember that it is the actual words underlying the subordinate (*that* . . .) clause that are the determining factor. Examples:

(a)	He says	(that)	they are here
	He says		'They are here'
	Mae'n deud		**'*Maen* nhw fan hyn'**
(b)	It's obvious	(that)	he is telling lies
	It's obvious		He is telling lies
	Mae'n amlwg		**'*Mae* o'n deud clwyddau'**

In particular, where the main clause verb is past in English, as in example (c) below, a rule of sequence of tenses requires the subordinate verb to be past also, but the original words (inside the quotation marks) may well have been present, and this is what matters here:

(c)	She said	(that)	the train was late
	She said		'The train is late'
	Wedodd hi		**'Mae'r trên yn hwyr'**

In all these cases, Welsh uses a special form of **bod** which varies for person and includes both the idea of 'that . . .' and the verb:

ⁿmod i	that I (am) . . .
°fod ti	that you (are) . . .
°fod e/o	that he (is) . . .
bod hi	that she (is) . . .
bod ni	that we (are) . . .
bod chi	that you (are) . . .
bod nhw	that they (are) . . .

These are sometimes heard, and often seen written, with the corresponding possessive adjectives (see §109) preceding, e.g. **fy ⁿmod i, eich bod chi** etc. The written language has a preference for using the possessive alone and dropping the following pronoun: **fy ⁿmod** *that I* (*am*) . . . , **ei °fod** *that he* (*is*) . . . etc.

In speech, examples (a) and (b) above will be:

Mae'n deud	***bod nhw***	**fan hyn**
He says	that they are	here

| Mae'n amlwg | °fod o | 'n deud clwyddau |
| It's obvious | that he is | lying |

Where a noun follows the *that* ... in this type of indirect sentence in English, as in example (c) above, the form can be either **bod** or °**fod**, and this has nothing to do with whether the noun in question is m or f:

| Wedodd hi | °fod/bod y trên yn hwyr |
| She said | that the train was late |

In many parts of Wales simplified forms with **bo** for all persons are in common use:

bo fi	that I (am) . . .
bo ti	that you (are) . . .
bo fe	that he (is) . . .
bo hi	that she (is) . . .
bo ni	that we (are) . . .
bo chi	that you (are) . . .
bo nhw	that they (are) . . .

488   Indirect sentences – present or perfect of bod starts negative subordinate original

The same broad principles apply where the subordinate clause is NEG, but there are two options for linking:

ⁿmod i . . . °ddim	or	nad ydw i . . . (°ddim)	that I (am) not . . .
°fod ti . . . °ddim	or	nad wyt ti . . . (°ddim)	that you (are) not . . .
°fod e . . . °ddim	or	nad ydy e/o . . . (°ddim)	that he (is) not . . .
bod hi . . . °ddim	or	nad ydy hi . . . (°ddim)	that she (is) not . . .
bod ni . . . °ddim	or	nad ydyn ni . . . (°ddim)	that we (are) not . . .
bod chi . . . °ddim	or	nad ydych chi . . . (°ddim)	that you (are) not . . .
bod nhw . . . °ddim	or	nad ydyn nhw . . . (°ddim)	that they (are) not . . .

The first options (and variants **bo fi** etc.) are probably the more common in speech. Examples:

Dan ni'n gobeithio bod chi °ddim yn siomedig

We hope (that) you're not disappointed

Mae'n amlwg inni i gyd nad ydych chi'n °barod i °gydnabod hyn

It's clear to all of us that you are not prepared to acknowledge this

Dw i'n eitha siwr nad ydy o (°ddim) isio creu trafferthion

I'm fairly sure (that) he doesn't want to make trouble

O'ch chi'n gwybod bod nhw °ddim yn °briod?

Did you know (that) they weren't married?

Wedodd e gynnau bo fe °ddim yn dod wedi'r cwbwl

He's just said that he's not coming after all

Rhaid i mi °gyfadde ⁿmod i °ddim wedi darllen y °ddogfen

I must admit (that) I haven't read the document

Note: in the last example the perfect of **bod** logically comes under this type because, formally, it is simply the present tense but with a following **wedi** instead of **yn** (see §268).

489 Indirect sentences – interrogative subordinate clause

Where the subordinate clause is INT, no linking element is required, and the original question is used as its own subordinate clause – in other words Welsh phrases *Do you know if (/whether) they are coming?* as *Do you know are they coming?* **Dach chi'n gwybod ydyn nhw'n dod?** Strictly speaking the word **os** *if* is not required in indirect clauses in Welsh, and its use in this way by some speakers – **Dach chi'n gwybod os ydyn nhw'n dod?** (echoing English usage) – is regarded as substandard by some speakers. Further examples:

Dw i °ddim yn sicr ydy hi'n siarad Cymraeg neu °beidio

I'm not sure if (/whether) she speaks Welsh or not

Cer i °ofyn iddyn nhw ydyn nhw'n moyn rhywbeth o'r siop

Go and ask them if (/whether) they want anything from the shop

°Allwch chi °ddeud 'tha i ydy hi'n iawn i mi °barcio fan hyn?

Can you tell me if (/whether) it's alright for me to park here?

Indirect
sentences –
verb other
than present
or perfect of
bod starts
subordinate
original

490   **Indirect sentences – verb other than present or perfect of** bod **starts subordinate original**

In these cases there is a simple choice of link-word depending on whether the subordinate clause is AFF, INT or NEG.

AFF: (y) – often not heard in ordinary speech; **yr** is used before vowels

INT: (a)° – often not heard in ordinary speech, leaving the SM only

NEG: na° (or MM) – with an optional (°ddim) following; **nad** is used optionally before vowels and always before **oedd**, etc.

For example, using the procedure already explained for finding the subordinate original:

I think (that)	you ought to tell him
I think	'You ought to tell him'
Dw i'n meddwl	**'Dylech chi °ddeud wrtho fe'**

This makes **dylech**, a verb-form that is not present tense of **bod**, the first element of the subordinate original, so the resulting complex sentence will simply be:

Dw i'n meddwl (y) dylech chi °ddeud wrtho fe

I think you ought to tell him.

Similarly, INT and NEG versions would be:

Dw i °ddim yn siwr (a) °ddylech chi °ddeud wrtho fe

I'm not sure if (/whether) you should tell him

Dw i'n siwr na° ddylech chi °ddeud wrtho fe

I'm sure you shouldn't tell him

Further examples of y/a°/na° indirect sentences:

Mae'n sicr (y) byddai hynny'n °beryglus dros °ben

It is certain that that would be extremely dangerous

Swn i'n meddwl (y) dôn nhw wedyn

I should think they'll be along later

Tybed (a) °geith hi °ddiwrnod rhydd wythnos nesa?

I wonder if she'll get a day off next week?

A i i °ofyn (a) leicsen nhw °gyfrannu

I'll go and ask if they'd like to contribute

Gobeithio na °bleidleisiodd e yn erbyn

I hope (that) he didn't vote against

Wedodd Geraint nad oedd ei °rieni gartre (°Ddydd Sadwrn diwetha)

Geraint said (that) his parents weren't home (last Saturday)

With the last example, note the difference between it and **Wedodd Geraint** °*fod* ei °rieni °*ddim* gartre which also translates as *Geraint said that his parents weren't home.* But in the **nad oedd** . . . example, what he actually said was '*Doedd* 'n rhieni °*ddim* gartre (°Ddydd Sadwrn diwetha)' (impf tense of **bod**) 'My parents *weren't* home (last Saturday)', while in the °fod . . . °ddim example what he actually said was '*Dyw* 'n rhieni °*ddim* gartre' (present tense of **bod**) 'My parents *aren't* home'.

491 Alternative constructions when a preterite begins the subordinate original

Alternative constructions are found in some parts of Wales where the verb at the start of the subordinate original is a preterite, as, for example, in *I know (that) the train went two hours ago:*

(a) it is treated as a perfect for the purposes of linking:

Dw i'n gwybod	*Aeth y tren °ddwy awr yn ôl*
Dw i'n gwybod	°*fod y trên wedi mynd °ddwy awr yn ôl*

(b) a completely different construction, comprising **i** + subj. + °VN, is substituted:

Dw i'n gwybod *i'r trên* °*fynd °ddwy awr yn ôl*

This second method, though less common than the **wedi**-construction, is not as alien to the spoken language as is sometimes claimed.

492 Indirect sentences – focused subordinate original

In this type, the first element of the subordinate original will be something that is not a verb (this includes VNs, which are not strictly speaking verbs – see §198), because the word-order in focused sentences is not VSO. If you are uncertain about this, review §§17–21 before proceeding.

Where the subordinate clause does not begin with the verb, Welsh has special 'that'-like words that simply join the two clauses as they stand.

AFF: **mai** (N and standard), **na** (widespread in many parts of the N, but not accepted in the standard), or **taw** (some parts of the S)

INT: **ai**

NEG: **nad**

To take an AFF example:

It's clear   (that)   you are to blame

There is nothing unusual about this in English, but the subordinate clause in Welsh is a focused sentence because it answers the notional question 'Who is to blame?' **Pwy sy ar °fai?**, for which the answer here is **Chi** [focused element] **sy ar °fai**. Since **chi** is not a verb (**sy** is the verb in this sentence), and the clause is AFF, then the only way to join the two clauses is with **mai** (or **na** or **taw**):

Mae'n amlwg   **mai chi sy ar °fai**

It's clear   that [it is] you [who] are to blame

Further AFF examples:

Dw i'n siwr na breuddwydio o'n i

I'm sure I was dreaming   [subordinate original: **Breuddwydio o'n i**]

Mae'n gwybod mai ni biau fe

He knows that it's ours   [subordinate original: **Ni biau fe**]

Wi'n gwybod taw Alun yw'r hena fan hyn

I know that [it is] Alun [who] is the oldest here

It is important for the non-native user to distinguish between **na°** (used in NEG indirect clauses beginning with a verb other than present **bod**) and **na** (common alternative to **mai**, and used, despite appearances, with AFF focused clauses). The two are easy to distinguish in practice, since the word after **na°** will be a verb, while the word after **na** will be anything but a verb.

493   Link-word ai

The INT link-word **ai** corresponds to *if/whether* where the subordinate clause is focused in Welsh:

Go and ask him   if   [it was]   Bert [who] said that

Dos i °ofyn   **ai**   **Bert wedodd 'ny**

This subordinate clause is focused because the sense is *was it Bert rather than someone else?* In this sense, the original question would be **Bert wedodd 'ny?** (focused element first, verb second). If the question had been a neutral one, for example *Did Bert say that (or did he not)?* this would have been **Wedodd Bert 'ny?** – and this would have converted to the indirect equivalent (**Dos i °ofyn) (a) wedodd Bert 'ny.** Further examples:

> **Dan ni °ddim yn siwr ai dyma'r ffordd °orau**
>
> We're not sure if this is the best way

> **Mae isio gofyn o °ddifri ai meddwl am y dyfodol dan ni am °wneud neu °boeni am yr hyn sy wedi bod**
>
> We need to seriously ask whether we want to think about the future or worry about the past
>
> [lit. whether thinking about the future (is what) we want . . .]

> **O'n i °ddim yn gwybod ai fo oedd o** (N)
>
> I didn't know if it was him

494   **Link-word** nad

The NEG link-word **nad** corresponds to *that (it is/was) not*, with a focused subordinate clause. It replaces the **Dim** or (rather literary) **Nid** which starts all NEG focused sentences (see §157(b)). Examples:

[simple]	**Dim Gerwyn °dorrodd y ffenest** It was not Gerwyn who broke the window
[complex]	**Dw i'n siwr *nad* Gerwyn °dorrodd y ffenest** I'm sure *that* it was *not* Gerwyn who broke the window
[s]	**Dim ni sy'n °gyfrifol am hynny** It is not we who are responsible for that
[c]	**Dw i'n siwr *nad* ni sy'n °gyfrifol am hynny** I'm sure *that* it is *not* we who are responsible for that
[s]	**Dim ceisio'n twyllo ni oedd e** He wasn't trying to deceive us
[c]	**Dw i'n siwr *nad* ceisio'n twyllo ni oedd e** I'm sure *that* he was *not* trying to deceive us

Summary of linking constructions for indirect sentences

first element in subordinate original	*AFF*	*INT*	*NEG*
pres. or impf of **bod**	bod/°fod . . . etc.	(a)°	nad . . . (°ddim) bod/°fod . . . (°ddim)
any other verb form	**y**	**(a)** °	**na°** . . . (°ddim)
VN or any non-verb element	**mai/na/taw**	**ai**	**nad**

Summary of indirect sentence types

(**a**)   present tense of **bod**:

   AFF   **Dw i'n gwybod bod nhw'n hwyr**

   I know (that) they are late

   INT   **Ewch i °weld ydyn nhw wedi cyrraedd 'to**

   Go and see if (/whether) they have arrived yet

   NEG   **Dw i'n gwybod nad ydy Fred (°ddim) yn dod**

   Dw i'n gwybod °fod Fred °ddim yn dod

   I know (that) Fred is not coming

(**b**)   other tenses of **bod** or other inflected verbs:

   AFF   **Dw i'n siwr (y) byddai hi'n iawn**

   I'm sure (that) it would be OK

   INT   **Ewch i °ofyn (a) °fyddai hi'n iawn**

   Go and ask if (/whether) it would be OK

   NEG   **Dw i'n siwr na °fyddai hi'n °deg**

   I'm sure (that) it would not be fair

(**c**)   non-verbal element (includes VNs):

   AFF   **Mae'n amlwg mai/na/taw breuddwydio o't ti**

   (VN is focused element - **breuddwydio**)

   It is obvious (that) you were dreaming

AFF	**Dw i'n siwr mai/na/taw Gerwyn naeth e**
	(non-verbal focused element - **Gerwyn**)
	I'm sure (that) it was Gerwyn who did it
INT	**Dw i isio gwybod ai rhybuddio neu °fygwth oedd o**
	I want to know if (/whether) he was warning or threatening (us)
INT	**Dw i isio gwybod ai Fred °dorrodd y ffenest**
	(non-verbal - **Fred**)
	I want to know if (/whether) it was Fred who broke the window
NEG	**Dw i'n siwr nad bygwth ni oedd o** (VN - **bygwth**)
	I'm sure (that) he wasn't threatening us
NEG	**Dw i'n siwr nad Fred °dorrodd y ffenest**
	(non-verbal - **Fred**)
	I'm sure (that) it wasn't Fred who broke the window

497 **Interrogative subordinate clauses**

INT subordinate clauses in indirect sentences can also be introduced by question words like lle?, pryd?, beth? etc. No linking word is required in these cases, and no change in word-order:

Dw i °ddim yn gwybod lle mae o

[Lle mae o?]

I don't know where he is

Cer i °ofyn pryd maen nhw'n bwriadu dod

[Pryd maen nhw'n bwriadu dod?]

Go and ask them when they're planning to come

Dw i °ddim yn siwr beth mae hi'n moyn °wneud

[Beth mae hi'n moyn °wneud?]

I'm not sure what she wants to do

Does neb yn gwybod pwy ydyn nhw

[Pwy ydyn nhw?]

Nobody knows who they are

Conjunctions

498 Definitions

Conjunctions are linking words that join two sentences or clauses and show
the relationship between them. There are four co-ordinating conjunctions
which can link either clauses or single words: a[h] (ac before vowels and
certain miscellaneous words) *and*, **ond** *but*, **neu**° *or* and **na**[h] (nac before
vowels) *nor*. Their use is straightforward and they are discussed separately
in §§510–513. The remaining large majority of conjunctions have a role in
the sentence similar to that in indirect speech sentences (see §486). But they
convey a variety of relationships between the clauses they join (e.g. purpose,
time, reason), and these clauses are of equal status – the resulting sentence
is more 'balanced' on either side of the conjunction. Examples in English:

I'm not going out *because* I have to wash my hair	[reason]
We'll help you with the decorating *if* we have time	[condition]
Make a note of that *so that* you don't forget	[purpose]
Let's wait here *until* Dafydd comes back	[time]
We had so much rain *that* the river burst its banks	[result]
I drink coffee *whereas* my wife prefers tea	[contrast]

499 Principles of construction after conjunctions

In modern Welsh, conjunctions come in three groups according to the
construction that follows them:

(a) indirect speech construction (**bod** etc.); you should review §§486–496
now if you are uncertain about indirect (or reported) speech in Welsh

(b) **i** + subject° + VN

(c) neither of the above

In the lists that follow, the appropriate construction will be indicated after each conjunction: (**bod**), (**i**) or neither. Broadly speaking, however, most time conjunctions are type (**b**), while the rest are mostly type (**a**) – there is some overlap between these two types. A handful of conjunctions (**os, pe, hyd, felly**, and to some extent **pan°**) take neither.

500 Indirect speech conjunctions

Indirect speech (type (a)) conjunctions will be followed by **bod** (or °**fod**, ⁿ**mod, bo** etc.), (**y**), **na(d)** or **mai** (or **na/taw**). This choice depends on the type of word following, exactly as in indirect speech proper. For example, **fel** (**bod**) means *so that* (result or purpose):

Siaradwch yn uwch fel ⁿmod i'n gallu clywed

Speak up so that I can hear

Siaradwch yn uwch fel (y) galla i °glywed

Speak up so that I can hear

Well i mi °dynnu map fel (y) byddi di'n deall yn union lle ydan ni

I'd better draw a map so that you'll know exactly where we are

Cuddia'r anrhegion nawr fel na °fydd y plant yn gweld nhw

Hide the presents now so that the kids won't see them

501 [I + subject + VN] conjunctions

I + [subj.] + VN (type (b)) conjunctions include most time conjunctions, and also **er mwyn** *in order to* and **rhag ofn** *in case*. The VN carries no indication of tense, and can be used regardless of the tense of the verb in English. Compare:

Dw i'n moyn cael gair 'dag e cyn iddo fe °fynd

I want to have a word with him before he *goes*

°**Ges i °air 'dag e cyn iddo fe °fynd**

I had a word with him before he *went*

In Welsh, the time referred to is indicated by the first verb in the sentence, and the simple VN is sufficient for *goes* or *went*.

Note that, if the subject is the same on both sides of the conjunction, then it need not be repeated, and the i is dropped. Compare:

°Elli di °olchi'r llestri ar ôl inni °wylio'r rhaglen 'ma

You can do the dishes after we've watched this programme

[different subjects: *you, we*]

°Elli di °olchi'r llestri ar ôl gwylio'r rhaglen 'ma

You can do the dishes after watching this programme

[i.e. *after you've watched* . . . – therefore same subj.]

In this second case, the Welsh and English versions are much closer (**ar ôl gwylio**, *after watching*).

502   Conjunctions taking neither bod nor i

The few conjunctions that take neither (**bod**) nor (**i**) are followed directly by the verb. They are **os, pe** (both meaning *if* – see §279), **hyd** (*as long as, until*) and **felly** (*so*):

Paid deud dim os daw e yn ôl nawr

Don't say anything if he comes back now

Byddwn i'n °barod i helpu pe gallet ti °ddangos ychydig mwy o °ddiddordeb

I would be willing to help if you could show a bit more interest

Arhoswch fan hyn hyd gwelwch chi'r golau gwyrdd

Wait here until you see the green light

Oedd y neuadd yn °wag, felly es i adre

The hall was empty, so I went home

Pan° *when* is followed directly by a verb, except that for the present tense NEG of **bod**, the indirect pattern **nad ydy** (°ddim) is often used:

. . . pan mae hi'n noson °dywyll

. . . when it's a dark night

but **. . . pan nad ydy'r goleuadau'n cael eu diffodd**

. . . when the lights are not put out

But otherwise:

. . . **pan o'n i'n °blentyn**	. . . when I was a child	[impf]
. . . **pan °fydd hi'n ôl**	. . . when she is [will be] back	[fut.]
. . . **pan °ddaeth Emrys adre**	. . . when Emrys came home	[pret.]

503   Time conjunctions

Time conjunctions are:

ar ôl (i)	after	**pan°**	when
cyn (i)	before	**tra (bod)**	while
erbyn (i)	by the time that	**unwaith (bod)**	once
ers (i)	since	**wedi (i)**	after
hyd	until; as long as	**wrth (i)**	while; as
nes (i)	until		

Notes:

(a)   as a conjunction, *after* is usually **ar ôl**; in this use (e.g. **wedi iddo fe °fynd** for **ar ôl iddo fe °fynd**), **wedi** is rather literary

(b)   **cyn** and **nes** are sometimes used with **(bod)** – see §509

(c)   **hyd** and **pan°** are directly followed by the verb

Examples:

Oes amser inni °gael panaid cyn i'r bws °fynd?
Have we got time for a cup of tea before the bus goes?

Erbyn iddyn nhw °gyrraedd, oedd y bwyd i gyd wedi diflannu
By the time they arrived, all the food had gone

Dw i °ddim wedi gweld y °fath °beth ers i mi °fod yn °fyfyriwr
I haven't seen such a thing since I was a student

°Gewch chi'ch dau °ddod mewn tra bod y lleill yn aros tu allan
You two can come in while the others wait outside

Unwaith bod chi wedi penderfynu, rhowch °wybod inni
Once you've decided, let us know

Wrth i John °ddod allan, es i i mewn
As John came out, I went in

504 Reason conjunctions

Reason conjunctions are:

achos (bod)	because	**am (bod)**	since; as
oherwydd (bod)	because	**gan (bod)**	since; as

Notes:

(a) **achos** and **oherwydd** are interchangeable as *because*; but **oherwydd** also has the related meaning of *because of*: **oherwydd y streic** *because of the strike* – **achos** requires a preceding **o** for this use: **o achos y streic**

(b) **am (bod)** and **gan (bod)** are to all intents and purposes interchangeable

Examples:

°Fydd 'na °ddim gwers heddiw achos °fod yr athro'n sâl

There'll be no lesson today because the teacher's ill

°Allwch chi °ddim galw yfory oherwydd na °fydd neb gartre

You can't call tomorrow because there won't be anyone home

°Dala i mo'r °ddirwy 'ma achos mai ti °barciodd y car yno

I won't pay this fine because it was you who parked the car there

Gan bo chi'n mynd allan beth bynnag, °ellwch chi °roi hwn yn y post?

Since you're going out anyway, can you put this in the post?

505 Result conjunctions

Result conjunctions are:

fel (bod)	so that	**felly**	so; therefore

Notes:

(a) **fel (bod)** is also a purpose conjunction (see §**507**)

(b) **felly** has no special construction, but is inserted in the sentence much as *so* in English.

Examples:

Fe °ruthrodd pawb mas fel na °ges i °gyfle i siarad â nhw

Everyone rushed out so (that) I didn't get a chance to speak to them

Mae Sioned yn teimlo'n °wael, felly mae Iona'n dod yn ei lle

Sioned's feeling unwell, so Iona's coming instead

Bydd yr ymgeisydd llwyddiannus yn ymdrin ag ymholiadau yn Saesneg a ʰChymraeg, felly byddai'r gallu i siarad Cymraeg yn °ddymunol

The successful applicant will be dealing with enquiries in English and Welsh, so the ability to speak Welsh would be an advantage

506   Contrast conjunctions

Contrast conjunctions are:

   er (bod) although   **tra (bod)** while (i.e. whereas)

Notes:

(a)   in the literary language **er** also has the meaning of spoken **ers** *since* (see §§**266, 503**). Note the set phrase **er cof am°** . . . *in memory of*

(b)   sometimes **er** (+ noun) is found with the related meaning of *in spite of* (more usually **er gwaetha**): **er ei holl °gyfoeth** . . . *in spite of all his wealth*

Examples:

Na i °geisio ffonio nhw er ⁿmod i'n sicr bod hi'n rhy hwyr

I'll try phoning them though I'm sure it's too late

Mae Llafur o °blaid tra bod y Rhyddfrydwyr yn erbyn

Labour is in favour while the Liberals are against

507   Purpose conjunctions

Purpose conjunctions are:

   er mwyn (i)   in order to/that   **fel (bod)** so that   **i°** to

Notes:

Notes:

(a) **er mwyn** is fundamentally a compound preposition (see §§475–476) meaning *for the sake of*: **er ei °fwyn e** *for his sake*. In practice, however, its use as a conjunction is more common

(b) **fel (bod)** is also a result conjunction (see §505)

(c) **i°** is of course the preposition (see §460). As a conjunction it is frequently used with a VN like English *to . . .* where some idea of purpose is intended

Examples:

Dere'n nes ata i er mwyn i mi °glywed yn °well

Come closer so that [in order that] I [can] hear better

Dw i'n deud hyn fel bod neb yn camddeall y sefyllfa

I'm saying this so that no-one misunderstands the situation

508 Conditional conjunctions

Conditional conjunctions are:

os, pe if   **rhag ofn** in case, lest   **onibai** unless

Notes:

(a) **os** and **pe** are discussed fully under conditional sentences (§279) Broadly speaking, **pe** is used with conditional verbs, and **os** with others

(b) **onibai** and **rhag ofn** appear with either (**i**) or (**bod**) – see §509

Examples:

Na i °ddim aros os dôn nhw yn ôl fan hyn

I'm not staying if they come back here

°Allwn ni °ddim llofnodi onibai bo chi'n llofnodi hefyd

We can't sign unless you sign too

Gwna nodyn ono fo rŵan rhag ofn i ti anghofio (N)

Make a note of it now in case you forget

509 **Conjunctions used with either (bod) or (i)**

As well as having their normal use with i (see §501), cyn *before* and nes *until* can appear with bod:

Tacluswch y stafell 'ma cyn bod eich tad yn dod yn ôl

Tidy this room up before your Dad gets back

[= . . . cyn i'ch tad °ddod yn ôl)

Arhosa i fan hyn nes bod y gweddill yn cyrraedd

I'll wait here until the others arrive

[= . . . nes i'r gweddill °gyrraedd]

Constructions of the type . . . cyn daeth e adre . . . *before he came home* are regarded as substandard for . . . cyn iddo °ddod adre.

Er *although* occasionally appears with (i) instead of (bod), usually where a past sense is involved:

Nes i °wrthod er iddo °geisio argyhoeddi fi

I refused even though he tried to convince me

[= . . . er °fod e wedi ceisio . . .]

Rhag ofn *in case* sometimes appears with (bod), but the (i) construction is more common and does not require inflected tenses of the verb, which are in any case implied in the other part of the sentence.

Na i °ddangos y map i ti rhag ofn i ti °fynd ar °goll

Na i °ddangos y map i ti rhag ofn °fod ti'n mynd ar °goll

I'll show you the map in case you get lost   [non-past]

Bydden ni'n poeni rhag ofn i ti °fynd ar °goll

Bydden ni'n poeni rhag ofn (y) byddet ti'n mynd ar °goll

We'd be worried in case you got lost   [unreality]

510–513 CO-ORDINATING CONJUNCTIONS

510 **A[h]**

A[h] *and* becomes ac before vowels, and also before mae, fel *so, as*, felly *so, therefore* and wedyn *then*. Ac is often heard as ag in many areas. In the standard language, however, the spelling convention a/ac *and* is retained to distinguish from **â/ag** *with*. There is similarly no pronunciation difference in normal speech between **a**[h] and **â**[h].

In the literary language **a** is followed by AM: **bara a** [h]**chaws** *bread and cheese*, **halen a** [h]**phupur** *salt and pepper*, **mam a** [h]**thad** *mother and father*. This usage is often disregarded in the spoken language, particularly for [h]**th-**, except in set or common expressions as above (see §9).

Sometimes **a**[h] is used with a following noun or pronoun with a contrastive or resultative sense:

Naethon nhw °ofyn inni °ganu a ninnau heb °fwyta dim ers brecwast

They asked us to sing even though we hadn't eaten anything since breakfast [lit. 'and us without eating . . .' – a neat colloquial way of saying . . ., **er nad o'n ni wedi bwyta . . .**]

Note the idiom **cael a** [h]**chael** *touch and go*:

°Ddaethon ni adre yn y diwedd, ond [h]**cael a** [h]**chael oedd hi**

We got home eventually, but it was touch and go.

511 Ond

Ond *but* is used as in English, but note **dim ond** for *only*, frequently heard as **'mond**: **'Mond fi sy 'ma** *It's only me here*. An alternative expression is **yn unig** *only*, but the two are positioned differently:

'Mond tair punt sy ar ôl 'da fi (S)

Tair punt yn unig sy ar ôl 'da fi (S)

I've only got three pounds left

512 Neu°

Neu° *or* is used as in English

Gyda siswrn neu °gyllell?

With scissors or a knife?

Ti neu fi sy'n gyrru?

Is it you or me who's driving?

Where **neu** is followed by an imperative (command form – see §377) rather than simply a noun, VN or adjective, the SM is cancelled. Compare:

°Ellwch chi aros fan hyn neu °*ddod* 'da ni (VN after **neu°**)

You can stay here or come with us

but:

Arhoswch fan hyn neu *dewch* 'da ni (imperative)

Stay here or come with us

In cases involving a choice between two options, an alternative for *or* – **ta** or **'ta** – is sometimes heard:

Heddiw ta fory dach chi am °fynd?

Do you want to go today or tomorrow?

P'un leiciech chi, te 'ta coffi?

Which would you like, tea or coffee?

Either . . . or . . . is **naill ai . . . neu°**, while *neither . . . nor . . .* is **dim/na . . . na . . .** (see §513).

Examples:

Dan ni ar °frys – cymer naill ai'r un neu'r llall, nei di?

We're in a hurry – take (either) one or the other, will you?

Naill ai mae'n ymguddio, neu mae wedi dianc

Either s/he's hiding, or s/he's escaped

513 Na[h]

Na[h] *nor* is followed by AM in the literary language, a usage often disregarded in speech, as also with a[h] *and*. **Nac** (usually pronounced **nag**) is used before vowels.

Does dim llaeth na caws yn yr oergell 'ma

There's neither milk nor cheese in this fridge

At the end of a sentence, *neither* or *not/nor . . . either* is **chwaith**, with a preceding NEG verb (sometimes with **°ddim** omitted) or other NEG element (**dim** or **na(c)**):

Dw i °ddim yn mynd i'r sinema'n aml dyddiau 'ma. – Na fi chwaith

I don't go to the cinema much these days. – Me neither.

Dw i heb °lofnodi'r °ddeiseb 'na hyd yn hyn. – Na ninnau chwaith.

I haven't signed that petition yet. – Neither have we.

°Fuon ni erioed yn Louisiana, nac yn Arkansas chwaith

We've never been to Louisiana, nor to Arkansas either.

FUNCTIONS AND SITUATIONS

Functions and situations

I   General greetings

The all-purpose general greeting for any time of the day is **S'mae** (N) or **Shw mae** (S), corresponding to *Hi!* or *Hello!*, or *How are things?* The same expression can be used in reply, or alternatively **Iawn, Go lew, Yn °o lew, Dim yn °ddrwg** or **Gweddol** are possible responses, and these may also be used in response to the phrase **Sut wyt ti?, Sut dych chi?** (and variants) – *How are you?*

Slightly more formally, the greetings associated with times of the day and night are:

Bore da

Good morning

P(ry)n(h)awn da

Good afternoon

Noswaith °dda

Good evening

But note that, as in English, the phrase **Nos da** *Good night* cannot be used as a greeting, but only when taking one's leave.

II   Leavetaking

The basic term for *Goodbye!* is **Hwyl!**, which occurs on its own or in the extended variants **Hwyl nawr!** and **Hwyl °fawr!** – there is little to choose between any of these, and all are heard with great frequency in all situations.

Very common also these days are forms derived from **gweld** *see*:

°Wela i di!, °Wela i chi!

(I'll) see you!

°Welwn ni di!, °Welwn ni chi!

(We'll) see you!

Expressions involving **tan°** *till* (§467) are also standard:

Tan yfory!

Till tomorrow!

Tan wythnos nesa!

Till next week!

Tan °Ddydd Sadwrn, 'te!

Till Saturday, then!

Tan y tro nesa!

Till next time!

The phrase **Da boch (chi)** also corresponds to *Goodbye*, but is more formal and consequently of somewhat less frequent occurrence in everyday speech. The **ti**-variant is **Da bo (ti)**, which is perhaps more current.

At night, **Nos da!** is the standard phrase (note no mutation of **da** even though **Nos** is feminine – see §102), with an extended variant **Nos dawch!** quite common with N speakers.

III Attracting attention

The usual way of politely attracting someone's attention is to use:

Esgusodwch fi

Excuse me

used broadly as in English, and in comparable circumstances.

Esgusodwch fi, ydy'r sedd 'ma'n rhydd?

Excuse me, is this seat free?

Esgusodwch fi, °ga i °ddod drwodd?

Excuse me, can I come through?

Other possibilities are:

°Ga i eiliad?

Can I have a second/moment?

Dal eiliad!

Daliwch eiliad!

Hold on a second/moment!

IV Seasonal greetings

These are straightforward in use:

Nadolig Llawen

Merry Christmas

Blwyddyn Newydd °Dda

Happy New Year

Nadolig Llawen a Blwyddyn Newydd °Dda!

Merry Christmas and a Happy New Year!

Cyfarchion y Tymor

Season's Greetings

Pasg Hapus

Happy Easter

In all these cases, the reply can be:

A tithau!

A chithau!

And (the same to) you!

V Personal greetings and congratulations

To wish someone a Happy Birthday, use:

Penblwydd hapus!

Other occasions for congratulation use the basic terms **llongyfarchiadau** *congratulations* (**ar°** *on* + noun or VN) and **llongyfarch** *congratulate*:

Llongyfarchiadau!

Congratulations!

Llongyfarchiadau ar eich swydd newydd!

Congratulations on your new job!

Llongyfarchiadau ar °gael dy °benodi / . . . ar °gael eich penodi

Congratulations on your appointment

Llongyfarchiadau ar °basio dy °brawf gyrru

Llongyfarchiadau ar °basio'ch prawf gyrru

Congratulations on passing your driving test

**Llongyfarchiadau ar °enedigaeth eich mab bach newydd/eich
merch °fach newydd**

Congratulations on the birth of your new little son/daughter

Llongyfarchiadau ar dy °ganlyniadau ardderchog

Llongyfarchiadau ar eich canlyniadau ardderchog

Congratulations on your excellent results

Gad i mi dy °longyfarch di

Gadewch i mi'ch llongyfarch chi

Allow me to congratulate you

Less formally, *Well done!* is usually expressed as follows:

Da iawn ti!

Da iawn chi!

Dw i wedi gorffen ⁿngwaith cartre.	**– Da iawn ti!**
I've finished my homework.	– Well done!

VI Good wishes

General phrases for wishing someone good luck are:

Pob lwc!

Pob llwyddiant!

Good luck!

In the second of these, **llwyddiant** means *success*, so this option is particularly appropriate where some element of achievement is involved. When the

circumstances are specified in the wishes, however, **pob lwc** is perhaps more common:

Pob lwc gyda'r arholiadau

Good luck with the exams

Pob lwc yn eich cartre newydd

Good luck in your new home

Wishes for a return to health:

Gwella'n °fuan!

Get well soon! (also used on cards)

Gobeithio y byddwch chi'n teimlo'n °well cyn hir

Gobeithio y byddwch chi'n teimlo'n °well yn °fuan iawn

I hope you'll be feeling better (very) soon

Miscellaneous other good wishes include:

    Mwynhewch!

or **Mwynheuwch!**

    Enjoy yourself/yourselves

Mwynhewch/Mwynheuwch y gwyliau

Enjoy the holidays

Bendith!

Bless you! [when someone sneezes]

Iechyd da!

Cheers! [when drinking]

Cysga'n °dawel

Cysgwch yn °dawel

Sleep well/tight

Dal ati!

Daliwch ati!

Keep at it!/Keep it up!

To 'wish' someone something is **dymuno**:

Gad i mi °ddymuno pob llwyddiant i ti

Gadewch i mi °ddymuno pob llwyddiant i chi

Let me wish you every success

In more formal and written style, this verb is found with endings:

Dymuna'r corff llywodraethol Nadolig Llawen i °bawb

The governing body wishes everyone a Merry Christmas

Dymunwn Nadolig Llawen i chi

We wish you a Merry Christmas

In normal speech, however, these would be **Mae'r corff llywodraethol yn dymuno . . .** and **Dyn ni'n dymuno . . .**, using the VN in the present tense as usual (see §210).

VII Introductions

More formal introductions are done using **cyflwyno** *introduce*:

°Ga i °gyflwyno . . .?

May I introduce . . .?

Mr Williams, °ga i °gyflwyno Iwan Edwards, cadeirydd y cwmni?

Mr Williams, may I introduce Iwan Edwards, the chairman of the company?

Less formally, a third party can introduce someone to someone else by asking:

Wyt ti wedi cwrdd â^h . . .?

Dych chi wedi cwrdd â^h . . .?

Have you met . . .?

or **Wyt ti'n nabod . . .?**

Dych chi'n nabod . . .?

Do you know . . .?

Marc, wyt ti wedi cwrdd â ^{n}ngwraig?

Marc, have you met my wife?

Dych chi'n nabod 'n chwaer Josephine?

Do you know my sister Josephine?

or by simply saying:

Dyma° . . .

This is . . .

Dyma Elwyn Jones, sy'n byw drws nesa

This is Elwyn Jones, who lives next door

Once you've been introduced to someone, you can say:

Neis cwrdd â chi

Nice to meet you

or, more formally:

Mae'n °dda gen i °gwrdd â chi

I'm pleased to meet you

VIII   Eating and drinking

Hunger and thirst are expressed in the normal way for temporary states, using the preposition **ar°** (see §398) – in other words, *I am thirsty*, for example, is phrased as *There is thirst on me*.

Mae eisiau bwyd arna i

I'm hungry

Mae syched arna i

I'm thirsty

Oes eisiau bwyd arnat ti?

Oes eisiau bwyd arnoch chi?

Are you hungry?

Oes syched arnat ti?

Oes syched arnoch chi?

Are you thirsty?

If you are really famished, you can say:

Dw i'n llwgu!

or **Dw i bron â llwgu!**

I'm (almost) starving!

Making suggestions to have food or drink is straightforward:

Beth am °gael rhywbeth i °fwyta?

How about having something to eat?

Beth am °gael rhywbeth i yfed?

How about having something to drink?

Beth am °ddiod?

How about a drink?

Beth am °bryd o °fwyd?

How about a meal?

Similarly, if one is contemplating going out for food or drink:

Beth am °fynd allan i °gael rhywbeth i °fwyta?

How about going out for something to eat?

Beth am °fynd allan i °gael pryd o °fwyd?

How about going out to have a meal?

Beth am °fynd allan am °ddiod?

How about going out for a drink?

In all the above examples, **Awn ni** *Let's go* (§307) can be substituted for **Beth am °fynd** – so, for example:

Awn ni allan am °bryd o °fwyd

Let's go out for a meal

Similarly,

Awn ni i'r °dafarn

Let's go to the pub

Awn ni i °dŷ bwyta rhywle

Let's go to a restaurant somewhere

IX   Giving and receiving compliments

For giving compliments on something achieved, the all-purpose phrase is

Da iawn!

or   **Da iawn ti/chi!**

Well done!

Other useful constructions are of the following patterns:

Mi oedd hi'n °berfformiad gwych/ardderchog!

It was a great/excellent performance!

Mae hwnna'n edrych yn °dda arnat ti/arnoch chi

That looks good on you

Ti 'n chwarae'n °dda

Dych chi'n chwarae'n °dda

You play well

Ti wedi gwneud yn °dda iawn

Dych chi wedi gwneud yn °dda iawn

You've done very well

Nest ti hynny'n °dda iawn

Naethoch chi hynny'n °dda iawn

You did that very well

Roedd y canlyniadau'n ardderchog

The results were excellent

Mi °ddylet ti °fod yn °falch

Mi °ddylech chi °fod yn °falch

You should be proud/pleased

Complimentary comments on things made or produced can be done simply
with Am° . . .!

Am °bryd o °fwyd gwych!

What a great meal!

Am °fyns ardderchog!

What excellent buns!

On receiving a compliment, you can say:

Diolch!

Thanks!

Ti 'n °garedig iawn

Dych chi'n °garedig iawn

You're very kind

Ti 'n rhy °garedig (o °lawer)

Ti'n (llawer) rhy °garedig

Dych chi'n rhy °garedig (o °lawer)

Dych chi'n (llawer) rhy °garedig

You're (far) too kind

X Commiserations

To say that you're really sorry, use:

Mae'n °wir °ddrwg gen i . . . (/ . . . °ddrwg 'da fi . . .)

Mae'n °wir °ddrwg gen i °glywed am eich nain

I'm really sorry to hear about your grandmother

Similarly,

Roedd yn °ddrwg gen i °glywed eich newyddion

I was sorry to hear your news

In a similar vein, the following are also fairly formal expressions of sympathy:

Dw i'n cydymdeimlo

I sympathize

O'n i'n °drist iawn o °glywed eich newyddion

I was very sad to hear your news

Gadewch i mi °fynegi ⁿnghydymdeimlad

Allow me to express my sympathy/condolences

°Druan ohonot ti

°Druan ohonoch chi

Poor you

The latter expresses commiseration, but is perhaps better suited to less serious circumstances.

Dw i wedi colli Tedi.	– **°Druan ohonot ti**
I've lost Teddy.	– Poor you

To say that something is a pity, use any of the following:

'Na °drueni (predominantly S)

'Na °biti

What a pity

Piti garw! (N)

What a terrible pity!

Finally, if someone has suffered a disappointment, you can say either 'Na °drueni as above, or:

'Na siom!

What a disappointment!

'Na siomedig (i ti / i chi)!

How disappointing (for you)!

XI Giving and receiving thanks

There are many variations of and extensions to the basic term

Diolch

Thank you/Thanks

In roughly ascending degree of gratitude these are:

Diolch yn °fawr

Thanks a lot

Diolch yn °fawr iawn

Thanks very much

Llawer o °ddiolch

Many thanks

Dw i'n °ddiolchgar iawn

I'm very grateful

Diolch o °galon

Thank you from (the bottom of my) heart

To specify what the thanks are for, use am° *for*, either with a noun or a VN.

Diolch am y . . .

Thank you for the . . .

Diolch am dy °gymorth

Diolch am eich cymorth

Thanks for your help

Diolch am °bopeth

Thanks for everything

417

Diolch am yr anrheg

Thank you for the present

Diolch am y noson °fendigedig

Thank you for the marvellous evening

Diolch am °ddod 'da ni

Thanks for coming with us

Diolch am °barcio'r car i mi

Thanks for parking the car for me

The verb *to thank* is **diolch**, and note that it is normally used with **i°** to link to a following person:

Fe °ddiolchon nhw inni am °gyfrannu

They thanked us for contributing

Mae'n °bleser i mi °gael diolch i chi am° . . .

I'm delighted to be able to thank you for . . .

Mae'n °bleser i mi °gael diolch i Mr Williams am °dderbyn ein gwahoddiad i siarad heno

It's my pleasure to be able to thank Mr Williams for accepting our invitation to speak tonight

One final expression with **Diolch** is

Diolch byth!

Thank God!

Thank goodness!

Expressions of thanks not involving **Diolch** include:

Doedd dim angen, °wir i ti/chi

You needn't have, really!

Ti'n °garedig iawn

Dych chi'n °garedig iawn

You're very kind

'Na °garedig!

How kind!

In response to someone thanking you, you can simply say:

Dim o °gwbwl!

Not at all

Note that *thankfully* is sometimes used in English in the sense of *fortunately* – where this is the case, **ffodus** is the usual translation:

Yn ffodus iawn, °ddigwyddodd dim byd

Thankfully, nothing happened

XII Apologies

The basic phrase for apologizing is

Mae'n °ddrwg gen i

Mae'n °ddrwg 'da fi (S)

Mae'n °flin 'da fi (parts of the S)

I'm sorry

Its range corresponds closely to that of the English expression, and it can be used not only for apologizing but also for sympathy or condolence (see also section **X**)

Mae'n °ddrwg gen i am yr oedi

I'm sorry for the delay

Mae'n °ddrwg gen i am °beidio ysgrifennu

I'm sorry for not writing/I'm sorry I didn't write

Mae'n °ddrwg gen i ⁿmod i'n hwyr

I'm sorry I'm late

Mae'n °flin 'da fi bod hyn wedi digwydd unwaith eto

I'm sorry that this has happened again

Mae'n °ddrwg gen i °fod pethau wedi mynd yn chwith

I'm sorry that things have gone wrong

Mae'n °ddrwg gen i, o'n i °ddim yn gwybod

I'm sorry, I didn't know

If you are really sorry, this can be done by inserting °wir:

Mae'n °wir °ddrwg gen i am yr holl °drafferth

I'm really sorry about all the bother

Mae'n °wir °ddrwg 'da fi am anghofio dy °benblwydd

I'm really sorry for forgetting your birthday

As in English, *excuse* can be used as an alternative way of apologizing:

Esgusodwch fi am °fod yn hwyr

Excuse me for being late

Esgusodwch ni am °beidio ffonio'n ôl yn °gynharach

Excuse us for not phoning back earlier

The verb *apologize* is **ymddiheuro** – this word is sometimes associated with more formal styles:

Ymddiheurwn am yr oedi

(= **Dan ni'n ymddiheuro am yr oedi**)

We apologize for the delay

but is the norm even in less formal styles where the phrasing requires a VN:

Roedd rhaid iddi ymddiheuro am y camgymeriad

She had to apologize for the mistake

°Ga i ymddiheuro am ddoe?

May I apologize for yesterday?

Gad i mi ymddiheuro (i ti)

Gadewch i mi ymddiheuro (i chi)

Allow me to apologize (to you)

Gadewch i mi ymddiheuro am yr hyn °ddigwyddodd ddoe

Allow me to apologize for what happened yesterday

More heinous offences may require:

Maddau i mi!

Maddeuwch i mi!

Forgive me!

Maddeuwch i mi am °ddweud y °fath °bethau – mae'n °wir °ddrwg gen i.

Forgive me for saying such things – I'm really sorry

Various possibilities are available for responding graciously to apologies:

Paid poeni

Peidiwch poeni

Don't worry (about it)

Dim problem

No problem

Dim problem o °gwbwl

No problem at all

Gad inni anghofio'r cyfan

Gadewch inni anghofio'r cyfan

Let's forget the whole thing

Nawn ni °ddim sôn mwyach amdani

We won't say anything more about it

Wedi'i anghofio ('n °barod)

(Already) forgotten

Asking for and giving help

Asking for help usually involves either **gallu, medru** (N) or **cael** (§§326ff):

°Alli di/°Elli di helpu fi gyda'r . . .?

°Allwch chi/°Ellwch chi helpu fi gyda'r . . .?

°Fedri di helpu fi gyda'r . . .? (N)

°Fedrwch chi helpu fi gyda'r . . .? (N)

Can you help me with the . . .?

°Allet ti helpu fi?

°Allech chi helpu fi?

°Fedret ti helpu fi? (N)

°Fedrech chi helpu fi? (N)

Could you help me?

°Allet ti helpu fi i °drwsio'r to?

°Allech chi helpu fi i °drwsio'r to?

°Fedret ti helpu fi i °drwsio'r to? (N)

°Fedrech chi helpu fi i °drwsio'r to? (N)

Could you help me mend the roof?

°Ga i °ofyn i chi am help/am °gymorth?

Can I ask you for help?

°Ga i °ofyn i chi am °roi cymorth?

Can I ask you to give (me some) help?

°Fyddech chi mor °garedig âʰ . . .?

Would you be so kind as to . . .?

Dw i angen eich help i °olchi'r car

I need your help to wash the car

Positive responses to requests for help include:

Iawn

OK

Wrth °gwrs

Of course

Yn °bendant

Definitely

Dim problem

No problem

Gad i mi helpu fan hyn/fan'na

Gadewch i mi helpu fan hyn/fan'na

Let me help here/there

If you are unable to help:

°Alla i °ddim

°Fedra i °ddim (N)

I can't

Yn anffodus, °alla i mo'ch helpu chi

Yn anffodus, °fedra i mo'ch helpu chi

Unfortunately I can't help you

Dim ar y °foment

Not at the moment

Dim ar hyn o °bryd

Not just now

Dyw hwnna/hynna °ddim yn °bosib, mae arna i ofn

That's not possible, I'm afraid

Mae'n anghyfleus

It's not convenient

Dw i ar °frys

I'm pushed for time

°Allet ti °ofyn i °rywun arall?

°Allech chi °ofyn i °rywun arall?

°Fedret ti °ofyn i °rywun arall? (N)

°Fedrech chi °ofyn i °rywun arall? (N)

Could you ask someone else?

XIV   Asking and giving advice

There are various ways of asking for advice, depending on the particular
situation:

Beth °fyddet/°faset ti'n °wneud?

Beth °fyddech/°fasech chi'n °wneud?

What would you do?

Beth ydy (/yw) 'r ffordd °orau o °ddelio â hyn, dych chi'n meddwl?

What's the best way of dealing with this, do you think?

Beth dych chi'n °gymeradwyo?

What do you recommend?

Beth ydy (/yw) 'ch cyngor?

What's your advice?

°Ga i °ofyn i chi am °gyngor?

May I ask you for some advice?

Similarly, there are a number of ways of offering advice:

°Ga i °gynnig rhai geiriau o °gyngor i chi?

Can I offer you some words of advice?

Mae gen i °air o °gyngor i chi

I have a word of advice for you

Taswn i yn dy °le di, swn i'n . . .

Taswn i yn eich lle chi, swn i'n . . .

Pe byddwn i yn dy °le di, byddwn i'n . . .

Pe byddwn i yn eich lle chi, byddwn i'n . . .

If I were in your place/position, I'd . . .

To accept advice, or show that you are at least considering it, the following may be of use:

Efallai °fod hynny'n °bosib

Hwrach °fod hynny'n °bosib (N)

That may be possible

Efallai bod chi'n iawn

Hwrach bod chi'n iawn (N)

You may be right

Diolch am °dynnu 'n sylw at hynny

Thanks for drawing my attention to that

O'n i °ddim wedi ystyried yr agwedd 'na

I hadn't considered that aspect

Dych chi wedi bod o °gymorth i mi

You've been a help to me

XV **Asking for something to be done**

By far the most common way to ask someone else to do something for you is by using **Nei di° . . .?/Newch chi° . . .?** (§382) *Will you . . .?*, followed by the VN of the action you want performed:

Nei di °gasglu'r plant o'r ysgol?

Will you collect the children from school?

Newch chi °ddiffodd y teledu?

Will you switch off the television?

Newch chi aros tu allan, os gwelwch yn °dda?

Will you wait outside, please?

Nei di °fwydo'r °gath?

Will you feed the cat?

There are various more oblique alternatives (*Could you . . .?*) that work in the same way:

°Allet ti° . . .?

°Allech chi° . . .?

°Fedret ti° . . .? (N)

°Fedrech chi° . . .? (N)

Could you . . .?

°Fyddai/°Fasai modd i ti°/chi° . . .?

°Fyddai/°Fasai'n °bosib i ti°/chi° . . .?

Would it be possible for you to . . .?

°Allech chi °gael gair ag e?

°Fedrech chi °gael gair efo fo? (N)

Could you have a word with him?

°Fasai modd i chi °gau'r ffenest?

Would it be possible for you to close the window?

°Fyddai'n °bosib i ti °dalu drosta i?

°Fasai'n °bosib i ti °dalu drosta i?

Would it be possible for you to pay for me?

Tybed (S) and Sgwn i (N), both meaning *I wonder*, can be used in conjunction with the above to make the request even more oblique:

Tybed °fyddai'n °bosib i ti helpu fi?

I wonder if it would be possible for you to help me?

Sgwn i °fasai modd i chi °lofnodi'r °ddeiseb 'ma?

I wonder if you could/would sign this petition?

More direct requests can be phrased as in the following examples:

°Alla i °ofyn i chi am °ddychwelyd y llyfrau'n syth?

Can I ask you to return the books straight away?

Gwnewch yn siwr bod chi'n archebu'r tocynnau, newch chi?

Make sure you order the tickets, will you?

Mae'n °bwysig (iawn) °fod ti'n rhoi gwybod i mi

It's (very) important that you let me know

Mae'n hanfodol bod chi'n cael trwsio'r car erbyn diwedd yr wythnos

It's vital that you have the car repaired by the end of the week

XVI   Expressing needs, wishes and desires

Need and *want* are expressed in Welsh by the pseudoverbs **angen** and **eisiau**, used for the most part as if they were verbs although they are grammatically nouns – see §396 for fuller discussion.

Dw i angen . . .

I need . . .

Dw i angen rhagor o amser

I need more time

Wyt ti angen . . .?

Dych chi angen . . .?

Do you need . . .?

Dw i °ddim angen y llyfr 'ma bellach

I don't need this book any more

Dan ni °ddim angen pobl fel 'na ar ein wiki!

We don't need people like that on our wiki!

With **angen** an alternative construction, treating it as a true noun and with **ar°** before the person, is also possible:

Mae angen . . . arna i

I need . . .

Oes angen . . . arnat ti?

Oes angen . . . arnoch chi?

Do you need . . .?

Does dim angen . . . arna i

I don't need . . .

To say that you want something, **eisiau** is the standard word, and is nearly always treated as a verb (but, as with **angen**, without the linking **yn** that a true VN would require):

Dw i eisiau . . .

I want . . .

Dw i eisiau gweld y canlyniadau ar unwaith

I want to see the results at once

Dych chi eisiau help?

Do you want help?

Wyt ti eisiau dod 'da ni?

Do you want to come with us?

Dw i °ddim eisiau aros fan hyn

I don't want to stay here

In some S areas, the VN **moyn** (or **mofyn**) is used instead, so:

Wi'n moyn gwylio'r teledu (S)

I want to watch TV

Ych chi'n moyn rhagor? (S)

Do you want any more?

Beth ych chi'n mofyn? (S)

What do you want?

Note also that, when *want* is followed by a verb, there is an alternative construction available in Welsh using **am°** + VN (see §448 (e)):

Dw i am °weld y canlyniadau ar unwaith

I want to see the results at once

Wi am °wylio'r teledu (S)

I want to watch TV

But a less direct and more common way to say that you want something is
to say *would like* (see §341):

Hoffwn i° . . .

I would like . . .

Leiciwn i° . . . (or Leicsiwn i° . . .)

I would like . . .

There is no difference in meaning or usage at all between these two verbs.
Hoffi is officially promoted, but the older **leicio** is by far the more common
among native speakers everywhere.

Hoffwn i °docyn i'r gêm °fawr yfory

I'd like a ticket to the big game tomorrow

**Mi leiciwn i °wybod sut yn union mae hyn yn mynd i °weithio'n
ymarferol**

I would like to know quite how this is going to work in practice

Hoffwn i °fynd i'r Eidal eleni

I'd like to go to Italy this year

Asking someone else if they would like something, or like to do something,
involves the same verbs:

Hoffech chi °banaid o °goffi?

Would you like a cup of coffee?

Hoffet ti °ddod i'r cyngerdd heno?

Would you like to come to the concert tonight?

Leiciech chi °gael cipolwg?

Would you like to have a look?

XVII   Expressing objections and complaints

If you want to put somebody right about something, you can start with

Esgusodwch fi, . . .

Excuse me, . . .

and then continue with one of the following:

> **. . . ond dw i'n meddwl °fod rhywbeth o'i °le fan hyn**
> . . . but I think something's wrong here

> **. . . ond mi °ddylech chi ailedrych ar hyn, dw i'n meddwl**
> . . . but I think you should have another look at this

> **. . . ond mae camgymeriad fan hyn, dw i'n meddwl**
> . . . but there's a mistake here, I think

> **. . . ond mae'n ymddangos bod chi wedi gwneud camgymeriad**
> . . . but it looks like you've made a mistake

If you want to be a little more forthright, use:

> **Dw i °ddim yn meddwl °fod hynny'n iawn**
> I don't think that's right

> **°Alla i °ddim derbyn hynny**
> **°Fedra i °ddim derbyn hynny** (N)
> I can't accept that

And if you want to express your feelings very strongly, then:

> **Dw i °ddim yn °barod i °dderbyn hynny**
> I'm not prepared to accept that

> **Mae hynny'n (°gwbwl) annerbyniol**
> That's (completely) unacceptable

The best way to make a complaint without inviting confrontation is to simply say:

> **Dyw/Dydy hynny °ddim yn iawn**
> That's not right/That's not on

or, with the offence specified:

> **Dyw/Dydy hi °ddim yn iawn bod chi'n troi lan yn °ddirybudd**
> It's not on for you to just turn up unannounced

For making official, or at least formal, complaints, you can use either **cwyn** *complaint* or the derived verb **cwyno** *complain*:

> **Mae gen i °gwyn** (N)
> **Mae cwyn 'da fi** (S)
> I've got a complaint

Mae gen i °gwyn am y gwasanaeth fan'ma yn °ddiweddar (N)

Mae cwyn 'da fi am y gwasanaeth fan hyn yn °ddiweddar (S)

I've got a complaint about the service here lately

Dw i eisiau cwyno am° . . .

I want to complain about . . .

Hoffwn i °gwyno am °gyflwr y stafell molchi

I would like to complain about the state of the bathroom

In the case of an absolutely intolerable slight or affront, you can say:

Mae'n °warthus!

It's disgraceful!

or **Mae hyn yn °warth!**

This is a disgrace!

or even:

Mae'n annioddefol!

It's insufferable!

And if you want to take matters to the top, say:

Ewch i nôl y rheolwr

Go and get the manager

or **Dwedwch wrth y rheolwr ⁿmod i eisiau cael gair ag e'n syth**

Tell the manager that I want a word with him right now

XVIII Giving and seeking promises and assurances

Making a promise involves the VN **addo** *promise* (with i°), or the noun
addewid *a promise*:

Dw i'n addo i ti/chi

I promise you

Mae hynny'n addewid

That's a promise

Wyt ti'n addo?/ Dych chi'n addo?

Do you promise?

Wyt ti'n addo y byddi di yno?

Dych chi'n addo y byddwch chi yno?

Do you promise that you'll be there?

Dych chi'n addo rhoi'r gwahoddiadau yn y post?

Do you promise to post the invitations?

Common phrases of assurance are:

Iawn

OK

| **Byddwch yma erbyn saith, iawn?** | **– Iawn** |
| Be here by seven, OK? | – OK |

Wrth °gwrs

Of course

| **°Fydd y car yn °barod yfory?** | **– Wrth °gwrs** |
| Will the car be ready tomorrow? | – Of course |

Popeth yn iawn

Everything's OK (i.e. Don't worry)

| **Rhaid inni °beidio colli'r bws.** | **– Popeth yn iawn** |
| We mustn't miss the bus. | – OK |

Don't worry can be expressed in a number of ways, with both **poeni** and **pryderu** meaning *worry*:

Paid poeni

Peidiwch poeni

Paid pryderu

Peidiwch pryderu

Don't worry

An enhanced level of reassurance can be conveyed by these extended versions incorporating the pronouns:

Paid ti â poeni

Paid ti â ʰphoeni

Peidiwch chi â poeni

Peidiwch chi â ʰphoeni

Don't you worry

General requests for reassurance such as

Dych chi'n siwr y bydd popeth yn iawn?

Are you sure everything will be OK?

and

Does dim eisiau poeni, nag oes?

Does dim eisiau pryderu, nag oes?

There's no need to worry, is there?

can be answered by such expressions as the following:

Bydd popeth yn iawn

Everything will be OK

°Fydd 'na °ddim problem

There'll be no problem

Mae popeth dan °reolaeth

Everything's under control

Mi °fyddwn ni'n ymdopi, siwr iawn i chi

We'll manage, you can be sure

Bydd popeth yn iawn, siwr o °fod

Everything's sure to be OK

Finally, in more formal style, sicrhau *assure* can be used in various ways:

Mi °alla i'ch sicrhau °fod popeth yn mynd yn °ddidrafferth

Mi °fedra i'ch sicrhau °fod popeth yn mynd yn °ddidrafferth

I can assure you that everything is going fine

Gadewch i mi'ch sicrhau °fod 'na °ddim achos i °boeni

Let me assure you that there's no cause to worry

XIX Issuing, accepting and declining invitations and offers

Informal invitations can be made in the following ways:

Beth am inni° . . .?

How about if we . . .?

Beth am inni ymweld â nhw wythnos nesa?

How about if we visited them next week?

Beth am° . . .?

How about . . .?

Beth am °fynd allan heno?

How about going out tonight?

Hoffet ti° . . .? / Hoffech chi° . . .?

Would you like to . . .?

Leiciet ti° . . .? / Leiciech chi° . . .?

Would you like to . . .?

Hoffech chi °ddod efo ni?

Would you like to come with us?

To accept invitations of this type, use:

Iawn

OK

O'r gorau

Alright

'Na syniad

That's an idea

Syniad da/gwych

Good/great idea

Pam °lai?

Why not?

To decline invitations and suggestions:

Dim diolch

No thanks

Dw i °ddim yn teimlo fel (mynd allan heno)

I don't feel like (going out tonight)

Dw i °ddim eisiau (gwylio'r teledu) ar hyn o °bryd

I don't want to (watch TV) at the moment

433

°Well gen i° . . . (N)

°Well 'da fi° . . . (S)

I'd rather . . .

°Well gen i aros gartre

I'd rather stay at home

and the refusal can be softened with:

. . ., ond diolch am y cynnig

. . ., but thanks for the offer

. . ., ond efallai y tro nesa

. . ., but maybe next time

. . ., ond efallai °rywdro arall

. . ., but maybe another time

When discussing offers to do with transactions, the following types of phrases can be of use:

Beth °allwch chi °gynnig i mi?

Be' °fedrwch chi °gynnig i mi? (N)

What can you offer me?

Beth ydy/yw 'ch cynnig gorau?

What's your best offer?

Ai dyna'ch cynnig gorau?

Is that your best offer?

Mae hynny'n °gwbwl annerbyniol

That's completely out of the question

°Alla i °ddim derbyn hwnna o °gwbwl

°Fedra i °ddim derbyn hwnna o °gwbwl (N)

I can't accept that at all

Mae hynny'n swnio'n rhesymol/°wych

That sounds reasonable/great

Byddai/Basai hynny'n °dderbyniol, swn i'n meddwl

That would be acceptable, I should think

°**Allwn ni °gytuno ar hynny, 'te?**

°**Fedrwn ni °gytuno ar hynny, 'ta?** (N)

Can we agree on that, then?

XX   Seeking, granting and denying permission

The primary verb for asking and giving permission is **cael** in its specialized modal sense (§340), though other constructions using **modd** *way* and **posib** *possible* are also common.

°**Ga i° . . .?**

Can/May I . . .?

°**Gawn ni° . . .?**

Can/May we . . .?

°**Ga i °fynd nawr?**	– **Cei/Cewch**	– **Na ʰchei/Na ʰchewch**
Can I go now?	– Yes	– No

Oes modd i mi° . . .?

Can I . . .?

Oes modd inni° . . .?

Can we . . .?

Oes modd i mi aros fan hyn?	– **Oes/Nag oes**
Can I stay here?	– Yes/No

Ydy hi'n iawn i mi° . . .?

Is it OK for me to . . .?

Ydy hi'n iawn i mi °barcio fan hyn?	– **Ydy/Nag ydy**
Is it OK for me to park here?	– Yes/No

°**Fyddai/°Fasai'n °bosib i mi° . . .?**

Would it be possible for me to . . .?

°**Fasai'n °bosib i mi °dalu â ʰcherdyn credyd?**	– **Basai**
Would it be possible for me to pay by credit card?	– Yes

These four methods of asking permission are really interchangeable, and so the last example could equally well be phrased as:

°Ga i °dalu â ʰcherdyn credyd?

or   **Oes modd i mi °dalu â ʰcherdyn credyd?**

or   **Ydy hi'n iawn i mi °dalu â ʰcherdyn credyd?**

though the yes/no answers would, of course be different (**Cewch/Na ʰchewch; Oes/Nag oes; Ydy/Nag ydy**).

To grant permission, use either the *yes* responses detailed above in accordance with how the request for permission was phrased, or any of the expressions below:

Iawn

OK

Iawn, 'te

OK, then

O'r gorau

Alright

Mae hynny'n iawn gen i (N)

Mae hynny'n iawn 'da fi i (S)

That's alright with me

Digon teg

Fair enough

Ewch amdani!

Go for it!

Gwnewch fel y mynnoch (chi)

Do as you please

Gwna fel y mynnot ti/mynni di

Do as you please

Does gen i °ddim byd yn erbyn (y syniad) (N)

Does dim byd 'da fi yn erbyn (y syniad) (S)

I've got nothing against (the idea)

To refuse permission, use either the *no* responses appropriate to how the request was phrased, or alternatively choose from the following, which appear roughly in ascending order of vehemence:

Wyt ti'n siwr °fod hynny'n syniad da?

Dych chi'n siwr °fod hynny'n syniad da?

Are you sure that's a good idea?

Dw i °ddim yn meddwl °fod hynny'n syniad da (o °gwbwl)

I don't think that's a good idea (at all)

Wyt ti'n siwr °fod ti eisiau?

Dych chi'n siwr bod chi eisiau?

Are you sure you want to?

Dw i °ddim o °blaid hynny o °gwbwl

I'm not in favour of that at all

Rhaid i mi °ddweud ⁿmod i yn erbyn

I have to say that I'm against

Nage °ddim!

Certainly not!

Nage °ddim, mae hynny'n °ormod!

Certainly not, that's too much!

Cer o 'ma! / Cerwch o 'ma! (S)

Dos o 'ma! / Ewch o 'ma! (N)

Get lost!

XXI   Making, accepting and declining suggestions

Making suggestions can be done either with **awgrymu** *suggest* or more informally by means of Beth am° . . .?

Dw i'n awgrymu bod ni'n . . .

I suggest that we . . .

Dw i'n awgrymu bod ni'n ffonio nhw wedyn

I suggest we phone them later

Beth am inni°...?

How about if we ...?

Beth am inni °gael panaid rhywle?

How about if we had a cup of tea somewhere?

Beth am °ofyn yn y siop 'ma?

How about asking in this shop?

You can preface these with:

°Ga i awgrymu rhywbeth?

May I suggest something?

A more neutral way is to elicit suggestions from the other person:

Beth dych chi (/Beth wyt ti) 'n awgrymu?

What do you suggest?

Oes gynnoch chi (/Oes gen ti) °rywbeth i awgrymu? (N)
Oes rhywbeth 'da chi (/'da ti) i awgrymu? (S)

Have you got any suggestions?

A more oblique way to suggest something uses dylwn (§336):

Oni °ddylech chi°...?
Oni °ddylet ti°...?

Shouldn't you ...?

Oni °ddylech chi °ofyn iddo °gynta?

Shouldn't you ask him first?

Oni °ddylen ni°...?

Shouldn't we ...?

Oni °ddylen ni aros nes i'r lleill °gyrraedd?

Shouldn't we wait till the others arrive?

For accepting suggestions:

Syniad da!

Good idea!

Pam °lai?

Why not?

I'r dim!

Perfect!

Dw i'n meddwl bod chi (/°fod ti)'n iawn

I think you're right

'Na syniad

That's an idea

Cytuno'n llwyr

Completely agree

Nawn ni hynny, 'te

Let's do that, then

If, on the other hand, you wish to decline the suggestion that has been made:

Dw i °ddim yn meddwl °fod hynny'n syniad da

I don't think that's a good idea

Gadewch (/Gad) inni °drio meddwl am °rywbeth arall

Let's try and think of something else

Dw i °ddim eisiau gwneud hynny

I don't want to do that

°Alla i °ddim gwneud hynny, yn anffodus

°Fedra i °ddim gwneud hynny, yn anffodus (N)

I can't do that, unfortunately

Dw i yn erbyn y syniad, mae arna i ofn

I'm afraid I'm against the idea

XXII Issuing and responding to warnings

The basic term for issuing a warning is

Gofal!

Gofalwch!

Watch out!

In less urgent circumstances, where you simply want to tell someone to be careful:

Bydd yn °ofalus!

Byddwch yn °ofalus!

Be careful!

Gan °bwyll, nawr!

Easy does it/Steady, now

Admonitions to do things can be expressed as follows:

Gofalwch bod chi'n . . .

Take care that you . . .

Gwnewch yn siwr bod chi'n . . .

Make sure that you . . .

Gwnewch yn siwr bod chi'n bwcio'r tocynnau

Make sure you book the tickets

Gofalwch bod chi'n archebu digon

Make sure you order enough

Rhaid i chi (/ti) °ofalu bod chi (/°fod ti) 'n . . .

You must take care to . . .

Rhaid i chi °ofalu bod chi'n arwyddo pob tudalen o'r °ddogfen

You must take care to sign every page of the document

For warnings not to let things happen, you can of course use the expressions above followed by negatives:

Gofalwch na °ddaw gormod o °bobol

Make sure that not too many people come

Gwnewch yn siwr bod chi °ddim yn hwyr

Make sure you're not late

or you can simply issue negative commands using:

Paid!

Peidiwch!

Don't!

Peidiwch eistedd ar °bwys y dyn 'na!

Don't sit next to that man!

Note also:

Rhaid i ti °ofalu bod °fod ti °ddim yn . . .

Rhaid i chi °ofalu bod chi °ddim yn . . .

You must take care that you don't . . .

Rhaid i ti °ofalu °fod ti °ddim yn colli marciau ar y cwestiwn 'ma

You must take care that you don't lose marks on this question

To thank someone for warning you about something, you can use:

Diolch am y rhybudd

Thanks for the warning

Diolch am °rybuddio fi

Thanks for warning me

Diolch am hynny

Thanks for that

or, where the warning was in sense of a reminder:

Diolch am atgoffa fi i °wneud hynny

Thanks for reminding me to do that

Diolch am °beidio gadael i mi anghofio gwneud hynny

Thanks for not letting me forget to do that

XXIII Asserting and denying the truth of something

When people don't believe what you've said, you can reinforce your position with:

°Wir i chi!

Honest!

Alternatively, you can act pre-emptively by prefacing or finishing your assertion with:

Credwch neu °beidio . . .

Coeliwch neu °beidio . . .

Believe it or not

**Credwch neu °beidio, dw i'n °frawd-yng-nghyfraith i Claudia
Winkleman**

Believe it or not, I'm Claudia Winkleman's brother-in-law

When other people tell you things, on the other hand, while you may wish
to indicate that you believe what they're telling you:

Dw i'n credu °fod hynny'n °wir

Dw i'n meddwl °fod hynny'n °wir

I think that's true

Rhaid bod/°fod hynny'n °wir

That must be true

Mae hynny'n °gywir

That's correct

It is of course perfectly in order to deny the truth of them – use any of the
following:

Dw i °ddim yn credu °fod hynny'n °wir

Dw i °ddim yn meddwl °fod hynny'n °wir

I don't think that's true

°All hynny °ddim bod yn °wir

°Fedr hynny °ddim bod yn °wir (N)

Rhaid bod/°fod hynny °ddim yn °wir

That can't be true

Dyw hynny °ddim yn °gywir

That's not correct

Mae hynny'n anghywir

That's wrong/incorrect

If it's blatant nonsense, why not say so?

Sothach!

Rubbish!

Sothach ydy hwnna!

That's rubbish!

XXIV   Remembering and forgetting

The basic verbs are cofio and anghofio.

Dw i'n cofio

I remember

Dw i'n cofio (ei) gweld hi fan hyn llynedd

I remember seeing her here last year

Dw i °ddim yn cofio

I don't remember

Dw i °ddim yn cofio dweud hynny

I don't remember saying that

Dw i wedi anghofio

I've forgotten

Nes i anghofio'r diodydd

Anghofies i'r diodydd

I forgot the drinks

Wyt ti 'n cofio . . .?

Dych chi 'n cofio . . .?

Do you remember?

°Fyddi di'n cofio dod â'r tocynnau?

°Fyddwch chi'n cofio dod â'r tocynnau?

Will you remember to bring the tickets?

°Alla i °ddim anghofio . . .

°Fedra i °ddim anghofio . . .

I can't forget

    °Fydda i °ddim yn anghofio hynny

or **Na i °ddim anghofio hynny**

or **Anghofia i mo hynny**

    I won't forget that

Anghofiwch y cyfan!

Anghofia'r cyfan!

Forget the whole thing!

443

Efallai bod chi °ddim yn cofio

Perhaps you don't remember

Er cof am° . . .

In memory of . . .

Cofiwch fi at eich rhieni

Remember me to your parents

Peidiwch anghofio dychwelyd y llyfrau

Don't forget to return the books

Cofiwch °ddychwelyd y llyfrau

Remember to return the books

XXV Expressing future intentions

The best way to indicate that you intend to do something is by using the inflected future of **gwneud** (§305) to form the Future III of the verb in question, as detailed in §306.

Na i° . . .

I'll . . .

Nawn ni° . . .

We'll . . .

Na i ('ch) ffonio chi pan °gyrhaeddwn ni

I'll phone you when we arrive

Nawn ni aros amdanoch chi

We'll wait for you

Neith e mo hynny

He won't do that

Dere 'ma, na i °ddangos i ti

Come here, I'll show you

A less direct way is to use **penderfynu** *decide*:

Dw i wedi penderfynu siarad ag e yfory

I've decided to speak to him tomorrow

for which one could just as easily say

Na i siarad ag e yfory

Longer-term plans are best done with **bwriadu** *intend*, or by using the preposition am° in its specialized meaning, with a following VN, of *want to* (§448(e))

Dw i'n bwriadu teithio o °gwmpas Iwerddon °flwyddyn nesa

I intend to travel round Ireland next year

Dw i am °fynd i'r Eisteddfod eleni

I want to go to the Eisteddfod this year

To ask about someone else's intentions:

Be(th) nei di?

Be(th) newch chi?

What will you do?

Beth wyt ti'n mynd i °wneud?

Beth dych chi 'n mynd i °wneud?

What are you going to do?

Beth ydy/yw dy °fwriad?

Beth ydy/yw'ch bwriad?

What's your intention?

Beth wyt ti'n bwriadu °wneud?

Beth dych chi'n bwriadu °wneud?

What are you intending/do you intend to do?

Beth sy gen ti ar y gweill? (N)

Beth sy 'da ti ar y gweill? (S)

Beth sy gynnoch chi ar y gweill? (N)

Beth sy 'da chi ar y gweill? (S)

What have you got planned?

Beth sy gen ti mewn golwg? (N)

Beth sy 'da ti mewn golwg? (S)

Beth sy gynnoch chi mewn golwg? (N)

Beth sy 'da chi mewn golwg? (S)

What have you got in mind?

XXVI **Expressing likes and dislikes**

To say what things you like, or what you like doing, the basic (and inter-changeable) verbs **hoffi** and **leicio** can be used with either a following noun or following VN:

> **Dw i'n hoffi/leicio . . .**
>
> I like . . .
>
> **Dw i'n leicio hufen iâ**
>
> **Dw i'n hoffi hufen iâ**
>
> I like ice-cream
>
> **Dw i'n leicio chwarae gwyddbwyll**
>
> **Dw i'n hoffi chwarae gwyddbwyll**
>
> I like playing chess

And if you like something a lot, you can say:

> **Dw i'n dwli ar° . . .**
>
> I'm crazy about . . .
>
> **Dw i'n hoff iawn o° . . .**
>
> I'm very fond of . . .
>
> **Dw i wrth 'y ⁿmodd yn . . .**
>
> I like nothing better than to . . .
>
> **Dw i'n dwli ar Elin Fflur**
>
> I'm crazy about Elin Fflur
>
> **Dw i'n hoff iawn o °gerddoriaeth °ganoloesol**
>
> I'm very fond of medieval music
>
> **Dw i wrth 'y ⁿmodd yn gwrando ar °gerddi Meinir Gwilym**
>
> I like nothing better than to listen to Meinir Gwilym's songs

Saying that you don't like something can be done in the following way, in increasing order of dislike, all of them again followed by either a noun or a VN:

> **Dw i °ddim yn leicio . . .**
>
> **Dw i °ddim yn hoffi . . .**
>
> I don't like . . .

°Alla i °ddim diodde(f) . . .

°Fedra i °ddim diodde(f) . . . (N)

I can't stand . . .

Dw i'n casáu . . .

I hate . . .

°Gas gen i° . . . (N)

°Gas 'da fi° . . . (S)

I hate . . .

Dw i °ddim yn leicio codi'n °gynnar

I don't like getting up early

°Alla i °ddim diodde bresych

I can't stand cabbage

°Gas gen i °fod ar ⁿmhen 'n hun (N)

I hate being on my own

°Gas 'da fi °flodfresych (S)

I hate cauliflower

To ask someone else if they like something, or like doing something, say:

Wyt ti'n leicio . . .?

Dych chi'n leicio . . .?

Wyt ti'n hoffi . . .?

Dych chi'n hoffi . . .?

Do you like . . .?

Dych chi'n hoffi afalau?   – Ydw/Nag ydw

Do you like apples?   – Yes/No

Wyt ti'n leicio eistedd yn yr °ardd?   – Ydw/Nag ydw

Do you like sitting in the garden?   – Yes/No

XXVII   Indicating and asking about preferences

There is no commonly used verb in Welsh for *prefer*, and a paraphrase
involving °**Well** *better* with the prepositions **gan**° (§455) or **(gy)da**ʰ (§457)
is used instead – this construction is dealt with in §354.

°**Well gen i°** . . . (N)

°**Well 'da fi°** . . . (S)

I prefer . . .

°**Well gen i'r un coch**

I prefer the red one

°**Well 'da fi° hwnna**

I prefer that one

Than in this construction is na[h]:

°**Well gen i °weithio gartre na gweithio yn y swyddfa**

I prefer working at home to working in the office

°**Well gen i °de na [h]choffi**

I prefer tea to coffee

To enquire about someone else's preferences, use:

P'un sy ('n) °well gynnoch chi? (N)

P'un sy ('n) °well 'da chi? (S)

Which do you prefer?

and note that the word order of the answer mirrors that of the question:

Yr un coch sy ('n) °well gen i (N)

Yr un coch sy ('n) °well 'da fi (S)

I prefer the red one

On a more hypothetical level, you can ask what someone would prefer by
using the conditional of **bod** in the same basic construction:

P'un °fasai'n °well gynnoch chi heno, aros i mewn neu °fynd allan? (N)

P'un °fyddai'n °well 'da chi heno, aros i mewn neu °fynd allan? (S)

Which would you prefer tonight, staying in or going out?

°**Fyddai'n °well 'da chi °drafod hyn oll nes ymlaen?** (S)

°**Fasai'n °well gynnoch chi °drafod hyn oll nes ymlaen?** (N)

Would you prefer to discuss this later on?

XXVIII Expressing indifference

There are various expressions to indicate indifference:

Dim ots gen i° . . . (N)

Dim ots 'da fi° . . . (S)

I don't mind . . .

Dw i °ddim yn malio

I don't mind . . .

Does gen i °ddim ots yr un ffordd neu'r llall (N)

Does dim ots 'da fi yr un ffordd neu'r llall (S)

I don't mind/care one way or the other

Dim ots gen i os dych chi'n dweud wrthi neu °beidio

I don't care whether you tell her or not

Beth ydy'r ots?

What does it matter?

Does a °wnelo hynny â fi

That's got nothing to do with me

If your indifference inclines you to leave decisions to someone else, you can say:

Gwnewch fel y mynnoch (chi)

Gwna fel y mynni di

Gwna fel y mynnot ti

Do as you please

Na i °adael i chi °benderfynu

Na i °adael i ti °benderfynu

I'll let you decide

XXIX Voicing opinion

Welsh has two words for *think* in the sense of *be of the opinion* – meddwl and **credu**; they are interchangeable in this sense, though **credu** is more associated with S areas. You should use a *that . . .* clause (§§486–497) after either.

Dw i'n credu/meddwl bod ni'n hwyr

I think we're late

Dw i'n credu/meddwl y dylen ni aros

I think we should wait

Similarly when your opinion is that something *isn't* the case:

Dw i °ddim yn credu/meddwl y dylen ni aros

I don't think we should wait

If you're more certain of your opinion, you can use:

Dw i'n siwr/sicr . . .

I'm sure . . .

Dw i'n eitha siwr/sicr . . .

I'm fairly sure . . .

Dw i'n °gwbwl siwr/sicr . . .

I'm quite sure . . .

Dw i'n eitha siwr °fod hynny'n anghywir

I'm fairly sure that's wrong

'Y "marn i yw/ydy . . .

My opinion is . . .

To ask someone else's opinion, you can use:

Beth wyt ti'n °feddwl?

Beth dych chi'n °feddwl?

What do you think?

Beth dych chi'n °feddwl am° . . .

What do you think about . . .?

Beth yw/ydy dy °farn am° . . .?

Beth yw/ydy'ch barn am° . . .?

What is your opinion of . . .?

Beth dych chi'n °feddwl am °ddatganoli?

What do you think about devolution?

Beth ydy'ch barn am ei °wraig?

What's your opinion of his wife?

or, in the past:

Beth o't ti'n °feddwl . . .?

Beth o'ch chi'n °feddwl . . .?

What did you think?

Beth oedd dy °farn?

Beth oedd eich barn?

What was your opinion?

Beth o'ch chi'n °feddwl am y cyngerdd?

What did you think of the concert?

Reporting opinions of third parties can similarly be done either with meddwl/credu or with **barn**:

Roedd llawer ohonyn nhw'n meddwl °fod eisiau cyfaddawdu

Many of them thought that compromise was needed

Barn llawer ohonyn nhw oedd °fod eisiau cyfaddawdu

The opinion of many of them was that compromise was needed

For voicing an opinion that you think may not be to the liking of all those listening, you can begin with:

Rhaid i mi °ddweud . . .

I have to say . . .

Rhaid i mi °ddweud °fod hyn oll yn swnio'n arwynebol braidd

I have to say that all this sounds rather superficial

and to interject your opinion into a conversation, you can say:

Os °ga i °wneud sylwad fan hyn, . . .

If I may make an observation here . . .

Agreeing with what someone has said is easy:

Cytuno'n llwyr

(I) completely agree

Dych chi yn llygad eich lle fan'na

You're spot on there

°Fyddai/°Fasai neb yn anghytuno â chi fan'na

Nobody would disagree with you there

If you want to be non-committal, just say:

Mae'n anodd dweud

It's hard to say

or **Mi °allai hynny °fod yn °wir**

    Mi °fedrai hynny °fod yn °wir (N)

    That might be true

Finally, if you wish to disagree with someone's opinion, the following are good general-purpose expressions:

Dim felly dw i'n gweld y sefyllfa

That's not how I see the situation

Dim felly mae'r sefyllfa'n edrych i mi

That's not how the situation looks to me

Rhaid i mi anghytuno â chi fan'na

I have to disagree with you there

Dyw hi °ddim yn °bosib bod chi'n meddwl felly

You can't possibly think that

Mae hynny'n safbwynt dadleuol, wedwn i

That is a controversial point of view, I would say

XXX   Expressing agreement and disagreement

Central to agreeing and disagreeing with someone are **cytuno** (â[h]) *agree* and its derivative **anghytuno** (â[h]) *disagree*, though of course many other phrasings and constructions are available.

All the following are standard ways of agreeing with someone:

Dw i'n cytuno

I agree

Dyn ni'n °gytun

We are in agreement

Dych chi'n iawn

You're right

Mae hynny'n °gywir

That's correct

I'r dim!

Exactly!

Yn °bendant!

Definitely!

Yn °ddi-os!

Heb os nac onibai!

Without any doubt!

Does dim dwywaith amdani

There's no two ways about it

When you *don't* agree with someone, say:

Dw i °ddim yn cytuno

I don't agree

Dw i'n anghytuno

I disagree

°Alla i °ddim cytuno

°Fedra i °ddim cytuno (N)

I can't agree

Rhaid i mi anghytuno

I have to disagree

Dych chi °ddim yn iawn

You're not right

Mae hynny'n anghywir

That's incorrect

Dyw hynny °ddim yn °gywir (o °gwbwl)

That's not right (at all)

If you want to agree to differ, you could say:

Yn °bersonol, dw i'n meddwl . . ., ond dw i'n gweld °fod eich barn chi'n °wahanol

Personally I think . . ., but I can see that you think differently

And if you want to bring the discussion to an end, or change the subject:

Gadewch inni °adael y pwnc fan'na

Let's leave it at that

Awn ni ymlaen at °drafod rhywbeth arall

Let's go on to discuss something else

Expressing happiness, fear and sadness

While *happy* in the sense of *joyful* is **hapus**:

Ti'n edrych yn hapus iawn bore 'ma

You're looking very happy this morning

the usual word for *happy* in the sense of *glad* is **balch**:

Dw i'n °falch o °glywed hynny

I'm glad/happy to hear that

Sen ni'n °falch iawn pe gallech chi ymweld â ni wythnos nesa

We would be very glad if you could visit us next week

Note the idiomatic expression for being very happy with the way things are:

Dw i wrth 'y ⁿmodd!

I'm in my element!/I'm as happy as can be!

To say that you're looking forward to something, use **edrych ymlaen at°**:

Dyn ni'n edrych ymlaen at eich gweld chi i gyd yfory

We're looking forward to seeing you all tomorrow

Wyt ti'n edrych ymlaen at y gwyliau?

Are you looking forward to the holidays?

If you want to indicate that you are happy about a situation or circumstance, you can include **yn ffodus** *fortunately* or **wrth lwc** *luckily*:

Yn ffodus iawn, ʰchafodd neb ei anafu yn y °ddamwain

Fortunately, no-one was injured in the accident

Wrth lwc, fe °ddes i o hyd iddo mewn pryd

Luckily, I found it in time

If you wish to express formal pleasure at doing something, use **pleser** in the following construction:

Mae'n °bleser gen i'ch croesawu fan hyn heno

It's a pleasure for me to welcome you here this evening

To talk about being afraid, there is a verb **ofni** *fear*, but a different construction using the noun **ofn** *fear* with **ar°** + person (§398) is more common:

Dw i'n ofni stormydd

Mae ofn stormydd arna i.

I'm afraid of storms

Dych chi'n ofni cŵn?

Oes ofn cŵn arnoch chi?

Are you afraid of dogs?

In the metaphorical sense of *I regret to say*, the construction with **ar°** is preferred:

Mae'n rhy hwyr, mae arna i ofn

It's too late, I'm afraid

Note that it is usually added to the end of the phrase in Welsh, even where the English equivalent starts the sentence:

Bydd rhaid i chi °adael nawr, mae arna i ofn

I'm afraid you'll have to leave now

Sadness is generally covered by the word **trist**:

Mae e'n °drist (braidd)

He's (rather) sad

O'n i'n °drist iawn o °glywed eich newyddion yn °ddiweddar

I was very sad to hear your recent news

To say that someone is feeling a bit low or depressed, use the following:

Mae e (braidd) yn isel ei ysbryd

He's (rather) depressed

Roedd hi'n isel ei hysbryd

She was feeling down

Dw i'n isel 'n ysbryd ar hyn o °bryd

I'm feeling down at the moment

XXXII Expressing hopes and disappointment

For dealing with *hope* generally, Welsh has an all-purpose word **gobeithio** (§433), which corresponds both to *I hope* and *we hope*, as well as to the useful and unfairly maligned *hopefully* in English:

Gobeithio bod chi'n °barod

I hope you're ready

Gobeithio y byddwch chi'n °barod mewn pryd

I hope you'll be ready in time

Gobeithio na °gawsoch/ʰchawsoch chi'ch siomi

I hope you weren't disappointed

Gobeithio na °fyddan nhw'n hwyr

I hope they won't be late

Bydd y lleill yn dod wedyn, gobeithio

Hopefully the others will be along later

Dw i'n °obeithiol iawn

I'm very hopeful

Dydy'r sefyllfa °ddim yn °obeithiol iawn

The situation isn't very hopeful

For disappointment, **siomi** means *disappoint* and is generally used in a passive construction with cael (§§362–363)

°Gest ti dy siomi?

°Gawsoch chi'ch siomi?

Were you disappointed?

°Ges i 'n siomi o'i °weld e yn ôl ar y strydoedd

I was disappointed to see him back on the streets

Peidiwch °gael eich siomi – archebwch heddiw!

Don't be disappointed – order now!

The adjective **siomedig** means both *disappointed* and *disappointing*:

Siomedig iawn oedd yr ymateb

The response was very disappointing

Roedd pawb yn siomedig braidd

Everyone was rather disappointed

When talking about a disappointment, you can also use the noun **siom**:

Roedd hi'n siom

It was a disappointment

°Ges i siom °fawr wrth °wylio'r ffilm

I was very disappointed in the film

XXXIII Expressing surprise

There are a number of interjections for indicating surprise:

Duw! Duw!

Nêfi blŵ!

'Rargian!

Or you can say:

'Na syndod!

What a surprise!

If you are surprised at something someone tells you, say:

Ti °ddim o °ddifri!

Dych chi °ddim o °ddifri!

You're not serious!

Mae hynny'n anhygoel!

That's incredible!

Pwy °fyddai'n meddwl?

Pwy °fasai'n meddwl?

Who would have thought that?

The usual way to tell someone that you or someone else was surprised is to use **synnu** in a passive construction with **cael** (§§362–363):

°Ges i 'n synnu o'ch gweld chi

I was surprised to see you

°Gawsoch chi'ch synnu?

Were you surprised?

Rather more formally, unforeseen circumstances and events can be commented on with:

O'n i °ddim wedi disgwyl hynny

I hadn't expected that

Mi oedd hynny yn erbyn pob disgwyl

That was against all expectations

O'n i °ddim wedi rhagweld hynny

I hadn't foreseen that

XXXIV Expressing enjoyment and pleasure

The general word for *fun* is **hwyl**; **hwyl a sbri** is used for *all sorts of fun*, and **sbort** is encountered as well (*sport*, on the other hand, is **chwaraeon**)

Am sbort!

What fun!

Fe °gawson ni (°gryn dipyn o) hwyl

We had (quite a bit of) fun

°Gawsoch chi hwyl?

Did you have fun?

Naethoch chi °fwynhau?

Did you enjoy (it/yourself/yourselves)?

Dych chi wedi cael amser da?

Have you had a good time?

Roedd hi'n °brofiad arbennig (o °dda)

It was a great experience

Rhaid inni °wneud hyn (hynny) eto °rywbryd (cyn hir)

We must do this (that) again some time (soon)

XXXV Asking for and giving directions

There are a number of ways of asking the whereabouts of a place or building you are looking for:

Oes banc rhywle fan hyn?

Is there a bank somewhere (round) here?

Lle mae'r banc agosa?

Where's the nearest bank?

°Allech chi °ddweud wrtha i lle mae'r swyddfa °bost?

°Fedrech chi °ddweud wrtha i lle mae'r swyddfa °bost? (N)

Could you tell me where the post office is?

Dw i'n chwilio am swyddfa °bost

I'm looking for a post office

Once you've received directions (see below), you might like to ask:

Ydy hi'n °bell?

Is it far?

Pa mor °bell ydy hwnna?

How far is that?

And if the directions were not quite as simple as you had hoped, you could always try:

°Allwch chi °ddangos i fi ar y map 'ma? (S)

°Fedrwch chi °ddangos i mi ar y map 'ma? (N)

Can you show me on this map?

(to avoid embarrassment, make sure you have a map handy before you try this one).

Giving and understanding spatial directions is generally a straightforward business involving a limited number of patterns and phrases in obvious combinations:

Mae'n (°ddigon) syml

It's simple (enough)

459

Ewch . . .

Go . . .

yn syth ymlaen

straight on/ahead

ffordd yma

ffordd hyn

this way

hyd at y °groesffordd

as far as the crossroads

hyd at y goleuadau

as far as the traffic lights

Yna . . .

Then . . .

trowch . . .

turn . . .

i'r °dde

right

i'r chwith

left

Cymerwch . . .

Take . . .

y stryd °gynta

the first street

yr ail stryd

the second street

y °drydedd stryd

the third street

ar y °dde

on the right

ar y chwith

on the left

Mi/Fe °welwch chi'r °orsaf . . .

You'll see the station . . .

yn syth o'ch blaen

straight in front of you

gyferbyn

opposite

ar y °dde

on the right

Other phrases you may encounter or have to use yourself are:

Dw i ar °goll

I'm lost

Dw i wedi anghofio'r ffordd i'r . . .

I've forgotten the way to the . . .

Mae'n ddrwg 'da fi, . . . (S)

Mae'n °ddrwg gen i, . . . (N)

I'm sorry, . . .

Does gen i °ddim syniad (N)

Does dim clem 'da fi (S)

I've no idea

Dw i °ddim yn nabod y lle 'ma 'n hun

I don't know this place myself

Bydd rhaid i chi °ofyn i °rywun arall

you'll have to ask someone else

XXXVI Dealing with money

The units of currency are **punt** (*f*) *pound* and **ceiniog** (*f*) *penny*. Both these units tend to be found in the singular when used with numbers, for example **dwy °bunt** *£2*, **wyth punt** *£8*, **ugain punt** *£20*, **hanner can punt** *£50*; **pum ceiniog** *5p*, **hanner can ceiniog** *50p*, **wythdeg ceiniog** *80p*. For more information on this see §181.

To ask how much something is, use any of the following models:

Faint ydy/yw hwnna?

How much is that?

Faint ydy/yw'r esgidiau 'na?

How much are those shoes?

Beth ydy/yw pris y car 'ma

What is the price of this car?

Beth/Faint dych chi eisiau am y peth 'ma?

What/How much do you want for this?

If you want to haggle, these may be of use:

Ai dyna'ch pris gorau?

Is that your best price?

Dych chi °ddim o °ddifri!

You can't be serious!

°Allwn i °ddim talu cymaint (am y peth)

°Fedrwn i °ddim talu cymaint (am y peth) (N)

I couldn't pay that much (for it)

Gadewch i mi °feddwl a dod yn ôl atoch chi

Let me think about it and come back to you

°Allwch chi °gynnig gostyngiad i mi?

°Fedrwch chi °gynnig gostyngiad i mi? (N)

Can you offer me a discount?

Ydy'r pris 'na'n cynnwys popeth?

Is that price all-inclusive?

°Fydda i °ddim yn siopa fan hyn eto

I won't be shopping here again

And you can use the following to cover eventualities when paying for things:

'Na chi

Here you are [when handing over the money]

Mae'n °ddrwg gen i, dim ond papur ugain punt sy gen i (N)

Mae'n °ddrwg 'da fi, dim ond papur ugain punt sy 'da fi (S)

Sorry, I've only got a twenty

°Allwch chi newid hwn?

°Fedrwch chi newid hwn? (N)

Can you change this?

Mae'r newid 'ma'n anghywir (, dw i'n meddwl)

This change is wrong (, I think)

°Alla i °dalu â siec?

°Fedra i °dalu â siec? (N)

Oes modd i mi °dalu â siec?

Can I pay by cheque?

°Alla i °dalu â ʰcherdyn credyd?

°Fedra i °dalu â ʰcherdyn credyd? (N)

Oes modd i mi °dalu â ʰcherdyn credyd?

Can I pay by credit card?

Dych chi'n derbyn cardiau fan hyn?

Do you accept cards here?

You might need some of these phrases in the bank:

°Ga i °dalu'r siec 'ma i mewn?

Can I pay this cheque in?

Mae'r peiriant wedi llyncu ⁿngherdyn

The machine has swallowed my card

O'n i'n gobeithio trafod gorddrafft gyda rhywun

I was hoping to discuss an overdraft with someone

Dw i eisiau gweld y rheolwr

I want to see the manager

Mae'r rheolwr eisiau ⁿngweld i

The manager wants to see me

Dyma'r trydydd tro i hyn °ddigwydd y mis 'ma

This is the third time this has happened this month

Dw i eisiau trosglwyddo arian o ⁿnghyfrif cyfredol i ⁿnghyfrif cadw

I want to transfer some money from my current account to my savings
account

Dw i angen benthyciad sylweddol

I need a substantial loan

Pam bod chi'n edrych arna i fel 'ny?

Why are you looking at me like that?

XXXVII Talking about health and illness

To tell the doctor how you're feeling, you'll probably need to make an
appointment first:

°Ga i °wneud apwyntiad i °weld y meddyg heddiw?

Can I make an appointment to see the doctor today?

If it's urgent, you can say:

Mae'n °bwysig

It's important/urgent

Dw i eisiau gweld rhywun ar °frys

I want to see someone urgently

As detailed in §398, temporary states of mind and body are often expressed
using ar°, and this includes many illnesses:

Mae annwyd arna i

I've got a cold

Similarly:

Mae'r ffliw arna i

I've got (the) flu

Mae'r °ddannodd arna i

I've got toothache

Mae peswch arna i

I've got a cough

Mae gwres arna i

I've got a temperature

But some types of ailment, particularly where a part of the body is specified, use the **gan/gyda** possession construction (§§455, 457). N areas use **cur**, S areas use **tost** – both meaning *painful* or *ache*.

Mae pen tost 'da fi (S)

Mae gen i °gur pen (N)

I've got a headache

Questions are phrased differently depending on whether the definite article appears with the illness. So:

Oes annwyd arnoch chi?

Have you got a cold?

Oes peswch arnoch chi?

Have you got a cough?

Oes pen tost 'da chi?

Have you got a headache?

but:

Ydy'r ffliw arnoch chi?

Have you got (the) flu?

Ydy'r °frech °goch arni hi?

Has she got measles?

Things the doctor may ask:

Lle mae'n brifo?

Lle mae'n rhoi dolur?

Lle mae'n doluro?

Where does it hurt?

Ers pryd dych chi'n teimlo'n sâl?

How long have you been feeling ill?

Ers faint dych chi wedi bod fel hyn?

How long have you been like this?

Dych chi wedi cymryd moddion o °gwbwl?

Have you taken any medication?

Ydy hyn yn rhoi dolur?

Does this hurt? [lit. '. . . give pain?']

At the end of the consultation, the doctor's advice may well include one or more of the following:

Rhaid i chi °fynd yn syth i'r gwely

You must go straight to bed

Rhaid i chi aros yn y gwely nes bod chi'n (teimlo'n) °well

You must stay in bed until you're (feeling) better

Rhaid i chi °beidio mynd yn ôl i'r gwaith am °weddill yr wythnos

You mustn't go back to work for the rest of the week

Dylech chi °gadw'n °gynnes

You should keep warm

Dylech chi °gael gorffwys

You should get some rest

Peidiwch mynd allan

Don't go out

Peidiwch gorwneud pethau

Don't overdo things

Ewch â hyn at y fferyllydd

Take this to the chemist's

Dewch yn ôl i ⁿngweld i ymhen wythnos (os na °fydd pethau wedi gwella)

Come back and see me in a week's time (if things haven't improved)

Na i °drefnu i chi °weld arbenigwr

I'll arrange for you to see a specialist

XXXVIII–XL ENGLISH WORDS CAUSING PARTICULAR TRANSLATION PROBLEMS

XXXVIII Translation of *have*

Translation of *have* is problematic for two reasons:

(a) for its primary meaning of *possess*, for which Welsh simply has no corresponding verb in addition to meaning *possess*, *have* is used in five other senses in English, and for each of these there is a different translation in Welsh

Have – possession

Where *have* means *possess*, a paraphrase using the existential verb (§252) with **gan°** (N) (§455) or **(gy)da^h** (S) (§457), both meaning *with*, must be used – i.e. for *John has a car* the Welsh construction is 'There is a car with John' – **Mae car 'da John**. Similarly, *Have you got a car?* will literally be 'Is there a car with you?' – **Oes car 'da chi?**, and so on. Note that the N construction with **gan°** and the S construction with **(gy)da^h** have differing word-order:

(N) **Mae gan John °gar**

(S) **Mae car 'da John**

Further examples:

Mae gen i'r holl °fanylion fan hyn (N)

I've got all the details here

Doedd dim car 'da Gerwyn pan °weles i fe tro diwetha (S)

Gerwyn didn't have a car when I saw him last

Oedd plant 'da nhw o °gwbwl °bryd 'ny? (S)

Did they have any children at that time?

'S gen i °ddim bwyd yn y tŷ (N)

I haven't got any food in the house

Note that, in British English at least, the present tense of this *possess* use is often *have/has got* and that this should not be confused with simple *got*, which implies the different idea of *receive* – generally **cael** in Welsh.

Have – receive

Where *have* means *receive*, the appropriate Welsh equivalent is **cael**. The only problem for the learner here (apart from **cael** being an irregular verb) is distinguishing the *receive* and *possess* senses in English. If *have* can be replaced by *receive* in the English sentence without change of meaning, then **cael** is the right choice. Compare:

(a) Rhian had a big red book when I saw her

(b) Rhian had a big red book for her birthday

The clear sense of (a) is possession – there is no implication of Rhian receiving the book, but simply of having it with her at the time. Therefore:

Oedd gan Rhian °lyfr mawr coch pan °weles i hi

In sentence (b) the whole point is that she did receive the book – someone gave it to her as a present. Therefore:

°Gafodd Rhian °lyfr mawr coch i'w ʰphenblwydd

Have – take

Sometimes have has the sense of take, and here the usual Welsh equivalent is **cymryd** (cymer-):

°Gymerwch chi °ragor o °gacen?

Will you have some more cake?

°Gymera i °ddau °ddwsin o'r rheina, os gwelwch yn °dda

I'll have two dozen of those, please

Have something done

The English idiom *have (something) done* uses **cael** + VN in Welsh, in the following construction:

Ti wedi cael torri dy °wallt!

You've had your hair cut!

Dan ni wedi cael trwsio'r ffenestri

We've had the windows repaired

Note the difference in word-order from English, with the object coming after both **cael** and the VN.

Have to

English *have to* is a synonym for *must*, and is used both in the present as an alternative to it, and in other tenses where *must* is not possible. Obligation, then, is the basic idea here, and this is expressed in Welsh by the non-verbal modal **rhaid** (§§349–350). Examples:

Rhaid inni °adael erbyn deg o'r °gloch man pella

We have to leave by ten o'clock at the latest

Oes rhaid iddyn nhw °fynd a'u gwisg nofio 'da nhw?

Do they have to take their swimming costumes with them?

Have as auxiliary

Finally, *have* is used as an auxiliary in English to form the perfect tense – *I have lost my money*. Welsh uses **bod** (with **wedi**) as the auxiliary for the perfect (§268) – dw i wedi colli 'n arian i.

Mae Siôn wedi cicio'r °bêl i °ardd Mrs Tomos unwaith eto

Siôn has kicked the ball into Mrs Tomos's garden yet again

°Fyddan nhw °ddim wedi cyrraedd 'to

They won't have got there yet

XXXIX Translation of *take*

Cymryd (**cymer-**) is the right verb for nearly all English uses of *take* except *accompany* (see below):

Faint °gymerith y °daith?

How long will the journey take?

Cymerwch °daflen wrth °fynd allan

Take a leaflet as you leave

°Gymerwch chi siwgwr yn eich te?

Do you take sugar in your tea?

When *take* implies duration of time, **para** (literary **parhau**, but hardly ever so pronounced) can be used:

O'n i'n poeni, ond naeth hi °ddim para'n rhy hir yn y diwedd

I was worried, but in the end it didn't take too long

Take – accompany

Where *take* means *accompany*, **mynd â**[h] (lit.: *go with*) is preferred:

Ewch â'ch sbwriel adre!

Take your rubbish home!

Nei di °fynd â'r plant i'r ysgol i mi bore 'ma?

Will you take the kids to school for me this morning?

The position of âʰ serves to differentiate *take* and *go with*, because it must immediately follow **mynd** when *take* is meant:

Dw i'n mynd â Siân adre	I'm taking Siân home
Dw i'n mynd adre â Siân	I'm going home with Siân

Alternatively, the unambiguous **gyda**ʰ can be used for *with*:

Dw i'n mynd adre gyda Siân	I'm going home with Siân

 Translation of other miscellaneous problem words

ACTUALLY

The parenthetical expression **a dweud y gwir** is often given a literal translation in learners' manuals – 'To tell (you) the truth', but in practice it occurs far more frequently in Welsh than this rather laboured English expression. In frequency and use it corresponds almost exactly to *actually*, a similarly parenthetical expression that often serves no other purpose than to soften the force of the original statement, or gently qualify a preceding one.

Faint °dalon nhw amdano fo? – A dweud y gwir, 's gen i °ddim clem

How much did they pay for it? – I've no idea, actually

BECOME (or GET in this sense)

There is no word corresponding to *become* in Welsh – a variety of strategies are available for translating it. Of these the most common are **mynd yn°** and **dod yn°**, of which **mynd yn°** is the more common, being of more general meaning, while **dod yn°** is less frequent, being perhaps restricted to a connotation of improvement .

Mae'n mynd yn hwyr

It's getting late

Bydd hi'n mynd yn oerach nes ymlaen heddiw

It will become colder later on today

Mae hi am °fynd yn °feddyg

She wants to become a doctor

Mi 'steddais i lawr tan iddi °ddŵad yn °deg (N)

I sat down until it [the weather] cleared up [lit. 'became fair']

The verb **troi** *turn* (again with following **yn°**) is another alternative, used intransitively much as its English equivalent:

Yn sydyn iawn mae hyn oll yn troi'n °ddifrifol

All of a sudden all of this is becoming serious

Roedd y cyfan wedi hen °droi'n °ddadl °gron

The whole thing had long since become a circular argument

In addition, Welsh has the facility to make verbs from some adjectives which convey the meaning of 'become' – common examples are **oeri** *become/get cold* (< **oer** *cold*), **poethi** *become/get hot* (< **poeth** *hot*), **tywyllu** *become/get dark* (< **tywyll** *dark*).

Gobeithio y byddan nhw'n cyrraedd adre cyn iddi °dywyllu

I hope they arrive home before it gets dark

Cofiwch °gymryd y camau canlynol cyn iddi °boethi

Remember to take the following steps before it gets hot

BRING

Just as Welsh uses **mynd â**[h] (*go with*) for *take*, so **dod â**[h] (*come with*) is used for *bring*:

Cofiwch °ddod â'r plant

Remember to bring the children

Dewch â'ch cwpanau gyda chi

Bring your cups with you

°Ddo i â nhw draw nes ymlaen

I'll bring them over later

JUST

Where *just* means *only*, **dim ond** (**'mond**) is the usual translation:

Dim ond gofyn o'n i!

I was just asking!

'Mond papur pum punt sy ar ôl 'da fi

I've just got a fiver left

Where *just* means *exactly*, (yn) **union** is required:

Dyna yn union beth oedd gen i mewn golwg

That's just what I had in mind

Ar yr union °foment lle °ddaeth o i mewn . . .

Just as he came in . . . [lit.: at the exact moment . . .]

In constructions of the type *They have just left*, the perfect tense is used with **newydd°** replacing **wedi**:

Maen nhw newydd °adael, mae ofn arna i

They've just left, I'm afraid

(cf. **Maen nhw wedi gadael** – *They've left*)

PROBABLY

Tebyg *likely, probable* is the most obvious choice, but in the sense of *probably* it is mostly used in its own verbal phrase **mae'n °debyg** (*it is probable*), which is placed either at the start of the sentence or, more often, in the manner of an afterthought at the end.

    °Ddaw hi °ddim rŵan tan yfory, mae'n °debyg

or **Mae'n °debyg na °ddaw hi °ddim tan yfory rŵan**

    She probably won't come till tomorrow now

°Fyddi di'n cael gair ag e am hyn?   **– Mae'n °debyg**

Will you be having a word with him about this?   – Probably

As an answer, **Digon tebyg** *Quite probably* is also common enough.

QUITE

Where *quite* means *completely*, a number of Welsh words are available as translations: **hollol** or **llwyr** *complete*, or **perffaith** *perfect*:

Dw i'n °berffaith siwr nad fo naeth hyn

I'm quite sure he didn't do this

Cytuno'n llwyr!

(I) quite agree!

Mae'n hollol amlwg °fod rhywbeth o'i °le

It's quite clear that something is wrong

Where *quite* means *reasonably*, *fairly*, then **eitha** or (less frequently) **go°** (see §95) are the most likely:

Oedd hyn yn syniad eitha da wedi'r cwbwl, on'd oedd?

This was quite a good idea after all, wasn't it?

Golwg go °wael sy arno fo erbyn hyn

He's looking pretty/quite ill these days

Other problem words

Problem words *may*, *might*, *could* and *should* are dealt with under verbs – see §§333, 335, 339, 436.

Problem words *now* and *then* are dealt with under adverbs – see §§407, 408.

XLI–XLIII AFFIRMATIVE AND NEGATIVE RESPONSES

XLI   *Yes and no*

Answering *yes* to a question depends in Welsh on what word the question started with, because the literal response to (for example) *Are you going into town today?* will be not *Yes* but *I am*. The verb of the question is repeated by way of confirmation. With 3rd pers. questions, this procedure will simply involve exact (or near-exact – no SM in responses) repetition of the INT verb, without the accompanying pronoun:

Ydy hi'n oer tu allan?	– **Ydy**
Is it cold out?	– Yes [, it is]
Oedd dy °frawd yno?	– **Oedd**
Was your brother there?	– Yes [, he was]
°Fyddan nhw'n °barod?	– **Byddan**
Will they be ready?	– Yes [, they will be]

Note in the present, however, that while in the language generally **ydy** = **yw** and the two are largely interchangeable (see §223), this is not the case with questions and responses, where **Ydy** is the only option for *Yes* (i.e. you cannot simply say **Yw** for *Yes*). In some S areas **Yw** is used as an INT form (so: **Yw hi'n oer tu allan?**), but even here, the *yes*-response is still **Ydy** (though the *no*-response can be either **Nag ydy** or **Nag yw** – see below).

473

Yw hi'n dod, 'te?   – **Ydy** (S)

Is she coming, then?   – Yes

With 1st and 2nd pers. questions, these persons will naturally alternate between question and answer:

Dych chi'n dod?   – **Ydw**

Are you coming?   – Yes [, I am]

O't ti'n hwyr?   – **Oeddwn**

Were you late?   – Yes [, I was]

°Fydda i'n °barod?   – **Byddi**

Will I be ready?   – Yes [, you will be]

°Allen ni aros?   – **Gallech**

Could we wait?   – Yes [, you could]

This combination of person-switching and cancellation of SM accounts for two very common response patterns:

[Polite request]	**Newch chi °fynd ag e?**	– **Gwna**
	Will you take it?	– Yes [, I will (do)]
[Asking permission]	**°Ga i °fynd ag e?**	– **Cei** (sing.), **Cewch** (formal)
	Can I take it?	– Yes [, you can]

No in all the above types is expressed by preceding the appropriate *yes-* answer with (or MM), or **Nag** before vowels. Examples:

Ydy hi'n oer tu allan?   – **Nag ydy**

Is it cold outside?   – No

Yw hi'n oer ?   – **Nag ydy** or **Nag yw** (S)

Is it cold?   – No

Oes car 'da chi?   – **Nag oes**

Have you got a car?   – No

°Fyddi di fan hyn yfory?   – **Na °fyddaf**

Will you be here tomorrow?   – No

Ti'n siarad Pwyleg?   – **Nag ydw**

Do you speak Polish?   – No

°Ga i °fynd allan?   – **Na ʰchei**

Can I go out?   – No

Note, however, that in the spoken language an all-purpose **Na** is frequently heard in place of the standard person-specific responses. The same is not true for *yes*, for which the appropriate form must be used.

XLII   Do/naddo

All questions phrased with a preterite tense (see §§292, 293, 298, 301, 302), regardless of person, and whatever type of preterite (I, II or III) it is, require **Do** for a *yes* answer, and **Naddo** for *no*; see below.

°Gaethoch chi amser da, 'te? – **Do**

Did you have a good time, then?   – Yes

Ddaru nhw °weld o? (N)   – **Do**

Did they see him?   – Yes

Nes i °glywed hwnna'n iawn? – **Do**

Did I hear that right?   – Yes

This usage extends in many areas to the **wedi**-tenses (see §§268, 273) which, although not preterite in form, share with the preterite a past-time connotation. The response pattern, therefore, can be dictated either by grammatical form or by meaning:

Ydyn nhw wedi gorffen?   – **Ydyn/Do**   – **Nag ydyn/Naddo**
Have they finished?   – Yes   – No

XLIII   Ie/nage

Focused questions, which must begin with a non-verbal element (see §18), use **Ie** for *yes* and **Nage** for *no* in all cases:

Chi sy wedi gwneud hyn?	– **Ie**	– **Nage**
Did *you* do this?	– Yes	– No
Fan hyn mae o, 'te?	– **Ie**	– **Nage**
It's here, is it?	– Yes	– No
Y dyn yma °welsoch chi?	– **Ie**	– **Nage**
Was it this man you saw?	– Yes	– No

XLIV **Words differing in North and South Wales**

The following are the main differences in vocabulary between the North and the South. Where one option is preferred over the other in the standard language, this is in italics.

North	South	
allan	mas	out
agoriad	allwedd	key
bwrdd	bord	table
chdi	*ti*	you (sing.)
dallt	*deall*	understand
dos	cer	go (sing. command form)
dŵad	*dod*	come (VN)
'ddchi	chimod	y'know (pl.)
efo	*gyda*	with (see §§**454, 457**)
geneth	*merch*	girl
i fyny	lan	up
i ffwrdd	bant	away; off
isio	moyn	want (**isio** usually written **eisiau**)
llefrith	*llaeth*	milk
mai/na	taw	that (focused sentences – see §**492**)
nain	mam-gu	grandmother
o/fo	e/fe	he/him
pres	*arian*	money
rŵan	*nawr*	now
'sti	timod	y'know (sing.)
taid	tad-cu	grandfather
tyrd	dere	come (sing. command form)

North and South also differ slightly in syntax, notably in the constructions with **gan°** (N)/**gyda^h** (S) used to express possession – see **XXXV** in this section.

XLV   Using fillers

Fillers are words and phrases that we put into the conversation to give ourselves time to think and react – the following are very common in Welsh:

timod, chimod (S)

°wyddost ti, °wyddoch chi (N)

all meaning *you know, y'know* (§322)

Wi °ddim yn siwr, timod

I'm not sure, y'know

Wel, °wyddoch chi, mi °allai °fod yn iawn

Well, y'know, it might be OK

Similarly, various formations from **gweld** *see*

ti'n gweld

chi'n gweld

gweli di/°weli di

gwelwch chi/°welwch chi

dach chi'n gweld

are used in much the same circumstances as their equivalent *you see* in English:

Ond, °welwch chi, dw i heb °gwrdd â fo

But, you see, I haven't met him

°Well 'da fi'r stwff go iawn, ti'n gweld

I prefer the real stuff, you see

Another handy filler phrase is:

hynny yw

hynny ydy

that is

When you can't quite think of the word you want, you can say:

Beth oedd y gair 'na eto?

What was that word again?

477

When you just want to let the person you're talking to know that you need
a moment, try:

Dal eiliad

Daliwch eiliad

Hold on a moment

Gad i mi °feddwl (eiliad)

Gadewch i mi °feddwl (eiliad)

Let me think (a moment)

And these near-meaningless phrases are also useful in helping the flow:

Yn y bôn

Basically

A dweud y gwir

Actually

XLVI Keeping the channel open

Some words and phrases are used in normal conversation to keep the
listener involved and engaged when the speaker has a lot to say in one go
– these are like cues to the listener to elicit confirmation that he or she is still
engaged. The best all-purpose one of these in Welsh is:

yntefê?

or **yndefê?**

or **yndê?**

which, like its broad counterparts *n'est-ce pas?* and *nicht wahr?* in French
and German, really has no intrinsic meaning other than to ask for agreement:

Caws o't ti am °brynu, yntefê

It was cheese you wanted to buy, wasn't it?

O'n i'n mynd lawr y stryd, yndê, ac yn sydyn . . .

I was going down the street, wasn't I, and suddenly . . .

Another tactic is to ask for confirmation that the listener is understanding:

ti'n deall?

chi'n deall?

do you understand?

Equally, the speaker needs to receive clues that the listener is still engaged – any of the following, dropped in while the main speaker is speaking, will serve this purpose perfectly well:

°wir?

really?

iawn

OK; sure

wrth °gwrs

of course

yn hollol

quite

wel, efallai

well, perhaps

i'r dim

exactly

dim o °gwbwl

not at all

If communication is in danger of breaking down because you either didn't hear or didn't understand something the other person said, there are various strategies that can be deployed to get the conversation back on track:

Newch chi ailadrodd, os gwelwch yn °dda?

Nei di ailadrodd, os gweli di'n °dda?

Will you repeat that, please?

°Allech chi ailadrodd, os gwelwch yn °dda?

°Allet ti ailadrodd, os gweli di'n °dda?

°Fedrech chi ailadrodd, os gwelwch yn °dda? (N)

°Fedret ti ailadrodd, os gweli di'n °dda? (N)

Could you repeat that, please?

Beth (°dd)wed(s)och chi gynnau?

Beth (°dd)wedest ti gynnau?

What did you just say?

Eto?

Again?

O'n i °ddim yn deall hynny

Nes i °ddim deall hynny

I didn't understand that

O'n i °ddim yn clywed chi'n iawn

O'n i °ddim yn dy °glywed di'n iawn

Nes i °ddim clywed chi'n iawn

Nes i °ddim clywed ti'n iawn

I didn't hear you properly

Ydw i wedi'ch deall chi'n iawn?

Ydw i wedi dy °ddeall di'n iawn?

Have I understood you properly?

If you need clarification about what the other person's getting at, try:

Beth ydy/yw'ch pwynt?

Beth ydy/yw dy °bwynt?

What's your point?

Pa °bwynt dych chi'n trio °wneud?

Pa °bwynt wyt ti'n trio °wneud?

What point are you trying to make?

Beth mae hwnna i °fod i °feddwl?

What's that supposed to mean?

XLVII Asking for spoken linguistic cues

Sometimes you won't know the Welsh word for something – in these cases it's important to keep the conversation in Welsh and ask in Welsh for the information:

Sut mae dweud hynny yn °Gymraeg?

How do you say that in Welsh?

Sut mae dweud 'hovercraft' yn °Gymraeg?

How do you say 'hovercraft' in Welsh?

Beth yw/ydy 'hovercraft' yn °Gymraeg?

What's 'hovercraft' in Welsh?

If the item is to hand or at least visible, you can point and say:

Beth dych chi'n galw hwn/hwnna yn °Gymraeg?

What do you call this/that in Welsh?

If you can't catch the word when it's said to you, you can ask:

°Allech chi ailadrodd, os gwelwch yn °dda?

°Allet ti ailadrodd, os gweli di'n °dda

°Fedrech chi ailadrodd, os gwelwch yn °dda? (N)

°Fedret ti ailadrodd, os gweli di'n °dda? (N)

Could you repeat that, please?

Unwaith eto, os gwelwch yn °dda

Once again, please

Unwaith eto, ond yn arafach (y tro 'ma), os gwelwch yn °dda

Once again, but slower (this time), please

And if you're still at sea, you could resort to:

Sut mae sillafu hwnna?

How is that spelt?

°Allech chi sillafu hwnna i mi?

°Allet ti sillafu hwnna i mi?

°Fedrech chi sillafu hwnna i mi? (N)

°Fedret ti sillafu hwnna i mi? (N)

Could you spell that for me?

Failing all else, make sure you have pencil and paper handy, and say:

°Allech chi sgrifennu fe i lawr i mi?

°Allet ti sgrifennu fe i lawr i mi?

°Fedrech chi sgwennu fo i lawr i mi? (N)

°Fedret ti sgwennu fo i lawr i mi? (N)

Could you write it down for me?

If there are signs that your difficulties are in danger of leading the person
you're talking to to take pity on you and turn to English, you can prevent
this by saying:

> **Peidiwch troi i'r Saesneg os gwelwch yn °dda, dw i eisiau sgyrsio
> yn °Gymraeg**
>
> Don't turn to English, please – I want to speak in Welsh

Then follow this up with a request for them to reformulate what they said:

> **°Allech chi °ddweud fe mewn ffordd °wahanol?**
>
> **°Allet ti °ddweud fe mewn ffordd °wahanol?**
>
> **°Fedrech chi °ddeud o mewn ffordd °wahanol?** (N)
>
> **°Fedret ti °ddeud o mewn ffordd °wahanol?** (N)
>
> Could you say it in a different way?
>
> **Oes ffordd arall o °ddweud hynny?**
>
> Is there another way of saying that?

XLVIII Shaping the course of the conversation

To develop the topic of conversation – in other words, to reiterate or restate
something you've just said – the best all-purpose phrases are:

> **hynny yw**
>
> that is
>
> **mewn geiriau eraill**
>
> in other words

To change the topic – in other words to steer the conversation in a different
direction – use one of these strategies:

> **Gyda llaw . . .**
>
> By the way . . .
>
> **Gyda llaw, dych chi wedi clywed y newyddion am Aled?**
>
> By the way, have you heard about Aled?
>
> **Wrth i mi °feddwl . . .**
>
> While I think of it . . .
>
> **Wrth i mi °feddwl . . . mae llythyr i ti yn y °gegin**
>
> While I think of it . . . there's a letter for you in the kitchen

To actively drop the subject or indicate that you no longer want to pursue the topic, there are a number of possibilities, in ascending degrees of forcefulness:

Gad/Gadewch inni siarad am °rywbeth arall

Let's talk about something else

Nawn ni °adael y pwnc 'ma am y tro

Let's leave this subject for the time being

°Well gen i siarad am °rywbeth arall (N)

°Well 'da fi siarad am °rywbeth arall (S)

I'd rather talk about something else

Dyn ni wedi sôn am hyn yn °barod

We've talked about this already

Ie, ie – dw i'n gwybod hynny'n °barod

Yes, yes – I know that already

Dw i wedi cael digon o'r pwnc 'ma

I've had enough of this subject

Rhowch °derfyn ar y pwnc nawr!

Rho °derfyn ar y pwnc nawr!

Put an end to the subject now!

If, on the other hand, the other person has changed the subject and you want to steer things back to what *you* were talking about, these models may come in useful:

Nawr 'te – beth o'n i ar °fin dweud?

Now then – what was I just going to say?

Ond, i °droi'n ôl at beth oedden ni'n °drafod . . .

But, turning back to what we were discussing . . .

Ond, fel o'n i'n dweud gynnau . . .

But, as I was just saying . . .

Ond mae hynny'n beth gwahanol

But that's something else entirely

Ond mater arall ydy (/yw) hwnna

But that's another issue

Ond dyw (/dydy) hwnna °ddim yn °berthnasol fan hyn (, nag ydy?)

But that isn't relevant here (, is it?)

Ond mae hynny'n °gwbwl amherthnasol

But that's completely irrelevant

To narrow the topic – in other words to single out some element for particular consideration – the two most useful terms are:

yn enwedig

especially

Dw i'n hoffi'r tŷ, yn enwedig y °gegin

I like the house, especially the kitchen

and, for naming and itemizing:

sef

namely

Mae dau ohonyn nhw yn erbyn, sef Aled a Sioned

Two people are against, namely Aled and Sioned

Mae 'na un °broblem, sef argyhoeddi'r lleill

There is one problem, namely convincing the others

APPENDICES

Appendix A

Summary of mutations

Soft Mutation (SM) – *Treiglad Meddal*		
B > **F**	G > (disappears)	P > **B**
C > **G**	LL > **L**	RH > **R**
D > **DD**	M > **F**	T > **D**

Words directly followed by SM:

(a)° [relative – see §481]	fe° [verb particle]	pur°
	gan°	rhy°
am°	go°	tan°
ar°	heb°	trwy°/drwy°
at°	hyd°	un°
dacw°	i°	wrth°
dan°	(y)ma°	y° [feminine only; not ll-, rh-]
dau°	mi° [verb particle]	
dros°	mor° [not ll-, rh-]	yn° [complement marker before nouns and adjectives; not ll-, rh-]
dwy°	(y)na°	
dy°	neu°	
dyma°	o°	
dyna°	pa°	
ei° 'his'	pan°	

[*also any noun or pronoun that is the grammatical OR notional/semantic subject of the sentence*]

Aspirate Mutation (AM) – *Treiglad Llaes*

C > **CH**	P > **PH**	T > **TH**

Note: in some dialects, radical M and N are also susceptible to this mutation, though this is regarded as non-standard:

m > **mh**   n > **nh**

Words directly followed by AM:

a^h 'and'	ei^h 'her' (possessive)	tua^h
â^h	gyda^h	
chwe^h	tri^h	

Nasal Mutation (NM) – *Treiglad Trwynol*

B > **M**	C > **NGH**	D > **N**
G > **NG**	P > **MH**	T > **NH**

Words directly followed by NM:

fy^n, '(y)n^n "my"   yn^n "in"

Summary overview

Original consonant	SM	AM	NM
c	g	ch	ngh
p	b	ph	mh
t	d	th	nh
g	(disappears)	–	ng
b	f	–	m
d	dd	–	n
ll	l	–	–
m	f	(mh)	–
rh	r	–	–
n	–	(nh)	–

Words resistant to mutation:

1) words that already have fixed mutation – e.g. **ddoe, beth**

2) personal names

3) (generally) non-Welsh place-names – but special Welsh names for places outside Wales do mutate; similarly certain well-known foreign capitals

4) loanwords (mostly from English), especially beginning with **g-**

5) miscellaneous Welsh words: **dy°, pan°, mae, mai, taw, mor°, tua**[h] (sometimes seen with AM, however), **byth** in the sense of 'ever/never', **lle** (sometimes) in the sense of 'where', **tu** (usually) in location expressions of the type **tu allan** 'outside', **tu hwnt** 'beyond', etc.

Appendix B

Verb: tense arrays

Verb system tense array (example 3sg hi) by type

INFLECTED TENSES

PRETERITE (I)	talodd hi	she paid
	°dalodd hi?	did she pay?
	ʰthalodd hi °ddim	she didn't pay
FUTURE (I)	talith hi	she will pay
	°dalith hi?	will she pay?
	ʰthalith hi °ddim	she won't pay

YN-TENSES

PRESENT	mae hi'n talu	she pays/she is paying
	ydy hi'n talu?	does she pay?/is she paying?
	tydy hi °ddim yn talu	she doesn't pay/she isn't paying
IMPERFECT	roedd hi'n talu	she was paying
	oedd hi'n talu?	was she paying?
	doedd hi °ddim yn talu	she wasn't paying
FUTURE (II)	bydd hi'n talu	she will pay
	°fydd hi'n talu?	will she pay?
	°fydd hi °ddim yn talu	she won't pay
CONDITIONAL	basai/byddai hi'n talu	she would pay
	°fasai/°fyddai hi'n talu?	would she pay?
	°fasai/°fyddai hi °ddim yn talu	she wouldn't pay

490

WEDI-TENSES

PERFECT	**mae hi wedi talu**	*she has paid*
	ydy hi wedi talu?	*has she paid?*
	tydy hi °ddim wedi talu	*she hasn't paid*
PLUPERFECT	**roedd hi wedi talu**	*she had paid*
	oedd hi wedi talu?	*had she paid?*
	doedd hi °ddim wedi talu	*she hadn't paid*
FUTURE PERFECT	**bydd hi wedi talu**	*she will have paid*
	°fydd hi wedi talu?	*will she have paid?*
	°fydd hi °ddim wedi talu	*she won't have paid*
COND. PERF.	**basai/byddai hi wedi talu**	*she would have paid*
	°fasai/°fyddai hi wedi talu?	*would she have paid?*
	°fasai/°fyddai hi °ddim wedi talu	*she wouldn't have paid*

OTHER AUXILIARY

FUTURE (III)	**neith hi °dalu**	*she will pay*
	neith hi °dalu?	*will she pay?*
	neith hi °ddim talu	*she won't pay*
PRETERITE (II)	**naeth hi °dalu**	*she paid*
	naeth hi °dalu?	*did she pay?*
	naeth hi °ddim talu	*she didn't pay*
PRETERITE (III)	**ddaru hi °dalu**	*she paid*
	ddaru hi °dalu?	*did she pay?*
	ddaru hi °ddim talu	*she didn't pay*

491

Verb system tense array quick view (example AFF 3sg hi) by type

INFLECTED TENSES

PRETERITE (I)	**talodd hi**	*she paid*
FUTURE (I)	**talith hi**	*she will pay*

YN-TENSES

PRESENT	**mae hi'n talu**	*she pays/she is paying*
IMPERFECT	**roedd hi'n talu**	*she was paying*
FUTURE (II)	**bydd hi'n talu**	*she will pay*
CONDITIONAL	**basai/byddai hi'n talu**	*she would pay*

WEDI-TENSES

PERFECT	**mae hi wedi talu**	*she has paid*
PLUPERFECT	**roedd hi wedi talu**	*she had paid*
FUTURE PERFECT	**bydd hi wedi talu**	*she will have paid*
COND. PERF.	**basai/byddai hi wedi talu**	*she would have paid*

OTHER AUXILIARY

PRETERITE (II)	**naeth hi °dalu**	*she paid*
FUTURE (III)	**neith hi °dalu**	*she will pay*
PRETERITE (III)	**ddaru hi °dalu**	*she paid*

Verb system tense array (example AFF 3sg hi) by structure

PRESENT	**mae hi'n talu**	*she pays/she is paying*
[pres. **bod**] + **yn** + VN		
PERFECT	**mae hi wedi talu**	*she has paid*
[pres. **bod**] + **wedi** +VN		
IMPERFECT	**roedd hi'n talu**	*she was paying*
[impf **bod**] + **yn** + VN		
PLUPERFECT	**roedd hi wedi talu**	*she had paid*
[impf **bod**] + **wedi** + VN		
FUTURE (II)	**bydd hi'n talu**	*she will pay*
[future **bod**] + **yn** + VN		
FUTURE PERFECT	**bydd hi wedi talu**	*she will have paid*
[future **bod**] + **wedi** + VN		
CONDITIONAL	**basai/byddai hi'n talu**	*she would pay*
[condt **bod**] + **yn** + VN		
CONDITIONAL PERFECT	**basai/byddai hi wedi talu**	*she would have paid*
[condt **bod**] + **wedi** + VN		
PRETERITE (I)	**talodd hi**	*she paid*
[stem] + [prêt. endings]		
FUTURE (I)	**talith hi**	*she will pay*
[stem] + [fut. endings]		
PRETERITE (II)	**naeth hi °dalu**	*she paid*
[pret. **gwneud**] + VN		
FUTURE (III)	**neith hi °dalu**	*she will pay*
[fut. **gwneud**] + VN		
PRETERITE (III)	**ddaru hi °dalu**	*she paid*
ddaru + VN		

Irregular verbs – official spoken forms

				MYND – *go*	DOD – *come*	CAEL – *get*	GWNEUD – *do*
PRETERITE	sing.	1		es i	des i	ces i	nes i
		2		est ti	dest ti	cest ti	nest ti
		3		aeth e/hi	daeth e/hi	cafodd e/hi	naeth e/hi
	pl.	1		aethon ni	daethon ni	cawson ni	naethon ni
		2		aethoch chi	daethoch chi	cawsoch chi	naethoch chi
		3		aethon nhw	daethon nhw	cawson nhw	naethon nhw
FUTURE	sing.	1		a i	do i	ca i	na i
		2		ei di	doi di	cei di	nei di
		3		eith e/hi	daw e/hi	ceith e/hi	neith e/hi
	pl.	1		awn ni	down ni	cawn ni	nawn ni
		2		ewch chi	dewch chi	cewch chi	newch chi
		3		ân nhw	dôn nhw	cân nhw	nân nhw
CONDITIONAL (N)	sing.	1		elwn i	delwn i	celwn i	nelwn i
		2		elet ti	delet ti	celet ti	nelet ti
		3		elai fo/hi	delai fo/hi	celai fo/hi	nelai fo/hi
	pl.	1		elen ni	delen ni	celen ni	nelen ni
		2		elech chi	delech chi	celech chi	nelech chi
		3		elen nhw	delen nhw	celen nhw	nelen nhw
CONDITIONAL (S)	sing.	1		awn i	down i	cawn i	nawn i
		2		aet ti	doet ti	caet ti	naet ti
		3		âi fe/hi	dôi fe/hi	câi fe/hi	nâi fe/hi
	pl.	1		aen ni	doen ni	caen ni	naen ni
		2		aech chi	doech chi	caech chi	naech chi
		3		aen nhw	doen nhw	caen nhw	naen nhw

Anomalous verb: GWYBOD – *know*

			PRESENT	IMPERFECT/CONDITIONAL
sing.	1		gwn i	gwyddwn i
	2		gwyddost ti	gwyddet ti
	3		gŵyr e/hi	gwyddai fe/hi
pl.	1		gwyddon ni	gwydden ni
	2		gwyddoch chi	gwyddech chi
	3		gwyddan nhw	gwydden nhw

Verb: regular paradigm

PRESENT *spoken forms (further variants may be encountered)*

			NORTH	SOUTH	SOUTH-WEST
AFF	sing.	1	dw i'n talu	wi'n talu	
		2	ti'n talu	ti'n talu	
		3	mae o/hi'n talu	mae e/hi'n talu	
	pl.	1	dan ni'n talu	ŷn ni'n talu	
		2	dach chi'n talu	ŷch chi'n talu	
		3	maen nhw'n talu	maen nhw'n talu	
INT	sing.	1	ydw i'n talu?	ydw i'n talu?	
		2	wyt ti'n talu?	wyt ti'n talu?	
		3	ydy o/hi'n talu?	ydy e/hi'n talu? *or* yw e/hi'n talu?	
	pl.	1	ydan ni'n talu?.	ŷn ni'n talu?	
		2	ydach chi'n talu?	ŷch chi'n talu?	
		3	ydan nhw'n talu?	ŷn nhw'n talu? *or* ydyn nhw'n talu?	
NEG	sing.	1	dw i °ddim yn talu	wi °ddim yn talu	smo fi'n talu / sa i'n talu
		2	dwyt ti °ddim yn talu	ti °ddim yn talu	smo ti'n talu / so ti'n talu
		3	tydy o/hi °ddim yn talu	dyw e/hi °ddim yn talu	smo fe/hi'n talu / so fe/hi'n talu
	pl.	1	(ty)dan ni °ddim yn talu	ŷn ni °ddim yn talu	smo ni'n talu / so ni'n talu
		2	(ty)dach chi °ddim yn talu	ŷch chi °ddim yn talu	smo chi'n talu / so chi'n talu
		3	tydan nhw °ddim yn talu	ŷn nhw °ddim yn talu	smo nhw'n talu / so nhw'n talu

IMPERFECT official and spoken forms (further variants may be encountered)

			OFFICIAL	SPOKEN
AFF	sing.	1	roeddwn i'n talu	o'n i'n talu
		2	roeddet ti'n talu	o't ti'n talu
		3	roedd e/hi'n talu	oedd e/hi'n talu
	pl.	1	roedden ni'n talu	o'n ni'n talu
		2	roeddech chi'n talu	o'ch chi'n talu
		3	roedden nhw'n talu	o'n nhw'n talu
INT	sing.	1	oeddwn i'n talu?	o'n i'n talu?
		2	oeddet ti'n talu?	o't ti'n talu?
		3	oedd e/hi'n talu?	oedd e/hi'n talu?
	pl.	1	oedden ni'n talu?	o'n ni'n talu?
		2	oeddech chi'n talu?	o'ch chi'n talu?
		3	oedden nhw'n talu?	o'n nhw'n talu?
NEG	sing.	1	doeddwn i °ddim yn talu	o'n i °ddim yn talu or do'n i °ddim yn talu
		2	doeddet ti °ddim yn talu	o't ti °ddim yn talu or do't ti °ddim yn talu
		3	doedd e/hi °ddim yn talu	oedd e/hi °ddim yn talu or doedd e/hi °ddim yn talu
	pl.	1	doedden ni °ddim yn talu	o'n ni °ddim yn talu or do'n ni °ddim yn talu
		2	doeddech chi °ddim yn talu	o'ch chi °ddim yn talu or do'ch chi °ddim yn talu
		3	doedden nhw °ddim yn talu	o'n nhw °ddim yn talu or do'n nhw °ddim yn talu

PRETERITE (optional affirmative particles Fe°/Mi° omitted from I and II AFF)

			PRETERITE I (OFFICIAL SYSTEM)*	PRETERITE II	PRETERITE III (N)
AFF	sing.	1	tales i	nes i °dalu	ddaru mi °dalu
		2	talest ti	nest ti °dalu	ddaru ti °dalu
		3	talodd e/hi	naeth e/hi °dalu	ddaru o/hi °dalu
	pl.	1	talon ni	naethon ni °dalu	ddaru ni °dalu
		2	taloch chi	naethoch chi °dalu	ddaru chi °dalu
		3	talon nhw	naethon nhw °dalu	ddaru nhw °dalu
INT	sing.	1	°dales i?	nes i °dalu?	ddaru mi °dalu?
		2	°dalest ti?	nest ti °dalu?	ddaru ti °dalu?
		3	°dalodd e/hi?	naeth e/hi °dalu?	ddaru o/hi °dalu?
	pl.	1	°dalon ni?	naethon ni °dalu?	ddaru ni °dalu?
		2	°daloch chi?	naethoch chi °dalu?	ddaru chi °dalu?
		3	°dalon nhw?	naethon nhw °dalu?	ddaru nhw °dalu?
NEG	sing.	1	ʰthales i °ddim	nes i °ddim talu	ddaru mi °ddim talu
		2	ʰthalest ti °ddim	nest ti °ddim talu	ddaru ti °ddim talu
		3	ʰthalodd e/hi °ddim	naeth e/hi °ddim talu	ddaru o/hi °ddim talu
	pl.	1	ʰthalon ni °ddim	naethon ni °ddim talu	ddaru ni °ddim talu
		2	ʰthaloch chi °ddim	naethoch chi °ddim talu	ddaru chi °ddim talu
		3	ʰthalon nhw °ddim	naethon nhw °ddim talu	ddaru nhw °ddim talu

*Mutation patterns for PRETERITE I official forms may vary in spoken varieties – see §294.

FUTURE (optional affirmative particles Fe°/Mi° omitted from I and II AFF)

			FUTURE I (OFFICIAL SYSTEM)*	FUTURE II	FUTURE III
AFF	sing.	1	tala i	bydda i'n talu	na i °dalu
		2	tali di	byddi di'n talu	nei di °dalu
		3	talith e/hi *or* taliff e/hi	bydd e/hi'n talu	neith e/hi °dalu *or* naiff e/hi °dalu
	pl.	1	talwn ni	byddwn ni'n talu	nawn ni °dalu
		2	talwch chi	byddwch chi'n talu	newch chi °dalu
		3	talan nhw	byddan nhw'n talu	nân nhw °dalu
INT	sing.	1	°dala i?	°fydda i'n talu?	na i °dalu?
		2	°dali di?	°fyddi di'n talu?	nei di °dalu?
		3	°dalith e/hi? *or* °daliff e/hi?	°fydd e/hi'n talu?	neith e/hi °dalu? *or* naiff e/hi °dalu?
	pl.	1	°dalwn ni?	°fyddwn ni'n talu?	nawn i °dalu?
		2	°dalwch chi?	°fyddwch chi'n talu?	newch chi °dalu?
		3	°dalan nhw?	°fyddan nhw'n talu?	nân nhw °dalu?
NEG	sing.	1	ʰthala i °ddim	°fydda i °ddim yn talu	na i °ddim talu
		2	ʰthali di °ddim	°fyddi di °ddim yn talu	nei di °ddim talu
		3	ʰthalith e/hi °ddim *or* ʰthalith e/hi °ddim	°fydd e/hi °ddim yn talu	neith e/hi °ddim talu *or* naiff e/hi °ddim talu
	pl.	1	ʰthalwn ni °ddim	°fyddwn ni °ddim yn talu	nawn ni °ddim talu
		2	ʰthalwch chi °ddim	°fyddwch chi °ddim yn talu	newch chi °ddim talu
		3	ʰthalan nhw °ddim	°fyddan nhw °ddim yn talu	nân nhw °ddim talu

*Mutation patterns for FUTURE I official forms may vary in spoken varieties – see §294.

CONDITIONAL (optional affirmative particles Fe°/Mi° omitted from AFF) ('I would pay', etc.)

			SOUTH	NORTH
AFF	sing.	1	byddwn i'n talu	baswn i'n talu
		2	byddet ti'n talu	baset ti'n talu
		3	byddai fe/hi'n talu	basai fo/hi i'n talu
	pl.	1	bydden ni'n talu	basen ni'n talu
		2	byddech chi'n talu	basech chi'n talu
		3	bydden nhw'n talu	basen nhw'n talu
INT	sing.	1	°fyddwn i'n talu?	°faswn i'n talu?
		2	°fyddet ti'n talu?	°faset ti'n talu?
		3	°fyddai fe/hi'n talu?	°fasai fo/hi'n talu?
	pl.	1	°fydden ni'n talu?	°fasen ni'n talu?
		2	°fyddech chi'n talu?	°fasech chi'n talu?
		3	°fydden nhw'n talu?	°fasen nhw'n talu?
NEG	sing.	1	°fyddwn i °ddim yn talu	°faswn i °ddim yn talu
		2	°fyddet ti °ddim yn talu	°faset ti °ddim yn talu
		3	°fyddai fe/hi °ddim yn talu	°fasai fo/hi °ddim yn talu
	pl.	1	°fydden ni °ddim yn talu	°fasen ni °ddim yn talu
		2	°fyddech chi °ddim yn talu	°fasech chi °ddim yn talu
		3	°fydden nhw °ddim yn talu	°fasen nhw °ddim yn talu

CONDITIONAL 'if' clause alternatives ('if I paid . . .' etc.)

			SOUTH	NORTH
AFF	sing.	1	pe byddwn i'n talu	taswn i'n talu
		2	pe byddet ti'n talu	taset ti'n talu
		3	pe byddai fe/hi'n talu	tasai fo/hi i'n talu
	pl.	1	pe bydden ni'n talu	tasen ni'n talu
		2	pe byddech chi'n talu	tasech chi'n talu
		3	pe bydden nhw'n talu	tasen nhw'n talu
NEG	sing.	1	pe byddwn i °ddim yn talu	taswn i °ddim yn talu
		2	pe byddet ti °ddim yn talu	taset ti °ddim yn talu
		3	pe byddai fe/hi °ddim yn talu	tasai fo/hi °ddim yn talu
	pl.	1	pe bydden ni °ddim yn talu	tasen ni °ddim yn talu
		2	pe byddech chi °ddim yn talu	tasech chi °ddim yn talu
		3	pe bydden nhw °ddim yn talu	tasen nhw °ddim yn talu
AFF	sing.	1	pe bawn i'n talu	petawn i'n talu
		2	pe baet ti'n talu	petaet ti'n talu
		3	pe bai fe/hi'n talu	petai fo/hi i'n talu
	pl.	1	pe baen ni'n talu	petaen ni'n talu
		2	pe baech chi'n talu	petaech chi'n talu
		3	pe baen nhw'n talu	petaen nhw'n talu
NEG	sing.	1	pe bawn i °ddim yn talu	petawn i °ddim yn talu
		2	pe baet ti °ddim yn talu	petaet ti °ddim yn talu
		3	pe bai fe/hi °ddim yn talu	petai fo/hi °ddim yn talu
	pl.	1	pe baen ni °ddim yn talu	petaen ni °ddim yn talu
		2	pe baech chi °ddim yn talu	petaech chi °ddim yn talu
		3	pe baen nhw °ddim yn talu	petaen nhw °ddim yn talu

Appendix D

Welsh linguistic and grammatical terms

adjective	**ansoddair** (m., pl. **ansoddeiriau**)	nasal	**trwynol**
adverb	**adferf** (f., **-au**)	negative	**negyddol**
affirmative	**cadarnhaol**	noun	**enw (enwau)**
article	**bannod** (m./f., **-au**)	object	**goddrych**
aspirate	**llaes**	passive	**goddefol**
auxiliary	**cynorthwyol**	past	**gorffennol**
clause	**cymal** (m., **-au**)	plural	**lluosog**
comparative	**cymharol**	preposition	**arddodiad (arddodiaid)**
conditional	**amodol**	present	**presennol**
conjunction	**cysylltair (cysyllteiriau)**	pronoun	**rhagenw (rhagenwau)**
definite	**penodol**	radical	**cysefin**
equative	**cyfartal**	sentence	**brawddeg** (f., **-au**)
feminine	**benywaidd**	singular	**unigol**
form	**ffurf** (f., **-iau**)	soft	**meddal**
future	**dyfodol**	subject	**gwrthrych**
grammar	**gramadeg**	subordinate	**israddol**
indefinite	**amhenodol**	superlative	**eithafol**
interrogative	**gofynnol**	syntax	**cystrawen**
linguistic	**ieithyddol**	verb	**berf** (f., **-au**)
masculine	**gwrywaidd**	verbnoun	**berfenw (berfenwau)**
mutation	**treiglad (-au)**		

Further reading

Awbery, G.M. (1986) *Pembrokeshire Welsh: A Phonological Study*. Amgueddfa Genedlaethol Cymru.

——(2009*) The Syntax of Welsh* (Cambridge Studies in Linguistics 18). Cambridge: CUP.

Ball, M. (ed.) (1988) *The Use of Welsh*. Clevedon: Multilingual Matters.

Ball, M. and Müller, N. (1992) *Mutation in Welsh*. London: Routledge.

Borsley, R., Tallerman, M. and Willis, D. (2012) *The Syntax of Welsh* (Cambridge Syntax Guides). Cambridge: CUP.

Carter, R. and McCarthy, M. (2006) *Cambridge Grammar of English*. Cambridge: CUP.

Davies, C. (1994) *Y Geiriau Bach: Idioms for Welsh Learners*. Llandysul: Gwasg Gomer.

——(1996) *Torri'r Garw: Idioms for Welsh Learners Based on the Verb-noun*. Llandysul: Gwasg Gomer.

Davies, J. (2014) *The Welsh Language: A History*. Cardiff: University of Wales Press.

Fife, J. (1990) *The Semantics of the Welsh Verb*. Cardiff: University of Wales Press.

——and King, G. (1998) 'Celtic (Indo-European)'. In: Spencer and Zwicky (1998).

Fynes-Clinton, O.H. (1913) *The Welsh Vocabulary of the Bangor District*. Oxford: OUP. Reprint (two vols): Llanerch Publishers, Felinfach (1995).

King, G. (1996) *Intermediate Welsh: A Grammar and Workbook*. London: Routledge.

——(2007) *Modern Welsh Dictionary*. Oxford: OUP.

——(2008) *Colloquial Welsh*. 2nd edition. London: Routledge.

——(2013) *The Routledge Intermediate Welsh Reader*. London: Routledge.

——(2014) *Basic Welsh: A Grammar and Workbook*. 2nd edition. London: Routledge.

Knell, J. (2013) WJEC GCSE Welsh (2nd Language): Revision Guide. Glasgow: HarperCollins.

Lewis, D. (1960) 'Astudiaeth eirfaol o Gymraeg Llafar gogledd-orllewin Ceredigion'. (Dissertation) Aberystwyth: University of Wales.

Further reading

MacAulay, D. (ed.) (2008) *The Celtic Languages* (Cambridge Language Surveys). Cambridge: CUP.

Morris-Jones, J. (1913) *A Welsh Grammar Historical & Comparative*. Oxford: Clarendon Press.

Rowland, T. (1876) *A Grammar of the Welsh Language*. London: Simpson, Marshall.

Spencer, A. and Zwicky, A.M. (eds) (1998) *The Handbook of Morphology*. (Blackwell Handbooks in Linguistics). Oxford: Blackwell.

Stephens, M. (1973, 1979) *The Welsh Language Today*. Llandysul: Gwasg Gomer.

Thomson, A.J. and Martinet, A.V. (1980) *A Practical English Grammar*. Oxford: OUP.

Watkins, T.A. (1961) *Ieithyddiaeth*. Caerdydd: Gwasg Prifysgol Cymru.

Williams, S.J. (1959) *Elfennau Gramadeg Cymraeg*. Caerdydd: Gwasg Prifysgol Cymru.

——(1980) *A Welsh Grammar*. Cardiff: University of Wales Press.

Internet sites and resources:

www.bbc.co.uk/wales/learning/learnwelsh/ – online course from the BBC
http://clwbmalucachu.co.uk/ – popular site for Welsh learners
www.gwales.com/intro/ – Welsh Books Council
www.bangor.ac.uk/cio/ – University of Bangor Welsh for Adults class listings
www.geiriadur.net/ – University of Lampeter free online dictionary
www.learn-welsh.net/ – basic vocabulary and interactive materials for beginners

Index

This index covers both English and Welsh words and grammatical terms, as well as functions and situations. Arabic numbers refer to sections in the 'Grammar section' of the book, Roman numerals refer to sections in the 'Functions and Situations section' of the book. Welsh digraphs ch, dd, ff, ng, ll, ph, rh and th, which are additional and distinct letters in the Welsh alphabet, are disregarded here and treated strictly alphabetically. So, for example, **angen** comes after 'allowed' and **am°**. A semi-colon separates a main reference from other incidental occurrences.

CPSIA information can be obtained
at www.ICGtesting.com
Printed in the USA
BVHW04s1204270718
522813BV00022B/94/P